MASS COMMUNICATION:
AN INTRODUCTION

theory and practice
of
mass media in society

JOHN R. BITTNER *DePauw University*

PRENTICE-HALL, INC., Englewood Cliffs, New Jersey 07632

Library of Congress Cataloging in Publication Data

BITTNER, JOHN R (date)
  Mass communication, an introduction.

  Includes bibliographies and index.
  1. Mass media. I. Title.
P90.B515   301.16′1   76-44455
ISBN 0-13-559310-7
ISBN 0-13-559302-6 pbk.

9 2 0 2 6

for my family

© 1977 by Prentice-Hall, Inc., Englewood Cliffs, New Jersey 07632

PRINTED IN THE UNITED STATES OF AMERICA

10   9   8   7   6   5   4   3   2   1

PRENTICE-HALL INTERNATIONAL, INC., *London*
PRENTICE-HALL OF AUSTRALIA PTY. LIMITED, *Sydney*
PRENTICE-HALL OF CANADA, LTD., *Toronto*
PRENTICE-HALL OF INDIA PRIVATE LIMITED, *New Delhi*
PRENTICE-HALL OF JAPAN, INC., *Tokyo*
PRENTICE-HALL OF SOUTHEAST ASIA PTE. LTD., *Singapore*
WHITEHALL BOOKS LIMITED, *Wellington, New Zealand*

contents

books, direct mail, outdoor, and the emergence of specialized media   66

CHAPTER FOUR

media delivery systems: the atmosphere, microwave, cable, satellites, and computers   82

CHAPTER FIVE

the broadcasting networks   110

CHAPTER SIX

advertising messages   164

CHAPTER NINE

mass media news: the selection and treatment of stories   190

CHAPTER TEN

target audiences   268

CHAPTER FOURTEEN

feedback in mass communication: the print media   288

CHAPTER FIFTEEN

feedback and the electronic media   305

CHAPTER SIXTEEN

media business   333

CHAPTER SEVENTEEN

media control in the 20th century   365

CHAPTER EIGHTEEN

careers in mass media   456

CHAPTER TWENTY-TWO

notes   487

glossary of media terms   494

index   505

preface
and
acknowledgments

This book is designed primarily for use in introductory courses in mass communication and courses studying the role of mass media in society. The aim has been to help the student understand the full impact of mass media through coming to know the operational aspects of each medium and then relating these aspects to basic theoretical concepts. Human beings, of course, respond to many aspects of their environment, and that environment in turn responds to and is modified by their behavior. As far as mass communication is concerned, we must keep in mind that exposure to one message on one medium is not sufficient to explain human behavior. For this reason, this book examines the many different mass media—newspapers, magazines, radio, television, film, books, direct mail, and outdoor—and their relationship to one another and to society.

The points of departure are the traditional components of the communication process—senders, receivers, media, messages, feedback, and control. Of necessity the book deals with the hardware components that make communication possible through each medium. Two of the book's practical concerns are reflected in the chapters on media business and careers in mass media. The book also examines ethics and social issues related to mass media. It attempts to gain a historical perspective by glancing back at the development of each medium as well as discussing a prognosis for its future. In sum, it is hoped that this book will prove useful for those who aspire to be either practicing professionals or responsible consumers of mass media in society.

acknowledgments

To list everyone who participated in the development of this book would take far more space than is permitted here. And although there is always the risk of offending someone not mentioned, some attempt must be made to recognize those who did provide considerable assistance. It is these colleagues and friends who are responsible for all of the good and none of the bad parts of this book. Certainly not the least of these are those whom I have had the fortunate opportunity to know and to work closely with as practicing professionals in mass media—Hal Youart, F. Pat Nugent, and Thom Brown. Colleagues who deserve a special mention include James Carroll, Alfred G. Smith, James Harless, and Robert Avery. Many illustrations, including the cartoons, are the result of Chris Loeffler's creative hand, Byron Daugherty's camera, and the processing of Taylor Graphics Corporation.

A special acknowledgment is made to those people who contributed through indepth interviews. These include Walter Bagot, Ian Ballentine, John Bergen, Eric Bernsee, Wanda Duel, Beverly Green, Kathy Klassen, David Lawrence Jr., Lucian Lupinski, David G. Markle, Donald Roberts, Henry Romersa, Rupert Stow, and Robert Waiss. People at all levels of commercial and non-commercial mass media have provided tremendous assistance.

A special acknowledgment is made to Cornell Chulay for contributing the description of a week's activity "behind the scenes" of the *Mary Tyler Moore Show.* A special acknowledgment is also made to David Tucker and Bill Hogen who provided especially valuable information on the subject of, and their experiences with, city magazines.

The friendships and professional associations made through the International Communication Association are also a part of this book.

In addition, appreciation is expressed to Ted Arnold, Brian Walker, Barbara Christenberry, Larry Barker, and Robert Kibler for their efforts in the book's development and their belief in the product.

In a special way the faculty of the Department of Communication at Purdue University is part of this book for contributing professional spirit. Charles J. Stewart, William D. Brooks, Gus Friedrich, and G. Wayne Shamo are thanked for special friendships and support. Warm experiences shared at Purdue and the University of Oregon flow within these pages.

Thanks goes to Mildred Hancock, Virginia Scheline, and Rea Ziner who typed the manuscript.

And no one deserves more credit than Denise.

introduction

What is mass communication? It's the deadline of the investigative journalist, the creative artistry of documentaries, the bustle of a network newsroom, the whir of a computer, the hit record capturing the imagination of millions, the radio disc jockey setting the pace of a morning show, and the advertising executive planning a campaign. It's radio, research, recordings, resonators, and ratings. It's television, talent, telephones, and tabloids. It's satellites, storyboards, systems, and segues. It is all these things and many more. It *is* dynamic and exciting, but it is not new. Let's go back for a moment to the dawn of civilization—more than two and a half million years ago.

If you will, try to imagine our prehistoric ancestors emerging from their caves and reacting to their environment. Archeologists, who refer to this era as the Ramapithecus age, tell us that "cave men" possessed the basic senses of sight, hearing, touch, smell, and taste. Genetically different from creatures of the twentieth century, they resembled the ape more than man. However, as their brain and central nervous system began slowly to evolve, later generations gradually acquired the basic tools for communication. They began to distinguish between pleasurable and unpleasurable experiences. Finer tuning of perception and a more sophisticated brain and central nervous system developed hand in hand and aided them in satisfying their basic needs—light to see, air to breathe, food to eat, water to drink, sleep for strength, and shelter to protect them from the environment. By the year 300,000 B.C., their nervous system and brain as well as their genetic features began to resemble human characteristics.

Two hundred thousand years later, an embryonic language began to develop. Prior to this time people communicated mostly through touch. Anthropologists are still debating whether this language developed through learning or instinct. Nevertheless, genetic evolution had now been joined by language evolution. By about 7000 B.C., Homo sapiens had evolved genetically to his present form, and the ability to communicate had gained another medium, pictographics. These wall etchings on the inside of caves and temples still remain vivid picture messages that depict the life and religious beliefs of these first humans. In the period from 3000 to 2000 B.C., these etchings became highly stylized and the first symbols came into existence. Primitive alphabets, sometimes consisting of more than 600 characters, marked the beginning of recorded history. Mankind was now able to note down sociocultural events, to record attitudes, values, and habits, and to trace the development of moral codes.

Society's survival and growth depended on a number of things, among them a system of communication through which we could exchange symbols and thus propagate learning at a much accelerated rate; a system of production to create goods and services both for our own needs and for barter and exchange; systems of defense to protect our domain against intruders; a method of member replacement sufficient to counteract disease and other elements of member destruction; and a method of social control so that order could be possible in the society. In the centuries that followed, each of these functional requirements was (and is still being) fulfilled by ever more sophisticated and efficient systems, especially communication.

As civilization continued to expand, the process of interpersonal communication was applied cross culturally. Relay runners would carry messages to distant places and different people. However, learning about people living in different ways was still a very slow process—mostly determined by how fast a messenger could run or ride. In some cases, the messages literally took months and even years to reach their destination.

Cave paintings called pictographies were early forms of mass communication. (© The Bettmann Archive, Inc.)

In the fifteenth century, however, our ingenuity created a major breakthrough in technology, the invention of moveable type, and its introduction to the European continent. We could now produce and disseminate messages much faster. From this point on (and we should recall man's hypothetical emergence ca. 1,500,000 B.C.), breakthroughs in communication technology literally mushroomed. The facility with which we could now record knowledge made possible a much more rapid exchange of information. Two important developments followed the invention of moveable type. First, the invention of a paper-making machine in the early 1800s made it possible to mass produce and cut paper in specific sizes, reducing the cost of production. The second was the application of steam power to the printing press. Steam power, the first alternative to manpower, made possible true mass production of printed material. The use of power, the improved printing presses, and improved paper manufacturing processes developed continuously during the nineteenth century. Such devices as cylinder-fed paper rolls and type cylinders continued the advancement of printing. Mechanical typesetting machines also become part of the printing process. With the aid of larger and faster presses, newspapers could print editions with as many as a dozen pages.

Three other nineteenth-century inventions further aided our ability to communicate. First, the development of major transportation systems permitted large quantities of newspaper to be carried to people residing outside the major cities. Railroads became the key to this network and distribution system. Second, just as railroads began to prosper, we invented the telegraph, permitting us to communicate over long distances with considerable speed. By means of the mechanical transmission of short and long sounds, dots and dashes, representing the letters of the alphabet, a skillful telegraph operator could easily send or receive twenty words per minute. However, only those centers equipped with telegraph lines could receive messages.

Newspapers used the telegraph to communicate bulletins, and when the Atlantic Cable was completed, news of commerce and political events could be exchanged between the United States and England via Newfoundland. By the late 1800s, a network of telegraph lines had developed over the United States. The third major development of the nineteenth century, the device that enabled us to send voices over the wires, soon supplanted the telegraph signal because of the immediacy of communication it achieved. Although the telephone helped us to communicate with each other on a one-to-one basis over long distances, its impact was minor compared to that of the next technological revolution which loomed on the horizon.

Just as the twentieth century dawned, we perfected a system whereby electromagnetic impulses could be sent through the air without wires carrying voice transmission over long distances. This new invention was to become known as a radio. We developed low-cost receivers which could be purchased by almost everyone for a few dollars, enabling us to listen to mass-produced messages from thousands of transmitters located all over the world. Societies and cultures were within an instant of communicating with each other, and a news event on one side of the world could be transmitted almost simultaneously to any other point in the world. For the first time in the history of civilization, we had a medium of mass communication that just a century before had belonged to the world of science fiction.

In the same century, we further perfected our ability to capture moving visual images with the camera. We also discovered ways of capturing movement as well as sound on film to produce the motion picture and the electronic system called videotape. Scientists, determining the manner by which these motion pictures could be transmitted over wires and subsequently without wires, created a new medium called television. Much in the same way that steam aided the printing presses, jet propulsion took television to the galaxies and beyond. Utilization of the computer in our mass communication system aided in the transmission, monitoring, and logical development of information. Philosophers speculated about "technological determinism" and man's unquenchable desire to invent machines and grasp the power they produce.

These developments in mass communication did not, of course, go unnoticed by government. Control of some systems lay in the hands of nations and world governing bodies cooperated in the control of others. Now we find ourselves constantly needing to reanalyze and revitalize the balance between freedom and control in this new world of mass media, but, most important, seeking to develop new psychologies to better understand our interactive processes. In our desire to be exposed to as much information as possible, we also feel the presence of a technological monster over us and grope for individual identity. We have become schizophrenic, torn between the human and the technological world, searching for each without sacrificing the other.

The historian Allan Nevins notes that history is like a sextant on a ship, charting where we are so we may know where we are going. This is not a history book, but we have attempted to arrest time for a brief interlude to view our world of mass media; to stop for a moment and see where we have been and where we are now, so we can better understand where we are going.

processing

media messages

CHAPTER ONE

To understand how messages are processed through the media we must first understand the distinction between mass communication and other types of human communication, specifically intrapersonal communication and interpersonal communication. One of the best ways to do this is through the use of a *communication model*. This pictorial representation of the communication process sets forth the basic components of communication. Figure 1–1 shows the relationships between the *sender, medium, message, receiver, feedback,* and *noise*. With this model in mind, let's begin by discussing *intra*personal communication.

intrapersonal communication

We can assume, even before history recorded such things, that early humans used their senses to help them understand their world. If they looked into a clear midday sky, light and heat touched their eyes and were communicated to their brain via the central nervous

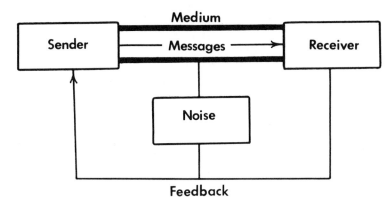

Figure 1-1 Basic model of communication.

system. If they felt cool rain on a hot day, this pleasant feeling was also communicated to the central nervous system. Cold winter air probably initiated an avoidance reaction. Our prehistoric subjects thus began to perceive, make judgments, and act accordingly. Perhaps the next time the temperature was hot and it began to rain, they went outside the cave and cooled off. When it was cold, they built a fire. The process of sunlight entering the eye and communicating brightness to the central nervous system, tactile sense organs communicating the feeling of cold air, the thought processes of deciding whether to brave the cold or build a fire, stay inside or walk in the rain—all were the result of communication taking place *within* the individual. This is the electrochemical action of the body taking part in the process of *intrapersonal communication*— communication within ourselves.

Intrapersonal communication is the basis of all other forms of human communication. Without an effective system of intrapersonal communication an organism is unable to function in its environment; i.e., to be open to external forms of communication. Ideally, this communication system allows one to make decisions based on information received through the senses. For instance, when you watch television, your eyes and ears receive information and communicate it to your brain. If what you see and hear is pleasurable and/or interesting, your intrapersonal communication system gives the green light and you attend to it. If you don't like it, your brain sends a message to your muscles which results in a decision to change stations or push the "off" button.

Sorting Out Stimuli

Just as the electronic components in your television set prohibit more than one station from being received at a time, your central nervous system also sorts out the different stimuli so that you can concentrate on one immediate thought—which station to watch.

7

Perhaps the telephone rang just as you began to think about changing stations. Instead of answering the phone, your central nervous system may give priority to the television message and you may continue to pay attention to that. However, if you had been anxiously awaiting a call from a close friend, then your central nervous system will probably give the telephone message priority, and you'll answer its ring. The entire process, however, involves intrapersonal communication. Now imagine the phone rings, and just as you get up to answer it, the doorbell rings. You stop. You can't decide whether to answer the door or the telephone. You just stand there. The doorbell has interfered with your intrapersonal communication processes. Or perhaps just as you get up to answer the phone, you drop back in your chair with a splitting headache. Again, you can't concentrate. The headache has also interfered with your process of intrapersonal communication.

Processing Stimuli

Now, applying our example of watching television to the components of our basic model of communication (Figure 1–1), we can see that your eyes and ears become the *senders* or transmitters of electrochemical impulses *(messages)* through a *medium* of communication, which in this case was your central nervous system. Your brain becomes the *receiver* of these impulses which transmits additional electrochemical impulses in the form of *feedback* to muscles, producing such physical activity as changing stations or answering the telephone. We also saw interference to successful intrapersonal communication. The doorbell produced external *noise* which interfered with this process. You also experienced internal noise in the form of a headache. The headache and doorbell interrupted the normal flow of electrochemical impulses, thus adding new factors to your decision-making task and temporarily distorting the process of intrapersonal communication.

interpersonal communication

With the crude beginnings of language, the process of *interpersonal communication* — communication in a face-to-face situation — bridged the gap from the concrete to the abstract. It became possible to communicate about persons or things not directly in view. If we apply our basic model to interpersonal communication, a typical situation might be as follows: You (sender) may speak (medium) words (message) to a friend (receiver) across the room, and the friend replies with an approval (feedback). While you are speaking and while your friend is reacting, intrapersonal communication is also taking place. Now if, when the two of you are talking, a baseball (noise) comes flying through the window, it will disrupt both the process of intrapersonal communication and that of interpersonal communication. Perhaps one of you uses a cliché or phrase which the other person doesn't understand; as a result, *semantic noise* interferes with the communication process. The possibility of semantic noise is one reason why a basic rule of journalism is to avoid using clichés.

For example, put yourself in the position of the television reporter from Idaho who visited New York to be interviewed for a job with a major television network. During the interview, the reporter commented how after a hard day on the job, he would literally "come apart at the seams" before sitting down for dinner. The network executive conducting the interview jotted down in her notes that the reporter "can't withstand pressure, becomes mentally deranged, and goes berserk before dinner!" To the Idaho reporter, "coming apart at the seams" simply meant totally relaxing before eating dinner. Obviously, the reporter didn't get the job. Semantic noise obstructed the process of interpersonal communication and consequently the job interview.

Every day we engage in the process of interpersonal communication. However, the number of people we can reach with our ideas is limited if this is the only means of communication available to us. To understand the full potential of our communication processes, we need to look beyond interpersonal communication to the process of mass communication.

mass communication

To understand mass communication as a process distinct from interpersonal and intrapersonal communication, imagine you are attending a party where a politician is mingling and conversing with guests. About an hour later, the party ends and you join a few thousand people in an auditorium to hear the politician deliver a major address. Stop and ask yourself whether mass communication was taking place either at the party or in the auditorium where a large number of persons was present. The answer is *no*. For mass communication to exist, we need an intermediate transmitter of information, a *mass medium* such as newspapers, magazines, film, radio, television, books, billboards, direct mail, or combinations of these. The politician who delivered a major address without the aid of the mass media would be forfeiting his chance to reach thousands, even millions of persons not physically present. Essentially, then, *mass communication is messages communicated through a mass medium to a large number of people.* By way of further clarification, we shall use the word "mass" to refer to a large body of persons.

The Gatekeeper Concept

The process of mass communication requires additional persons, most often complex societal organizations and institutions, to carry messages from the speaker to the audience. Returning to our simplified example: Sitting next to you in the auditorium is a reporter who hears the politician's speech, writes a story about it, and delivers it to the local newspaper that publishes it the next morning. In this example, relay people become involved in carrying the speaker's remarks beyond the auditorium to the reading public. The reporter who wrote the speech, the newspaper editor who edited the reporter's remarks, the typesetter, the printer, all helped relay this information through a medium of mass communication. Both the individuals (termed "relay people") and the organizations are called *gatekeepers.*

The term gatekeeper was first employed by the Austrian psychologist Kurt Lewin who used it to refer to individuals or groups of persons who govern "the travels of news items in the communication channel."[1] We will expand Lewin's definition and define gatekeeper as *any person or formally organized group directly involved in the relay or transfer of information from one individual to another through the use of a mass medium.* A gatekeeper can be a film producer who cuts a scene from the original script, a propaganda artist who prepares leaflets to be dropped from an airplane, the engineer at the local control center for cable television, or any other individual involved in the processing or control of messages disseminated through mass media to the public.

We can readily see that such an individual has the ability to *limit* information we receive from the mass media. A magazine editor may "kill" or eliminate a feature story judged to be of little interest or importance to the magazine's readers. A reporter may edit a story about the work of a congressional committee or a meeting of Parliament by deleting parts of the story he or she feels may be irrelevant. On the other hand, a gatekeeper can also *expand* information to the public by supplying facts, attitudes, or viewpoints his audience would not normally receive. The reporter who covers the congressional hearing or reports on Parliament's deliberations increases the total amount of information we receive—in this case, in absentia—from our environment. The reporter may also *reorganize or reinterpret* the information we the public receive. Facts may be rearranged or a new slant may be given to the story of the politician's speech. This is not always the case but it can take place.

Thus, it is important to remember that there are three functions of the gatekeeper: (1) to *limit* the information we receive by editing this information before it is disseminated to us; (2) to *expand* the amount of information we receive by increasing our informational environment; and (3) to *reorganize* or *reinterpret* the information.

Delayed Feedback

Returning to our example of the politician, perhaps the next day after reading about the speech in the local newspaper, an angry constituent writes a letter to the editor of the newspaper criticizing the politician's stand on an issue. Another constituent, somewhat more upset, decides to write directly to the politician. A lobbyist who heard the speech on radio may personally approach the politician and express approval of the speech. Each example is a form of *delayed feedback*, which differs from the immediate feedback the politician received from the members of the live audience. In the auditorium, for example, reporters could ask questions about certain ideas they didn't understand. The politician could in turn clear up any misunderstandings or project new messages for further thought. The difference between the reporters' responses and those of the constituents and the lobbyist may be accounted for by the time delay. Delayed feedback of course is not unique to the mass communication situation. It can occur on an intrapersonal level, as when one is temporarily baffled by an optical illusion. It also very often occurs on the interpersonal level when one person temporarily refrains from commenting about another's remark or suggestion. However, since delayed feedback will in many cases result from the mass communication situation, we shall use it as one of our distinguishing characteristics. Adding the concepts of the gatekeeper and delayed feedback to our basic model of communication gives us the model of mass communication illustrated in Figure 1–2. Another form of delayed feedback can be public reaction in the form of a telephone call to a local radio station broadcasting the speech. Still another form of delayed feedback is television ratings which can show that very few people cared about the politician's speech and were content to watch another program.

As noise can interfere with interpersonal and intrapersonal communication, so can it disrupt the process of mass communication. The politician may have had a headache and have difficulty concentrating (intrapersonal communication). The air conditioner may have been too loud for the reporter to hear everything the politician

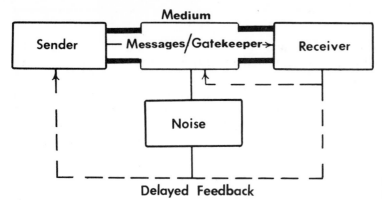

Figure 1–2 Model of mass communication.

was saying (interpersonal communication). The printing press at the newspaper may have failed, creating blurred pages and making it difficult to read the story (mass communication). Figure 1–3 shows the politician's speech broken down into the various components of our communication model. Keep in mind that the components present in intrapersonal and interpersonal communication are also part of mass communication. Note, for instance, that in the case of the receiver, for there to be a "public" to receive mass communication, there also has to be a "reporter" to receive interpersonal communication and a "brain" to receive intrapersonal communication. All three components are part of the process of human communication.

The Social Context of Mass Communication

Up to this point, our model of mass communication has been primarily concerned with how we send and receive messages. But there are also forces which affect the messages themselves and affect how consumers react to these messages. Specifically, these forces consist of society's social groups and systems.

Mass communication does not operate in a social vacuum like a machine. When a computer receives a message, for instance, it will provide an answer based on that original message. If the computer is functioning properly, the same answer will appear every time we send it the identical message. Now contrast this process with what occurs in mass communication. Imagine you, a consumer of mass media, read the newspaper story about the politician's speech. After you have talked with your family, friends, and co-workers about it, you decide to write a letter to the politician. It is thus possible that three social groups—your family, friends, and co-workers—affected your reaction to the speech.

Now imagine you are the newspaper reporter responsible for writing about the speech. Social groups will also affect your reporting of the story to the public. Perhaps you are a member of a union that goes on strike just as you return to your office to write the

	Intrapersonal	Interpersonal	Mass
Sender	Sense Organs	Politician	Politician
Receiver	Brain	Reporter	Public
Messages	Electro-Chemical Impulses	Language	Language
Medium	Central Nervous System	Voice	Newspaper
Feedback	Electro-Chemical Impulses	Questions	Letters
Noise	Headache	Breaking Glass	Blurred Printing

Figure 1-3 The politician's speech broken down into various components of the communication model.

story. Perhaps you belong to a journalism association with a code of reporting ethics to which you personally adhere. The code states you can't accept gifts as part of your job as a reporter. Your morning mail brings an invitation from a major oil company to be their guest on a flight to Kuwait for an on-the-spot story about oil exploration. You are faced with accepting the free trip and doing the story or rejecting the free trip and permitting other media in your city to obtain the story. You are obviously faced with a dilemma attributable at least in part to the influence various social groups have upon you. Your decision is not made easier if you take seriously your role in affecting the news received by the public. The hypothetical situation we have presented may seem rather remote to you. If so, try to think through a decision—discuss the problem with some of your friends—and then justify your decision to yourself.

We have viewed some of the specific components of communication and how they relate to the total communication process. We have also learned how mass communication differs from intrapersonal and interpersonal communication. In Chapters 2, 3, and 4, we'll look further into the process of mass communication by learning about specific media.

summary

There are certain basic components to the process of human communication—senders, receivers, messages, and a medium of communication. Two additional components are feedback and noise.

Feedback occurs when a receiver reacts to a message. Noise is anything that interferes with the communication process. Mass communication is just one of three basic types of human communication. The other two are intrapersonal and interpersonal communication. Intrapersonal communication is communication within ourselves, involving electrochemical impulses sent from the sense organs of sight, sound, touch, smell, and taste through the central nervous system to the brain. The brain, in turn generates electrochemical impulses that activate the muscular system. Interpersonal communication involves communication in a face-to-face situation. It involves the same basic components of the communication model as does intrapersonal communication. Mass communication differs from both intrapersonal and interpersonal communication in that it involves a mass medium, such as television or newspapers. It also involves the presence of gatekeeper(s), people, and/or systems that control and process the information before it is disseminated to the public. In addition, mass communication almost always involves delayed feedback rather than the immediate feedback present on the other two levels of communication. Mass communication also operates within a complex social context. Messages are affected by the attitudes of the various gatekeepers, and audience response is in turn affected by social context. How we react to mass media is partially self-determined, however. To some extent we choose to associate with specific social groups, friends, neighbors, co-workers, members of professional, religious, and political organizations, and so on. The people and groups we associate with influence how we respond to messages received via the mass media.

opportunities for further learning

DeFleur, Melvin L., *Theories of Mass Communication.* New York: David McKay Company, Inc., 1970.

Innis, Harold A., *The Bias of Communication.* Toronto: The University of Toronto Press, 1964.

Nierenberg, Gerard I., and Henry H. Calero, *Meta-Talk.* New York: Trident Press, 1973.

Webb, Ralph, Jr., *Interpersonal Speech Communication.* Englewood Cliffs, N.J.: Prentice-Hall, Inc., 1975

Wright, Charles R., *Mass Communication: A Sociological Perspective* (2nd Ed.). New York: Random House, 1975.

the media of newspapers and magazines

CHAPTER TWO

Newspapers are an economic and social phenomenon of our society. They are a major force in forming public opinion the world over and thus mightily affect national and international efforts toward economic progress and global understanding. Specialty newspapers exist for elementary school students, major financial dailies appeal to the commerce tycoons of the world, tabloids dress the newsstands of city transportation hubs, and popular underground publications appear and go defunct at the change of a trend or movement. Newspaper stories have turned ordinary men and women into heroes and removed world leaders from power. Huge presses spew out hundreds of pages in a single edition, and modern transportation and communication systems can put that same edition on a breakfast table 3,000 miles away. Today, the newspaper industry has become one of the largest in the world. It employs hundreds of thousands of people, from managing editors to investigative reporters to carriers. It has survived wars, economic collapse, and social destruction, yet remains essentially the same type of medium that it was centuries ago—pages of print communicating information to readers.

an international beginning

Scholars have never quite agreed on what could be considered the first true newspaper. This is partly because they could not reach a consensus on how to define the beginnings of the press.

The Posted Bulletins

In Italy, messengers disseminated mass news as early as 60 B.C. with the publication of a daily events bulletin titled *Acta Diurna.* It was posted in a public place for all to read and kept on file as an official record of historical events. There are indications that the bulletin may have been copied and reproduced by hand for distribution to other countries by messenger and ship. Obviously, the ability of the publication to transmit messages to a mass audience was minimal based on today's standards. The number of "subscribers" were the number of persons who happened to read the poster. The Romans also developed a system of news dissemination whereby a "reader" would announce the day's news events at a given time and place, and those wishing to hear him would be charged admission. You would have paid one Italian *gazetta* to hear the news. Such contemporary newspapers as the *Sydney Gazette* of Australia and our own *Georgia Gazette* and *Colorado Springs Gazette,* among many others, trace their name to this ancient custom. No one country can claim the foundation of the modern press. The earliest forerunner of the modern newspaper can, however, be credited to the Chinese. A publication resembling a court journal appeared about 500 A.D. and was titled *Tsing Pao.* The publication had its origin in Peking and remained in publication into the twentieth century.

European Foundations of the Modern Press

As the technological advances of printing made their way across the continent of Europe, newspapers cropped up frequently in almost all areas. Certain political atmospheres helped and in some cases hindered the development of the press, but for the most part it flourished. Figure 2–1 is a representative sampling depicting the international origins of the modern newspaper. We can see that the seventeenth century was deluged with this medium. During this period, the press flourished in England, the Scandinavian countries, France, Germany, and the United States. The turmoil of the Thirty Years' War during the first half of the seventeenth century contributed to the development of journalism in Europe primarily by providing a backdrop against which many different issues could be aired. In general the war did more to liberate journalism than hinder it.

The first newspaper published in Germany was founded by Egenolph Emmel, a bookseller, who started a Frankfurt weekly in 1615. A competing Frankfurt newspaper published in 1617 by Johann von den Birghden led to the first legislation over a newspaper monopoly. Von den Birghden asserted in a lawsuit brought on by Emmel that as postmaster, Birghden had an exclusive right to publish a newspaper. Similar controversies did not in any way discourage entrepreneurs from entering the business, however, as is indicated by the fact that in 1633 there were no fewer than 16 newspapers in Germany.

In England, the *Weekly News* was the first regularly published newspaper. It was started in 1622 by Nicholas Bourne and Thomas Archer. A rival newspaper called *Newes from Most Parts of Christendom*, published by Nathaniel Butter, eventually merged with its competitor to form *The Newes of the Present Week*.

Characteristics of a True Newspaper

In 1928, a German scholar, Otto Groth, developed a set of standards which modern scholars generally hold as acceptable criteria for determining the structure of a true newspaper.[1] Groth's first standard is that a newspaper must be *published periodically* at intervals not less than once per week. Second, *mechanical reproduction* must be employed. Obviously, our examples of early Roman and Chinese publications would not qualify here. Third, anyone who can pay the price of admission must have *access to the publication*. In other words, it must be available to anyone, not to a chosen few. No orga-

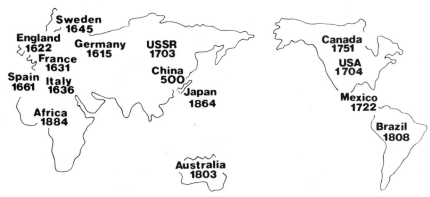

Figure 2–1 International origins of the modern newspaper.

nization can have an exclusive right to read or obtain the publication. Groth also places definitions on the content of the publication. He notes that it must *vary in content* and include everything of public interest to everyone, not merely to small, select groups. The publication must also be *timely* with some *continuity of organization.*

newspapers in america

If you had arrived among the first colonists in America, publishing a newspaper would not have been one of your first thoughts. There are a number of obvious reasons why not, even though skilled printers were among the first people to arrive from England. Basic needs of survival had to be met first: forests had to be cleared, fields plowed, houses built, and crops harvested. Second, news of international events arrived regularly via ships from London. In addition, you would have had little need for news about your own government, because that scarcely existed. Fourth, the close-knit geographical location of the New England communities facilitated news dissemination via interpersonal communication. Town meetings thus became the colonists' primary means of communication. Based on today's standards, early America was a closed society.

Early Colonial Newspapers

The first attempt at a newspaper in the colonies was one started by the English printer Benjamin Harris.[2] Harris had been banished from England for operating the modern day equivalent of an underground newspaper. Coming to Boston, he published in 1690 an edition of a newsletter entitled *Publick Occurrences, Both Forreign and Domestick.* In the publication, he made the mistake of taking a stance not favorable to the Indians in the area. The government of Massachusetts, one of whose primary aims was to win the favor of the Indians, didn't appreciate Harris' ill-timed and undiplomatic remarks. As a result, Harris' publication was promptly confiscated, but the government gave him a subsidy to continue printing. He accepted. This may seem a rather cowardly act by today's journalistic standards, but the seriousness of Harris' financial position dictated a practical response. According to Groth's standards, Harris' publication would not have been considered a true newspaper since it appeared only once before its publisher returned to England. The first publication to meet all of the standards of a true newspaper made its appearance fourteen years later.

In 1704 postmaster John Campbell joined with printer Bartholo-mew Green to publish a newspaper called the *Boston News-Letter.* Campbell had several advantages including a postmaster's free use of the mails. He also had been appointed by the Crown and re-ported directly to the Governor of Massachusetts, *and* when he ran into financial trouble a government subsidy was waiting.

The John Peter Zenger Case

The year 1733 saw a landmark case concerning freedom of the press. It involved John Peter Zenger, an immigrant from Germany who had been a colleague of William Bradford, a printer in the New York colony. Bradford's newspaper, the *New York Weekly Journal,* mostly expressed the government line. Upon Zenger's as-sumption of ownership, the tone of the paper, specifically that of the December 3, 1733, issue, became critical of the colonial govern-ment. Shortly thereafter, Zenger was arrested and brought to trial for *seditious libel,* criminal libel against the government. Famous Philadelphia lawyer Andrew Hamilton defended him in one of the classic cases of American journalism. Hamilton argued that the jury had the right to determine (1) whether or not Zenger printed the paper, and (2) whether or not the material was in fact libelous. In arguing his point, he stressed that the jury had the right to deter-mine law as well as fact. The prosecutor in the case took the posi-tion that though the jury could determine whether Zenger had in fact published the paper, it remained the judges' prerogative to de-termine whether the material was indeed libelous. When Hamilton argued that the jury had the right to both decisions, he won its fa-vor; a not guilty verdict established, at least in principle, the freedom to truthfully criticize public officials.

Surviving the Revolution and the Civil War

With the coming of the American Revolution, the press became no-ticeably more politically oriented. Strife between the colonies and the Crown was bound to be aired in a press that reflected the colo-nists' deep-seated mistrust of the political control they had fled to avoid. The Crown's attempt to place controls on the press was also a natural reaction. Newspapers, the stalwart of information during the Revolutionary War, quenched the people's thirst for information during a time of crisis. Thus, despite all the economic tribulations of war, 75 percent of the newspapers that commenced production during the Revolutionary War were still in existence at its con-clusion. Those that survived were healthier for the experience. The war had made them more aware of their role in a free society, and their content became much more than a regurgitation of commerce and government news. The press was on its way to becoming a true political force that would later join the ranks of the executive, legislative, and judicial branches of government as America's *fourth estate*. Although not the most objective press by modern day standards, these newspapers were nevertheless the training grounds for several notable persons who raised the prestige of the early colonial printer to that of publisher and editor. Horace Greeley, editor of the *New York Tribune,* used the medium to launch himself into politics, only to have the reputation of his political stands in editorials haunt him to defeat in the election that sent Ulysses S. Grant to the Presidency in 1872.

The Telegraph and Instant News

During the nineteenth century, technology significantly aided the newspaper industry. In 1844, Samuel Morris invented the telegraph, and news could now be transmitted rapidly over long distances to major cities and rural communities. No longer did important information have to wait upon ship, pony express, or stagecoach, conveyors that sometimes took weeks and months to reach their destination. The era of the "bulletin" meant that news could be reported on the same day that it occurred. Consider your reaction had you been used to receiving news from distant places weeks and months after it happened, when suddenly you could be in touch with events the day they occurred. Certainly your awareness and desire for information would increase. This thirst for "instant" news often resulted in the common practice of newspapers' preceding their headlines by the word *TELE-GRAPHIC* (Figure 2–2).

The Atlantic Cable: A Link with Europe

Along with an improved domestic relay system, another development, the Atlantic Cable, provided the international link for news coverage. Completed in 1866, the Atlantic Cable prompted predictions that the European mails would become little more than waste paper. "The profound discussions of the old world press will pass un-read," stated the *New York Times.* Although plagued with periodic breakdowns, the cable provided the first direct link between the United States and Europe and helped disseminate news of international happenings both in the United States and abroad. The American student of economics and politics could open the *New York Times* and read news of British commerce and the activi-

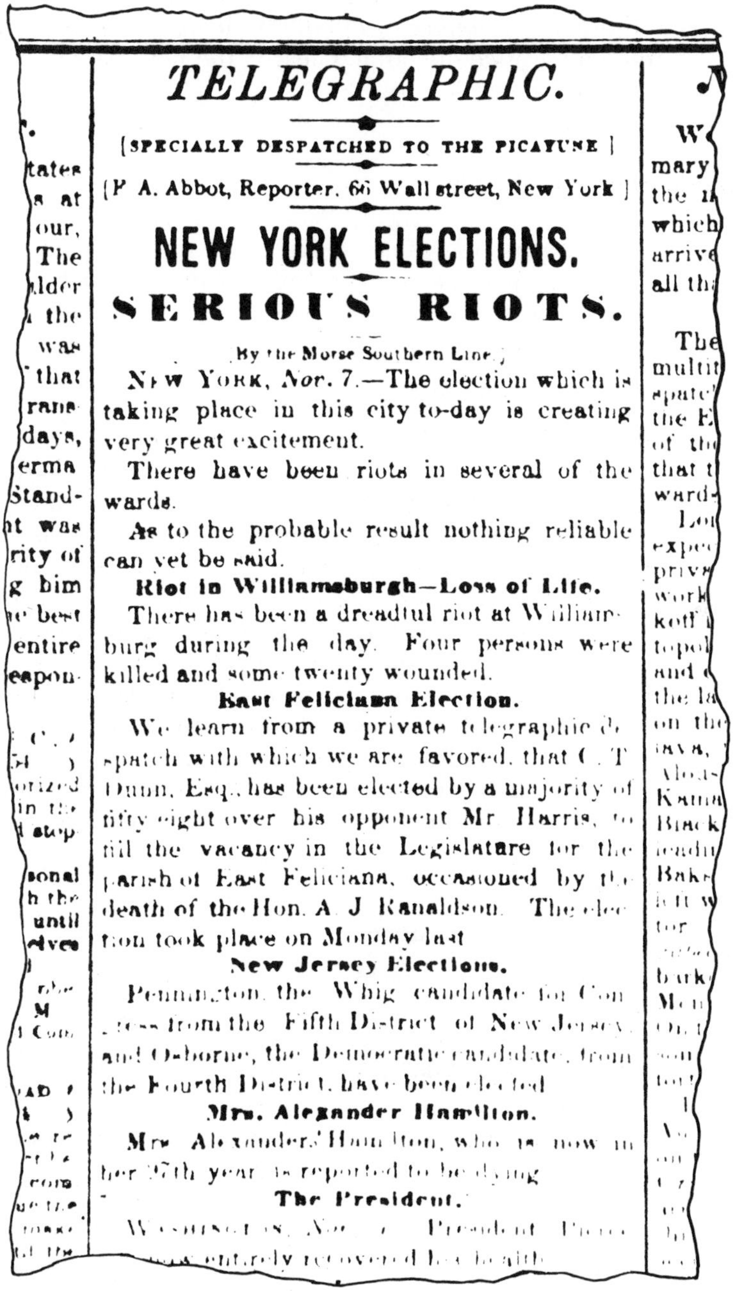

TELEGRAPHIC.

[SPECIALLY DESPATCHED TO THE PICAYUNE]

(P A. Abbot, Reporter. 66 Wall street, New York)

NEW YORK ELECTIONS.

SERIOUS RIOTS.

By the Morse Southern Line.

NEW YORK, Nov. 7.—The election which is taking place in this city to-day is creating very great excitement.

There have been riots in several of the wards.

As to the probable result nothing reliable can yet be said.

Riot in Williamsburgh—Loss of Life.

There has been a dreadful riot at Williamsburg during the day. Four persons were killed and some twenty wounded.

East Feliciana Election.

We learn from a private telegraphic despatch with which we are favored, that C T Dunn, Esq., has been elected by a majority of fifty eight over his opponent Mr Harris, to fill the vacancy in the Legislature for the parish of East Feliciana, occasioned by the death of the Hon. A J Kanaldson. The election took place on Monday last

New Jersey Elections.

Pennington the Whig candidate for Congress from the Fifth District of New Jersey, and Osborne, the Democratic candidate, from the Fourth District, have been elected

Mrs. Alexander Hamilton.

Mrs Alexander Hamilton, who is now in her 97th year is reported to be dying

The President.

WASHINGTON, Nov 7 — President Pierce has entirely recovered his health

Figure 2–2 Newspapers in the mid-1800s would supersede headlines with the word TELEGRAPHIC, calling attention to the immediacy of the news item.

ties of Parliament. The student in England could check the latest edition of the *Times of London* to learn the actions of Congress and the going price of cotton. Clearly, the newspaper had become an international organ.

newspapering gains an identity

As newspapering came of age as an international news medium, it simultaneously began to develop a professional identity among its practitioners.

The Birth of the ANPA

By the late 1800s, enough newspapers existed and publishers had enough in common to join together and form a trade organization called the American Newspaper Publishers Association (ANPA), founded in 1887. Its presidents consisted of seasoned veterans in newspaper publishing. Men like Don C. Seitz of the *New York World* and John Norris of the *New York Times* were typical of the leaders who made the ANPA a viable organization. Today the Association offers publishers a number of services, including a weekly bulletin with news on management, circulation, laws, and advertising. Special publications distributed by ANPA deal with specific issues such as political advertising, sales, and "primers" on current subjects making news. The ANPA also sponsors meetings, training programs, and supports research which directly aids the membership.

Sigma Delta Chi is Formed

The impact of new technology, the increase in the number of newspapers, and the jump in readership also spawned a new emphasis on the "profession" of journalism. This emphasis first became visible on college campuses. In 1909 an organization was formed that was later to become known as the Society for Professional Journalists, Sigma Delta Chi.[3] The constitution for the then "secret fraternity" read:

> In Order to associate college journalists of TALENT, TRUTH and ENERGY into a more intimately organized unit of good fellowship, with the element of mysticism as a binding force in order to assist the members in acquiring the noblest principles of journalism and to cooperate with them in this field. . . . In order to advance the standard of the press by fostering an ethical code, thus increasing its value as a social up-

lifting agency, we do hereby establish and ordain this Constitution of the Sigma Delta Chi fraternity.

Through the years, the organization has grown to about 30,000 members; it has modified its thrust to publish a journal, *The Quill;* admit women into its membership; and allow journalists with an advertising or public relations emphasis to remain within its ranks. It actively lobbies for such issues as freedom of information laws, laws protecting the confidentiality of reporters' news sources, and others.

the electronic newsroom

If you had been a large city newspaper publisher in the early 1900s, you would most likely have set your news copy by the linotype or "hot type" method. With linotype, the linotype operator works at a typewriter-like keyboard. There is a series of steps, some performed by the operator and some performed automatically by the machine. The end product of the process is a line of type which has been cast in molten metal (thus the name "hot type"). These lines of type, or "slugs," are assembled into pages and finally a special curved metal plate is made for rotary presses. In a small newspaper, printing is done from the original type in a flatbed press.

From Hot to Cold Type

Linotype machines did not eliminate any of the processes in typesetting, but they did mechanize and accelerate typesetting. Because of increased speed and efficiency in typesetting the news, publishers could produce larger newspapers and produce them faster than when type was hand set. With the exception of the steam-powered printing presses, linotype machines did more than any other invention to launch the newspaper industry forward into the twentieth century.

The invention of lithographic printing, commonly called "offset," to augment letterpress printing, increased printing efficiency in the 1950s. Offset differs from letterpress printing in the following ways: (1) in offset a proof is pulled from the hot metal, and (2) this proof is used to make a smooth surface plate from which to print the newspaper; the image is not transferred to the paper by raised typefaces.

The advantages of offset printing for the newspaper publisher over letterpress are lower cost of offset plates and better quality of printing, especially illustrations, obtainable.

The 1970s brought another change to the typesetting process— the computer. Computer-set type is also called "cold type." The operator types the copy on the computer's electronic keyboard. The computer sets the type electronically, using a memory system to position every letter in place. Each line and margin is set according to the input commands in the computer. The output is strips of special paper with columns of type just as they will appear in the newspaper. These strips are then pasted up in columns on a "mechanical" for each page. Headlines can be added by hand or programmed in the computer, and illustrations are put in by hand. The entire page is then photographed and ready for the next step, the production of the offset printing plate.

Goodbye to Typewriters?

Electronic keyboards and visual display terminals (VDTs) that look like television screens have been interfaced with the computer and are actually replacing typewriters in the newsroom (Figure 2–3). Reporters now type their copy on electronic keyboards and watch the letters appear before them on the VDTs. They can automatically "store" their story in the computer for later perusal by an editor. The headline writer then uses the computer to call up the story and prepares a headline for it. With yet another push of a button, the completed story is electronically set in type, photographed on the photosensitive printing plate, and rolls off the press minutes later. Although the newspaper looks much the same as the one composed

Figure 2–3 The visual display terminals (VDT), also called cathode ray tubes (CRT), are replacing the typewriter in many news rooms. (Courtesy, Dow Jones & Company, Inc.)

by linotype, the actual process is radically different—it has become a product of the electronic revolution.

Most major newspapers have made the change to cold type and are adding computer technology to their newsroom. Publishers can justify the change by reduced labor and materials costs. Labor unions, however, are slowing the transition in many areas as they try to protect the jobs of workers who operate the older machines. With a union contract staring them in the face, publishers can't fire a linotype operator the way they fired the typesetter at the turn of the century—at least without facing a strike. As these employees retire or can be retrained, more newspapers will undoubtedly switch to electronic printing.

For the journalist, computer technology brings two primary advantages. First, more money can be devoted to the actual process of gathering and reporting the news, since fewer people are needed to actually produce the paper. This doesn't mean that converting to computer technology will necessarily mean an increase in the reporting staff. However, there are some cost savings which can usually be realized. Second, computers speed up the process of placing a news story into print. If there is a 10:30 a.m. deadline in order for news to roll off the press and hit the street by 5:00 p.m., reporters will obviously be unable to get a late breaking story into print. With the arrival of radio and television, media that can air news almost instantaneously, this time factor has become even more crucial. Now, along with having the edge over radio and television in the amount of coverage that it can give to an event, the newspaper has more time to report complete and accurate stories to its readers.

Computer Technology in Advertising and Distribution

Computer technology has also become a part of other phases of newspaper publishing such as advertising and distribution. If you are a business executive and want to place an advertisement in the evening edition of your local paper but want to reach only one part of the city, a computer-based distribution system will put your ad in newspapers going exclusively to that section of the city, and you will be charged for the appropriate circulation. Even satellites and microwave transmission systems are part of the production of large newspapers. A facsimile of a major metropolitan daily can be sent via satellite to another country and incorporated into one of its newspapers. It is now possible for newspapers with regional editions, such as the *Wall Street Journal,* to use computers and satellite technology to transmit entire pages from one city to another, electronically, in a matter of minutes.

Electronic distribution systems give newspapers a flexibility never before possible. Little more than a century after a crude method of dots and dashes was utilized to send individual letters across a telegraph wire, satellites now link news bureaus all over the nation and can almost instantaneously transmit news stories to any of these bureaus. Computers can automatically set the stories into type and start the presses rolling. The development of cable television systems can be expected to open up new frontiers for newspaper distribution. Future newspaper subscribers will be able to "tune in" the evening edition of the local paper on cable television instead of having it delivered. By the twenty-first century, the era of the paper carrier may be a thing of the past.

the changing industry

As we look at the growth trends of the newspaper over the past twenty-five years, we notice that circulation rose very slowly. The increase in circulation between 1946 and 1973 did not keep up with the general population growth (Figure 2–4). This did not, however, spell financial gloom; quite the contrary. Income of most newspapers, through both advertising and sales, increased steadily. Newspapers still claim the major share of the advertising dollar. Economic data show that the growth of the newspaper industry has generally equalled and in several ways exceeded the growth of the economy (Figure 2–5). Expenditures for advertising, for instance, have more than kept pace with the gross national product, and employment in the industry has expanded at a more rapid rate than composite United States employment indicators. The success of the industry is due in large part to its adaptability to the new technology developed over the last fifty years. Supplementary features of the modern newspaper have also widened its appeal; such things

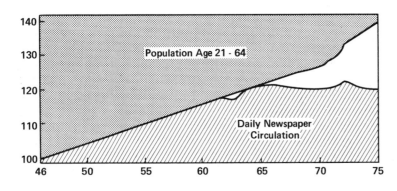

Figure 2–4 Daily newspaper circulation growth compared to population growth among 21- to 64-year olds. (Source: *Editor & Publisher*, U.S. Department of Commerce, Bureau of the Census. From American Newspaper Publishers Association publication *Facts About Newspapers*, 1976.)

as special features and syndicated columns grasp our attention just as much as news. The evening sports page, *Dear Abby, Ann Landers,* and *Peanuts* all provide a lure for us to spend more time reading a daily newspaper.

The Economic Indicators

But along with the positive indicators have come signs of caution for newspaper publishers. A research study by the Bureau of Business Research and Service at the University of Wisconsin highlighted these concerns.[4] *First,* as consumers we are finding it increasingly difficult to read more than one newspaper per day. Newspapers are becoming larger; a major city edition may include sixty pages instead of the ten or twenty that comprised the major city editions at the turn of the century. *Second,* other media vie for our attention. We have at our disposal a wealth of magazines, we listen to the radio, we watch television, we receive direct-mail literature, and we go to the movies. *Third,* the shorter work week of many businesses and the new technology give us more free time, longer vacations, and higher income to spend on recreational activities. Again, these activities take away from time spent reading. *Fourth,* deterioration of the central city means we're not as apt to go downtown after dark and purchase an evening edition from the corner newsstand. The convenience of listening to the radio on the drive to work is another factor to be considered. *Fifth,* wire services carrying news and information from around the world are available at moderate fees to even the smallest newspapers, and these papers are taking advantage of that fact. Thus, their ability to carry national and international news cuts into the circulation of the major metropolitan dailies. *Sixth,* raw paper costs and labor costs are steadily increasing. All of these considerations will be examined closely by publishers who are planning their corporation's growth over the

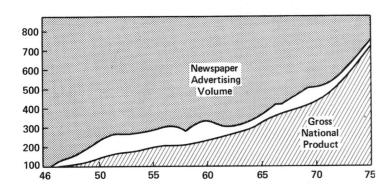

Figure 2–5 Newspaper advertising volume compared to Gross National Product. (Source: U.S. Department of Commerce; McCann Erickson, Inc.; Newspaper Advertising Bureau. From American Newspaper Publishers Association publication *Facts About Newspapers, 1976.*)

next quarter century. Uncertainties about the number of employees, about possible strikes affecting not only advertising dollars but also the supply of raw paper, and about the growth of competing media have prompted some major changes in the structure and organization of major newspapers.

Expanding Enterprises

These changes have made many modern newspapers much like other corporate conglomerates; that is, they have diversified into areas surprisingly different from merely publishing the local edition. *The Peoria Journal Star* of Peoria, Illinois, for example, has a rapidly developing broadcasting chain and publishes such magazines as the *Shooting Times.* Dow Jones and Company, Inc., for another example, publishes more than one newspaper; it serves the reading public with *National Observer,* the *Wall Street Journal,* and *Barron's National Business Financial Weekly.* In addition to publishing, its specialized services include the Dow Jones-Bunker Ramo News Retrieval Service, Inc., a jointly operated computerized news retrieval service available to stock brokerage firms, banks, and other businesses. The AP-Dow Jones Economic Report in conjunction with the Associated Press operates an international wire service. Operating 24 hours a day, six days a week, news is gathered by AP and Dow Jones and sent out around the world through AP facilities. Also part of the Dow Jones enterprises is the Ottaway Newspapers, Inc., a wholly owned subsidiary, and Dow Jones Books, yet another enterprise.

Pros and Cons of the Media Conglomerate

Arguments both for and against the wisdom of such major holdings under one roof have been espoused. Some argue that this arrangement seriously hampers the public's ability to gain access to the media. This is especially true when the media holdings are in the same community. Concerned over this issue, the FCC has moved in to break up combinations of newspapers, television, and radio outlets when all are owned by the same party and serve the same people. Place yourself in the position of a politician running for office who discovers that a certain journalist works for more than one medium. Perhaps the journalist writes a political column for the newspaper and also anchors a major radio newscast. You might feel that crossing this reporter could seriously jeopardize your campaign's publicity efforts either in the newspaper or on the radio station, and unfavorable publicity in one medium would surely be reflected in the other. Other arguments against multi-holdings deal with the lack of incentive to improve facilities. If a newspaper-owned radio station is merely a hobby for newspaper management, then even if the station is neglecting its community's needs, its personnel are underpaid, and morale is low, there may be a temptation to retain the status quo. In addition, when one media outlet must report on another commonly-owned outlet, objectivity may not prevail.

Despite these drawbacks of monopolistic ownership, other examples reveal that rival media under the same owner can be as fiercely competitive as two football teams. When the same boss oversees both and can readily make a comparison, the incentive for excellence can far outweigh any concern over the identity of the owner. Similarly, when a broadcast division, a magazine division, and a newspaper division have equal voice and vote in a board of directors meeting, and when each, in the presence of the others, must be accountable for its own operating procedures and profits, each will put forth maximal efforts. Such competition can effectively eliminate any bias in news reporting as well. When a broadcasting station owned by a major newspaper loses a court battle, for example, there may be little hesitancy about publishing the story. When the newspaper is sued, this story may be just as apt to headline the evening news on the co-owned television station across town. As a consumer of messages from mass media, the important thing to remember is newspaper ownership of other media outlets can be both harmful *and* beneficial to a community.

The newspaper industry has remained prosperous, in some instances because of these diversified investments. Moreover, there is no indication that the public's thirst for news is waning. For as both government and international politics become more complex, and as new communication technology puts each individual in touch with people all around the world, newspapers in their traditional sense and in their allied services will continue to be a vital and prosperous part of the world economy.

magazine publishing

The latter quarter of the nineteenth century fostered the climate for the birth of what we today view as the modern magazine. The United States had survived the Civil War, and its economy had regrouped for a fiscal start that signaled the thrust of the industrial revolution. Economic and geographical expansion brought with it a sharpened social awareness. Fields could be plowed beyond the Alleghenies, and people knew that they were part of the excitement that caught up thousands in the trek across miles of hills and dales to reach the ever new western frontier. The new generation's background consisted of more that Main Street U.S.A., for they were familiar with the great railroads which spanned the Continent, the telegraph which brought messages from afar, and the newspaper which was published via rotary press with far greater speed and efficiency than its predecessors in the earlier part of the century.

Magazines Find an Audience

And as the nation prospered, a growing audience began to yearn for entertainment, entertainment that took the form of major magazines. Entrepreneurs immediately realized that if they could provide light, diversionary reading at nominal prices, they could capture this mass audience. And they did. The magazine publishing boom set in. Between 1865 and 1885, the number of periodicals jumped from 700 to 3,300.[5]

As competition developed, so did trends in pricing and content. The name of the game was circulation. Circulation lured advertisers who could pay the price to reach a mass audience. That price was high enough to allow a decrease in subscription prices, making magazines still more attractive to the public. Distribution was also becoming more efficient, as the rails spread their network into hitherto inaccessible rural areas. Many magazines were specifically seeking a mass audience, just the opposite of what would happen fifty years later.

An Era of Prosperity and Transition

America's phenomenal industrial growth during the early twentieth century also helped spur the magazine publishing industry. The era saw major strides in corporate expansion and the ability to effectively produce mass goods for the consumer. With that ability came the need to make the consumer aware of these goods and of the various brand names the products assumed on grocery shelves, in new car showrooms, on fashion racks, and in furniture stores. Magazines filled the bill, and advertisements filled magazines. Although there were ups and downs, many of the publications achieved wide national acclaim. Among them were *Life, Look,* and *The Saturday Evening Post.* The classic issue of prosperity was the *Saturday Evening Post* of December 7, 1929. "Weighing nearly two pounds, the 272-page magazine kept the average reader occupied for twenty hours and twenty minutes. From the 214 national advertisers appearing in it, Curtis took in revenues estimated at $1,512,000."[6]

For the mass circulation magazine, the glory of that era would not survive. Television already loomed on the horizon. It would signal the growth of specialized magazines and the decline of mass circulation publications. The exact time of this turning point is debatable. The mass national magazines survived the golden era of radio and at first seemed to be holding their own with television. Advertising revenues for *Life* increased in the early 1960s. "A single issue of *Life* in October, 1960 carried $5,000,000 worth; another in November, 1961 had revenues of $5,202,000."[7] But the figures were deceiving. A period followed in which many industry spokesmen argued that television was making gains on the magazine publishers; magazine publishers countered that more than ever was being spent on advertising—magazines were not only holding their own, but gaining. To some extent, both arguments were correct. Magazines in general were still experiencing a period of growth, but television was bound to make an impact. It would expand until it dealt a terminal blow to the mass circulation magazines. Skyrocketing postal rates also contributed to their demise.

decline of mass circulation magazines

Inability to direct themselves to a specialized audience was another reason for the demise of such well-known magazines as *Look* and *Life*. These were magazines in the true sense of the word "mass," having something within their pages that was of interest to everyone. With the advent of television, however, advertisers could reach the same mass audience as with *Look* and *Life*, but cheaper and more efficiently. Besides cutting into the major advertising revenues of the mass magazines, television also surpassed them in distributing visual messages on a mass scale. The new medium could in addition offer both motion and sound accompaniment. With increased operating costs, mass circulation magazines folded. *The Saturday Evening Post* shared the fate of the other mass circulation magazines but was reintroduced a few years later as a specialty magazine. The new *Saturday Evening Post* espouses the theme of traditional, conservative America. With good writers, sound management, and a more specialized audience, the publication finds itself again on the newsstands where it had been started, ironically enough, as a specialty publication of Benjamin Franklin in 1778.

The Marketing Dilemma

Tough problems and decisions await the publishers of specialty magazines. For instance, when a market analysis reveals that audience profile is changing, both publishers and advertisers may need to take immediate action, most of it based on hypothetical projections. Advertisers who buy space in the hope of reaching a specific audience as verified by market data must now decide whether or not to switch media. Put yourself in the position of an advertising manager, say of your school magazine. According to market data, the audience you are reaching is the school audience. All of a sudden, your audience begins to shift. Your magazine's circulation remains the same, but student interest now begins to ebb while subscriptions among the housewives living near campus increase. Your first reaction may be, "So what?" Your advertisers don't want to reach housewives, that's what. They want to reach the students. What do you do? Do you change the editorial or news content of the paper to reflect the needs of the student audience? That might work, but what if the trend is already too deeply rooted, and by changing the content you don't regain the students but you do lose the housewives in the process. By now your circulation has dwindled and advertising rates must be cut. But in order to stay in business and meet expenses you must keep the same advertising rate. Tough decisions? Absolutely. Now imagine how hard it is for magazine publishers dealing with millions of dollars in revenue and millions of readers.

Business Week was one magazine that did not go the way of *Look* and *Life*. It offers advertisers a select group of management level readers by regularly refusing to take subscriptions from non-management level people. Other magazines adhere to similar practices, such as the executive edition of *Newsweek*, which requires you to make a fairly high annual income before you can "qualify" for a subscription. Even living in a certain section of the country may determine if you qualify for a specialized magazine subscription. For example, *Sunset*, called "the magazine of Western living" is sold throughout the western United States. If you want to subscribe to the publication but do not live in the West, then you pay extra. The rationale is not based on postage or shipping rates, but on the magazine's desire to keep its readership exclusively western. This is an implicit understanding for the advertiser purchasing ad space.

Joining Forces to Cut Costs

Some magazine publishers actually join forces to help each other maintain a strong position in the market. The Society of National Association Publications (SNAP) is one vehicle that helps publishers cuts costs, in this case by sharing cover designs. The magazine

Hardware Retailing, published an issue featuring a cover design of Uncle Sam eyeing a consumer. The title of the special issue was "Consumer Protection . . . How Far is Too Far" (Figure 2–6). This cover was subsequently made available to any other member of SNAP who wanted to copy it. The other publishers needed only to substitute the title of their own magazine. Four others did, including *Mutual Review,* whose issue was entitled "A Look at Government/Industry Cooperation."

Growth of Regional Editions

Many magazines also have special regional editions. For example, *Playboy* has Eastern, Central, Western, Southeast, Southwest, New York Metropolitan, Chicago Metropolitan, Los Angeles Metropolitan, San Francisco Metropolitan, Urban Market, International, Overseas Military, and United Kingdom editions. The centerfold isn't any different in the New York Metropolitan edition than in the Los Angeles Metropolitan edition. However, an advertiser wanting to reach only the New York audience can do so by buying advertising space in just the New York Metropolitan edition.

magazine growth patterns

An analysis of the growth of magazines shows continued development of the medium in both circulation and revenue. For example, using 1921 as a base year, we see that 365 magazines were published that year in the United States. That figure, with minor fluctuations, rose steadily through 1962 when it reached a high of 706 magazines in print. At that time television reached a significant saturation point in American households. However, magazines concomitantly began to reorganize both their content and distribution system to reach more specialized audiences. During this readjustment period, magazines entered a slight period of decline, their number dropping to a low of 649 in 1966 (Figure 2–7). By 1972, however, with 704 magazines in print, they had almost recouped their earlier position. With minor fluctuations circulation also increased. The year 1929 saw annual United States circulation at approximately 1.8 billion, jumping to 5.4 billion by 1972.

Magazine Reader Loyalty

A major reason for the overall steady growth of magazines has been their ability to adapt with remarkable efficiency to the changing media habits of readers and the unpredictable changes in the economy. Magazines have also fared well because of their ability to reach specialized audiences, audiences whose *loyalty* is considered fairly steadfast. Stop and consider your own media experiences. Naturally you watch television, if not as much when in school, then certainly when you are at home in the evening, on weekends, during the summer, or on vacation. But do you have a loyalty to one channel? Probably not. You switch freely from channel to channel. However, if you have a keen interest in a hobby, you may very well have a strong loyalty to a magazine which devotes its contents to your hobby. If you enjoy skiing, you might regularly read *Ski;* if you are a gun enthusiast, you might regularly read *Shooting Times;*

Figure 2–6 Magazines sharing cover designs can help cut some production costs.

a horse enthusiast might subscribe to *Western Horseman* or the *Chronicle of the Horse.* You may even be involved in your hobby to the point where you avidly read the editorial content of the magazine. Editorials may champion financial support for the United States Olympic team, gun control, or new interstate commerce regulations for transporting horses over state lines.

How strong is your own loyalty to a magazine? You might test this by asking yourself if you would sacrifice reading one issue of the newspaper each week to continue the opportunity to read your favorite magazine. Would you give up the chance to watch a TV channel one or two nights a week so that you could continue to receive your favorite magazine? Regardless of your own answers,

keep in mind that millions of people would react with a definite "yes" to these questions. A business executive, for example, might need an industry publication to understand business trends and assure his or her continued livelihood.

How New Magazines Develop

Usually a prospective magazine will first determine the need of an audience, then develop distribution methods and economic means to reach that audience. Many times an organization will provide a ready and waiting readership. For example, one of the most familiar magazines in the journalism profession is the *Quill*, the official publication of the Society of Professional Journalists, Sigma Delta Chi. The organization's growth finally spawned the need for a publication which could reflect the common concerns of all journalists. A sport that recently provided the impetus for a new specialty magazine is hang-gliding. The publication, entitled *Ground Skimmer*, hit the press not long after the sport began in earnest in the early 1970s. Subscribers can now read more about the activities of other participants, where they can purchase equipment, what meetings are scheduled, and which are the best mountains with the most favorable wind currents. Moreover, the magazine helps the sport itself to prosper, which in turn gains more readership for the magazine. The same type of mutual aid and growth occurred between the colonial economy and its newspapers. When a colonial businessman needed to advertise, newspapers fulfilled the function of advertising medium; commerce and trade in turn expanded because people could learn more about available goods and services.

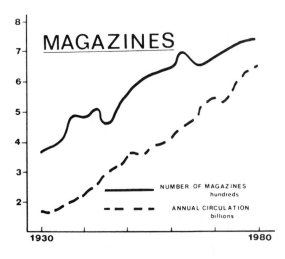

Figure 2-7 Magazine growth patterns. (Source of data through 1974: Magazine Publishers Association, Inc., New York. Circulation #3, pp. 1–2. Included are Audit Bureau of Circulations (ABC) magazines, including comics, plus all general and farm non-ABC magazines listed in Standard Rate and Data Service.)

characteristics and types of magazines

Magazines are primarily of four types—*farm, business, consumer,* and *religious magazines.* Each has subcategories. For example, farm publications consist mainly of *state* and *vocational* publications. State publications are directed toward a particular geographic area, such as the *Montana Farmer-Stockman* and *The Pennsylvania Farmer.* Vocational farm publications, on the other hand, are directed toward a particular type of farmer, and include such magazines as the *Citrus and Vegetable Magazine* and *Dairy Herd Management.*

Business publications include *professional* magazines such as those dealing with law, medicine, or education. Here the publisher may be a professional organization such as the American Dental Association. Another subcategory of business publications include *trade* magazines dealing with specific businesses, such as the *Hardware Retailer.* A third subcategory consists of *industrial* publications. Edited for specific industries, they can include magazines directed to specific processes, for example, manufacturing or communication. Two examples of industrial publications of the printing and broadcasting industries respectively are *The Printing*

City magazine stand. (Photo: Courtesy Main Lafrentz and Company.)

News and *Broadcast Management and Engineering. Institutional* business magazines also abound, e.g., *Hotel-Motel News.* Publications that are sent to a group of people belonging to an organization are usually termed *house organs.* Copies of house organs may, of course, be sent to the news media for public relations purposes. In content, the house organ will consist primarily of information of special interest to its select readers.

In addition to these major categories of business publications, you should understand the difference between *vertical* and *horizontal* publications. Vertical publications reach people of a given profession at different levels in that profession. For instance, a major vertical publication of the radio and television industry is *Broadcasting.* Its content is geared for every person working or interested in the broadcasting industry, whether it be the television camera operator, the radio station manager, or even the advertising executive who needs to know about new FCC regulations affecting broadcast commercials. Horizontal magazines, on the other hand, are aimed at a certain managerial level but cut across several different industries. *Business Week,* for example, is directed at management level personnel in many different facets of the business world. Two other examples of magazines directed at management include *Forbes* and *Fortune.*

Consumer magazines are usually of two types. Magazines directed at audiences with an interest in a special area, such as *Sailing* or the *Model Railroader,* are *specialized* magazines. The others are *general* magazines directed toward people with more varied interests. *Playboy* would fit into this category as would *Better Homes and Gardens.*

Religious publications also comprise various subdivisions, usually based on specific religious denominations. Typical religious publications include *The Catholic Voice, The Jewish News, The Episcopalian, The Lutheran* and many more regional publications which deal with specific denominations within a city.

Magazines have a bright future despite the increases in cost for labor, printing, and postage that are continually confronting the industry. With the ability to successfully distribute and produce content directed at specialized audiences, magazines should continue to experience a steady growth rate.

summary

Scholars, although unable to pinpoint the beginnings of the press, have generally concurred that for a newspaper to be considered legitimate, it must be published periodically, be mechanically reproduced, be accessible to all who can pay its subscription price, display both variation in content and continuity of organization, and be timely. Early newspapers went through a transition which included changing from primarily a medium of economic news and politically slanted government publicity sheets, to more modern and less biased transmitters of news and information. As the newspaper industry grew, so did the profession of journalism. It has gained an identity primarily through the increasing importance of newspapers in society. The industry, like other businesses, experienced and survived both the industrial and electronic revolution. Today, computers and offset presses have created the electronic newsroom, a totally automatic system which can compose and print a newspaper within a fraction of the time it took the manual typesetter of the past.

Magazines have experienced some of the most stable growth patterns of all mass media. The major change in their development occurred with the demise of the mass circulation magazines such as *Look* and *Life*. Now, by directing themselves toward specialized audiences, magazines have boosted both their circulation and their income. There are four basic types of magazines—farm, business, consumer, and religious magazines. Most persons are likely to have a strong loyalty to a particular magazine. It may be a magazine that deals with their hobby or an organization to which they belong. Business people regularly read magazines telling about new products that can increase the efficiency of their business. Many major magazines publish regional editions. Advertisers desiring to reach a certain area of the country can specify that their ad appear in only a particular regional edition.

As society has changed, so have newspapers and magazines. They remain active competitors of other media, because they have adapted to changing life styles that necessarily affect reading habits. Increased production costs have also forced each medium to diversify and specialize its operations.

opportunities for further learning

EMERY, EDWIN, *The Press and America* (3rd Ed.). Englewood Cliffs, N.J.: Prentice-Hall, Inc., 1972.

HARRISON, STANLEY, *Poor Men's Guardians.* London: Lawrence and Wishart, 1974.

LYONS, LOUIS M., *Newspaper Story: One Hundred Years of the Boston Globe.* Cambridge, Mass.: Harvard University Press, 1971.

MERRILL, JOHN C., *Elite Press: Great Newspapers of the World.* New York: Pitman Publishing Corp., 1969.

MOTT, FRANK LUTHER, *American Journalism* (3rd Ed.). New York: The Macmillan Company, 1962.

PETERSON, THEODORE, *Magazines in the Twentieth Century* (2nd Ed.). Urbana, Illinois: University of Illinois Press, 1964.

SWANSON, WALTER S. J., *The Thin Gold Watch: A Personal History of the Newspaper Copleys.* La Jolla, Calif.: The Copley Press, Inc., 1970.

TEBBEL, JOHN, *Compact History of the American Newspaper.* New York: Hawthorn Books, Inc., 1969.

TEBBEL, JOHN, *The Media In America.* New York: Thomas Y. Crowell Company, 1974.

WOLSELEY, ROLAND E., *Understanding Magazines* (2nd Ed.). Ames, Iowa: The Iowa State University Press, 1969.

non-print media:

radio, television, film

CHAPTER THREE

The completion of the Atlantic Cable between North America and England was hailed as the dramatic breakthrough of the nineteenth century. But it was only a foretaste of the mass communication revolution yet to come. The development of wireless communication would make the cable antiquated. Radio would beam its signals across continents, making communication possible in areas that could never be conquered with a cable. Within the same century, television would enable us to watch in living color as men walked on the moon. Film would also become an international medium of communication. And, all of these non-print media would become art forms in their own right. Recordings of old-time radio would deck record shops as nostalgia became a craze. Old movies would be revived and become the core of film-art classes in schools everywhere. Even centers for experiments in television would develop this medium to be used as a video palette of colors and sound just as the painter works with a brush. Non-print media would literally surround us.

radio

A woman recently called a midwestern radio station during a thunderstorm to find out why the station had not provided a forecast for the impending weather conditions. The announcer at the station replied courteously that the station antenna had been hit by a bolt of lightning, the inside of the transmitter had burned out, and that it had been off the air for more than two hours. Indignantly the woman replied, "Then why don't you have the courtesy to at least make an announcement?" Her reaction typified how people view radio today and what they expect of the medium. Radio, while being a background sound of society, is still a dominant information medium. Radio is also a portable medium and can accompany us to picnics, to the beach, on hikes, on a walk downtown, or to the study room. Because of its portability, radio becomes the primary medium responsible for communicating information during such crisis events as major power blackouts. It can stop panic, disseminate information to almost any location regardless of the terrain, and be a constant companion.

Radio's Early Development

The concept of radio evolved almost 100 years ago when a German physicist named Heinrich Rudolph Hertz utilized an 1864 theory of James Clerk Maxwell that electrical impulses travel through space at the speed of light. Hertz discovered the *electromagnetic waves* passing through the air. He used an oscillating spark to demonstrate the production and transmission of these electromagnetic waves which were then received by a special grid a short distance away. All of us have had the experience of a nearby power tool's causing static in radio reception. The sparks generated by the power tool's electric motor produce signals of the same sort that Hertz experimented with. The name Hertz became synonymous with radio frequencies. Such terms as *megahertz* and *kilohertz* representing positions on the electromagnetic spectrum are named after him.

Less than ten years after the application of Hertz's work, a young Italian inventor named Guglielmo Marconi furthered the principle of electromagnetic waves when he developed a device called the wireless, which was capable of receiving "spark" signals over long distances. Receiving a British patent on his wireless, Marconi formed a company to continue developmental work. By 1898, the wireless transmitted signals from the Eiffel Tower in Paris to receivers across the Bristol Channel in England. In 1901, Marconi traveled to Newfoundland for a gamble that shook the scientific world. On the morning of December 12, 1901, his assistants flew a large kite with an antenna into the Newfoundland air. At 11:30 a.m., the transmitter in England began to send a series of successive *s*'s in the form of three short dots. Marconi and his assistants received the transatlantic transmission, marking a new era in the history of broadcasting.

Radio Programming Makes Strides

With the development of equipment to send voices via the wireless, the concept of "radio" was born. In 1909, Dr. Charles David Herrold constructed a small transmitter and sent newscasts to friends for whom he provided free receiving sets.[1] KDKA in Pittsburgh, Pennsylvania, went on the air in 1920 as the first commercially licensed radio station and provided extensive coverage of the Harding-Cox election. From then on, the medium hummed with exciting new developments.

In 1923, Robert McCormick, editor and publisher of the *Chicago Tribune,* wrote his mother saying, "I have written to arrange to have an operator come to your room with a radio set and give you an exhibition. I don't think you will want to keep one, but you cannot help being thrilled at the little box that picks sounds from the air. . . ."[2] McCormick's *Chicago Tribune* had its own station, WDAP, which later became WGN, a major station in American broadcasting. The ambitious and creative people at WGN helped bring radio into its own. A warm May afternoon brought the microphone of WGN's A. W. "Sen" Kaney to the famed Indianapolis 500 auto race for seven hours of live sports broadcasting, the first time the Indy 500 had ever been heard on radio. In October of 1924, the crack of the bat kept listeners glued to their radios as sounds of Chicago Cubs' and Chicago White Sox' baseball came over WGN's air waves. That same month, the University of Illinois and the University of Michigan met for a football clash, again broadcast by WGN. The famed Scopes trial of 1925 heard WGN broadcast the voices of Clarence Darrow and William Jennings Bryan as they argued the case of the Tennessee school teacher, John Thomas Scopes, accused of teaching the theory of evolution.[3] Radio journalism made its debut as an attentive nation listened to:

> **Bryan:** I want the world to know that this man, who does not believe in God, is trying to use a court in Tennessee—
>
> **Darrow:** I object to that!
>
> **Bryan:** —to slur at it, and while it will require time, I am willing to take it!

> **Darrow:** I object to your explanation! I am examining you on your fool ideas, ideas that no intelligent Christian on earth believes!

The next decades saw radio blossom into mass popularity. Variety shows, dramatic productions, and comedy series elevated such radio personalities as Jack Benny and George Burns to national stars. Radio heroes dominated the medium. *The Lone Ranger, The Shadow*, and many more kept listeners spellbound. Radio also developed as a news medium. A study by educator Wilbur Schramm in 1945 asked college students what medium they would most likely believe in the face of conflicting news reports. Radio led by far.[4] Broadcasts of events as they happened—the actual "sounds" of the news—made radio one of the most credible news sources. The radio schedule of the evening newspaper became important and popular reading for everyone, especially the radio critics' columns. When WSB in Atlanta pioneered the airways, the *Atlanta Journal* noted in wordy adjectives:

> As may be instantly surmised by a casual glance at telegraphic tributes printed elsewhere on this page today, Sig Newman, astonishing virtuoso of the saxophone, and his orchestra of New York, entrancingly aided by the vocal brilliance of Mrs. Susan Reese Kennedy, Atlanta soprano, not only took Atlanta but half of the United States by storm at WSB's 10:45 concert Monday night, following proportionate glittering success at the 7:00 radio debut of the *Journal's* radio telephone station.[5]

For the time being, the thrill and novelty of radio were conveyed to the public by a press only too eager to cover every new programming and technical development of the new medium.

The Medium Becomes Specialized

This massive audience appeal began to waver, however, when television made its appearance. Forced into new formats, radio began a period of transition. It found its niche as a "specialized" medium. Major radio networks which once carried entertainment programming began to specialize in news. Each station began to forge its own individual identity. An examination of radio stations in any major metropolitan area illustrates the extent to which this specialization has been accomplished. One station may specialize in Top 40 or rock music, while another may devote itself exclusively to foreign broadcasts. Still others may concentrate on educational programs or all-news formats. Starting at one end of the AM spectrum, your first encounter might be a "personality" station. By the time you had turned the dial to the other end of the spectrum, you would probably have heard a country-western station, a station that plays solely hit records from the past, an automated station, a foreign language station, a top-forty station, and more than a dozen others. If you were to turn to the FM dial, you would hear an equally large selection among almost three dozen stations, each with its own identity.

The Invisible Medium

Much different from the tubes and wires that held together the early stations of the 1920s, today's radio station is a complicated combination of electronic sophistication and creative mastery. Radio commands more than just the attention of the audience; it commands the imagination as well. But radio's ability to conjure up creative imagery had disadvantages as well. Images triggered by auditory stimuli perhaps more than visual cues depend heavily on the listener's own experience. For the child in the ghetto, for example, the sound of a crackling fire might create a vision of a burning tenement house. For a child from a well-to-do family, it might recall an open hearth fireplace in a sunken living room or the crackling logs beyond the doorstep of a motor home. Radio's coverage of civil unrest has suffered from the same drawback, resulting in the criticism that it wasn't objective and accurate. A news report about a shouting demonstrator and a milling crowd could easily give the impression of a mob out of control in the minds of many listeners.

With all of this criticism, though, radio has the ability to communicate messages with special qualities. Intangible products, for instance, can sell well on radio. Thus, the added "visual costs" of television are sometimes unnecessary, and less expensive radio advertising can do the job with equal effectiveness. Moreover, radio journalism is experiencing considerable new growth and recognition.

The Constant Companion

A portable audio background medium, radio can be part of our lives when we are busy doing other things. It is often part of our "media experience" without our even realizing it. Consider the businessman who walked into an advertising agency one morning to inquire why the agency selected radio to advertise his products. He approached the head of the agency and said to her:

Businessman: Listen, we have to have an understanding about this account. I really don't think it's a good idea to have these commercials running on radio. Everyone

Executive: watches TV, and that's the medium we want to hit. Cost isn't an item, and as I mentioned at lunch yesterday, no one listens to radio anymore!

Executive: Well, let's talk about it. Can I get you a coffee?

Businessman: Yes, thank you.

Executive: What's the weather going to be like today? It seemed cold this morning.

Businessman: It's supposed to reach a high of 65 with a chance of rain.

Executive: Well, it looks like the baseball game might be called off.

Businessman: I hope not. After that win of a double-header last night, they ought to be keyed up enough to win.

Executive: Did you go to the game?

Businessman: No, I had to work. We're getting a new import shipment ready. Wow, that trouble abroad this morning is causing shaky economic conditions.

Executive: Yes, I heard. By the way, do you mind if I ask you some personal questions?

Businessman: What kind of personal questions?

Executive: Well, how did you find out what the weather would be today?

Businessman: While shaving, the reporter on the radio said it was going to rain.

Executive: And about the double-header and the trouble abroad?

Businessman: Well, I heard about it riding to work this morning on the car radio.

Executive: And now what is this about no one listening to radio anymore?

Our discussion between the executive and the businessman illustrates some of the qualities that make radio a unique medium. For one thing, the businessman didn't even realize he was listening to radio. Moreover, as a mobile medium it accompanied him on his drive to work. Try reading a newspaper or watching television while driving home from a date!

The Special Qualities of FM

FM radio signals are transmitted directly from transmitter to receiver without being rebounded from layers of the atmosphere as are AM signals. We'll learn more about this process in Chapter 6. Suffice it to say that this enables FM to transmit high-quality musical sounds, and it was this which caught the attention of the public during the 1960s when FM's primary format was classical music. The development of FM stereo also gave FM stations the ability to broadcast music of a quality and distinction previously limited to the stereo record player. FM stereo broadcasts the two tracks of a stereo record on two separate FM frequencies. A special FM stereo receiver picks up these signals. Even stereo news is coming into its own. With stereo speakers a morning news interview with a local politician assumes immediacy as the interviewer's voice emanates from one speaker and the politician's from the other. When a reporter airs a report from the scene of a parade, the listener hears the parade bands first on one speaker and then gradually on the other speaker, as though the band were marching through her dining room. In addition to these technical advantages, the FM band has the practical advantage of a wide range of frequencies still open for station expansion. Since most AM frequencies had been allocated by the FCC during the '60s, FM has been surging with new allocations.

Many industry professionals expect the real growth of radio audiences to be in FM. From a low figure of 35% of the radio audience in America's top 25 markets in 1973, research predicts an increase to 43% in 1980 and then to a majority figure of 55% by 1985 (Figure 3–1).[6] In short the real future of radio seems to be in FM. AM is in no danger of going out of existence but the obvious advantages of FM programming—better signal, stereo, and less frequency crowding—signal a popularity surge for FM. Today it is not unusual for FM broadcasting stations to sell for millions of dollars, a price unheard of in the 1960s.

AM/FM SHARE OF AUDIENCE
(TOP 25 MARKETS)

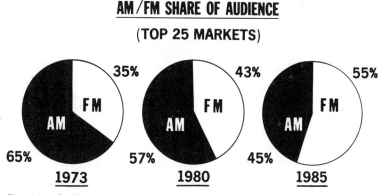

Figure 3–1 Predicted growth patterns of FM radio. (Source: Cox Broadcasting Corporation.)

Radio's Acceptance and Potential

Despite the enormous impact of television in the 1950s, radio has continued to grow and prosper. Since its early development in 1920, it has achieved and maintained a growth factor rivaling that of all other media in the history of mass communication. Estimated percentages through the 1980s see growth up over 225% from the early 1950s. Despite a penetration of more than 100% of the population, radio set sales continue to climb. We might well ask why, with virtually every household equipped with more than one radio, people continue to buy radios. A cursory glance at the market will give us some answers. For one thing, a transistor radio has become a widely accepted gift, coming in all shapes and sizes from complex shortwave sets, to combinations of radios and other gadgetry such as cigarette lighters, liquor decanters, and pencil sets. Miniaturization of parts has made it possible to place a radio in virtually all kinds of imaginable items in the home, from intercoms to popular home entertainment combinations of television, AM/FM radio, and stereo record players. Moreover, increased use of FM bands has sparked still more sales. Now the public's appetite has been whetted for FM sets which can receive FM in stereo or quadrophonic four-channel sound.

Educational Radio

In many countries where television systems are not well developed, radio remains the dominant medium. Consequently, it has become a major teaching medium for people in these underdeveloped nations. Researchers at the Institute for Communication Research of Stanford University have compared the effectiveness of instructional media in various international locations. The Institute has tested both instructional radio and instructional television. In a recent summary report, researchers concluded:

> There is nothing in the research evidence to cast doubt on the proposition that a motivated student can learn from any medium. One of the most surprising results to researchers was the absence of any clear and consistent evidence of difference between the efficiency of learning from the complex and costly media like television and the less costly ones like radio. . . .[7]

Installation of relatively inexpensive transmitters in local areas enables radio to disseminate information in the local language and to reflect local cultures. This is especially important in areas where social and cultural identities are threatened—Liberia being a good example. In the United States, cultural identity is sought in radio programming aimed toward American Indian reservations. Certain New Mexico stations broadcast special language programs and music of the Navajo Indians. Major universities are also awarding credits to listeners who complete courses taught completely by radio. With this emphasis on the outreach function of colleges and universities, radio is beginning to realize another of its potentials.

Radio's Future Perspective

The future of radio is bright both in terms of technological developments and the all-important economic considerations which face any mass medium. The ability of radio, for example, to reach a great number of people at a comparatively small cost is a distinct advantage over television. For corporations with small to moderate advertising budgets, radio affords the opportunity to reach their public. Many radio news departments operate with a small number of personnel, a few inexpensive cassette tape recorders, and an automobile equipped with a two-way radio. For television news to function, it takes thousands of dollars worth of equipment, trained personnel for operating the equipment, and a costly television transmitter and studio equipment to edit, compose, and send the program to the viewers.

Stereo FM will continue to develop. The full potential of stereo news has yet to be tapped. It will permit radio to develop and stretch the audio picture of an event even beyond what television can do as a single video dimension. The medium has come a long way since Marconi first lifted his kite antenna above Newfoundland and received signals across the Atlantic. Throughout the world, radio serves the masses with entertainment, news, and instructional programming. It has survived television and gained its own identity as a medium with distinct advantages and the ability to reach specialized audiences in our society.

television

Television has been called everything from an educational panacea to a boob tube projecting images of a vast wasteland. People have labeled it biased, accurate, liberal, conservative, and have accused it of everything from wrecking the family structure to robbing us of our individuality. Somewhere in between all this lies the truth. One thing is certain. The medium has become one of the most powerful communicative forces in the history of civilization. Today satellites cross paths in space to transmit television pictures from one country and culture to another. It too has come of age as a world medium.

Television's Early Development

To fully appreciate the great technological strides television has made in the past decades, we need to examine the history of the medium.

The concept of television can be traced back to 1839. In that year French physicist Alexandre Edmond Becquerel observed the electrochemical effects of light. In 1884, the German scientist, Paul G. Nipkow, devised a method whereby a spiraling disc could pass over a picture and create a scanning effect. Nipkow punched holes in his disc to create the pattern of a spiral, beginning at the outer edge and circling toward the center of the disc. When the disc revolved, the holes would pass over the picture, and in one complete revolution of the disc the total picture would be scanned. Nipkow transferred the light passing through each hole into electrical energy and transmitted this electrical energy through wires to a receiver which also had a synchronized disc connected to a transmitter. When the transmitter changed pictures at rapid intervals, a very crude picture with a semblance of motion could be achieved. Nipkow's device represented a mechanical adaptation of the principle used in the old penny arcade in which a series of cards would turn down, each with a slightly different picture than the one before it, thus creating the illusion of movement.

Electronic Breakthrough: The Iconoscope Tube

A breakthrough came in 1923 with Russian physicist V. K. Zworykin's patent for the iconoscope-tube television camera. In Zworykin's invention, electricity picked up where mechanics left off. Zworykin's process used electrons to scan lines in a sweeping motion. To understand this principle, think of a flag with red and white stripes. The electron scanning process first scans the entire field of white stripes and then scans the entire field of red stripes. Now imagine a flag with 500 stripes and all of these being alternately scanned. That's how the electron scanning process increases the optical clarity of a picture as compared to the mechanical process. Changing each picture as in the penny arcade technique, then using a fast scanning process results in a clear illusion of motion. Why illusion?—because motion is not inherent; it is your eyes and brain that lend the illusion of motion.

To better understand the illusion, we'll return to our discussion of intrapersonal communication in Chapter 1. In intrapersonal communication, your eye becomes the receiver of visual stimuli which are transmitted via your optic nerve to your brain. When you look at an object, your brain retains the impression of that object for a fraction of a second. Since television projects images more rapidly than your eye and brain can comprehend them, the television picture being scanned for a fraction of a second creates the illusion of motion. And because television pictures change so rapidly that you cannot possibly perceive their movement, the illusion is of smooth motion, not rough as when you watch a slow motion picture projector jerk each frame.

The Illusion of Color Television

A similar process takes place in color television. Again, your intrapersonal communication enables you to see color. Your eye actually has the capacity to intercept three primary colors—red, blue, and green (Figure 3–2). Combinations of these wavelengths of light are responsible for all other colors. In color television, a separate television tube detects each of these three primary colors in an image and each transmits its results to a television receiver. Your eyes and brain then see a cohesive picture based on tiny elements of red, blue, and green appearing on your television screen.

Improved versions of the iconoscope tube, including the image orthocon tube and Amperex Corporation's plumbicon tube, per-

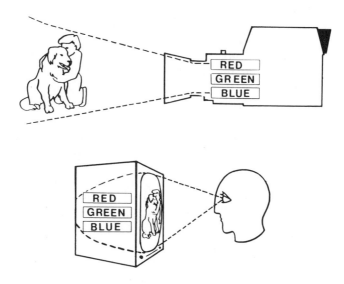

Figure 3–2 Three primary colors of light, red, blue, and green produce all other combinations of color resulting in the illusion of a composite color television picture.

fected Zworykin's concept. Further developments enabled camera tubes to scan color with a clarity equal to that of the human eye.

Criticism of Television

The medium has become embroiled in many social issues since its impact was first felt in the late 1940s. In the nationally televised debates between presidential candidates Richard Nixon and John Kennedy, the public saw television communicate the "images" of candidates and alter political campaigns. The medium's attempts to sell candidates through the use of political commercials much as it promotes soap or other products came under intense criticism. As political candidates began to regard television exposure seriously, consulting firms popped up offering candidates high-priced advice on how to use TV to influence voters.

Television news came under criticism in the 1960s during the era of campus unrest. A college administrator of one of the nation's universities condemned the media by saying, "TV stations have almost no interest in reporting the truth, rather they are interested only in sensationalism." His reaction was typical of many other college administrators who experienced the presence of media on their campuses during a time of turmoil. Television news coverage of politics also came under scrutiny with the special Kerner Commission's investigation into the coverage of the 1968 Democratic Convention in Chicago.

Television advertising has also become the subject of congressional inquiries. When cigarette smoking was determined "hazardous to your health" by the Surgeon General, Congress admitted the tremendous impact of television and promptly banned cigarette advertising on the medium. The television industry complained of its rights under the First Amendment, but the complaints were of little avail. Many television advertising executives were concerned about the crippling economic effects of removing cigarette advertising, yet the medium recovered from the economic pinch within six months after the rulings went into effect.

Televised violence in children's programming is another controversial issue facing television. Results reported by the Surgeon General's commission on televised violence still spur debates by educators, media professionals, and politicians. Follow-up studies continue to research the issues. Many university communication research centers, institutes, and even the television networks are supplying funds to examine more closely the true relationship between televised violence and aggressive behavior. It has been estimated that children see as many as 1200 hours of violence on television by the time they are sixteen, and some claim that this constant exposure to violence plants the seeds of aggressive behavior. Another view is that children fully realize the fictional nature of these shows and are thus not tempted to imitate the televised acts. Self-regulating organizations such as the National Association of Broadcasters continually view television programming and encourage voluntary restraint of violence. In Mexico, the government intervened and banned some American television programs because of the violence they portrayed. No simple solution to this complex problem exists.

Some nations have become alarmed at the wholesaling of cultural programming from one society to another. They argue that television is destroying the cultures of many nations because programming from America and other major nations dominates the media. In some cases, nations have even passed regulations requiring a certain amount of local cultural programming be reflected in a day's television schedule. Yet the positive side of international programming is television's ability to inform people of one country and culture about the activities of another, thus fostering harmony and understanding in international relations. Criticism of television will undoubtedly continue.

Television's Impact and Use

The public has widely accepted the medium ever since its first year of significant operation in 1948. Television Bureau of Advertising estimates list television as commanding 48% of our time spent with media as opposed to 32% for radio, 13% for newspapers, and 7% for magazines. Television set ownership increased dramatically after World War II. Networks began to develop major distribution systems at that time to reach affiliate stations in most areas of the United States and many foreign countries. Nielsen estimates listed more than forty-three million households with televisions in 1950. By the mid-1970s, that figure had increased to approximately seventy million. Other countries have experienced similar growth patterns. For example, Nielsen estimates for Canada report 3.7 million households had television sets in 1954, and approximately 6 million had them by the mid-1970s. New developments in satellite communication have made television possible in outlying areas of Canada and other countries where the cost of transmitting signals via relay towers is prohibitive. The amount of time we spend with television has also steadily increased. In the United States, we averaged more than five hours of television consumption per day, per household in 1963, and this had increased to six by the mid-1970s. This translates into actual years spent in front of television by the time we reach adulthood.

Educational television (ETV) and instructional television (ITV) have been designed specifically to capitalize on the teaching-learning process. ETV refers to *any non-commercial television program*, whether or not the program is used for direct classroom instruction. ITV refers to *programming especially tailored for use in the classroom or in a direct teaching role.* Industries as well as schools have incorporated ITV in many areas of training. The ability to transmit ITV programs directly into the home makes it possible for many corporations to conduct home training programs. Similar programs have been developed through colleges and universities.

Much of the medium's impact cannot be measured in statistics. The changes in our life styles since the advent of television are too numerous and in some cases too subtle to measure fully. An international television spectacular from one country can set a new trend in another country's clothing styles. A breakfast cereal commercial may show someone participating in the sport of hang-gliding. The sale of the breakfast cereal soars, and so does the sale of hang-gliders. A stomach medicine is advertised as a man stuffs pizza into his mouth. The sale of the stomach remedy stays constant, but pizza sales increase. A student sits in the classroom and has little desire to learn from lectures. The teacher introduces a televised segment to the lesson, and the student's interest and attention span increase. Researchers in a university prepare a comedy series to teach reading to underprivileged children. When their examples seem unreal to the children's preconceptions about television, the series fails miserably. All of these examples show that at present we are still unaware of the total impact of the medium. It has only been during the last decade that college students have become the first total-television generation, living with the medium from birth. What will occur when you become the first television-parent generation, and your children will be part of a home which has seen every member of the family molded by television since birth? It is easy to see why it is so important to realize the impact of the medium now, and to become responsible consumers and molders of its future.

What the Future Holds

What television holds for society as it approaches the end of the 20th century is open to considerable speculation. Already we can sit in front of "big screen" television, which can cover an entire wall. A special television receiver collects the signal and then projects it onto a wall like a slide projector. Research has also developed slim screen television to replace the cumbersome models of the past that saw television tubes as large as two feet thick. The new picture tubes aren't much thicker than a picture frame and can be hung on the wall in much the same manner. Portable "mini-cams" and "micro-cams" give television reporters the flexibility of the radio journalist, although still not at the reduced cost which radio enjoys (Figure 3–3). Held easily with two hands, these small cameras permit live TV coverage of many news events that was previously impossible because of the difficulty in transporting cumbersome television equipment. Side-line interviews with football coaches, traffic flow observations from a helicopter, and streetside interviews at a political rally have thus become commonplace. Although we may not see the wholesale marketing of Dick Tracy-type wrist televisions in our lifetime, the miniaturization of electronic components will increase television's portability.

Increases in Channel Capacity

Television programming will also change as cable television grows, making available more channels than are possible with direct over-the-airways reception. We'll see an increase in the amount of local access to cable television, and community groups will be responsible for this programming. Public television supported through public contributions and government subsidies from the Corporation for Public Broadcasting will be providing more alternatives to

Figure 3–3 KSD-TV crew operates a small portable television camera and recorder used in an on-the-scene news interview in St. Louis.

the mass appeal programs seen on commercial network television. The future of pay television on a mass scale is somewhat uncertain, but limited experiments have proved successful in a number of communities. A coin dropped into a slot in the top of your home television set permits you to see programming not available on other channels. All this adds up to more selective viewing, which, along with technological improvements, will play an important part in television's development as a medium of the future.

film

In May 1896, the excitement and enthusiasm of his first sight of a motion picture caused Russian critic, 73-year-old Vladimir Stasov to exclaim:

> What joy I had on Monday, seeing the *moving photography*, that magnificent new invention of the genius Edison. It was Glazunov who took me to see it. He had been there earlier and his tremendous enthusiasm persuaded me to see it too. It is really extraordinary, resembling nothing previously known, and indeed it could not have existed before our century. Glazunov and I were in such ecstasy that at the end we applauded noisily and shouted, "Vivat Edison! . . ."[8]

Less than a month before, similar excitement and enthusiasm for the new medium had been expressed in America, when on April 23, 1896, the American premiere of motion pictures took place in Koster and Bial's Music Hall in New York. The following day, the *New York Times* reported:

> When the hall was darkened last night, a buzzing and roaring was heard in the turret and an unusually bright light fell upon the screen. Then came into view two precious blonde young persons on the variety stage in pink and blue dresses, doing the umbrella dance with commendable celerity. Their motions were all clearly defined. When they vanished, a view of the angry surf breaking on a sandy beach near a stone pier amazed the spectators. . . . A burlesque boxing match between a tall, thin comedian and a short, fat one; a comic allegory called 'The Monroe Doctrine'; an instant of motion in Hoyt's farce, the 'Milk White Flag' repeated over and over again and a skirt dance by a tall blonde completed the views, which were all wonderfully real and singularly exhilarating.[9]

The beginning of motion pictures at the turn of the century drew many predictions for the impact and growth of the medium. As the industry came into its own and developed the added dimension of sound, and then technicolor and cinemascope became household words, there seemed to be no limit to the imagination. Film was now regarded as a serious art form: the world recognized the expertise and creative talents of such men as Cecil B. De Mille, Otto Preminger, D. W. Griffith, Mack Sennett, Alfred Hitchcock, Stanley Kubrick, and countless others. The motion picture moved out of the peephole boxes of the arcades into the giant screen of cinerama in the plushest theaters, holding thousands of viewers in velvet-cushioned comfort. A California town called Hollywood became the glittering motion picture capital of the world. Yet as directors grew more skillful and equipment became more portable, the industry called its home "on location," any place the scenery fit the story. The large movie houses of the city gradually evolved into the smaller cinemas, as the population took over suburbia. Thus, the best actors and most famous films could be seen not only in downtown major metropolitan areas but also down the street at the closest shopping center. The film industry began to cater to the automobile as drive-ins popped up across the countryside. The world experienced a new medium equally capable of reflecting the social climate of nations as dramatic theater or great literature.

The Early Years of Film

In theory, the concept of motion in pictures can be traced all the way back to pictographics in caves of prehistoric times. Animals, objects of the hunt, were frequently portrayed in motion. The penny arcade was, however, the real forerunner of the modern motion picture. A coin dropped into a slot and the turn of a crank brought cards flipping past your viewfinder. Each card had a picture slightly different than the one before it, and the speed of your crank determined the speed and authenticity of their motion.

Thomas Edison played a major part in the development of early motion pictures with his *kinetoscope* machine, a crude device with a peephole through which you could see pictures move. But the real development of a projecting device must be credited to two French brothers, Louis and Auguste Lumière. They opened a public theater called the Grand Café and charged admission to see a short series of films. One of the most famous early films, *Arrival of a Train at a Station*, showed a train moving directly forward on the screen, an amazing spectacle for the era.

As more movie theaters opened, the public flocked to the new medium in numbers unheard of for any art form in previous history. An average theater could see box office receipts increase as much as three thousand percent within two weeks of business! Certainly, part of this popularity was due to the medium's novelty. Yet for those with a serious interest in the arts, motion pictures held an opportunity for a new type of creativity. At this period in time, Americans were just witnessing the full impact of the industrial revolution, bringing with it a new life style—leisure time. This newfound freedom fostered a desire for relaxation, amusement, and entertainment. If they were going to be successful, the movies could not have arrived at a more opportune time in history.

The early motion pictures were cumbersome to produce. The first bulky photography cameras did not lend themselves to such modern feats as being positioned on the front of a racing car or being strapped to the shoulders of a skydiver. These cameras were big, complex machines that needed a lot of light to take pictures. The early films could only capture action in front of the lens; refined techniques where the lens would follow the action had to wait upon technology. Some of the most famous early productions included D. W. Griffith's *Birth of a Nation,* a controversial story of the Civil War era that dealt with the rights of blacks in the South following the defeat of the Confederate army. *Birth of a Nation* altered the entire concept of American movie making, developing the close-up, cross-cutting, rapid-fire editing, the iris, the split-screen shot, and realistic and impressionistic lighting, creating images and sequences yet to be surpassed. The film's magnitude and epic grandeur swept audiences off their feet. In a private White House screening, President Woodrow Wilson exclaimed, "It is like writing history with lightning!"[10]

International Film

Other nations besides America witnessed the serious development of film. In Italy, for example, industrialists invested heavily in the Italian film industry in the early 1900s, and some of the most famous Italian films dealt with the historical development of the nation and much of Europe. Enrico Gauzzoni directed many early Italian films. He produced *Brutus* and another extravaganza entitled the *Last Days of Pompeii,* the latter bringing in box office receipts three times as much as its production costs. Despite oppression and intense censorship, films also began to make headlines in the Soviet Union. Soviet films in the early 1900s were known for their literary content and elaborate costumes.[11] Credit for part of this goes to the ruling Tolstoys, who felt it important that the cinema recapture important moments in Russian history. Hungary carried on similar controlled film production. In 1919, the entire film industry of Hungary became nationalized. Little protest was heard from producers, actors, or those associated with the basic foundation of the industry, since nationalization was a welcome change from a corrupt production and distribution system.[12]

In Japan, film also made great strides. One of the men who had a major effect on the Japanese film industry was Norimasa Kaeriyama, an engineer by trade who developed a love for film and published a text entitled *The Production and Photography of Moving Picture Drama.* He was noted for bringing three major improvements to the Japanese film industry. These were the introduction of longer films and close shots, a major emphasis on editing films to perfect their development and artistry, and the use of women in women's roles. Prior to this time, men impersonators had played the part of females.[13]

Film had truly gone international, yet the directions the new medium took in different areas of the world were strikingly different. The Soviets wanted to record history, the Hungarians decreed national economic control of the medium, and the Americans revered it as a source of entertainment. Whatever purpose it served, film became firmly fixed as an expressive art.

The Stars Are Born

Not long after film technology overcame many of its cumbersome hurdles, the novelty of the medium evolved into a novelty of film actors and actresses. They became the stars of the new medium, and the public idolized their every professional and personal move. Each nation had its own stars, and many of these national film stars grew to be international stars.

Perhaps the most famous was Charlie Chaplin, the little man with the moustache, the derby, and the baggy pants, who captured the hearts of viewers around the world. Audiences shared his disappointments, his frustrations, and his continual confrontations with the obstacles in life that prevent people from reaching their dreams. In the era of silent films, Charlie Chaplin became an institution. He was a star in the truest sense of the word, both in tangible box office receipts and in his achievement of immortality. Today, his films still draw large audiences at film festivals all over the world. Chaplin needed no sound; he was able to communicate through movements and gestures. He was a master of nonverbal subtleties, and his slightest motion could shake an audience into uncontrollable fits of laughter. In one of his most famous films, *The Tramp,* he perfected his role as the underdog in society's many predicaments, always seeking victory but usually winning humorous frustration. His was a slapstick form of comedy, credited in many ways to the film theory of director Mack Sennett. Sennett's theory conformed to three primary approaches.[14] One method was to take a melodramatic plot and insert well-placed gags in it. Another was to take a given "place or situation and then run through all of the gags they can think of that might occur there." His third approach shaped individual gags to fit the theme of the picture. Sennett also developed various mechanical innovations for film. He found that by photographing in slow motion and playing the film back at regular speed, the animated, mechanical, robot-like trademark of Chaplin could be achieved with great satisfaction. Chaplin himself became a distinguished director, often acting in his own pictures. Other famous stars glittered in Chaplin's era, including the famous slapstick comedy team of Laurel and Hardy.

Trends in Theater Construction

With the advent of television, motion picture theater popularity began to dip. For example, in 1945 there were about 17,000 indoor theaters in the United States (Figure 3–4). That figure dropped to slightly more than 14,500 by 1954 and hit a slump of 9,150 in 1963. From that point on, the motion picture industry moved into a new era.

A Medium in Transition: The 1960s

The 1960s brought two major developments to film. First, it became a true art form, much more so than in the past. Drawing on a fifty-year foundation of experience, film now had the means to perfect its craft. International film producers, directors, and scholars began to

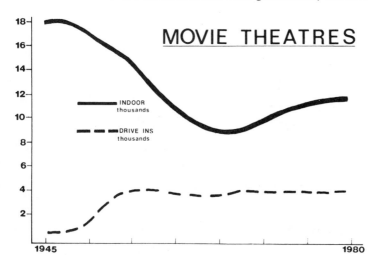

Figure 3–4 U.S. motion picture theatres — indoor and drive-ins — projected thru 1980. (Source of data to 1973: U.S. Dept. of Commerce, Domestic and International Business Administration, Bureau of Competitive Assessment and Business Policy.)

exchange ideas. Journals, trade publications, and film reviews all added to the scholarly acceptance of the medium as art. By the 1960s enough films had been produced to prompt specialization in the study of film. For example, you could study a certain film form or a certain director's technique. Federico Fellini and his creation of reality on the big screen was one example of many specific "styles" that emerged in this new inquiry. The westerns, foreign films, the slapstick comedy of the silent era, and the cartoon empire built by Walt Disney all provided avenues for a student to view, study, perceive, and write about film.

The second major impact of the motion picture industry came when television gave film a new channel of distribution. Not only were the movies of the big screen aired on television at prime time, but special production companies started developing films specifically for the purpose of showing them on television. The portability of the camera and the financial backing of the television networks permitted this new film industry to develop side-by-side with the older one. Many of the people involved in the production of traditional films found themselves adapting easily to the production of films for television.

Film's new era also produced internationalism. From the Orient came the brilliant directorship and acting of Bruce Lee and a rising popularity of films depicting man's hand-to-hand physical combat in the art of Kung Fu. Similarly, American western heroes became just as popular in Japan. Foreign stars such as Italy's Sophia Loren and England's Richard Burton became popular in America.

New Directions in the 1970s

The early 1970s saw the serious emergence of black stars in films designed to capture the unique experience of the black American. Such screen figures as James Earl Jones, Lola Falana, Roscoe Lee Brown, James Brown, Sidney Poitier, and many others were seen in theaters throughout the country in such box office attractions as *Shaft* and *Superfly*. Pam Grier added to the appeal of such box office attractions as *Coffy*, *Foxy Brown*, and *Sheba Baby*.

The screen also saw the advent of social commentary films. One of the most popular of these attractions was *Billy Jack*. What started out to be a very underpublicized, low-budget film turned into one of the biggest sleepers in motion picture history. It was the story of an Indian ex-Marine who came home from the war to live on an Indian reservation and ended up trying to protect a free school against a prejudiced community. The picture had such popularity that a sequel entitled the *Trial of Billy Jack* followed two years later, which again set opening week box office records. And that was followed by *Billy Jack Goes to Washington.*

Even the physical qualities of the "theater experience" have been the object of experimentation. The film *Earthquake* added the dimension of "Sensurround," in which the illusion of actually experiencing an earthquake was perfected. Sensurround was followed by the technique of "halographics" which achieved three-dimensionalism in the film *Logan's Run.* In *Logan's Run,* producer Saul David created a mythical society of the twenty-third century where the characters actually appeared to stand out from the screen. The technique eliminated the need to wear special 3-D glasses utilized by 3-D films of the 1950s.

But of all the films, none produced such mass reaction as *Jaws* (Figure 3–5). It was the brainchild of author Peter Benchley who wrote a book and publicized it in serial form in a leading magazine. The movie was released at the beginning of the summer of 1975. It wasn't long before the "Jaws" fad took the country by storm. Not since the famous undershirt uproar when Clark Gable was seen

Figure 3–5 The movie JAWS, along with setting box office records also set off a series of fads resulting in everything from editorial cartoons to inflatable sharks. (From the Motion Picture "JAWS," Courtesy of Universal Pictures.)

without one in *It Happened One Night* did the public become so "aware" of something produced on the silver screen. The film was successful enough to give Universal City Studios a 25 percent share of the United States and Canadian film market for 1975 and to become the all-time box office record breaker. For the producers, Richard Zanuck and David Brown, it meant millions in personal income. The director, Steven Speilberg, also reaped millions. Other box office receipts from re-releases, foreign showings, and eventually television would place the movie at the pinnacle of motion picture success.

Popular "Jaws" trinkets hit the mass market in waves, almost unequaled by memorabilia evoked from any other motion picture. Stores flaunted T-shirts, rubber floating sharks, shark greeting cards, books about sharks, shark posters, and even fake shark fins that could be placed in one's favorite lake or bathing area to start the panic of the season—literally. On beaches everywhere people hesitated to experience the rolling surf with the abandon of previous seasons. A child yelling shark could break the synchronized stroke of many an ocean swimmer. Small pieces of floating debris sent panic up the spine of surfers. On beaches where shark sightings had once been routine, such incidents now profoundly affected bathers and made national network news reports.

Other movies tried to capitalize on the bandwagon shark effect. Low-budget films about sharks lured the true "Jaws-crazy" fans back into the theater. And just as the growth of such disaster films as *Towering Inferno* and *Earthquake* can be traced to the *Poseidon Adventure*, it wasn't long before *Jaws* would spawn its own counterparts. Reports began to filter out to game management people that a movie was being prepared about a killer grizzly bear. The title of the movie—*Claws!*

The Future of Film

If any medium claims the distinction of coming into its own in the twentieth century, film will undoubtedly accept that title. From its early impact in the 1900s to its achievement as an art form by mid-century and finally its emergence as a significant mass medium 75 years later, film has justified its continuing existence as a mass medium to be reckoned with.

With the constant transformation of all mass media, uncertainties about the future of film abound which puzzle not only industry professionals but also social scientists. Will film continue to play a significant role in our lives? We have seen cassette videotapes and videodiscs develop into a home and educational medium. The ability to purchase videotapes of films for home television viewing opens a new outlet for much of the material previously reserved for theater viewing. The videotape explosion has also revolutionized the production of motion pictures. Many television programs are now produced just as inexpensively on videotape as they were on film, and to many videotape "artists," this medium is just as realistic as film. Yet the film artist would deny that statement with equal legitimacy and vigor. There has been no decrease in the production of major motion pictures. In addition, after the number of indoor theaters reached its nadir in 1963, approximately 50 new theaters have joined the ranks per year. Social scientists have also discovered that people still do not like a steady diet of home television entertainment. Perhaps the future of film will parallel that of professional sports. Despite the fact we can watch athletics on television, the excitement of watching a live game or event still seems to have no equal. It is this need to be part of a large audience, mutually watching an experience unfold that remains the lure of the film theater.

summary

Chapter 3 has dealt with the non-print media of radio, television, and film.

Radio's development can be traced to the pioneering work of German physicist Heinrich Rudolph Hertz who discovered the principle of electromagnetic waves in the atmosphere. The work of Hertz was followed by that of the Italian inventor Guglielmo Marconi, who perfected the wireless transmission of messages. Radio grew and prospered. It survived the challenges of television by diversifying and directing programming to specialized audiences. Its impact has been significant. Today as a world medium, it informs, entertains, and educates. In the United States, there are more radios than people. Radio is also a portable medium eminently suitable for our mobile life style.

Television's beginnings can be traced back to the work of the French physicist Alexandre Edmond Becquerel who studied the electrochemical effects of light. The mechanical transmission of pictures was achieved by the German scientist, Paul G. Nipkow. With the invention of the iconoscope tube by Russian inventor V. K. Zworykin, it was now possible to transmit pictures electronically. Both the medium itself and its at times unquestioned acceptance have been severely criticized. Television news has been criticized for its biased and sensationalistic coverage of civil unrest, and recent concern has emerged over the content of advertising directed toward children.

The international development of film corresponded closely to that of radio and television. Edison's early experiments with his kinetoscope paved the way for modern projection systems including cinemascope, or wide-screen motion pictures. Stars were also created by the new medium. Early favorites such as Charlie Chaplin were followed by stars who made it big in the era of the talkies. Within the century, the medium has become a legitimate art form.

opportunities for further learning

BARNOUW, ERIK, *The Golden Web*. New York: Oxford University Press, 1968.

BARNOUW, ERIK, *The Image Empire*. New York: Oxford University Press, 1970.

BARNOUW, ERIK, *A Tower in Babel*. New York: Oxford University Press, 1966.

BROWN, LES, *Television: The Business Behind the Box*. New York: Harcourt Brace Jovanovich, 1971.

FINCH, CHRISTOPHER, *The Art of Walt Disney*. New York: Harry N. Abrams, Inc., Publishers, 1975.

GREEN, MAURY, *Television News: Anatomy and Process*. Belmont, Calif: Wadsworth Publishing Company, Inc., 1969.

JOHNSON, JOSEPH S., and KENNETH K. JONES, *Modern Radio Station Practices*. Belmont, Calif: Wadsworth Publishing Company, Inc., 1972.

LICHTY, LAWRENCE W., and MALACHI C. TOPPING, *American Broadcasting: A Source Book on the History of Radio & Television*. New York: Hastings House, 1975.

MAST, GERALD, *A Short History of the Movies*. New York: Pegasus, 1971.

SAVARY, LOUIS M., and J. PAUL CARRICO, eds., *Contemporary Film and the New Generation*. New York: Association Press, 1971.

WHITAKER, ROD, *The Language of Film*. Englewood Cliffs, N.J.: Prentice-Hall, Inc., 1970.

WRIGHT, BASIL, *The Long View*. New York: Alfred A. Knopf, 1974.

books, direct mail, outdoor, and the emergence of specialized media

CHAPTER FOUR

Books, direct mail, and billboards are often the overlooked forms of mass communication. Yet they have the potential to influence our thoughts and actions just as much as the more flashy electronic media. These particular media do not have the instantaneous impact of the electronic media or even of the newspaper, yet they remain current and up-to-date. They are all multi-million dollar businesses in their own right, contributing to the economic growth of mass media industries in general. We'll begin our discussion of these "other" media with books.

books

When radio and then television became mass media, pessimists made dire predictions about the future of books, similar to the prognosis they had made for the mails upon completion of the Atlantic Cable. They suggested that we would become a visual society attuned to the giant screen instead of the printed page. The satirical movie *Fahrenheit 451* portrayed a future in which television would be the giant controlling medium, and it would be illegal to possess books. Although such a state is not beyond the realm of possibility in anything less than a free society, books have stood the test of time. They have survived and carry with them an important part of society's development. From Chaucer's *Canterbury Tales* to the latest best seller, books have remained a major part of our lives. We learn from them, we are entertained by them, we possess them, and they are indomitable through major reforms among men and nations. Books have been the object of political suppression and the stimulus for champions of liberation. They have been among the cherished possessions of kings and have helped lay the foundations of republican government. Radio and television programs come and go; at best we may remember a catchy word or phrase, or a fleeting image may haunt our memory. A book, however, like a good friend, can be looked up again and again without tiring of its acquaintance.

Early Book Publishing

The Saxons in the fifth century published some of the earliest books. They consisted of thin animal skins, crudely bound together. The animal skin was called vellum and was a major improvement over the clay tablets used to communicate messages thousands of years earlier. Later, in the cloisters and abbeys of medieval Europe, monks laboriously copied the Scriptures, embellishing them with crude hand engravings and placing them between hard covers for storage in the monasteries. There most of these early religious texts would remain to be used by men preparing for the priesthood. These early volumes were as large as two or three feet in length and width, obviously a far cry from the portability of modern paperbacks.

With increased use of the printing press during the sixteenth century, composition changed drastically. Engraved wooden blocks became printing plates to produce illustrations. Books could now be mass produced—of course on a scale we would consider moderate indeed. These early books were primarily hardback volumes, with content centered around religion, the writings of the ancient Greeks, and the trades. The audience for the early hard-bound volumes again was not the mass audience. It consisted mostly of students, who would borrow the books and pass them on from one class to another, the religious orders of the day, or the elite and wealthy who could afford the luxury of buying books.

Colonial Printers and Modern Paperbacks

The beginnings of book publishing in America can be traced as far back as the 1600s, when developing colonies needed to distribute documents to their colonists. Colonial governments would pay printers to assemble these documents into a form of paperback book. Such printing contracts constituted the major part of the trade of colonial printers. They earned additional income by printing religious publications, such as psalmbooks and collections of sermons. However, when they ventured beyond printing, they ran into trouble. When the lure of becoming journalists became too strong, printers began publishing colonial newspapers, at first with advertisements of economic news. Later on, they began publishing news of political developments, and then they got into trouble. As we learned earlier, some printers were even put out of business when they lost their government subsidies. From this time on, newspaper publishers and book publishers began to develop separately.

Beadle's Dime Novels

The impetus for major book publishing on a mass scale occurred shortly after 1850 when there appeared both the means and the desire to produce books that would become the foundation for much of the current publishing industry. At that time a New York publisher named E. F. Beadle decided he could sell books if they were cheap enough and if they quenched the public's thirst for entertainment and good literary prose. He started with the publication of a ten-cent paperback songbook. Shortly thereafter, he ventured into other paperback "dime novels" which were to become best-selling "dialogues," even by the modest standards of the late 1800s (Figure 4–1). Beadle's novels weren't long—only about 75 pages—and they dealt primarily with the American pioneer. Keep in mind that at that time much of the West was yet to be won. Yarns and tales of the lands west of the Allegheny Mountains made exciting reading for young and old alike.

A search for an escape into a fantasy world turned the dime novels into best sellers. They contained little truth but continued to prosper even into the Civil War era, when the troops found the books easy company on long hikes. Many other companies also ventured into dime novel publishing, and although the thrill of the original dime novel lessened, it left a sizeable impression on the history of book publishing. To it we owe the modern concept of the book as a medium of mass communication.

Distributing Paperbacks

One reason for the success of today's paperback book industry is its distribution system. Anytime you can distribute easily and inexpensively information that the public wants, then you have a chance for success. The first chapters of the paperback book success story are ease of transportation and wide availability. The distribution system, although not as efficient perhaps as that of radio or television, is still not cumbersome by any means.

Because of this ease of distribution, paperback books have also become an instrument of persuasion and, in some cases, propaganda. For example, politicians running for office may find that they can add to their prestige by writing a book that details their career in office. The book can be assembled into approximately one hundred pages and distributed on a mass scale to as many potential voters as funds permit. The cost of producing the book is minimal, and the means of distribution can be through political workers carrying an armload door-to-door. Portability is part of the reason you, as a consumer, chose a paperback book to accompany you on your last trip. It was light, and you could carry it for a long time even though you were walking through train stations or airport corridors. You could hold it easily or set it on the edge of your seat in the coach section of an airline or on a bus.

Paperback books can also be bought at places other than book stores. Sir Allen Lane, publisher of the famous Penguin books, during a visit to America in the early 1930s, surmised that if he could make buying books as easy as purchasing any other novelty, he could reach a substantial untapped market of readers. Sir Allen managed to negotiate a contract with the Woolworth stores to distribute his Penguin books.[1] The venture proved successful, and the new distribution system clinched the success of his enterprise. Today, you can find paperback books in virtually every type of retail establishment imaginable, from gas stations to grocery stores.

Personalized Books

The mid-1970s saw the dawn of what has become known in children's literature as the personalized book. This book is composed and printed entirely by computer. Stored in the computer is a complete text of the book but with computer programming arranged so as to permit the addition of specific names and places to be incorporated into the text. When the book is printed, the person ordering the book can request that certain names, dates, addresses, and places be incorporated into the text. For example, a parent wants to order a book for a child. Let us assume that the child has a family pet, a brother and a sister and lives in a small community. We'll call her Nancy Smith, the dog will be named Laddie, and the family will live on Peach Street. When Nancy's parent orders the book, all of this information is given to the publisher, who in turn programs the computer to print the book by personalizing it for Nancy. When Nancy opens the book, it reads: "This morning, Nancy and her dog Laddie were walking home on Peach Street when Laddie began barking loudly." The story would then continue with the names of the characters being Nancy's brothers, sisters, and relatives who are actually part of Nancy's real world. There is more to this concept than the novelty, however. What has made them of significant educational value and use as learning tools is the interest and motivation children acquire when they see their names in print.

Over the past centuries, books have become a foundation of

society. Like other media, they have helped to educate, inform, and entertain millions of people. With the aid of new types of printing, graphic design, and photographic processes, books will continue to be an important medium of mass communication.

direct mail

We don't often think of the mails as a form of mass communication. Yet they are exactly that. With the application of computer technology to the mailing process, mail is not only a vital form of mass communication but one that is growing by leaps and bounds.

Distribution of Direct Mail

In most countries, the direct-mail concept began when the postal system affixed postage to the simple postcard for a quick and inexpensive way to send messages. Cheaper postage rates for bulk mail also helped. But it was not, however, until 1972 that the true distribution of direct mail on a mass scale emerged. With the use of computers and satellite communication, direct mail came into its own as a mass medium. The 1976 presidential campaigns saw rapid, mass distribution come alive through computer assisted printing, processing, and distribution.

Today, a computer typewriter has the capacity to type 20,000 three-paragraph letters per hour and make every one of them look as though it were individually typed. When a donation is made to a political campaign, each contributor can thus receive a personal letter with the name of the contributor and the amount donated all included. The typewritten letter has the same personal "visual" appeal as if it were done on your own typewriter.

New Technology: Letter Scanners and Mailgrams

The system for using the mail as a mass medium is relatively simple. Imagine you are a candidate running for office and you want to solicit contributions from people whom you feel support your views. You would first secure a mailing list from the thousands available for sale from mailing list distributors. If you are politically conservative, you might purchase a mailing list of subscribers to conservatively-oriented magazines. A computer would then type and send a personal letter from you to every subscriber asking them for contributions. You could even send thank-you notes to everyone who contributed money, again using the computerized mailing system. To those whose contributions were not yet forthcoming you could send a personalized follow-up letter. Once deposited at the post office, the letters whiz through electronic Zip Code sorters called *letter scanners.* The scanners automatically read Zip Codes, computer check each one to make sure they match the city and address, and then send them on to the proper bin at rates of 50,000 pieces of mail per hour. Major cities process anywhere from five to ten billion pieces of mail annually.

In 1970 Western Union developed *Mailgram*^{TM}, a high-speed computer processing mail system for business and individual use (Figure 4–2). Between 1970 and 1974, the use of this system increased to a rate of almost 450,000 messages per week. Using *Mailgram,* an individual or a business can call a toll free number and dictate a message. The message is then processed through a computer and transmitted to regional offices of the postal service along with, but much faster than, the regular United States Mail. Special Western Union offices also accept computer tapes from businesses. The computer tapes, with messages for "mass distribution," are destined for distribution to millions of mailing list addresses. Companies whose computers are hooked into the Western Union teletype system can send these taped messages directly from their offices, eliminating the need to carry the computer tape to and from Western Union receiving centers. The system permits companies involved in major direct-mail campaigns to add the impact of a "telegram" message for distribution on a mass scale.

Western Union has now launched its two Westar^{TM} satellites. The satellites eliminate the need for lines and line charges and add to the efficiency of the distribution system. In slightly more than

Figure 4–2 Western Union's *Mailgram*^{TM}.

100 years from the time a pony express rider took almost a month to cross the United States with a letter, millions of direct-mail messages can now be transmitted between postal centers at the speed of light.

Types of Direct Mail

Many types of direct mail are used to communicate information to the public on a mass scale (Figure 4–3). Among these are *letters,* which can communicate all sorts of information, taking from one to sometimes ten pages to do so. They are usually printed on the letterhead stationery of a company or political organization. We have all received a direct-mail letter at some point in our lives. A military recruiter using a high school graduation mailing list may send a letter soliciting you to join the armed forces. An oil company using a college graduation mailing list may offer you the opportunity to apply for a credit card. Another type of direct mail uses *reply cards,* with a return address already printed on them. Some have preprinted postage; others require you to affix postage. *Postcards* are usually sent to notify you of a happening, perhaps a meeting, a special sale, or another event whose announcement requires a minimum amount of space.

Leaflets and folders can also come under the category of direct mail. Leaflets are usually a single sheet of paper folded as many times as is required to fit into an envelope. Folders may be printed on heavier paper with more extensive and expensive printing displays, often with multiple colors on special heavy-stock paper. Folders are preferred over leaflets for such things as advertising rate schedules, which will be handled frequently.

Three other types of direct mail include *broadsides, booklets,* and *catalogues.* Broadsides are single sheets of paper much larger than letters, folders, or leaflets. Usually folded in more than one direction, their message is colorfully displayed. A booklet, on the other hand, contains a number of sheets of paper, is usually fastened with staples, and opens like a book. It is normally cut to size so that it will fit into a business-size envelope for easy mailing. Everyone has leafed through the mail-order catalogues of major department store chains. Some of the most common, for instance, Montgomery Ward's, Spiegel's, and Sears' catalogues, have become a consumer tradition over the years.

Direct mail campaigns often use a combination of the above methods for maximum effectiveness. For example, a letter from the president of a company may describe a special offer displayed on a broadside. The consumer can order either the item on the broad-

Figure 4-3 Samples of contemporary direct-mail literature.

side or other gifts displayed in an accompanying booklet by simply returning a reply card.

Advantages of Direct-Mail Control

Direct mail has many advantages, the most important being *control.* Like no other form of communication except interpersonal communication, the direct-mail advertiser has the ability to control the message. He or she is not faced with having a radio commercial air at the ineffective hour, having an ad buried in an obscure corner of the newspaper, or reaching thousands of people who will never be interested in the product. The direct-mail advertiser can choose his audience.

Direct mail can also be very *economical.* Although it may seem expensive in terms of printing, postage, and distribution costs, actually the *impact* and *effectiveness* of the message in returned dollars may make it worth many times the original outlay. The direct-mail piece is personally addressed to each consumer, according him or her the kind of attention most other media overlook. Although the cost of reaching millions of people through television or radio may be less on a per thousand basis, many people reached by these messages may have no need for the product or service advertised. For example, one city recently passed a referendum to remove parking meters in a section of the downtown business district. The business district is part of two "twin cities" located next to each other. Since the voters of the second city don't have a say in the downtown parking problem, broadcasting on a medium like television which reaches the entire area would have wasted advertising dollars. The most efficient way to reach the specific voters was to use direct mail.

Advantages of the Direct-Mail Format

Another advantage of direct mail is its *format.* Some day you may be responsible for handling the advertising of a company or perhaps of your own business. You will find direct mail affords a considerable latitude for creativity in the use of visual displays. New printing processes provide extremely vivid colors, and when combined with special paper stocks, they yield a highly effective medium. Also, your message is permanent. It won't disappear when the next commercial pops into view.

As distribution costs become cheaper through increased technological efficiency, the use of direct mail will become more and more appealing. The speed of direct mail and its ability to reach millions on a personal basis are characteristics unmatched by any other medium. Cable television systems may also become a part of direct mail's role in the communication explosion. In the future, one of your television channels may be connected to the postal service, giving you access to direct-mail messages sent electronically via computer from thousands of miles away.

outdoor

Take a drive through any major city and count the number of billboards that line the sides and tops of buildings, hang from scaffolds, and dot the roadsides. Billboards, called *bulletins* or *outdoor* by the billboard industry, have mushroomed since the age of the automobile. They come in all shapes and sizes from the giant, illuminated spectaculars which appear on busy freeways to the small panels used for sidewalk theater advertising. There is some discussion on what exactly is a true billboard. The Institute of Outdoor Advertising, a trade association of member outdoor companies, is quick to explain that bulletins are not the on-premise signs found on business sites to advertise the particular brand of gasoline a service station sells or to popularize the name of a fast-food restaurant. To be a true bulletin, it must be located on land owned or leased by an outdoor company, commonly called a *plant*. The plant is responsible for maintaining the bulletins, handling the art work, selling advertising, and changing the messages whenever one advertisement is replaced by another.

Using Outdoor

If you wanted to purchase space on a bulletin, you would be concerned with a number of things. First, you would want to research traffic patterns of the community in which you wanted your ads to be located. You would want to be certain your ad appeared on bulletins which were in heavy traffic areas and seen by the audience you wanted to reach. If, for example, you wanted to reach blue-collar workers, you might have your ad placed on a bulletin near a factory where the workers would see it going to and from work. If you wanted to sell cereal, you might have your ad placed on a bulletin that was located near a supermarket where shoppers would see it. Another decision you would make would be on how many billboards you would buy space and for how long. Perhaps you would want to rotate your message among different locations; thus you would have to make both space and time buying decisions the same way you would if you were to buy an ad in the newspaper.

Changes in Outdoor

Outdoor has undergone considerable changes since the time when Model T Fords chugged down dusty roads. Back then, bulletins were placed anywhere automobiles could travel. Construction costs and concern over the environment were not serious issues as they are today. Few hesitated over cutting out a swatch of trees along a forest road to construct a bulletin or even contracting with a farmer to use the side of his barn for a complete repainting—the result being an outdoor advertisement for Mail Pouch Tobacco. However, in 1965, President Lyndon Johnson spearheaded highway beautification legislation establishing where bulletins could be placed, through a midnight session of Congress. The legislation even contained penalties for states that didn't adhere to the regulations. The legislation, for all practical purposes, went unnoticed. Except for news media publicity, there was little enforcement. It did, however, prompt some changes within the outdoor industry. Many outdoor companies realized that this legislation could be the first of much more to come if they themselves did not initiate certain procedures. Therefore, some outdoor companies began to clean up the ground around the base of their bulletins (Figure 4–4). Some actually hired landscapers to turn their bulletin grounds into mini parks. New manufactured bases also changed many billboards from the traditional utility pole supports to the more attractive metal and plastic

Figure 4-4 Improvements in outdoor construction have included the attractive "mini-parks."

sculptured bases. Although scattered, these improvements have lessened some of the criticism of bulletins. Future positive efforts like these will be determined by how much pressure is placed on outdoor companies to beautify their product.

Outdoor and Changing Life Styles

Changing life styles have also affected the outdoor industry. For instance, the move to surburban areas with multiple family dwellings and convenient shopping centers has eliminated the need for many people to drive to stores. They walk instead. Construction prices have also continued to climb as have art work, printing, and photography processes used in constructing modern outdoor advertisements. With the concern over the environment, some property owners may not be as apt to lease property for the construction of billboards. Other property owners realize the space they do have to offer is valuable, thus forcing many outdoor companies to purchase and pay taxes on land rather than leasing it. More centralized traffic patterns also mean that most commuters will use the main freeway arteries in and out of cities rather than the older two-lane streets and roads. The cost of constructing billboards on or near these freeways is becoming tremendous. Consequently, the cost of purchasing outdoor advertising is equally prohibitive, and many smaller businesses are placing their advertising on other media.

How well the outdoor industry survives the future will depend on all the factors mentioned here. Also, the increased cost of gasoline can cut down on the driving habits of many people, reducing total audience exposure to billboards. The efficiency of such other media as direct mail and cable television will also add to the competition. For the present, however, billboards play an important role in carrying messages to the public.

the emergence of specialized media

Media research has permitted us to make some fairly valid judgments about the future structure of mass media in society. Among these is the indication that media are becoming specialized.

Media and Media Delivery Systems

We have already seen examples of media adaptation in preceding chapters. For instance, we saw in Chapter 1 how mass circulation magazines such as *Look* and *Life* folded. Yet the total magazine market has prospered. Today, specialized magazines are directed at fruit farmers, cotton growers, the wool industry, retail merchants, model railroaders, religious groups, and almost any other group you can imagine.

As we learned in Chapter 3, radio presents another example of specialization. When radio first began in the 1930s, it was truly a mass medium. Today, it has become a specialized medium. What was once predominantly network programming directed at mass audiences is now local programming directed at specialized audiences. The radio network programming over ABC, NBC, CBS, and MBS has also diversified. ABC has broken down into four radio networks, each designed to reach a different audience with different demographic characteristics. Mutual Broadcasting System, besides its standard programming, has added the new Mutual Progressive Network, appealing to progressive rock music enthusiasts, and the Mutual Black Network. NBC has introduced its specialized NBC News and Information Service, designed for all-news radio stations which program to a highly educated and high-income audience. There has even been an outcropping of state radio networks directed at audiences in specific geographical regions.

Television is also appealing to diversified audiences. Cable television, for instance, can provide as many as forty or more separate channels with different types of programming for different viewers. In addition to the major network programs, special broadcasts can be produced by local colleges and universities, corporate programs can be used to train employees, and still other presentations can involve citizen discussion groups talking about community issues. No longer does television simply aim at the "masses."

Consider the case of newspapers. Although the large metropolitan dailies are still primarily serving mass audiences, new computer technology permits many of them to reach specific audiences with area edition inserts and refined distribution systems. Smaller suburban newspapers edited for communities adjacent to the metropolis attribute their success to content of interest to their own particular community.

Wire services have also gone the way of the other media. At the turn of the century, the United States was primarily served by two wire services, AP and United Press. In a sense, they were directed at the mass national audience via their subscribing newspapers. Today, however, although the two major wire services still function, numerous specialized wire services have come into existence. Some deal exclusively with weather information, "news" of prime importance to agricultural regions; others, directed at the business audience, deal with stocks and commodities. Grain farmers, chicken farmers, and people in the lumber business have specialized wire services. Even AP and UPI have become specialized. They now offer both print and broadcast wires for subscribers. They also offer audio services and special services to cable television operators.

Look at the recording industry. Back when the early television program *The Hit Parade* was popular, the ten songs performed each week were accorded a "mass" national audience. Today, a similar program would have a difficult time finding an audience large enough to justify its staying on the air. For there are now top-forty charts, top country and western charts, top classical charts, top easy listening charts, and many more.

Media and the Post-Industrial State

Richard Maisel has theorized that industrial society eventually necessitates the creation of specialized media. He contends that our present "post-industrial" society results in the growth of service industries, which are "great consumers of specialized media." He states, "The needs and tastes of specialized groups can only be satisfied by a form of specialized communication designed for a homogeneous audience."[2]

Although Maisel may seem to be discussing the industrial consumption of media, his concept applies just as well to many facets of nonindustrial consumption of media—e.g., the entertainment function of media. Even the radio commercials which serve to inform us of vital "services" in our post-industrial society are directed at local audiences.

Although it may at first seem that the growth of specialized media will conflict with the truly mass media, such is not necessarily the case. We now, however, have the *choice* of attending to the older, more generalized mass appeal media or the newer specialized media. The future of mass communication in the very broad sense is still open to speculation. Our society is centuries old; yet with the exception of books and newspapers, we are mere infants in our experience with mass media. What effect the growth of specialized media will have on society is open to further study.

summary

Chapter 4 has dealt with the mass media of books, direct mail, outdoor, and the emergence of specialized media.

Books have been an important means of mass communication for centuries. They were hand lettered and "published" as early as the fifth century. However, true mass distribution of books began with the publication of the dime novels in the 1800s and continued with the publication of the modern paperback book in the twentieth century. Paperbacks have become part of the mass culture because of their low cost and ease of distribution. Personalized books are also becoming popular. They have been used successfully as an educational tool to motivate children to read.

Direct mail, through the use of computer distribution, has become a mass medium in its own right. Its personalized messages reach specific audiences. Through the use of satellite communication, mass mailings can be dispatched coast-to-coast and delivered within twenty-four hours. Major direct-mail campaigns send millions of pieces of mail to select audiences. The eight basic types of direct mail are letters, reply cards, postcards, leaflets, folders, broadsides, booklets, and catalogues.

Billboards, commonly called bulletins or outdoor, are a mass medium of the automobile age. Major criticism of the environmental effects of billboards has resulted in some changes within the industry. Outdoor companies in certain areas have attempted to beautify the grounds around the base of billboards, making them less obtrusive to other landscaping. Competition from other media and the growth of suburban shopping centers, where people can walk to obtain goods and services instead of driving, will continue to be of concern to the outdoor industry.

Post-industrial society has brought with it a diversity that demands specialized media. Although true mass media are still with us, we now have before us an entire spectrum of specialized media to meet our individual needs.

opportunities for further learning

DESSAUER, JOHN P., *Book Publishing: What it Is, What it Does.* New York: R. R. Bowker Co., 1974.

MADISON, CHARLES ALLAN, *Book Publishing in America.* New York: McGraw-Hill Book Company, 1966.

YECK, JOHN D., and JOHN T. MAGUIRE, *Planning and Creating Better Direct Mail.* New York: McGraw-Hill Book Company, 1961.

YOUNT, JOHN T., *Mail Order Advertising Handbook.* San Angelo, Texas: Educator Books, 1970.

media delivery systems: the atmosphere, microwave, cable, satellites, and computers

CHAPTER FIVE

The use of the atmosphere, microwaves, satellites, cables, and computers all provide the basis for a modern, efficient technology. Mass communication systems make it possible for individual media to perform with speed and efficiency. In this chapter, we will learn more about these different systems of mass communication, how they function, and what role they play in our mass media society. As you study the material in the next chapter, think of the various mass media with which you come into contact in your daily life. Recall the different systems of mass communication which might aid these media in disseminating their information. Reflect also upon the efficiency of these systems, how they are controlled, and what forces act upon them. Now we will turn our attention to the most basic system of mass communication, the atmosphere, and its relationship to broadcasting.

the atmosphere and broadcasting

In our discussion of radio, we learned how Marconi sent and received messages without the use of wires. Utilizing the electrical properties of the atmosphere, he sent a message from one side of the Atlantic to the other. These properties make possible wireless electronic communication.

The Electromagnetic Spectrum

To understand how electronic media use the atmosphere to transmit signals, it is first necessary to understand the *electromagnetic spectrum,* which encompasses many different types of electromagnetic energy. Consider the analogy of a measuring stick. Radio waves, light, and X rays are all forms of electromagnetic energy. Each is located at a different place on the electromagnetic spectrum (Figure 5–1) or, using our analogy, at different points on the measuring stick. We refer to their position as a specific *frequency* on the electromagnetic spectrum. Radio waves, for instance, are found at the low end of the spectrum. Higher on the spectrum is visible light. This means that light waves actually differ from radio waves only in their higher frequency. Scientists using *fiber optics* have already determined ways to use light as a channel of communication. If we want to look much higher on the electromagnetic spectrum, we will find cosmic rays. Media which operate at different frequencies, such as the different stations heard on your standard radio, are actually operating at different points on the electromagnetic spectrum.

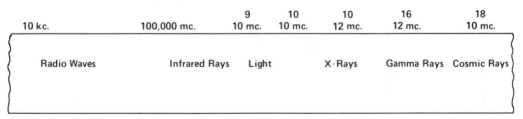

Figure 5–1 The electromagnetic spectrum.

Wave Propagation

The standard AM radio frequency is located at the lower end of the spectrum between 540 and 1600 Khz (kilohertz = 1000 hertz). Between these frequencies the FCC allocates each station a space of at least 10 Khz to broadcast; thus theoretically there would be room for more than 100 stations per city if they all operated at relatively low power and didn't interfere with stations in other cities. Yet not even large metropolitan areas can financially support this many stations through advertising, and certain characteristics of the atmosphere and terrain would make the total elimination of radio wave interference almost impossible.

To understand why interference occurs, let's examine the different routes a radio signal can take when it leaves the radio transmitter. The characteristics of those radio signals transmitted on the frequencies between 540 and 1600 Khz, the AM band, adhere to *sky wave* transmission patterns. This means that the signals will travel up and bounce off that portion of the atmosphere known as the ionosphere. Although some signals will escape into space, most will continue rebounding from the ionosphere back to earth in an ever weakening pattern. If a radio is too far away from the transmitter, the signal will simply no longer be audible. If a station has high power, then it is possible to transmit over a long distance. But simply increasing the station's power will not increase the strength of the signal proportionately. For example, if a 5,000 watt station wanted to effectively double the strength of its signal, it would have to increase its power by about 20,000 watts.

Frequencies higher on the electromagnetic spectrum send signals through line-of-sight, or *direct wave,* propagation. FM radio stations transmit signals in the 88 to 108 Mhz (megahertz = one million hertz) range of the electromagnetic spectrum. Since each FM station is assigned a 30 kilohertz range, there is an appreciable number of FM channels available for each market in the 88 to 108 Mhz band, yet there is no serious danger of overcrowding. The primary advantage of line-of-sight transmission is that there is much less distortion of the signal.

Many service agencies, such as fire and police departments and other two-way radio-equipped services, use frequencies in the FM band. Such agencies need reliable transmission systems unaffected by atmospheric conditions. Their transmission effectiveness is limited only by the height of their tower and their allocated power, the same considerations FM broadcasters have. An FM station's tower height is almost more important than its allocated power, however. Since line-of-sight transmission is used, it is critical to be above natural or man-made obstructions for your signal effectively to reach a wide coverage area.

Keep in mind that FM signals are not restricted to direct-wave propagation: United States FM stations use line-of-sight transmission simply because the FCC assigned them frequencies in that range of the electromagnetic spectrum. The same applies to AM signals, which are arbitrarily assigned to the 540 to 1600 Khz range — that band of energy transmitted by sky-wave propagation.

The sun also enters the communication picture; it heats the ionosphere during the day and thus decreases its ability to reflect radio waves. At night when the ionosphere cools, radio signals reflect better and can therefore travel farther. For this reason the FCC has required certain radio stations to either sign off the air or cut back their power at night to prevent interference signals from another station farther away but on the same frequency. We have all heard this take place. Just when your favorite song comes on the air, the station cuts back its power, and you're forced to turn up the volume or change stations. You may have also noticed that in the summer when the days are longer, certain stations stay on the air later than they do in the shorter days of winter. The reason for this is that the sun is still shining on the ionosphere and the reflective ability of the atmospheric layer is still at less than maximum efficiency. Stations required to sign off at sunset are called *daytimers*.

Which stations have the right to stay on the air while others must sign off? — usually the stations that were built first. The FCC grants stations operating time on a first come, first served basis. The original radio stations operating in a specific area are called *Class I* stations or *I-A Clear Channel* stations. Their broadcasting power is 50,000 watts, and they're authorized to operate 24 hours a day.

Wave Propagation and Policy Making

The qualities of the atmosphere directly affect mass communication policy decisions. Imagine you are the general manager of a daytimer AM radio station in a major city. Some of your management decisions would reflect your station's operating regulations. For instance, your station's revenue might be less than that of stations on the air full-time, because you would have proportionately less time for commercials. These daytime regulations would affect your audience ratings as well. When you sign off the air, most listeners will switch to another frequency, but some of them may not switch back the next morning when you sign on. Your payroll can also become a headache. A twenty-four hour station can easily schedule people for on-the-air shifts at regular intervals. But if your sign-off time varies with the sunset, then you will need to schedule employees on staggered shifts and pay them accordingly. This system can play havoc with your accountants and your personnel.

Now imagine you are a news reporter working at a daytimer, and just before sign off, a major story breaks in your community. You would face the frustration of sitting by while the competition provides extensive and perhaps live continuous coverage of the event.

Despite these seemingly endless hassles, there are also some definite advantages of managing a daytimer. For example, the majority of radio's listening audience tunes in during the daylight hours, so you would probably minimize costs and maximize profits by eliminating nighttime operating expenses. Also, there would be less wear and tear on the equipment, reduced maintenance costs, and a smaller payroll to meet as compared with the 24-hour station.

If you were a radio reporter and that big story broke at sign-off time, you would still have the advantage of having from ten to twelve hours to gather the facts before your early morning newscast. Thus, you wouldn't need to worry about "beating the competition" or possibly disseminating inaccurate information in the process. We will address these topics in detail in Chapters 10 and 11.

Along with restrictions on operating times, certain stations are also restricted in the size and shapes of their *contours*, that *geographic area covered by the station's signal*. If every station broadcast in all directions and covered the same area, their contour maps would be perfect circles, buildings and natural obstructions not included. You would also hear a jumbled mess on your radio receiver. By making certain changes in stations' antenna systems, however, it is possible to protect one station's signal from interfering with another. Most stations using these *directional antennas* (called directional stations) are designed for the crowded AM frequency range.

The next time you take an evening drive, notice the red lights of a cluster of radio towers. These multiple towers do not mean that the station decided to increase its coverage area by adding more antennas. The towers are strategically located so that the station's signal will radiate among the towers and transmit less power in a certain direction than in another, therefore protecting stations which may be located in that direction and transmitting on the same frequency. Figure 5–2 (right) graphically shows what the contoured coverage area map of a directional station looks like. Notice how it avoids interfering with the coverage area of the nondirectional station (left) operating on the same frequency. Three basic criteria determine the directional pattern of radio station signals: (1) the number of towers; (2) the relative positions of the towers — one tower is the primary reference tower, all others radiate the signal relative to the reference tower; and (3) the amount of current being fed into the antennas. By combining these factors, the signal in one or more directions transmits less power, thus protecting other radio stations' signals. In Figure 5–2 this would be the squeezed-in area of the right contour.

In summary, nondirectional antenna systems result in signals being radiated equally in all directions. In the directional antenna system, however, certain antennas deliberately interfere with the signals from the reference tower. All sorts of contour patterns are possible with different combinations of the three factors mentioned.

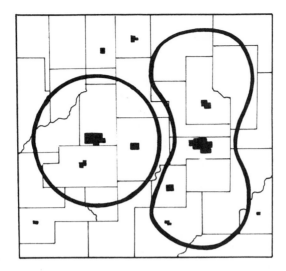

Figure 5-2 The 8-shaped contour on the right is that of a directional station. Notice how it avoids interfering with the contour of the nondirectional circular contour on the left.

Some stations may utilize as many as twenty towers just to create a signal contour which protects other stations.

Television Signals

Television signals travel through the atmosphere much like radio signals. In fact, a television picture is actually a series of radio signals. The audio portion of the television program is an FM signal; the video portion is transmitted by AM modulation but at a much higher frequency than that of AM radio. The frequencies of 54 to 72 Mhz and 76 to 88 Mhz are allocated for VHF (very high frequency) television transmission, and the frequency of 174 to 216 Mhz is allocated for UHF (ultra high frequency) television. The area of the electromagnetic spectrum allocated for each television station is much greater than that assigned to any AM or FM station. It consists of 6 Mhz, about half of which is used for transmitting video signals and the remainder for audio signals. To avoid interference, television stations in a single market have one channel separating them. In other words, if one station broadcasts on channel 5, another will broadcast on channel 7. In addition to separating audio from video signals to prevent interference, television employs the process of *scanning,* as discussed in Chapter 3. The picture components of each scanned line are converted to an AM signal and then decoded in your home television receiver.

Since the number of frequencies on the electromagnetic spectrum is finite, many federal regulations have been instituted to control the broadcast media. Scientists are working to increase the usable area of the electromagnetic spectrum to achieve better mass communication, within the range of frequencies allocated to AM, FM, and television broadcasting. Although these assignments represent only a small part of the current usable range of frequencies, we must keep in mind that the rest of the space is used for many other types of transmission, including microwave and the broadcasting needs of other nations. When we do discover how to tap the energy in other areas of the spectrum, then the potential for new and yet undiscovered types of electronic mass communication will evolve.

the many uses of microwave

We have all seen microwave antennas. They are usually large dish or horn-shaped devices attached to the top of towers or buildings. The term *microwave* means *a very short wave frequency located above the area on the electromagnetic spectrum where standard television transmission takes place.* Thus microwave transmission is line-of-sight transmission and not effective over long distances. Thirty miles in the earth's atmosphere is usually about the maximum distance microwave transmission can travel without considerable loss of signal quality. The real efficiency of microwave lies in its ability to send quality signals over distances in a more efficient and inexpensive manner than by wire transmission.

Television and Data Relay

In areas where it is difficult or expensive to string cable, such as over rugged terrain or water, microwave permits an effective link between a transmitter and receiver. The excellent quality of the line-of-sight microwave signal makes it ideal for transmitting television signals or computer data.

Most microwave systems consist of a series of relay transmitters and receivers. This type of "electronic-chain" arrangement permits microwave to be used for sending signals over long distances, the only limitation being the number of relay towers in the chain. For example, a television station in Boise, Idaho, receives its network programming over a distance of hundreds of miles from a main distribution transmitter located in Salt Lake City, Utah. A series of towers located at twenty-mile intervals on mountaintops is equipped with microwave receiving and transmitting antennas, commonly called *translators*. At each tower, the receiving antenna receives the incoming signal, amplifies it, and retransmits it to the next tower. Each tower's antenna system is in a line-of-sight path with every other tower's antenna system.

Portions of the microwave system may be owned by a private company or the telephone company. A television station or network may then lease one of the available microwave channels to transmit its signals. A mountainous terrain such as that between Idaho and Utah presents an ideal case for the use of microwave. However, a level terrain also lends itself to easy line-of-sight tower positioning.

The use of satellites has also opened up new vistas of communication using microwave. Satellites equipped with microwave antennas are capable of beaming signals around the world. They can transmit a correspondent's live report from the Middle East on an evening newscast, or they can relay the front page of the *Wall Street Journal* from coast to coast.

You should remember that microwave transmission is used to broadcast the network program to your local television station, not directly to your own home television set. Microwave frequencies received by your local television station are converted and retransmitted on a frequency receivable on your set. The quality network picture you receive, again because microwaves can transmit signals without much distortion, is virtually the same as that your local television station receives. Problems with microwave transmission may result during lightning storms, when ice forms on the antenna, or during dust storms; all these can interrupt the signal between two microwave relay towers.

Microwave and ENG

Recent developments in microwave systems accompanied by the miniaturization of equipment have permitted the portable microwave system to become an effective tool of local television programming and especially electronic news gathering (ENG). A portable microwave system consists of a motor van or truck equipped with portable batteries, television cameras, a small transmitter, and an antenna capable of sending signals via microwave (Figure 5–3). Back at the main television studio, another microwave antenna works as a receiving antenna for signals transmitted from the mobile van. When the mobile television crew arrives at the scene of an event, it simply focuses the van's microwave antenna on the antenna back at the television station. The signal received at the station travels through the studio's monitoring equipment to the station's main transmitter, which in turn broadcasts the signal to home television receivers. It permits great flexibility in local programming, especially news programming in which live coverage of an event can thus be accomplished anywhere the mobile van can go.

When microwave systems were first developed for local television coverage, it was always necessary for the microwave antenna on the mobile van to be in direct line-of-sight with the antenna at the main studio. This procedure was almost impossible when the van had to travel behind a large building or around a hill. Television stations then began locating microwave relay antennas on top of nearby buildings or on high terrain. The antenna on top of the van can thus transmit microwave signals to the relay station antenna which in turn will retransmit the signal to the main television studio.

New developments in microwave design have perfected the system even further. Small microwave horn antennas and a miniature transmitter about six inches long can now be mounted on a small tripod about three feet high (Figure 5–4). This portable tripod microwave transmitter is focused on the microwave transmitter at the mobile van (Figure 5–3), and the signal is then retransmitted back to the main studio. A television journalist with a portable camera connected to this portable microwave system can walk anywhere and broadcast live reports. Clear glass does not destroy the signal, so it's possible to take the portable tripod system inside a building and point the transmitting antenna through the window toward the antenna at the mobile van. The new portable microwave systems

Figure 5–3 A microwave receiver is mounted on a mobile van alongside the larger dish for the uplink to the news center at the television station. (CBS.)

Figure 5-4 A window unit microwave transmitter operating inside a building in St. Louis and sending the video signals to the support vehicle on the street below. (CBS.)

are also used for sports broadcasting. If you were part of a team of sports broadcasters covering a football game, you might be assigned to cover the sideline area of one of the teams with a portable system. Another member of your sports crew would take another portable system to cover the opposing team. Still another sportscaster would be high above the playing field with a portable system in a blimp taking aerial shots of the field. All portable antennas would focus on the mobile antenna, which in turn would relay their signals back to the main television studio.

The development of microwave systems has opened up whole new frontiers for involving society with mass media in general and with television in particular. The city council meeting once reported on the evening news and in the evening newspaper can now be televised live. Members of the local zoning board can be held accountable to the public in a far more direct and immediate manner. You can view documentaries broadcast live from such places as the inside of a nursing home, the office complex of a corporation executive, the parking lot of a shopping center, or the inside of a ghetto. Mobile television news crews can provide live coverage from the scene of a major event within a few minutes of the arrival of the mobile van. Microwave is yet another in the series of new technological inventions that aid the process of mass communication.

cable

The only communities capable of financially supporting several television stations are large population centers. The residents of these large cities have thus long enjoyed good reception of all the major network programs as well as those produced by independent stations. During television's early years, however, people living far away from these centers had no recourse but to sit in front of their sets, watching distant signals blurred by interference. People began investing in every type of complex antenna system imaginable, and a maze of television antennas graced rooftops everywhere. In the late 1940s there was a breakthrough in the previously fruitless efforts to receive clear, interference-free television signals from distant stations. It was the location of a large antenna on a hilltop high above the average terrain, from which point the distant signals would be carried by shielded wires, called cables, directly into home television receivers. Thus began the development of *cable television,* also called *community antenna television* or *CATV.* It soon became evident, especially in outlying areas, that the way to receive quality television signals and have a wide selection of channels was to link onto the local cable system. With the development of color TV sets, which accentuate poor reception, cable television gained in importance. Residents whose televisions are connected to a community antenna pay a monthly rental fee for the service. Others can, of course, still use their rooftop antenna, but usually sacrifice good reception.

Other important developments in CATV include the application of sophisticated transistorized electronic equipment and improvements in the construction of the cable. Both developments made it feasible to send many more channels via cable without needing to eliminate intermediate channels because of interference. Instead of receiving about half a dozen programs on the VHF spectrum, a cable subscriber could now receive all twelve channels if the cable system carried all twelve. Still further developments in cable expanded this twelve-channel capacity to carry as many as forty or fifty separate channels. Fiber optics can handle as many as 1,000 channels.

The FCC now requires that CATV systems, depending on the number of subscribers, permit local access to one of their channels. This means that in many communities a local organization or university may have access to one of the CATV channels and provide locally originated programming to subscribers. It also gives many systems the option of two-way transmission, something which, at least under current technology and development, broadcast systems cannot provide. The new two-way system, commonly called *broadband* communication, is opening up new possibilities. Two-way cable in New York, for instance, permits subscribers to scan the headlines of the news service and select with a home terminal the stories they want to read. But to comprehend the full potential of CATV, it's important to understand more about how it works.

Components of a Cable System

The basis of the CATV system is its community antenna. This, along with the amplifier, which retransmits signals to home subscribers, is called the *head end.* This term does not necessarily connote a specific location. Broadly speaking, it is *the human and hardware combination that is responsible for originating, controlling, and processing signals over the cable system.* In most cases, a separate antenna receives each individual signal; thus optimal reception is assured. In some cases, the head end will have the means to originate local programming. For example, it could contain a studio complex complete with a modest assortment of cameras and switching equipment. In other cases, the studio may be located at an adjacent site, such as a university campus or community center. In still

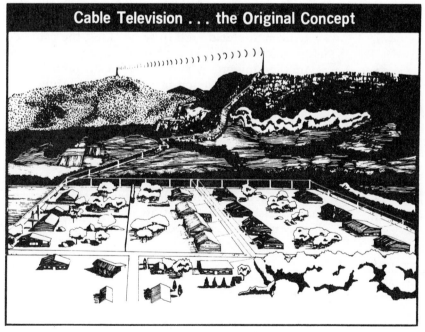

Figure 5–5 *(Communication News)*

other cases, the head end may include the local weather bureau which transmits emergency weather bulletins over the cable—for instance, small craft warnings.

The second major component of a cable system is its *distribution system*. As opposed to the head end, which originates, controls, and processes messages, the distribution system simply dispenses the system's messages. The most important component of the distribution system is the cable itself. The type of cable most commonly used is called *coaxial cable* and consists of an inner wire core surrounded by plastic, metal-webbed insulation and another coating of plastic. Coaxial cable, because of its thickness and shielding, is capable of carrying considerably more information than telephone lines. It is strung out over a community much in the same way that other utility lines are, usually connected to utility poles or installed as underground cable. A special line from the main cable then runs into a subscriber's home or office and connects directly to the television set.

The entire cable system can be likened to a tree. The main transmission line of the cable is called the *trunk*. Looking at a typical map, the trunk would usually parallel a community's main traffic arteries. Branching out from the trunk are *sub-trunks*, which convey the signal to outlying areas, some only a few streets away, others possibly miles from the main trunk line. *Amplifiers* are employed at strategic locations to give the signal a boost when it gets too far away from the head end. In some cases, the cable company owns or leases microwave links for long distance transmission.

Another important part of the distribution system is the *drop*. The drop is that section of cable which brings the signal from the trunk or sub-trunk directly to a subscriber's set. Usually about one to two hundred feet in length, it connects directly to the back of the television set, making the use of any other external antenna unnecessary.

The third part of the system is the *home terminal*. There are basically two types—*one-way* and *two-way* terminals. One-way terminals consist of the typical home television receiver. Two-way terminals consist of the television receiver, which is used as a visual display terminal, and a control board capable of sending commands into the system.

Uses and Issues

Our discussion of one-way CATV systems has already touched on some of the major uses this type of operation provides. One is the retransmission of television signals too weak for the average home antenna to pick up clearly. Another is the opportunity for universities to originate local programming, not only to train students preparing for careers in mass communication, but also to broadcast convocations, recitals, and even academic courses to cable subscribers. Local civic meetings can also be televised via the cable.

Two-way cable, or broadband communication, has an almost unlimited, still largely untapped potential. Consider the heart patient who at present must remain in the hospital for continual monitoring. With two-way cable, this same patient can return home and connect himself or herself to a home two-way cable terminal. The terminal connects to a computer at the hospital which monitors the heartbeat for a short period each day and signals the patient if anything is wrong. It will also automatically notify the hospital staff if emergency care is needed.

Central computers hooked up to home terminals can provide some that may seem pure science fiction—for example, performing complex mathematical formulas or giving you access to your checking account records. Mailing lists can also be sorted on the computer. If you had decided to send holiday greeting cards only to friends in your local community this year, you could ask the computer to sort those names from a master zip code list.

Additional tasks you can perform in your home via two-way cable include buying groceries, participating in group therapy sessions, and playing in chess tournaments. First-run current movies can also be part of your cable viewing. Instead of driving a date to the theater, you may want to stay at home to watch a movie. A channel on your two-way cable system will permit selection of any number of feature films. Using the two-way cable home terminal, you simply punch the code for the movie you want to watch.

Policy Concerns Affecting Cable

Although the subject of government control over cable television will be discussed in more detail in another chapter, we must raise several important issues here. One is the problem of public acceptance of new media. Over the past decades, we have become conditioned to resist such things as invasion of privacy, big government, corporate control, and similar factors that have an effect on our lives but over which we feel we have little or no control. History shows there has been similar resistance to new technology whenever it evolved. CATV did not suffer from excessive resistance since it was a logical extension of television. However, the concept of two-way cable is something entirely different. For many who don't understand the potential of the system, there is a feeling that "big

brother" has arrived and should be stopped at all cost. A typical reaction toward two-way cable envisions a super-spy electronic eye
lurking in the living room. Although it is possible to develop such a
system, that is not the current thrust of two-way cable. Until public
resistance to the new technology diminishes, it will continue to
stifle two-way cable's growth possibilities.

Government control also affects the cable industry. The use of microwave transmission systems placed cable companies under FCC
regulation, whose jurisdiction spread to such areas as local access and
eventually locally originated programming. However, unlike standard
radio and television broadcasters, cable companies are also accountable to local and state government. This may mean government-
controlled rate schedules or the adoption of guidelines for local access
programming. Inevitably jurisdictional conflicts will arise between local, state, and federal regulatory agencies. In one community, even
when the cable system owners were alleged to have violated federal
laws and the FCC wanted to take action, local officials said that they
had the authority to deal with the matter and that the FCC did not.
Similar conflicts are undoubtedly going to occur whenever several
governmental agencies have overlapping regulatory powers.

Pay cable will also become an increasingly contested issue. Pay
cable refers to an amount paid over and above the monthly rental
fee to see a particular program. With pay cable in your home, you
can see such selected features as major concerts, sports events,
plays, and other attractions. Opponents of pay cable argue that it
discriminates against those who cannot afford this type of "luxury
programming." Broadcasters are worried that it will take away from
their viewing audience. Proponents of pay cable argue that admission prices to movies and theaters are already discriminatory and
that pay cable will make available to the public a much greater variety of cultural and educational events. Obviously these arguments
are not easily resolved.

The fact that your home terminal would be connected to a central computer creates widespread anxiety. Questions immediately
asked are, How can the information I store in the computer remain
confidential? What if the computer feeds me misinformation? If I
am balancing my checkbook and someone finds out how much
money I have in my checking account, what would prevent that
person from making a computer withdrawal? If information about
my heart condition is stored in the computer at the local hospital,
what's to prevent my employer from finding out about it and stopping my next promotion? These questions are obviously practical
concerns that affect public acceptance of new media.

Cable television has tremendous potential. If trends toward specialized media continue, then there are even more growth possibilities for cable to carry much of this "specialized" communication on its many channels. Two-way systems will add a new dimension to the mass communication picture.

satellites

As we have already learned, various technological advancements throughout history have had a profound impact on our ability to communicate with each other. These included the printing press, radio, and television. Other developments increased the efficiency of these mass communication advancements; among them were the application of steam power to the printing press and the miniaturization of radio and television components. At the same time we were perfecting these developments, we were also gaining knowledge about the earth's orbital characteristics and about jet propulsion. Jet propulsion permitted us to launch instruments into space which could facilitate mass communication worldwide. We had reached the age of *satellites.*

Perhaps no other technological advancement in our history had or will continue to have such a tremendous impact on our lives. We have already mentioned some applications of satellite technology that have revolutionized communication. Newspapers such as the *Wall Street Journal* are printed in regional distribution centers using satellite communication. The postal system, through satellites and applied computer science, is already becoming a system of mass communication with a capacity to reach millions of people instantaneously. We are living in an age of satellite communication which links nations and cultures the world over.

Sputnik Through SYNCOM

When the Soviet Union launched Sputnik in 1957, it sent the world a message far more significant than "beep beep" signals. It signaled the beginning of a new era, in which we would experience groups of satellites hovering in a global communication network as well as manned space flights. Compared to today's satellites, Sputnik was very rudimentary indeed. It did not have a ground system relaying messages to the satellite for return transmission. There was no meaningful message broadcast, just the continual, intermittent tones. Sputnik's antenna was not directed toward any particular part of space or earth; thus it could be heard only when it passed over that area of the earth containing a receiving antenna.

In 1958, the United States launched the SCORE satellite, the first to carry a taped message. SCORE was followed in 1960 by Echo I, which became the first man-made *relay satellite* capable of bouncing messages back to earth. Satellite technology was now advancing rapidly. The United States' Courier 1-B, also placed into orbit in 1960, was the world's first *repeater satellite.* The repeater satellite differed from Echo I in that it was capable of receiving signals and then retransmitting them back to earth. With repeater satellites, it was now possible to send telephone and television signals via satellite.

But the real breakthrough was yet to come. For all practical purposes, there were two big liabilities facing satellite communication. First, satellites were only useful when they passed over an earth station's repeating or transmitting antennas. That meant if the United States wished to send a satellite signal to England, it was necessary for the satellite to be within "eye shot" of the two countries. As soon as its orbit placed it over another land mass, it could no longer function. Second, satellites had short life spans. Since the perigee, the point closest to the earth during an orbit, was at very low altitude, gravity would pull the satellite into the earth's atmosphere, and it would burn up after relatively short use. The solution to the two problems was first to launch a satellite which could be positioned so that its orbit would remain at a given altitude, making the *apogee*, the orbiting point furthest away from the earth, equal to the perigee. The second step was to position the satellite so that its orbit at 35,680 kilometers (22,300 miles) above the earth would travel at the same speed in proportion to the earth's rotation, resulting in a synchronous or *geostationary* orbit. Although the satellite would be orbiting at a faster rate than the earth because its circumference path was larger, the satellite would appear to remain stationary above the earth at a stationary point in space.

The feat was accomplished by Hughes Aircraft Company engineers Harold Rosen, Donald Williams, and Tod Hudspeth. In July, 1963, crews at a ground station in Lakehurst, New Jersey, and on board the Navy ship *Kingsport* stationed off the coast of Nigeria waited patiently for the launch. Then through the ship's speakers came a voice saying "*Kingsport* this is Lakehurst; *Kingsport* this is Lakehurst, how do you read me?" This crystal clear signal launched a new era of communication. It would also launch a new system of satellite development called the SYNCOM series, which stood for *synchronous orbit* satellite. Following the development of synchronous orbit satellites, engineers developed a satellite antenna system which rotated freely from the base of the unit. This enabled a microwave antenna system to point in one stationary direction. It was like having a satellite stopped in space pointed at a given spot on earth.

COMSAT and INTELSAT

To provide some form of regulation and control over the new developments in satellite technology, in 1964, the International Telecommunication Satellite Consortium (INTELSAT) was formed. INTELSAT is comprised of countries working together for the mutual cooperative development of satellite communication. The manager of INTELSAT is the United States Satellite Corporation called COMSAT. COMSAT was founded under the Communication Satellite Act of 1962, which provided for our commercial communication satellite system. Under the INTELSAT arrangements, there has been a systematic progression of satellite launches providing cooperative communication lines between nations. The INTELSAT series is capable of virtually all types of communication, including color television transmission (Figure 5–6). The first in the INTELSAT series was the Early Bird Satellite, which was then followed by INTELSAT II. INTELSAT II placed satellites over both the Pacific and Atlantic

Figure 5–6 INTELSAT satellites ringing earth. (Courtesy Hughes Aircraft Company.)

Oceans. The INTELSAT III series placed a satellite over the Indian Ocean, and the INTELSAT IV series greatly increased the circuit capability of the system.

Application to Mass Communication

The development of such hardware as satellites is meaningful only insofar as it can perform for consumers of mass communication. One of the most visible uses of satellite communication is the international transmission of television pictures, permitting us to be eyewitnesses to world events. Many Americans had their first glimpse of the Olympic games in 1964 when the summer games were brought into our living rooms via satellite from Japan. Through television, we were joined in an international bond of sportsmanship, unlike anything radio, newspapers, magazines, or delayed film had been able to accomplish in past Olympic games. The 1964 Olympics were only the beginning of the caption, "Live via Satellite," which high-lighted our television screens as we watched world events. We were eyewitness to the Pope's visit to Bogota and also to the 2500th anniversary of the Persian Empire. In 1969, we watched the first man land on the moon. In 1972, we saw President Richard Nixon disembark in the People's Republic of China. America and the world were able to see Nixon's visit live on the evening television news programs. This was a historic "first" in both international relations and international communication. That same year, the Summer Olympic games from Germany were broadcast via satellite. The 1976 Summer Olympics from Montreal were seen around the globe via satellite through the help of Canada's own satellite system fittingly called ANIK, the Eskimo word for "brotherhood."

We have touched on the use of satellites in newspaper publishing, and this field will experience great technological strides in the decades to come. It will be easy to publish an issue of the *Times of London* in New York by sending pictures of the pages to presses in America. It will be equally easy to publish a London edition of the *Wall Street Journal,* or facsimiles of magazines and specialized publications, such as business newsletters and financial bulletins.

Satellites and ETV

Perhaps one of the most promising feats of satellite technology will be its role in helping to educate the world's population, particularly in remote regions. An important experimental step in this direction was accomplished in 1974 with the regular operation of the Federation of Rocky Mountain States Satellite Technology Demonstration.

The satellite federation developed because mountainous terrain prevented many high schools in the Rocky Mountain states from receiving educational television programs. The federation thus linked a special system in each high school to a satellite and then to Denver where educational programs were produced and sent by satellite to the high schools.

Had you been a high school student in McCall, Idaho, for example, you might have joined your class in a special room with a television set and a control panel called the *blue box.* Your teacher would begin the class by turning on the television set, picking up a microphone in the blue box, and talking via a two-way radio to a synchronous orbit satellite traveling more than 20,000 miles away in space. The satellite would relay your teacher's voice to a special control center in Denver, Colorado, as she told the control center to begin transmitting ETV programs to your classroom (Figure 5–7). Sound like science fiction? Not at all. It is an experience satellite technology has enabled many students to share. At your high school in Idaho, you might also notice a special antenna system that, although much smaller, is similar to the antenna system used to track space capsules. Your teacher would be able to adjust the antenna automatically to ensure the clearest reception, all through a remote control panel inside the classroom. If you or your teacher had questions on the program's content, you would have the opportunity to ask the Denver experts via two-way radio and satellite. Periodically,

Figure 5–7 Satellite control center of the Federation of Rocky Mountain States Satellite Technology Demonstration.

you would also have the opportunity to evaluate these programs. If the production crew received negative comments about certain segments of the programs, they could change them accordingly. The entire system, although involving satellite communication, is still much less expensive than building a complex system of microwave towers over the Rocky Mountains. The results of this experimental satellite program are revealing to us some of the technical obstacles we will need to overcome in order to use satellites to bring knowledge into classrooms throughout the world.

Human Implications and Control

Our discussion of satellites cannot be complete without touching on some of the concerns which have arisen since the development of satellites. One concern is that as the communication network becomes tighter, and we increase our ability to communicate across international boundaries and cultures, ancient traditional heritages may be eliminated, creating negative consequences for the affected populations. Followers of an oriental religion may not look favorably upon an American church service which can be beamed around the world at the mere flick of a switch. The sacred dress of their elders may be rejected by younger members of a tribal culture when fads of other cultures cross the television picture. Even the first extensive televised trip of an American president to the People's Republic of China prompted stores in the United States to sell everything from dresses to lampshades printed with oriental symbols.

New developments in the miniaturization of satellite receiving systems will also result in important policy questions. No longer will only giant multi-antennas be able to receive satellite signals. Receiving antennas easily installed on housetops can bring satellite programming directly into your home. Questions posed theoretically now need immediate answers. Should communication from other nations via satellite be controlled, and how? What governments will control messages across international boundaries if individual homes can receive satellite communication directly? As students of mass communication, you will undoubtedly play an important role in finding the answers to these tremendously important questions. We'll touch upon them again in Chapter 19.

computer technology

When station KDKA broadcast the results of the Harding-Cox election returns in 1920, few people could have imagined that giant computers would someday predict with uncanny accuracy the outcome of national elections hours and sometimes days before all the votes were counted. The average citizen who sits in front of a television set and watches an election night broadcast is perhaps not aware of the full scope of the computer's power. For the publisher whose newspaper must go to press a short time after the polls close, however, with computer predictions there is far less chance of headline errors such as the famous boner made by the nation's major newspapers in predicting the outcome of the 1948 presidential election. Harry S. Truman, Dewey's opponent, went to bed listening to broadcast reports of his loss, only to awake the next morning as President-elect of the United States. The ability of the computer to analyze data from selected voting precincts, use voting trends from previous years, plot trends and probabilities, and predict victories has given added credibility to all media.

Today's newspaper owes its greatly increased efficiency to computer technology. The ability of a major national newspaper to compose pages and advertisements, edit copy, set type, and effect regional distribution, all by computer, has become commonplace. Computers have also reduced the error factor in newspaper production. In the past, "scissors and paste" manuscripts were marked with pencil and passed through many different copy desks. With computers, the copy is now clean, and erasures and changes are edited electronically instead of manually. Type is set automatically through electrical impulse instead of by hand. Even the spacing of the lines and margins has been computerized.

Operation and Application

In most applications for mass communication, the basic operation of a computer is one of information storage and retrieval. The three major components of the computer are *input, processing,* and *output.* Data, usually in the form of numbers, are entered into the computer and by one or more mathematical operations; the answer is then typed on a teleprinter or displayed on a visual display terminal. In our example of election night news coverage, information about prior voting trends is first stored in the computer. This might include the similarity in voting of key precincts to the total overall vote of a given area; how this has affected previous elections; and the percentage of voters eighteen to twenty-four years of age and how frequently they vote like their parents. On election night when the votes are tabulated in the sample precincts, the information previously stored in the computer is combined with the new vote totals and then processed. The result is a prediction of voting results based on sample data collected in the current election as well as information collected from previous elections.

Not every application of the computer requires a comparison of new data with information previously stored in the computer. If you were an executive of a major recording company, for instance, you might want to review all of the records on the *Billboard* "Easy Listening Chart" during the past ten years that also sold at least two million records. Perhaps you would then want to narrow the list to include only those records your company produced. By assigning the song titles separate codes to identify various characteristics, you could easily obtain this list of records. From this list, you then might want to make decisions on how many songs to release as "oldies but goodies," how many you should recommend for rewriting as possible new renditions, how many you should sell the copyright on, and so on. Without the computer, your job would have been much more difficult as well as time consuming. Integrating the computer with the operation of any mass communication enterprise increases its efficiency.

A large midwestern newspaper that also owns broadcast and magazine interests has most of the company's financial data stored on its computer. By means of sophisticated analysis, the company can take into consideration such factors as expansion trends toward specialized media, annual billings, rate of inflation, printing costs, plant expansion, and countless other factors, then use the computer to project these same cost factors over the next decade. With a mere command, the company president can have at his fingertips what percentage of his operating costs printing will consume by the next decade, how much paper he should stock, and what the price of advertising will be in the years ahead. Management might then decide to purchase more broadcast stations and sell some of its magazine interests, or just the opposite. Management might also decide that it needs to hire more employees to keep pace with the company's projected development over the next five or ten years. A composite sales chart can be developed by computer so that every person will know his or her quota. Perhaps, on the basis of cost data, management will even make the decision to move into other investments related to mass communication, such as purchasing a chain of movie theaters or starting a book publishing company.

A motion picture distributor can use the computer to tell where certain films are being shown and to plan film release dates for specific areas. For example, stored on the computer will be key demographic data for each area served by a given movie theater chain. When a certain type of movie is released, its prospective audience can be matched via computer with the theater serving a given neighborhood. Information on gross receipts can also be stored on the computer, and the distributor can instantly tell what films are showing upward trends in attendance and income. Perhaps a new movie is showing a surprising increase in gross receipts despite the fact that it has received little publicity. A review of the weekly computer printout of box office receipts for the film shows that attendance is high in areas with a large proportion of teenagers. You discover that your film has touched upon a subject that is of immediate and vital concern to teenagers. But the issue is one which will pass quickly, so it's important to make immediate decisions concerning your film. After computerized cost projections are made, you decide to order new advertising for the film and promote it as a major production instead of the low-budget picture you originally publicized. Without the computer, the data tipping you off to the film's success might not have been available for months, and your new cost projections would have been impossible.

One of the most frequent uses of the computer is to help mass media sales personnel sell advertising. If you were sitting in the office of a major advertiser selling a segment of network television programming, you would find the computer indispensable. Assume that the sale is in the neighborhood of $200,000 for a series of network commercials. You have just spent the past hour convincing the prospective advertiser how great your network programming is and how a commercial on your network will reach more prospective buyers than another network can deliver. Just then your client says, "OK, I'll buy *if* you can place all the commercials in a certain selection of afternoon programming, alternating them every other day and alternating programs as well, but with three commercials running every day in one very popular program." The complexity of the request may boggle your mind. Moreover, if the competing network's representative was outside in the waiting room, it could be even more serious. To return to your office, work out the schedule, and then call her back could mean the loss of $200,000 plus your commission. Her interest could dwindle after you left, and the competition could steal your sale. Instead, you simply call your office and ask the traffic director to check the time availabilities on the computer for the requested advertising schedule. In a matter of seconds, the computer feeds the information to the traffic director who tells you the requested time is free. The time slots you sell are then logged into the computer, and that action prevents another member of the sales force from selling them to another prospective advertiser. New developments in computer hardware also enable you to carry a miniature teleprinter in your briefcase. This teleprinter enables you to make direct contact with the computer by using the phone on the advertiser's desk, and both of you can watch the advertising schedule being printed right before your eyes.

The computer can also be utilized in broadcast engineering. For example, the chief engineer at a modern broadcasting complex can go directly to a teleprinter and read the computer printout data about the operation of the station's transmitter. In the past, the same engineer would have to spend considerable time each day walking around with a clipboard taking meter readings required by the FCC. Now, the computer receives data directly from the transmitter and translates this into a printout of the meter readings. The computer also stores these data for future reference. For example, by reviewing a list of the times the transmitter was off the air, the engineer can tell what the operating time of many key instruments is. He can then prepare for future equipment failures by replacing these instruments before they wear out.

New developments in computer technology have also been applied to radio and television production. A disc jockey can sit at the controls of a radio station and, with a keyboard and VDT nearby, automatically select the next song to be aired (Figure 5–8). A television program is recorded on magnetic videotape in much the same way that sound is recorded on magnetic audiotape. If a section of videotape needs to be edited, you locate that portion of the tape and then electronically edit it. You may have two videotapes and want to blend video from both of them onto a third tape. You may also want to dissolve or slowly change from one tape to another. Simply turn on the tape machines, and the computer automatically does the editing, stopping and starting the tapes exactly when you command it. Also, you might want to insert a sound effect at the moment a specific picture appears. By giving pre-edit commands to

Figure 5–8 Disc jockey Johnny Walker at Station CKXL in Calgary, Canada uses a computer-based system to select records for airplay. (Moffat Communications photo.)

the computer, the exact picture and sound combination will occur automatically. The time segments on the computer are very detailed, down to tenths and even hundredths of a second. The ability to edit in such detailed segments permits an almost error-free editing production.

Transition to Computer Technology

The integration of computer technology into mass communication did not occur overnight. There naturally has been some resistance to computers by segments of organized labor who see union jobs being eliminated or reduced. In many cases, these fears have been justified. Linotype operators who have spent their lives setting type face a bleak future when the linotype machine simply disappears.

Psychological adjustment also enters the picture. The reporter who has made a living pounding out stories on an old typewriter for the past twenty-five years may be hesitant to give up the "friend" that has served so well and replace it with an electronic keyboard and visual display terminal. In most cases, however, the remorse is only temporary, and after there has been ample opportunity to become accustomed to the new equipment, the changeover is welcomed. One newspaper made the transition to a computerized system by first installing electric typewriters. The feeling of the managing editor was that the electric typewriters were the real transition, not the electronic keyboards and visual display terminals. Most of the employees therefore easily made the adjustment to computers. However, one reporter did run into trouble when he wanted to use a slightly off-color word which had come into acceptable vogue. Programmed into the computer was a block system whereby a list of certain swear words would not appear in printed type. When the reporter wanted to use the word as an adjective, the computer refused to print it. Incidents like this are common. At a major wire service bureau, it was discovered that static electricity built up in the rug would, when an employee wore wool clothing, erase portions of completed stories from the visual display terminal. In both of the above cases, some minor adjustments solved the problem.

summary

The properties of the electromagnetic spectrum make wireless communication possible. Two types of wave propagation occur in the transmission of radio signals: sky-wave propagation, which uses the ionosphere as a reflective source, and direct-wave propagation, which creates line-of-sight transmission. The ionosphere becomes more reflective at night, allowing radio signals to travel farther by sky-wave propagation. This phenomenon is the reason the FCC requires some stations to sign off at night or cut back their power to avoid interfering with other stations' signals.

Microwave systems use line-of-sight transmission to relay signals between two points. These systems are especially well suited for relaying television signals and computer data over areas where the cost of cable transmission systems would be prohibitive. Microwave is also used in the production of local television programming, permitting the remote coverage of news or sports events.

CATV, called cable or community antenna television, first developed in the 1940s when large community antennas were shared by many people living far away from television stations. Later, cable developed as a two-way communication medium. Today, cable systems offer the potential for home hookups with central computers, medical monitoring, grocery shopping, and access to first-run movies. When public resistance to the new two-way cable systems begins to diminish, more opportunities for using the system will unfold.

Satellites have played an important role in fostering international mass communication. The first satellite in orbit was the Russian Sputnik. It was followed by the American SCORE satellite and then Echo-I, the first relay satellite. The United States' Courier 1-B was the first repeater satellite. The world body governing the development of satellite communication is the International Telecommunication Satellite Consortium called INTELSAT. The management of INTELSAT is under the United States' Communication Satellite Corporation (COMSAT). There are many policy issues still affecting the development and operation of satellites. Cultural invasion by television programs from other countries is one major concern.

Computers are also playing an important role in mass communication. From the rapid tabulation of election-night results, to making management decisions, to sales assistance, computers are yet another example of hardware systems making the process of mass communication more efficient.

opportunities for further learning

BAER, WALTER S., *Cable Television: A Handbook for Decision Making.* Santa Monica, Calif.: Rand, 1973.

KEMENY, JOHN G., *Man and the Computer.* New York: Charles Scribner's Sons, 1972.

LeDuc, Don R., *Cable Television and the FCC: A Crisis in Media Control.* Philadelphia, Pa.: Temple University Press, 1973.

Polcyn, Kenneth A., *An Educator's Guide to Communication Satellite Technology.* Washington, D.C.: Academy for Educational Development, Inc., 1973.

Walsh, John E., *Introductory Computer Language.* Toronto, Ontario: Sir Isaac Pitman (Canada), Limited, 1971.

Williams, Norman E., and John H. Savage, *Communicating with a Computer: Programming in Student Language.* Toronto, Ontario: Sir Isaac Pitman (Canada), Limited, 1971.

Yin, Robert K., *Cable Television: Citizen Participation in Planning.* Santa Monica, Calif.: Rand, 1973.

the broadcasting networks

CHAPTER SIX

As consumers of mass communication, we spend more time with the broadcast media than we do with any other medium. The great majority of this time is spent watching or listening to network programming, especially television networks. The three major commercial networks — CBS, NBC, and ABC — have come under all sorts of criticism and have been charged with being an information monopoly. Yet they still prosper: they continue both to distinguish themselves as major news media and to innovate in the mass entertainment and educational programming fields. We'll examine these radio and television networks to see how they developed, reflect upon their changing roles, and review their operations.

early network development

Broadcast networks began in very modest surroundings in the 1920s. At that time, although there was considerable growth in the number of radio stations as well as in listenership, there was serious concern that radio would collapse. Stations would engage in all sorts of experimental programming to capture the attention of the listening audience, but they would lose that audience as soon as the novelty wore off. Specifically, there was no means to provide a regularly scheduled diet of entertainment and news upon which the public could depend. Consequently, various cooperative ventures between stations were undertaken, such as joint broadcasts of major sports or news events. Yet, if radio was to survive, there had to be some way to give the public a regular schedule of programming, or else they would ignore the new medium. The answer was network radio.

NBC, ABC, and Mutual

NBC pioneered the network concept beginning with twenty-five stations, and on January 1, 1927, broadcast coast-to-coast the Rose Bowl Game from Pasadena, California. That venture followed with other types of radio "firsts," which included news and public affairs programming as well as entertainment in the form of comedy and radio drama.

NBC soon divided into dual networks, called the Red and Blue networks. In 1942, two historic legal cases of American broadcasting, *CBS* v. *U. S.* and *NBC* v. *U. S.*, broke up the dual network concept.[1] The decision was precipitated by the development of still another network, the Mutual Broadcasting System (MBS), which wanted to develop its own national network but found that the presence of the two NBC networks as well as CBS made it a difficult proposition. The outcome decreed the sale of the Blue network, and its name changed to the American Broadcasting Company (ABC).

Zworykin, Marconi, and Sarnoff

While NBC was developing its networks, its parent company, RCA, with the work of Vladimir Zworykin, applied for the patent on the iconoscope electron television tube in 1923. Two years earlier RCA had bought out the Marconi Wireless Co. One of the Marconi employees, David Sarnoff, was named general manager of the company and later rose to head RCA. The development of the iconoscope was promising enough for RCA to open its experimental television station W2XBS in New York on July 30, 1930.

Between 1930 and 1940, RCA continued to experiment. In 1931, the company placed an experimental transmitting tower on top of the Empire State Building. These experimental transmissions permitted the development of a 120-line transmitting system producing a clearer picture than had been previously possible. Continuing its television experiments, RCA announced in 1935 that it would spend one million dollars for television field testing. It was a sizeable business venture at a time when there were few viewers and much progress still to be made before the system could approach significant home use.

Experimental Programming Succeeds

In 1936, television receivers were able to pick up signals across a distance of one mile. In 1937, the antenna atop the Empire State Building went into "public" use, and NBC and RCA took television to the people. In an arrangement set up on the streets of New York, passersby could stop and see the operation of the new invention. A broadway play, *Susan and God,* was televised from the NBC studios on June 7, 1938. It was also the year David Sarnoff, President of RCA, announced to a meeting of the Radio Manufacturers Association that television sets would go on sale to the public when the World's Fair opened in 1939. During that year, television signals were transmitted a distance of 130 miles from New York City to Schenectady, New York. A year later on the first of February, as members of the FCC watched, television pictures were sent from New York to Schenectady and then *rebroadcast* to other points in upstate New York. On a small and experimental basis, the first television network began that first day of February in 1940.

David Sarnoff and Guglielmo Marconi at the RCA transmitting center at Riverhead, Long Island. (Courtesy RCA.)

the corporate development of CBS

All the time NBC and ABC had been making major strides in developing their networks, CBS had also become a landmark in communication systems development. It was a classic case of corporate brilliance and forethought which carried CBS into the mid-1970s on a 20-year trend as the world's largest advertising medium.

Paley's Cigar Company

The network started in the humble surroundings of a cigar company with an advertising manager named William S. Paley. Paley's cigar company, La Palina, had experimented with sponsoring a program on the UIB/Columbia radio network in 1927 and saw its business more than double. Paley, a year later at the age of twenty-seven, arrived in New York, and bought the network, which was later to become CBS.

Like the other networks, besides its regular entertainment and news programming, CBS experimented with broadcasts from trains, balconies, and underwater bathyspheres. Some unexpected outcomes sometimes resulted. A 1930 broadcast featuring George Bernard Shaw aired the playwright's comments without approving them beforehand. CBS officials gasped as Shaw began with, "Hello America! Hello, all my friends in America! How are you dear old boobs . . ." and ended up by praising Russia. When the broadcast was over, CBS decided it was in everyone's best interest to provide equal time for an opposing opinion.[2]

Promotion and Research: Kesten and Stanton

In 1930, Paul Kesten joined CBS as promotion manager and immediately began to whittle away at powerful NBC. First came a survey on radio listenership which refuted NBC's claim to be the most "listened to" network. Next came an era highlighted by a policy of attracting big-name radio personalities to CBS. This concept of using major entertainment to build up the business saw such stars as Bing Crosby and Kate Smith join CBS. In 1935, a 27-year-old instructor from the Ohio State University received a telegram from CBS. It read, "I don't know of any other organization where your background and experience would count so heavily in your favor or where your talents would find so enthusiastic a reception."[3] The instructor's name was Dr. Frank Stanton. He accepted CBS's invitation and began to work for $55 a week doing audience measurements and research. Later, he too climbed CBS's success ladder to become one of the leading spokesmen for the broadcasting industry.

When World War II broke out, many CBS employees began to make names for themselves in the field of broadcast journalism. Correspondents Eric Sevareid, Richard C. Hottelet, H. V. Kaltenborn, and many others reported from the front lines—a first in providing up-to-date wartime news coverage.

The Talent Raids

When the war ended, there was again a thrust to develop competitive programming, and CBS spared little in competing head-on with NBC. In what became known as the great "talent raids," CBS literally bought such NBC talent as Red Skelton and Jack Benny. CBS also developed a sizeable chain of its own radio and television stations serving major markets. The combination of its own stations, its network affiliates, and creative programming placed the network at the top in national popularity. Early television programs such as *I Love Lucy* and *Gunsmoke,* and soap operas like *As the World Turns* made CBS a leader in prime-time television programming. Financially, the network would see profits steadily climb and set records. As a corporation, CBS would also diversify into other fields to build a broad-based financial structure in which broadcasting is a major but not dominant part of the organization.

Over the next decade all three major networks, NBC, ABC, and CBS, expended great effort to improve television. NBC and CBS with their already well-established radio networks had the head start. ABC, however, pioneered innovative television sports programming that was competitive with NBC and CBS and succeeded as a major programming force in the industry. Major events between 1950 and 1970 gave the networks ample opportunity to "show their stuff." The presidential campaigns and nominating conventions were excellent television material as were major sporting events such as the Super Bowl, the Indianapolis 500, and the Olympics. From the great debates between candidates for the presidency Kennedy and Nixon to the live coverage of space shots from the surface of the moon, the networks came into their own as dominant and powerful suppliers of information through mass communication.

modern radio networks

While the three major television networks concentrated on spectacular entertainment programming with a broad mass appeal, local radio was moving toward a more specialized programming format. The major radio networks, however, had retained the same broad programming appeal of television. For many radio stations, network affiliation was therefore something to contend with rather than welcome as an asset to their total programming concept. A contemporary station, for instance, might devise programming to create a young, "up-beat" sound of music spiced with creative announcers who could blend in with the sound and retain the overall image of the station. Yet these same stations were faced with a radio network which had the slow drum of news tones and a newscaster with little creative appeal. The radio networks were simply out of touch with the times and were losing their affiliates because of it.

The ABC Split

Then, in what turned out to be one of the most novel decisions ever to affect radio network programming, on January 1, 1968, ABC split its operation into four different networks. These were the American Contemporary Radio Network, the American FM Radio Network, the American Entertainment Radio Network, and the American Information Radio Network. The idea was to develop news programming to meet the needs of different types of radio formats. For example, the American Contemporary Network was designed to integrate into the programming of contemporary-sounding stations. Sharp, quick tones preceded and concluded the newscast, stories were shorter and more direct, and the entire newscast was shortened to fit into the quick changes in sound and the fast transition that takes place on the contemporary station. The four-network concept proved to be extremely successful.

Mutual's Ethnic Radio

Mutual tried unsuccessfully to block ABC's four-network concept with repeated arguments before the FCC. Then in 1971, it decided to try the multi-network idea for itself. Its existing MBS system was joined by the Mutual Black and the Mutual Spanish Networks. The content of the two new networks was news appealing to the black and Spanish communities. Black announcers were often employed in network newscasts, and there was a continued emphasis on the feedback of news stories from affiliates close to the black community. For example, a sampling of reports aired during a single day's programming of the Mutual Black Network included a congressional black caucus press conference informing the public of the introduction of a Black Bill of Rights and a Black Declaration of Independence, the voice of the first black to serve on the security board of the National Democratic Convention, a black Congresswoman interviewed about her opinions on various issues including busing, and a report on the merging of a white and black Methodist church. The Mutual Black Network survived but the Spanish network was dropped.

NBC's All News (NIS)

In 1975, NBC also joined the ranks of the major networks offering more than one service. It retained its original radio network but introduced a separate operation called the NBC News and Information Service (NIS). The NIS is an all-news network, broadcasting approximately forty-five minutes of news every hour. The only programming local stations are responsible for is the ten to fifteen minutes not covered by NIS. The networks' purpose is to service the growing number of all-news radio stations in the United States. The all-news format is relatively new to modern radio because of the prohibitive cost of salaries for additional news personnel. NIS affiliates, however, share a number of advantages. Along with the image of a major network, they require fewer personnel to operate the local news department since most of the programming comes from the network. Also, by letting the network assimilate almost fifty minutes of programming every hour, the local news team can concentrate on preparing a truly professional local newscast.

The Role of Radio Networks

The role of radio networks in broadcasting is similar to those of television networks except that the individual station is not as dependent on the network for programming. As we learned earlier, radio has become a very specialized medium with considerable local programming directed to specialized and local audiences. It is, of course, much less expensive to program local radio than local television. For one thing, the recording industry provides countless hours of inexpensive recorded music which can fill local programming schedules. In addition, a single disc jockey can operate virtually all the controls in a radio station, including the transmitter, and originate local programming as well, all at the same time. Larger stations naturally require a larger number of personnel; but overall, the operation of a radio station is much less complicated and less expensive than a television station. This despite the fact that most radio networks provide only supplementary not primary programming (the notable exception being NIS).

Radio affiliates are sometimes reimbursed for airing network commercials, although the various contractual agreements with stations vary greatly. In many cases, the station may not realize a profit from affiliating with a network, but feel the network programming adds to the overall image of the station.

Despite their supplementary role, radio networks have thrived, and if the future can be predicated on their ability to specialize plus the burgeoning number of FM stations, all indications are that they will prosper. Also, we must keep in mind that the cost per thousand persons reached via radio advertising is low and that advertisers can aim at specific markets. For example, a cosmetics manufacturer wanting to reach teenagers could purchase a combination of the American Contemporary Radio Network and The Mutual Progressive Network.

public broadcasting

Along with the major networks, public broadcasting systems play a major part in the overall structure of broadcasting. Public broadcasting as defined here simply means *the operation of the various noncommercial radio and television stations in the United States.* The depth to which the public is involved in these broadcasting complexes varies considerably, but the underlying purpose of these stations is to serve the public—not to operate at a large profit. This does not mean that commercial radio and television stations don't serve the public; it means simply that staying in business, that is, making a profit, must be their primary concern. In many cases, commercial stations may be owned by a parent corporation which views them primarily as profit-making instruments. If they aren't, then there is a good chance that they will be sold for more profitable ones. Since public radio stations are not under the same financial pressure as their commercial counterparts, they can program to more select audiences without as much concern over losing a mass audience or winning a spot in audience ratings. Public broadcasting stations usually operate with a sizeable portion of their budget coming from listener contributions, direct appropriations, and grants from foundations and corporations.

Early Stations and NET

Although public broadcasting has attracted serious attention only in recent years, the roots of the system began back in 1919 at the University of Wisconsin in Madison. It was at that time that experimental radio station 9XM went on the air. The noncommercial station's call letters were later changed to WHA, which it remains today. In the late 1940s, the FCC authorized the operation of small, 10-watt noncommercial stations, and in 1952, it allocated exclusive channels for noncommercial television. Of these, 80 were located in the VHF range and 162 at the UHF end of the spectrum. This was just the assist that noncommercial television needed to develop along with radio. Also in 1952, noncommercial broadcasting received a major financial boost when the Ford Foundation created the Educational Television and Radio Center. This later became the National Educational Television (NET), involved in producing ETV programs for public television stations. In 1953, station KUHT at the University of Texas in Houston was the first noncommercial educationally licensed television station to sign on the air. The next nine years saw noncommercial broadcasting develop rapidly. In 1962, Congress passed the Educational TV Facilities Act which provided $32 million over a five-year period to develop state systems of educational broadcasting.

The Carnegie Commission and CPB

In 1965, planning began for what was to become a major policy document affecting the development of public broadcasting in America. A major industry-wide study of public television was undertaken by the Carnegie Commission for Educational Television. The Commission was "asked to 'conduct a broadly conceived study of noncommercial television' and to 'focus its attention principally, although not exclusively, on community owned channels and their services to the general public.' . . . The Commission will recommend lines along which noncommercial television stations might most usefully develop during the years ahead."[4] The Commission, whose report was published in 1967, was made up of a broad spectrum of industry leaders. It reached the conclusion that a "well-financed, well-directed educational television system, substantially larger and far more persuasive and effective than that which now exists in the United States, must be brought into being if the full needs of the American public are to be served."[5]

The Public Broadcasting Act

Acting on that recommendation, Congress passed the Public Broadcasting Act of 1967. Among other things, the Act allocated an appropriation of $3 million for the construction of facilities and the formation of a nonprofit corporation called the Corporation for Public Broadcasting (CPB). Specifically, CPB was charged with authorization to:

Facilitate the full development of educational broadcasting in which programs of high quality, obtained from diverse sources, will be made available to noncommercial radio or television broadcast stations, with strict adherence to objectivity and balance in all programs or series of programs of a controversial nature;

Assist in the establishment and development of one or more systems of interconnection to be used for the distribution of educational television or radio programs so that all noncommercial educational television or radio broadcast stations that wish to may broadcast the programs at times chosen by the stations;

Assist in the establishment and development of one or more systems of noncommercial educational television or radio broadcast stations throughout the United States;

Carry out its purposes and functions and engage in its activities in ways that will most effectively assure the maximum freedom of the noncommercial educational television or radio broadcast systems and local stations from interference with or control of program content or other activities.[6]

The concept of public broadcasting had received the beginning of a financial base. Now it could prosper and expand.

The Public Broadcasting Service — PBS

To help meet these goals, the CPB joined in cooperation with many of the licensees of noncommercial television stations in the United States in 1970 and formed the Public Broadcasting Service (PBS), which became the primary distribution system for programs serving public broadcasting stations. PBS is responsible for obtaining programs for national distribution from its member stations as well as from independent suppliers. In less than a decade, PBS has been responsible for a number of award-winning special programs as well as regular series, the most famous of which is *Sesame Street.* Another popular PBS program is the *Electric Company.* Along with its production and distribution system, PBS is also responsible for representing the interests of member stations before Congress and other governing bodies.

National Public Radio

A national system of distribution for public radio programming evolved in 1971 with the creation of *National Public Radio* (NPR). NPR is much like PBS, except that NPR is sometimes involved in *producing* programs. Affiliate stations also produce programs which are sent to NPR, then aired on the NPR network or syndicated by NPR to noncommercial stations not directly linked to the network. Like PBS, NPR has also had its share of award-winning programs, such as the nationally acclaimed *All Things Considered*, a daily news and public affairs program produced by NPR in Washington, D.C.

Affiliates, Organizations, and Licensees

Along with NPR, PBS, and CPB, other key components of public broadcasting include affiliated stations, state systems of educational radio and television, program libraries, producers, and the National Association of Educational Broadcasters (NAEB), a national organization of individuals associated either professionally or through interest with noncommercial broadcasting. Noncommercial radio and television stations are basically of four types. There are those licensed to state authorities or commissions; community stations, which are licensed to nonprofit community corporations; school stations licensed to school corporations; and university stations, usually licensed to the boards of trustees of both public and private colleges and universities.

The future of public broadcasting will be determined by its ability to adapt to changing life styles and habits of audiences while still retaining its uniqueness. As more and more channels of communication become accessible to the public, there is the real possibility that a new awareness of interaction between the public and media will take place. This in turn will generate even more interest in the activities and programming of public broadcasting. We'll learn more about public broadcasting in later chapters.

how networks operate

Most television stations operate on a profit. They derive their income from advertising, and their expenditures are primarily salaries to personnel. Paying the number of people necessary to produce eighteen hours of daily local programming would bankrupt the average television station. To produce a full day of local programming would require numerous sets, production crews, and theater and film crews, just to name a few. Obviously, because of the limited number of people a local station is capable of reaching, it can't charge enough for advertising to offset the cost of all that production. Thus, the network provides its affiliate stations with high-quality programming. Most stations need only to supplement this programming with two or three local shows per day, usually news programs. Since a network can charge more for advertising because of the large national audience it reaches, it can afford to provide programming with the talent capable of attracting and keeping sizeable audiences.

Networks also act as a distribution system for commercials as well as for entertainment, news, and other types of programming. A national advertiser, usually through an advertising agency, can purchase advertising time on a network and reach millions of people without having to contract with each individual station. The three major commercial networks are all in competition for a share of the total national television viewing audience. The number of viewers a network is able to capture, measured in ratings, determines how much money it can charge for a segment of advertising. Certain special audience characteristics such as the age and income of the audience will also affect charges for network advertising. For example, a certain type of sports programming may appeal to a special type of audience, such as a predominantly male viewership with an average income of over $15,000 a year. Obviously, this type of listener is much more capable of purchasing sponsors' products than an audience of equal size but with little buying power, such as a group of preschoolers. Thus, advertising on this type of programming will be more expensive. The local television station is bound by an *affiliate contract* with the network but is not obligated to carry all of the available network programming. Naturally, it is a rare occasion when a local affiliate will not carry network programming, although it does happen. It is the local station and not the network that is responsible to the FCC for meeting the needs of the station's local community. Thus, when a local station feels some type of programming may be objectionable to its audience, it may decide not to air the program or shift it to another time period.

The networks must keep attuned to the needs and desires of their local affiliates. A network couldn't survive if its affiliates objected to its programming and refused to broadcast it, because sponsors could no longer be guaranteed a specific audience for commercials. Some advertisers might also object to sponsoring programs that were distasteful to the public. Thus, it is easy to see that in the long run the networks, although competing with each other, still must program shows which appeal to the great majority of the national audiences.

production companies

Along with the programs produced by the networks, there are also programs produced by special production companies, commonly called *production houses*. These are growing increasingly common as the networks are becoming less involved in production and are instead concentrating on the distribution and sales aspects of their company. Since many of the networks have also diversified into other businesses, such as theaters and record companies, conflicts of interest may easily arise. Practices such as airing only programming produced by subsidiary companies of the network, although profitable (especially with major motion pictures), are frowned upon by the FCC. Since production companies have become specialists in their fields and networks are finding it hard to compete with them, purchasing their programs is now a common network practice. It's a case of each business doing its job best, the production companies producing the programs and the networks distributing and selling them.

Producing Programs

From a business standpoint, operating a production house is risky. Consider the gambles of producing expensive *pilot programs* which may never even see the light of day on the network. Some of the more successful production houses have, of course, produced award-winning shows which have set major trends in network programming. For example, the *Mary Tyler Moore Show* set a leadership posture for MTM Enterprises, the producers of the program. From the *Mary Tyler Moore Show* evolved the equally popular *Rhoda* and *Phyllis*. Another successful supplier of programs to the major networks is Quinn Martin Productions, responsible, among other things, for such popular drama as *The FBI* and *The Streets of San Francisco*.

In some cases, networks working in close liaison with production houses will sense the need for a particular type of program. As a result, the network will request that a pilot program be developed. The program may be advertised and aired as a special on the network, thus allowing an opportunity to monitor feedback on viewer acceptance. From this monitoring, the network and the production house can determine whether or not it would be profitable to produce an entire series of programs around the same stars and theme.

Getting into Syndication

Not all of the income of a production house is earned from programs sold to major networks. Some shows run a successful schedule on the network and are then syndicated, i.e., sold directly to individual television stations for local programming and sponsorship. Shows such as *Bonanza, Ironside, Star Trek, Mission Impossible, Gunsmoke,* and countless others have not only made a successful run on network television but are now reaping additional income through syndication. In certain instances, production houses may go directly to syndication instead of first through the network television route. An example of this type of direct syndication was Independent Television Corporation's *Space 1999.*

One of the most famous and successful programs to go directly into syndication is *Mary Hartman, Mary Hartman.* Having been turned down by networks for his program, creator Norman Lear resorted to this direct syndication approach. His success has even startled the networks. In the program, a fictitious Ohio housewife endures the trials and tribulations of everything that a 35-year-old housewife could possibly experience—and much more. The result is basically comedy, but comedy spiced with enough genuine soap opera to classify it as a hit among both the devotees of typical daytime drama and the person who seeks the comic escape of some of television's most humorous dialogue. The program also deals with formerly taboo social issues. Sex therapy and pot smoking, which had previously been left to late-night documentary fare, are dealt with openly in *Mary Hartman, Mary Hartman.* Understandably, some areas of the country reacted with outcries about bringing these subjects into the living room on a daily dramatic basis. Yet interestingly enough, stations haven't been content to schedule the very popular program merely in the daytime. Some bold, metropolitan stations back it up against their competitors' late evening news, scoring rating points that have sent news consultants into a tailspin.

Future Affiliate Decisions

Mary Hartman, Mary Hartman may have more long-range effects for television than simply attracting viewers. Local television affiliates of the major networks have been increasingly dissatisfied with the type of programming coming from network hoppers. And although other programs have gained success on the syndication circuit, *Mary Hartman, Mary Hartman* has been a first in the amount of attention and popularity that a program has captured going *directly* into syndication. Television station managers are suddenly realizing that perhaps the networks' distribution system might not always produce programming that suits their individual market. What's appropriate fare for Portland might not be appropriate for Paducah. Why should each city have to suffer with the other's programming? If the Portland television station manager can negotiate programming for Portland directly with production houses and syndicators, why make major commitments to the networks? Although it may be a while before the basic structure of the television networks changes and each individual station manager programs his or her own station much like radio now programs, this possibility does not escape either the management of the networks that turned down *Mary Hartman, Mary Hartman* or of the local station that has to compete with her.

Regional, Informal, and Sales Network

Along with the major radio and television networks, there are also other types of networks which affect the flow of information to the public. These are the regional, informal, and sales networks.

Regional networks provide programming and information to specific geographic areas. They're incorporated into the regular programming of the station in much the same way that national network programming is. The regionals' supplemental programming, especially in news, figures importantly in attracting local audiences. An audience in Maine, for instance, is more interested in news of Maine and New England than news of Alabama. The regional network thus provides an affiliate station gathering news from the state capitol and other major metropolitan areas in the state or region. With the advent of CATV, regional networks have become increasingly important for individual stations. CATV takes the station's signal beyond its primary broadcast contours into many outlying communities. Since, for most broadcasting stations, the cost of sending reporters to cover all these surrounding areas is prohibitive, the regional network solves the problem.

Informal networks are news networks created by a professional group of radio or television news personnel. There is no contract or written document spelling out services or agreements. Such networks are in existence everywhere and are a big help to participating stations.

Let's assume that you are working as a radio reporter in a large city and want to carry news of three surrounding cities. To do so, you develop an association with news personnel at a station in each of the three surrounding cities and call on them whenever you need information about a story in their community. The advantage of this informal network is that, because the desired story is important local news, the originating station will probably cover it in depth and can provide additional background information that other networks, including a wire service, might not have. Usually called *co-ops*, these informal networks can consist of two to as many as fifteen newspersons who exchange news on a fairly regular basis.

Sales networks are designed primarily for advertising purposes. Although participating stations may occasionally receive programming material, this is not the network's main role. A sales network is usually a group of stations linked together through some common bond to benefit all member stations financially. Like informal networks, this bond can be aided by a permanent communications system such as teletypes or leased transmission lines. The networks are often formed by advertising agencies or broadcast advertising representatives.

For example, one such network might be located in an area that is noted for its vacation opportunities or tourist attractions. Let's assume this area consists of three states and that you are responsible for buying advertising for a chain of restaurants located in the three-state area. You decide to purchase commercials on different radio and television stations in the area and are looking for an inexpensive group rate. However, since the stations don't often voluntarily cooperate — primarily because they are competing businesses and are perhaps miles apart — an advertising agency in the area might contact the group of stations and ask if they would like to join together in, for example, a "Tourist Network." The advertising agency or station representative would then sell commercials for all member stations, taking a commission on the total price of the commercials. All stations would benefit from the sale as would you, the advertiser, who would receive a group purchase discount. The difference between this type of a network and the previous ones we've learned about is the fact that dissemination of information is not the primary service provided by the network; its benefits occur through group purchasing power.

networks and other businesses

Up to now, our discussion has centered on the role of networks as systems used to supply programming and information to affiliate broadcasting stations. We should, however, be aware that the overall corporate structure of most major networks includes other business enterprises, which lend the networks a broader financial base than would programming alone. Often a common theme, such as ABC's entertainment basis, runs through all the ventures. Along with the ABC television and radio networks, ABC also owns a group of seven AM and seven FM radio stations. The seven AM stations include such famous call letters in broadcasting as WABC in New York, WXYZ in Detroit, KABC in Los Angeles, KGO in San Fransciso, KQV in Pittsburgh, KXYZ in Houston, and WLS in Chicago. Its profitable chain of theaters also gives ABC financial flexibility. There is no limit to the number of theaters a corporation can own, but the FCC limits to fourteen the number of AM and FM (seven of each) stations under single ownership.

All three of the major networks are involved in major publishing

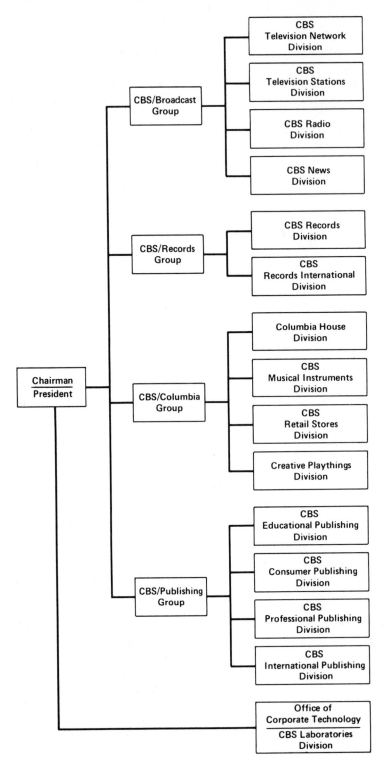

The corporate structure of CBS.

operations, including books, magazines, and specialty publications. CBS, for example, owns both Holt, Rinehart and Winston, Inc. and W. B. Saunders Company, which publishes specialty material in the health sciences field. CBS Consumer Publishing Division publishes *Field and Stream, Road and Track, World Tennis,* and *Cycle World.* ABC Publications include more specialized magazines, such as the *Wisconsin Agriculturist* and *Prairie Farmer.* RCA, of which NBC is a part, is involved in publishing through its subsidiary company, Random House. Allied publishing interests are also common, such as BFA Educational Media products, part of CBS, and RCA's Random House Enterprises, designed to compete in direct-mail sales.

One of the enterprises most closely allied to broadcasting is the recording business, in which both ABC and CBS have substantial interests. CBS's purchase of Columbia records in 1938 signalled the beginning of a lasting interest in the recording industry. Today, the CBS Records Group involves not only manufacturing and distribution but also talent scouting. Stars such as those of the early 1940s were the first on a long list of recording artists to include some of the most popular contemporary singers associated with all different types of music both here and abroad. Mounting interest in tapes has also helped the industry. Closely aligned to CBS's recording interests is the CBS Retail Stores Division. Headquartered in California, the division includes Pacific Stereo, a group of stores selling high fidelity and stereo components, and Discount Records, a chain of retail record stores. ABC also has a major records division, contracting many important recording stars. Its purchase of Duke/Peacock Records now permits ABC Records to produce its own black gospel recordings. Group-owned stations, theaters, publishing houses, and recording companies are just some of the many diversified interests in which the major networks are associated.

summary

Broadcasting networks make it possible to disseminate most of the information we receive from mass media. Their early beginnings can be traced back to the 1920s when radio was in its infancy. NBC pioneered in network development with the Red and Blue networks. A decision of the Supreme Court then split these two networks, and the Blue network became ABC. CBS and Mutual also grew steadily during this time.

Public broadcasting has also become an accepted part of American broadcasting. It is financed primarily through public contributions and the Corporation for Public Broadcasting. Programming is distributed to affiliate stations through the Public Broadcasting Service, which serves television, and National Public Radio, which serves radio.

Television networks are responsible for providing the majority of programming to their affiliate stations. Radio networks are primarily concerned with supplementary programming in the form of news to specialized audiences. Production houses, or companies, are responsible for providing television networks with a large share of their programming. Three other types of networks include regional, informal, and sales networks.

Along with broadcasting, the larger commercial networks are associated with other businesses through their parent companies. The ownership of motion theaters, radio and television stations, book and magazine publishing houses, and retail stores provides a broad base of financial support for the networks.

opportunities for further learning

BROWN, LES, *Television: The Business Behind the Box.* New York: Harcourt Brace Jovanovich, 1971.

CONANT, JAMES B., *et al., Public Television, A Program for Action: The Report and Recommendations of the Carnegie Commission on Educational Television.* New York: Harper & Row, Publishers, Incorporated, 1967.

EPSTEIN, EDWARD J., *News From Nowhere.* New York: Vintage Books, 1974.

FRIENDLY, FRED W., *Due to Circumstances Beyond our Control. . . .* New York: Random House, 1967.

MACY, JOHN W., *To Irrigate a Wasteland, The Struggle to Shape a Public Television System in the United States.* Berkeley, Calif.: University of California Press, 1974.

METZ, ROBERT, *CBS: Reflections in a Bloodshot Eye.* Chicago, Ill.: Playboy Press, 1975.

wire services, syndicates, and research services

The story reported by the television newscaster and the editorial in the newspaper may not be the sole result of the efforts of station's or newspaper's own staff. They may have utilized the assistance of wire services, syndicates, and research services to complete these assignments. Let's examine these media information systems in more detail.

the wire service concept

A major news commentator once described working in a wire service as being in the "hot seat" of journalism. His analogy is not far from the truth. Sometimes referred to as *press associations* or *news services*, wire services are major information support systems for many mass media. Radio and television stations, newspapers, and specialized publications such as news magazines all use wire services as a source for their presentations. The most familiar wire services are the Associated Press (AP), United Press International

(UPI), and Reuter. Stop and listen carefully to a television or radio news program. You'll hear many reporters introduce the news program with a reference to the wire service. The reporter may say, "and now from the wires of United Press International," or, "the Associated Press stated today. . . ." What follows is a story originally sent to subscribing media through a system of leased telephone lines and teletypes, or teleprinters. Much of the national and international news disseminated by radio and television stations or newspapers comes from the wire services. Even networks rely heavily on wire services. It is obviously impossible for every radio and television station or newspaper to have correspondents throughout the world. The wire service is an important link in providing information to these media and consequently to the public.

In the Beginning: AP and Reuters

The modern concept of wire services began in 1848 in the office of the *New York Sun* where New York newspaper publishers met and formed a news gathering organization called the Associated Press. Dr. Alexander Hones directed AP until 1851 when Daniel Craig, who had started AP's first foreign bureau two years earlier in Nova Scotia, became head of the organization under the title of "general agent." As we learned in Chapter 2, mass transportation systems not only increased the potential number of newspaper subscribers but also created a thirst for news content beyond the provincial reporting that permeated local presses of the era. In the same decade, the telegraph had become a major communication link. It provided instant news to places that just a few years earlier had waited for months to learn of events happening a mere hundred miles away.

Reuter's Pigeon Service

At the same time Craig took over at AP, Paul Julius Reuter began his first full year of operating a European carrier pigeon service relaying economic news to bankers between Aachen, in what is now West Germany, and Brussels, Belgium. The distance between the two points, 100 miles, was a major gap in the already developed telegraph network, and Reuter was able to successfully bridge this gap. Not long after, Reuter hired help to run his own pigeon service and moved to London to try to develop a stronger base for his operation and also have access to the coming Atlantic Cable. Although the London stockbrokers were eager for economic news, the London newspapers weren't. It was not until 1858, after Reuter had provided a free trial service to the newspapers, that they entered into an agreement allowing them to receive general news from Europe.

Dissension in the AP Ranks

In our own country, the AP was responsible for much of the news disseminated during the Civil War. The journalistic prowess and objective reporting of the AP even gave it exemption from censorship orders by the government. After the end of the war, the AP struggled under some organizational problems. Specifically, the Western Associated Press complained that it wasn't receiving enough quality news from the New York headquarters bureau, which was controlled by New York interests. The Western Associated Press claimed that when the New York press learned of a big story, instead of turning it into the wire service for distribution, they would simply hold on to it. Even today, if a major paper or a radio or television station wants to keep a scoop story from its competition, it may not immediately turn the story over to the wire service. Although the AP is legally entitled to all news gathered by its subscribers, there is no contractual agreement binding the subscriber to relay a major scoop immediately to the wire service.

The split between the two factions of AP temporarily healed, and the wire service expanded its operation with the development of its own leased lines for exclusive AP distribution. However, the split emerged again in 1891 when an investigative team of the Western group went to New York and discovered that some of the key AP people were in a secret news trade agreement with and were shareholders in a rival organization called United Press. The United Press was no relationship to the later service which eventually evolved into UPI. The outcome of the investigative team was the formation of the Associated Press of Illinois, which was incorporated as a nonprofit organization and became the foundation for the modern AP. AP of Illinois also entered into agreements with foreign press associations, including Reuter's, which increased its coverage of foreign news.

John Vandercook and United Press

In 1897, the old United Press went out of business and left the new AP without any real competition. At about the same time, a 25-year-old New York correspondent with the Scripps-McRae newspapers was getting his feet wet as a foreign correspondent and pursuing the opportunity to develop and enlarge the international wing of the Scripps-McRae Press Association. His name was John Vandercook. Seven years after his successful foreign assignment, he walked into his boss's office and asked E. W. Scripps for a promotion. He got it and began a fifteen-month position as editor of the *Cincinnati Post*. Not satisfied with his professional role as editor, Vandercook again approached Scripps with an even weightier proposition. Since the end of the old United Press in 1897, the Scripps papers weren't faring too well. Their own Scripps-McRae Press Association was no match for AP, but membership in the rival wire service was not an attractive prospect. Vandercook proposed consolidating the Scripps-McRae Press Association with the East Coast Publishers Association and the Scripps News Association, which served the West Coast members of the Scripps chain. Scripps bought the idea, and the three merged into a new press association called United Press. United Press prospered even after Vandercook's death a year later in 1907. In 1958, it merged with the International News Service to form United Press International. During the years between its founding and the merger, it also became the first major supplier of news to broadcasting stations and afforded the broadcast media equal status with newspapers in helping to determine wire service policies. It also launched UPI Audio to provide radio stations with audio actualities, correspondent reports, and regularly scheduled newscasts. AP began a similar audio service in 1974 called AP Radio.

Meanwhile Reuter was developing its own sizeable list of subscribers in the United States and especially in Europe. It continues to support many individual European bureaus that specialize in news services for specific countries. In 1967, it terminated agreements with AP and has since made great strides on its own, including the development of general and specialized services for the news media and such financial institutions as the Reuter Financial Report, Reuter Commodity Report, Reuter Money Report, and Reuter Metals Report.

using a wire service

To understand how wire services function and how they are used by individual media, let's eavesdrop on a conversation at a local radio station. We are standing in the news room as the news director walks in. It is 6:00 a.m., and part of the news team is already sitting around having coffee. The "sitting around" will stop shortly; the coffee will remain a constant friend throughout the day.

News Director: What's it look like today, gang?

      Reporter: We've had a big night. The jury on the Simpson case didn't get in until 1:30 this morning.

News Director: Did you get the story finished?

Reporter: I roughed out a draft and called it in to the wire service. They sent out a story on the morning split. They included some background information which we had overlooked. I had forgotten that Simpson had also been involved in that bank holdup five years ago.

News Director: Anything else breaking?

Reporter: Yea. Remember the hustler on the loan fraud case in Gainesville? Well, the wire says he tried it again last night and picked an undercover state trooper for his customer.

News Director: Call the state police headquarters and see if you can interview the trooper. We'll use it as an audio actuality.

Reporter: Already did that. Also there are some stories on the wire about the boy scout troop that uncovered the Indian ruins. It has some local interest for scouts in this area. There is even a good kicker story on the wire which should make you think about stopping your smoking, boss.

News Director: What's that?

Reporter: Some guy was out riding with his girlfriend in his new convertible last night. She was driving and he was sitting in the passenger seat smoking a cigarette. The wind hit the cigarette ashes and burned a hole in his pants. He jumped up in the open convertible just as his girlfriend took a sharp S-curve. He fell out of the car and is in the hospital with a concussion.

From our conversation, let's examine the uses of a wire service. Keep in mind that a similar conversation could have taken place in a television station or a newspaper news room.

Backgrounding Stories

From the wire, the news team acquired additional information about local stories. Although the reporter had the information about the jury in the Simpson trial, the wire service filled in the details that lent greater depth to the story. The wire service also added another dimension to the station's news programming, an *audio actuality,* the recording of the "actual" sounds in the news. A portion of the station's interview with the state trooper will be used in the local newscast as an audio actuality. A television station or newspaper could accomplish the same thing with videotape. Our radio reporter also used the wire service as a source of new information, here the story about the boy scout troop uncovering the Indian ruins. There was even a *kicker* story on the wire; this refers to the closing story of a newscast, which is in many cases a humorous anecdote, such as that about our friend who fell out of his new convertible.

We also heard some newsroom jargon during the conversation. For example, the word *split* was used to refer to a given news report sent over the wire. In wire service terminology, there are state splits, regional splits, morning splits, evening splits, etc. A split is simply a feature newscast dealing with a particular region or a specialized interest, such as business, agriculture, weather, or sports.

Audio Services

Along with the printed copy a subscriber receives over the teletype or teleprinter, a wire service also offers audio and video feeds to subscribers. A radio newscast acquires the dimension of sound, a television newscast, sight and sound, and newspapers receive pictures. The audio feed is sent via telephone lines to local radio stations where it is either recorded or aired live. Audio feeds can be a single story or a complete newscast, such as UPI Audio or AP Radio provide. When your local radio station airs an interview with an international leader, chances are the interview was first recorded on location, then sent to the wire service headquarters via telephone where it was recorded and added to an "audio file" with other prerecorded stories. At a given time, all of the prerecorded stories in the wire service's audio file are sent to all subscribing stations through leased telephone lines. If you were responsible for preparing a radio newscast, you would learn which prerecorded stories were available by checking the wire service audio *billboard* which periodically clears the teletype.

Picture Wires

Many of the pictures you see in the newspaper or view on television are also prepared by the wire services. Most newspapers subscribe to a *picture wire*. The next time you read the newspaper or look at a news magazine, examine the photographs. Chances are that under one of them will be the words AP WIRE PHOTO or UPI WIRE PHOTO. In each case, the picture was transmitted through a special photo transmission system to the newspaper or magazine. New developments in wire photo transmission have made it possible to transmit photos of almost lifelike quality. Using a process similar to color television, color pictures can also be transmitted.

Television stations can also benefit from wire service photographs. For example, video systems make it possible for television stations to receive daily video feeds, of both still and motion pictures, from the wire service. These are recorded on the station's videotape recorders and later used in television newscasts.

the bureau's role in gathering news

The major wire services have bureaus located throughout the world staffed with experienced reporters, photographers, and editors all responsible for gathering and disseminating news to subscribers (Figure 7–1). In the United States, wire service bureaus are located in state capitals and metropolitan centers. Many of the major bureaus are responsible for disseminating world news that they receive from other wire service bureaus. In wire services, then, we have one of the most important gatekeepers of mass communication. In any given twenty-four hour period, wire service bureaus determine the news that billions of people will hear, see, and read.

Reporters, Photographers, and Technicians

When a major story breaks, a wire service bureau may dispatch a reporter, photographer, and technician to cover the event. In many cases, one person performs all of these tasks. The nature of the wire

Figure 7–1 UPI in Chicago. A major wire service bureau serving many subscribers in both the print and broadcast media.

service as news supplier to subscribers over a wide region, necessitates that it carry the big stories and leave less important or local interest stories for individual broadcast stations and newspapers to carry. When major news does break, wire service reporters are under considerable pressure to get as much accurate information over the wire as soon as possible. After all, these reporters are actually doing the leg work for a large group of professional journalists who are dependent on their first-hand reports. Added to this is the pressure of competition among rival wire services.

Covering Major Events

An example of one enterprising wire service reporter in action is the account of UPI reporter, John Gregory, now assigned to the Chicago Bureau. Late one afternoon when Gregory was still with UPI's Indianapolis Bureau, a passenger jet collided with a small plane above Indianapolis Airport, and both planes crashed, killing all aboard. It was one of the country's major air disasters. Gregory left the office, and, in the process of driving to the scene of the event, pulled into a service station to ask directions. There he encountered a student on a school bus who had been an eyewitness to the event. Gregory directed the student to a telephone at the gas station, called UPI Audio headquarters in New York, and instructed the student to tell the wire service audio bureau about his eyewitness account of the crash. The New York bureau recorded the student's remarks. Continuing on his way to the scene, Gregory again stopped for the purpose of asking directions, this time at a nearby farmhouse. He was met at the door by a lady who had been picking vegetables outside when the crash occurred and had therefore been another eyewitness. In a few moments, Gregory had placed another call to UPI Audio in New York, and the woman was giving her eyewitness account of the event. Subscribers to UPI Audio thus had access to eyewitness interviews ready for airing on their evening newscasts, something which most other stations couldn't match. Gregory followed up the story that night with data on casualties, flight plans of the aircraft, and background information on the personal lives of passengers who were never to reach their destination. It was one example of what working at a wire service and being on the "hot seat" is all about.

the subscribers' role in gathering news

Not all of the work involved in gathering news falls on the shoulders of the wire service. It would be simply impossible for a wire service bureau to cover every news item in its assigned area. Wire services count on their subscribers to tip them off to major stories and provide in-depth coverage of others. It is this willingness on the part of subscribers to contribute news to the wire service that improves the quantity and quality of news sent to all subscribers, and consequently, to the public. For example, AP is organized as a news cooperative and is entitled to all of the news its subscribers gather. UPI is not automatically entitled to news which subscribers gather but does not operate at a disadvantage to AP. Both arrangements work equally well. AP simply puts into contractual terms what UPI has in a "shake hands" agreement. In some instances, subscribers are paid a nominal fee for their efforts. This token payment does not buy subscriber loyalty, however. The wire service's ability to provide a significant amount of important, accurate news on a regular basis is what keeps a subscriber renewing his contract.

Theoretically, the more subscribers a wire service has, the more information that can be fed back to the wire service from local areas and distributed to all other subscribers. In some states, the dominance of one wire service has created a lopsided situation, resulting in that wire service's disseminating more stories of better quality.

specialized wire services

Our discussion of wire services has centered on the major wire services of AP, UPI, and Reuter. Yet there are also many specialized wire services serving specific news markets. We have already dealt with those furnished by Reuter. Another example is the Commodity News Service headquartered in Chicago and Kansas City. The Commodity News Service provides a series of specialized market analysis wire services on specific types of information. For example, it offers the Lumber Instant News (LIN), carrying such specific information to the lumber industry as daily cash prices on plywood, forest ranger reports, construction trends, and mortgage and financial information. This information is not only of interest to the mass media located in the heart of the lumber country, but also provides an important service for the lumber industry, a subscriber to the LIN wire. Commodity News Service also offers the Farm Radio News (FRN) and Grain Information News (GIN), both dealing with crop reports, market quotations for the United States and Canada, and information on planting conditions. Also available are the Activity Commodity Trading News (ACT), Livestock Feed and Market News (LFM), and Poultry and Egg News (PEN).

Another example of a specialized wire service is the Public Relations Wire. It is for the exclusive use of companies or other institutions and individuals who want to disseminate press releases via a wire service rather then sending them through the mail. Disseminating a press release over a wire service provides an aura of importance and urgency that the mail cannot convey. The income for the wire comes from two sources—subscribers, such as newspapers, broadcasting stations, and networks; and the companies which pay a fee to have their news releases distributed.

At first you might ask, "Why would any medium want to subscribe to a public relations wire?" The answer lies in its content and speed of distribution. Certainly much of the information received from such a source is biased in favor of the company or institution that distributes it. On the other hand, special feature information from a particular company or institution—discussing a major industrial development, executive transfers, or quarterly earnings—may be of interest to a specific public. Highly competitive media, such as the networks, or media that carry a significant amount of financial news find the wire informative and rely on it for information a day or two in advance of the mails—and therefore well before competing media.

wire services and new technology

New technology has greatly helped to increase the efficiency of the wire service. For instance, it is now possible to transmit wire photos through the process of *electrostatic transmission*. Using specially prepared paper, this system processes pictures to subscribers as glossy prints on dry paper ready for printing. Before the electrostatic process, subscribers had still to develop wire photos for printing. The new system, pioneered by UPI, not only facilitates the work of the photo editor on a major newspaper but also makes it possible to use photos received only shortly before press time.

The computer has also played an important role in wire service operation and is now responsible for the storage and retrieval of most copy disseminated from wire service bureaus worldwide. No longer is the typewriter the standard piece of equipment in the wire service bureau. It has been replaced by the visual display terminal. As noted earlier, the VDT is a television screen with a keyboard on which are typed the stories to be sent to subscribers. The stories are then edited and stored in a computer until ready for transmission. At any point during the transmission process, an editor can call forth on the VDT a list of stories currently stored in the computer and then determine which stories and in which order they are to be sent.

Access to Stories

There are tremendous advantages to a computerized wire service system. Besides speed and efficiency, local news editors will have *access* to stories formerly available only to national wire service editors. An editor in Iowa, for example, might want a feature article on harvest conditions in other parts of the world. Previously the national editor would control the dissemination of such features. Now the Iowa editor can scan the list of news stories on file in New York and call forth to his own VDT a completed story about harvesting. If the editor likes the story, a command to the computer will order that complete story automatically typed on the editor's local teletype, ready for printing.

Even the teletype is succumbing to new technology and being replaced by the quiet and compact teleprinter. Used in many bureaus and news rooms throughout the world, the teleprinter eliminates the familiar drumming sound of the teletypes associated with radio newscasts for decades. The small, box-like machine sitting on a stylish base, joins the silent VDTs in news rooms of the future, where the only sounds will be those of conversation, not those of pounding typewriters and clicking teletypes.

Increased Channel Capacity

Channel capacity is another important consideration of wire services. By channel capacity, we mean *the number of words a wire service can transmit during a given time period.* In effect, this determines the amount of information a subscriber can receive. In the past, the channel capacity of standard teletype systems with information transmitted over telephone lines was limited to approximately 66 words per minute. However, new developments in technology, including high-speed teleprinters and cable systems, have the potential channel capacity of 70,000 words per second. Although the average news room won't ever receive that much news, developments such as these allow subscribers to receive an almost unlimited amount of news in any twenty-four hour period.

One of the most advanced concepts linking computer science and wire service technology is an arrangement started in 1974 between Reuter and Manhattan Cable Television (Figure 7–2). The system uses two-way cable to supply subscribers with news and information directly from the wire service on their home television set. Home subscribers can choose the stories they want to read by scanning headlines, then "calling up" the story on their television screen by pressing a button on their home response terminal hooked into the two-way cable system.

The future of wire services is dependent on their ability to remain free and independent suppliers of news. Currently, they are facing serious price squeezes because of increased costs for leased lines. If they can survive this era financially intact, and there is every indication that they will, new technology such as satellite communication may aid in disseminating the news to their subscribers much more economically.

feature syndicates

The next time you read the comics or your favorite feature column in the newspaper, notice in the corner of one of the panels or columns the small print reference to the copyright of a syndicate. The small print with the name King Features Syndicate, United Features Syndicate, National Newspaper Syndicate, or a similar reference spells the story behind one of the most important information systems for the newspaper and magazine industry. These publishers subscribe to syndicates in the same way they do to wire services. In the past seventy years, the role of the syndicates has steadily increased in size and importance. Moreover, newspapers long ago learned that the features they carry often determine the size and loyalty of their readers. Although people turn to the newspaper for news, they also depend on the newspaper for entertainment—entertainment which is just as important to the lifeblood of the newspaper as programming is to radio and television. It is mostly in this

Figure 7-2 Using two-way cable, subscribers can "call up" a complete news story selected having its own code number. (Photograph used by permission of Reuters.)

role that the syndicates, sometimes called *feature* or *press syndicates*, operate.

Even books can become a major part of syndicate publication. Many times a syndicate will purchase the rights to a book and release it piecemeal before the complete publication is made available to the public. Along with providing good reading material for many magazines, the author and publisher also receive beneficial promotion. King Features, for example, has syndicated such books as John F. Kennedy's *A Land of Immigrants* and J. Edgar Hoover's *Masters of Deceit.* Records of special events are also syndicated. Many of the Apollo astronauts syndicated the stories of their adventures in space. Famous explorers have done the same as have war heroes.

the comics

Of all the syndicated features, perhaps none reflects the concept of the feature syndicate more than the comics. Throughout this century, comic strips have reflected virtually every segment of life and have stereotyped such characters as the fighting soldier and the kid down the street. Every family with children can identify with such strips as *Dennis the Menace, Blondie,* and *Tiger.* The world of law enforcement has been accorded its share of attention through decades of *Dick Tracy.* We have watched this world-famous police officer tackle criminals with such crime fighting devices as two-way wrist radios and later two-way wrist television. The universal experience of romance has been captured in such popular strips as *Juliet Jones* and *Mary Worth.*

.Although not new, direct social commentary has become acceptable comic material and has gained popularity and loyalty among comic enthusiasts. One of the most successful is the strip *Doonesbury,* created by a 25-year-old Yale student named Gary Trudeau. The strip, an outgrowth of the turbulent unrest of the late 1960s, first appeared in the *Yale Daily News* before being discovered and syndicated by Universal Press Syndicate. This comic has taken an almost no-holds-barred approach to current issues. In fact, some newspapers have refused to run certain episodes that deal, by name, with some of the highest officials in government. Treatment of issues such as the energy crisis, protest marches, hippies, drugs, communal living, and life at the White House is common. Current estimates by Universal list the readership at eighteen million.

Syndicated artists and writers have emerged from some strange and unrelated backgrounds. Not atypical are the personal backgrounds represented by employees of King Features Syndicate. According to the Syndicate, Otto Soglow who created *The Little King* was a dishwasher, shipping clerk, and switchboard operator; the creator of *Prince Valiant*, Hal Foster, worked as a trapper, hunter, and boxer; Chic Young, who created *Blondie*, was once a mailcarrier; and Roy Crane, who created *Buz Sawyer*, claimed to have once been a hobo. But before you decide immediately to become a feature syndicate writer or artist, keep in mind that on the average, only about 1 in 10,000 attempted features ever reaches publication.

The Readership

Of those that do reach publication, the impact and readership are astounding. In comparison, syndicate publications hold their own among such media systems as the networks and wire services. Unofficial estimates for the comics alone range in the vicinity of 100

The Sunday comics, an American tradition reaching millions of readers daily.

million readers per day. The comic strip characters have also traveled beyond the pages of newspapers. Major radio serials have been developed around various comic strip personalities as have special radio and television programs. For example, Charlie Brown is not only a favorite among newspaper comic readers everywhere but has also starred in several prime-time television specials. In addition, his dog Snoopy adorns the dormitory rooms of countless students as a cuddly stuffed pillow dog, a perky poster, or in the form of countless other nicknacks. The character Ziggy, created by Tom Wilson of American Greetings Corporation and syndicated by Universal Press Syndicate, is also seen in stores as the little statue with the funny sayings inscribed on its base which seem to say anything you want about this charming little underdog.

Panel Cartoons

Panel cartoons are also popular syndicate features. These are cartoons which are contained in a single frame instead of a series of frames. Popular single frame cartoons include *Dennis the Menace, Marmaduke, Grin and Bear It,* and *Dunagin's People.* Editorial panel cartoons are syndicated in virtually every major newspaper in the free world.

As people continue to enjoy the escape that identification with characters whose experiences and life styles are similar provides, so will syndicate publications continue to thrive. With the ability to adapt to changing moods, issues, and experiences, the features of a syndicate can live almost indefinitely, appealing to generation after generation. Although the high cost of newsprint and other expenses associated with newspaper production have cut many pages from the print medium, the loyalty of readers to the comics and other features has been too steadfast for editors and publishers to gamble with removing some of the most popular characters of our daily lives.

early syndicate development

The beginning of the syndicate can be traced back to the late 1800s when Joseph Pulitzer published in the Sunday editions of his newspapers a comic character created by cartoonist Richard F. Outcault. However, Pulitzer didn't keep Outcault very long. The cartoonist succumbed to the monetary temptations of employment under William Randolph Hearst, who started the *New York Journal* in 1896. Hearst's success was in some ways directly attributable to Outcault's creativity with the character known as the Yellow Kid. Neither did Hearst's sense of competition rule out the use of sensational news to increase circulation. This practice, plus the fact that the Yellow Kid had been proselyted to Hearst's newspaper, spawned the phrase "yellow journalism," synonymous with sensational reporting techniques. The success of the syndicated features became apparent as newspapers realized there was more to attracting readers than just publicizing hard news. Following the Yellow Kid, the Katzenjammer Kids were born, and they were joined in the early 1900s by such strips as "Mutt and Jeff" and in 1917 by "The Gumps."

Hearst and King Features

Hearst also guided the founding of King Features Syndicate which was responsible for producing comic strips and other features for the Hearst newspapers as well as for subscribers. "Happy Hooligan" and "Bringing Up Father" appeared along with book reviews, fashion features, and reproductions of art. M. Koenigsberg became the first president of King, and some of his early writers included George Bernard Shaw and William Jennings Bryan. Today, King is responsible not only for its printed features but also for the production of radio features and cooperative ventures into motion pictures, such as the film *The Yellow Submarine*.

John Dille and Buck Rogers

Another syndicate pioneer, John Flint Dille, founded the National Newspaper Syndicate in 1916. Dille, who had an interest in science and the intellect, combined these qualities in 1929 to create the popular "Buck Rogers in the 25th Century." The series was the forerunner of science fiction. One of the characters evolving from the series, the famed Dr. Huer, differed from the usual athletic hero. He was an intellectual who was responsible for applying the discoveries of science to the imagination and creating mind-expanding adventures. He planted in many young readers of the era a thirst for scientific knowledge which undoubtedly influenced many of their professional careers. Yet along with becoming a successful and profitable entrepreneur, Dille wanted to confer some social significance to his enterprise. So at a time when the word "psychology" still belonged to the realm of skepticism and suspicion, Dille launched the feature called "Let's Explore Your Mind," authored by Dr. Albert Edward Wiggam. The reins of National have since changed to Dille's son Robert C. Dille.

Many other feature syndicates developed concurrently. The major wire services also entered the feature syndication field. Many major newspapers have syndicated their best writers and artists, including the *Washington Post, Chicago Tribune, New York Times, Los Angeles Times,* and *Denver Post.* Individual writers and artists have also independently syndicated their material for distribution.

the scope of syndicates: golf to gall bladders

The scope of content found in contemporary syndicate features is as broad as the tastes of the readership they serve. For example, our preoccupation with the sport of golf has prompted the syndicated "golf tips" of such sports immortals as Arnold Palmer, Gary Player, Sam Snead, Cary Middlecoff, Jack Nicklaus, and many others. "Mark Trail's Outdoor Tips" and the Publisher Hall Syndicate's "Jimmy 'The Greek' Snyder" plus many other sports cartoons are further examples. Syndicated columnists themselves are popular with many readers. Jack Anderson has become a journalistic legend with his inside scoops about happenings in government. Other syndicated political columnists gracing editorial pages include Rowland Evans, Robert Novak, and Carl Rowan. In some areas, regional columnists are also popular.

In addition, specialized features such as "Ann Landers" have gained tremendous loyalty among readers. Victor Reisel writes about the labor movement and has a wide following in areas where a significant percentage of the readership are union members or come from union families. Hobbies have always been popular syndicated subjects, and many run on a seasonal basis, such as those dealing with gardening and landscaping. Medicine is also a popular feature, and the number of famous doctors writing syndicated columns has increased steadily. One of the most famous is Dr. Spock, the "baby doctor," whose column is found not only in newspapers but magazines as well. Dr. Brady's health advice was syndicated by the National Newspaper Syndicate for over 50 years. National also syndicated the column by Dr. Lindsay Curtis entitled "For Women Only," which deals exclusively with women's health problems. The feature is a relatively new development in publishing, since in years past many conservative editors wouldn't have considered running such a column.

research services

Assume that you are a newspaper publisher and are responsible for preparing the editorial page of your newspaper. Your job necessitates your being well informed on various issues which are of concern to your readership. With all your other responsibilities at the newspaper, however, it might be difficult for you to take the time to do all the important research necessary to write intelligent editorials. You need to go to the local library, look through indexes, take notes, read through considerable material, and then write the editorial—every day. Having someone else do the basic research for you and summarize the material for your use would simplify your job greatly. This is the function of a *research service.*

There are many different types of research services. Many of them are based in Washington, D.C. and employ a large staff of researchers and writers who prepare background reports on major issues. The services then send these reports to subscribers, primarily newspaper and broadcast executives.

New Insights for Local Media

Research services can also aid media executives in other ways. For example, some of the issues raised in the reports may provide new insights for local stories. An example: You learn in a background report from Washington that a new energy bill lifting price controls on natural gas is being opposed by Congress. Congressmen feel it will cut into the profits of rural electric cooperatives, which operate with coal, and provide excessive profits to local gas companies. Your reading and observations may lead you to take an editorial stand on the legislation. One of your local reporters may then want to do a series of stories on rural electric cooperatives and their ability to compete. More stories might evolve from the different types of management structure found in the cooperative versus the gas company, or the different customer relations of the two companies and how this affects public attitudes. Thus both the editorial and the stories are outgrowths of the background report provided by the research service.

Background services are equally important for broadcasters. Some offer broadcasters a weekly newsletter filled with descriptions on how other broadcasters have covered a news story. Other services offer ideas for radio production techniques, jokes and humorous sayings for announcers, and special broadcast sales tips.

Tip Sheets

The same service may also provide *tip sheets,* which are lists of important events that will probably make news in the coming weeks. Reporters can then be assigned to prepare special features or investigative reports to accompany and complement coverage of the major event. The tip sheet might inform you of a bill in Congress making it a federal crime to injure a police officer. Learning of this, local reporters may examine local statistics on police assaults and compile a story appearing alongside the factual account of how your congressman voted on the bill.

As part of their public relations function, many companies and national organizations have their own research services and provide background reports on their own operations to the news media. For example, one insurance company's research service offers a telephone number that any member of the news media can call for information on no-fault insurance. Especially during campaigns, many politicians have telephone numbers the news media can call to learn the candidate's latest stand on an issue, usually provided by a voice recorder.

summary

In this chapter we have studied wire services, syndicates, and research services. Wire services are responsible for supplying the bulk of news to the mass media, which in turn disseminate it to the public through broadcast and printed news reports. Specialized wire services carry news designed for specialized audiences such as the agricultural and business communities.

The concept of a wire service actually found its first application in the 1800s with carrier pigeon service between towns not connected by telegraph. The first modern wire service was Associated Press, which did not take on its present form until a dispute between its western and eastern factions resulted in the formation of the Associated Press of Illinois. United Press International became the first supplier of news to broadcast stations. Reuter, AP, and UPI are the three major wire services in the world.

Syndicates are another major source of information for mass media, especially newspapers. The syndicate concept, which dates back to the end of the last century, has now been applied to everything from books to cartoons. Research services provide background information for editorials and stories.

opportunities for further learning

COOPER, KENT, *Kent Cooper and The Associated Press.* New York: Random House, 1959.

HORN, MAURICE, ed., *The World Encyclopedia of Comics.* New York: Chelsea House, 1976.

MORRIS, JOE A., *Deadline Every Minute: The Story of United Press.* Westport, Conn.: Greenwood Press, Inc., 1969.

NELSON, ROY PAUL, *Cartooning.* Chicago: Henry Regnery Co., 1975.

REITGERGER, REINHOLD, and WOLFGANG FUCHS, *Comics: Anatomy of a Mass Medium.* Boston, Mass.: Little, Brown and Company, 1972.

ROBISON, JERRY, *The Comics: An Illustrated History of Comic Strip Art.* New York: Putnam, 1974.

STOREY, GRAHAM, *Reuters.* New York: Crown Publishers, 1951.

the recording industry,
ad agencies,
and
public relations

CHAPTER EIGHT

Besides wire services and syndicates, other support systems produce different types of messages. The hit record on the radio, the commercial on television, or the feature article in a magazine may be the result of such support systems as the recording industry, advertising agencies, or a public relations firm. The purpose of Chapter 8 is to learn more about these industries and their important functions.

the recording industry

What images come to mind when one thinks of the recording industry? The support for virtually every type of electronic mass communication, the industry is synonomous with multi-million dollar studios, rock bands, promoters, albums, concerts, stars, excitement—and perhaps heartbreak. To the jet set it means London, Nashville, Chicago, New York, Paris, and Los Angeles, and to the electronic engineer it's echo chambers, reverbs, microphones, and synthesizers.

From 78's to 33-1/3's

In the early days of radio, the big bands, and live studio performances, music and music publishing affected every age group. Walking into a well-equipped music store, you would find someone sitting at a piano playing the latest tunes, and you could purchase sheet music for any popular tune. Matronly housewives were just as apt to purchase the latest popular song as were teenagers. But, as with other mass media, new developments in recording technology changed the industry. These included the development of the inexpensive 45 rpm (revolutions per minute) record and the 33-1/3 rpm albums. Because they were inexpensive, easily marketable, and of high fidelity, local stations found themselves doing more of their own programming and relying less on the networks. Competition from the new medium of television led to radio's catering to local, specialized audiences.

The Dawn of Rock and Roll

The 1950s brought forth a revolutionary new musical concept—"rock and roll." It changed the music industry, it helped change radio, it changed our culture, and it provided some of the largest profits that the entertainment world had ever seen. It also began to narrow its appeal to teens and young adults exclusively. Middle-aged people were attracted by the novelty of Elvis Presley's first appearance on national television, but it was the younger audience that became devoted fans of rock music and performers. By the time the Beatles arrived in the 1960s, these young fans were total rock converts. Meanwhile, the middle-aged recording fan had become a voice almost too small to be heard in the consumer market.

Disciples of the new music made up the larger portion of the population who tuned in rock radio stations to hear the "Top 100," the "Top 40," the "pick hit" of the week, the "number one song" in the area, and the occasional "oldies but goodies" which were never too old to be out of the real era of rock music. The music industry's new commodity commanded a loyalty and a following that sent thousands to concerts from Woodstock to the Thames. Because of radio's adaptability, it drew the same overwhelming loyalty, and disc jockeys became popular stars in their own right. Transistors even made it possible to take rock music and a favorite radio station almost anywhere.

But rock music did more than acquire its devotees—it also changed our culture. With the Beatles came long hair, and then still longer hair with the countless rock groups that followed. People began to realize that rock 'n roll was true cultural expression and not a passing fad. Country-western music, which normally commanded a loyal following, saw an even larger following in the young rock fans. From this evolved country-rock and an entire new generation of stars who managed to span two cultures.

Big Business and the Stars

The recording industry has become big business, its primary medium of distribution being radio and television programming. These introduce the public to the sounds destined to become national hits; the record stores take over from there. The industry has had to change radically from the era of the 1920s and 1930s when music publishers were in the business of printing sheet music. Today, a music publisher attracts and signs the stars, arranges to have their songs taped and pressed into records, distributes the records, and promotes them. The major publishers, such as RCA and Columbia, are multimillion-dollar corporations with many recording artists signed to contracts, ranging from major stars to those barely able to make a living.

The industry is closely tied to radio. Without the recording industry, most radio stations could not survive. On the other hand, the recording industry is equally dependent upon radio. It has come to rely on radio as a free method of advertising new songs. Radio becomes the first medium of distribution for the products of the recording industry, and the industry provides radio with programming to fill the many hours of the broadcasting day.

the making of a hit record

How does an idea become a hit record? Imagine you're driving down a main street in Nashville, Tennessee, with your guitar in the back seat, destined to become a star. About the second major recording company you pass, you decide that a walk through that door will turn your name into a household word to millions waiting to hear your latest songs and turn your life into fame and fortune. Through the front door you go, and to the first secretary you encounter you announce you are good, have some original material and a guitar, and would like to see the manager. The secretary in a nice way manages to tell you to get lost, just like she has told hundreds before you. With your confidence still intact, you learn that the correct place to start your claim to fame is at one of the performance rights societies, such as Broadcast Music, Inc. (BMI), or the American Society of Composers, Authors, and Publishers (ASCAP).

The Demo and Master Recording Sessions

Association with these organizations is important because they become responsible for collecting royalties from songs you write or perform. They collect licensing fees from broadcast stations, airlines, or rock groups that may be involved in playing your songs. After the performance rights societies, the next stop is a publishing company which specializes in your type of music. The publishing company may agree to let you have a demonstration or *demo session* and provide the basic accompaniment necessary to put your

A SONG

RECORDING SESSIONS

AIR PLAY

PUBLIC DEMAND

song on tape. After the manager and some of the staff listen to your tape, they decide whether or not you're hired to work with their major stars. Their reaction is positive. You now have the opportunity to learn from the professionals.

One day, you finally write some material you think has possibilities. The staff agrees, and they decide that you are worth the time and expense to have a *master session*. This session is immensely important for you and for the publishing company. To achieve authentic reproduction of every sound, the recording is done on a major control console having as many as thirty or more channels with a trained recording engineer and full orchestral accompaniment. The master session will involve an investment on the part of the publishing company of many thousands of dollars. After the master session, the tape is sent to be made into a *master record,* usually a 45 rpm, and from this, thousands of records are pressed and readied for distribution.

Promoting the Record

Promotion is the next step. So far, there isn't anyone interested in buying your records except you. No one else has even heard of you. But they will if they hear your song on the radio. Your publishing company thus sends complimentary copies of your record to radio stations all over the country, hoping the disc jockeys will listen to it, like it, and begin to play it. This process is not as easy as it sounds, though. At the average radio station, your record will be in competition each week with more than two hundred other records. At many stations, unless your name is known, your record won't even be taken out of its cover. Perhaps, however, you're lucky and someone does decide to play your record. Perhaps it even advances as a "pick hit." It is even possible that people select it in some of the jukeboxes where it's been placed.

The Billboard Charts

Now as these events begin to happen, perhaps your record is called to the attention of one of the recording industry trade magazines— for example, *Billboard*—and it later appears on one of *Billboard's* hit charts. Your chances for success, although not guaranteed, suddenly become a thousand times greater. Finally your record begins to rise on the charts. You record another song which also makes the charts, only this time the process is much easier. You have now reached stardom and are probably earning a considerable income. Before you rush out to purchase a guitar, however, it is important to remember two things: those who do make it to stardom are few and far between, and the time that transpires between your first signing with the publishing company and your reaching stardom may be decades. Moreover, you may never make it big. Although glamorous and profitable, the recording industry rests on a major element of risk.

payola and pirates

In its rather brief history, the recording industry has experienced many growing pains which have troubled both industry personnel and the public. Some of the most famous were the "payola" scandals. These involved record companies that allegedly paid disc jockeys to play certain records, thus making the songs appear popular and jump on the charts. The payola scandals brought to the surface a practice which had plagued honest operators and artists who were attempting to compete fairly in the open market. Disc jockeys and record companies alike were faced with a serious loss of credibility over the issue, and the public had its first glimpse at this murky activity which had exploited the recording industry as well as radio. Today, big payola is successfully policed, but other means of persuasion attempt to influence disc jockeys. It is not unusual for the program or music director at a typical radio station to open the mail and find paper weights, T-shirts, giant posters, or other gadgets all designed to promote a particular artist or song.

Although payola hurt the image of the industry, this was small compared to the monetary loss it experienced between 1970 and 1975 when the height of the record and tape piracy was in full swing. Pirating tapes and records is the illegal duplication of major records and tapes and their consequent distribution and sale at discounted rates. The practice reached epidemic proportions around 1971 and was even given support by certain court rulings which claimed major record companies were interfering with free trade when they tried to prevent their tapes and records from being duplicated and sold as pirated merchandise. Some organizations supporting free trade interests actually backed the pirate operators. Raids of pirate duplicating operations reached their peak in 1973 and 1974 with significant amounts of recording hardware and pirated tapes and records seized. It was determined that a major pirate operator could produce as many as 20,000 to 30,000 tapes in a single day and also operate major promotion and distribution systems. The breakthrough for the recording companies and artists who owned the original copyrights finally came with court rulings first in Europe and then in America. However, it was only after years of court battles accompanied by financial support from music organizations, recording artists, and the recording industry that pirating was controlled.

The prognosis for the future of the recording industry continues to be bright despite its almost total dependence on radio for marketing and distribution. There is little indication that the major purchasers of records, the young adults, will stop buying them. As long as television, film, and other types of communication entertainment prosper, the recording industry will continue to be a major support system for mass communication.

the functioning of ad agencies

As either industry professionals or future consumers of mass communication, we should be aware that there are many people responsible for the messages disseminated via mass communication. There are people and organizations whose primary responsibility is to produce and prepare messages, especially commercial messages. Advertising agencies are one of the most important and active organizations which influence every facet of mass media.

Ad agencies first appeared in the late 1800s when newspapers began to rely less on government subsidies and more on commercial advertising to survive. The improved distribution systems of railroads and highways made newspaper advertising an attractive means of reaching a large number of people. Yet advertising still met resistance, not from consumers but from merchants who felt it was unorthodox to market their products in any way other than a storefront display or a simple, typed paragraph in the paper. The creative ads which proliferate the pages of today's newspapers and magazines were unheard of in the late 1800s, mainly because the foundation for such an inventive service had yet to be laid. The newspaper publisher was primarily concerned with publishing, and the merchant was primarily concerned with running a business. There needed to be someone in the middle, someone who could develop the creative message necessary to lift the merchant's product out of the typed column and into the limelight of reader attention. Early efforts at advertising were primarily made by copywriters at the local newspaper. As the importance of their function was realized, however, they became independent agents, specialists whose talents were in great demand. Businesses realized that they needed the assistance of these specialists to compete successfully in the marketplace.

This modest beginning was the foundation of modern advertising and the ad agency. Today, ad agencies are found in virtually every major city in the free world, and their role in stimulating economic growth is being recognized. Advertising is an important link between products and the public, and the keys to its success are the systems of mass communication.

Talent: The Major Commodity

The basic commodity of an ad agency is *talent*. The creative efforts of the art director, the marketing savvy of the media buyer, the detailed analysis of the research director, and the political understanding of the campaign director are just a few examples of the many abilities ad agency personnel have to offer. A business, organization, or person will contract the services of an ad agency to help market a product. The product may be soap, the corporate image of

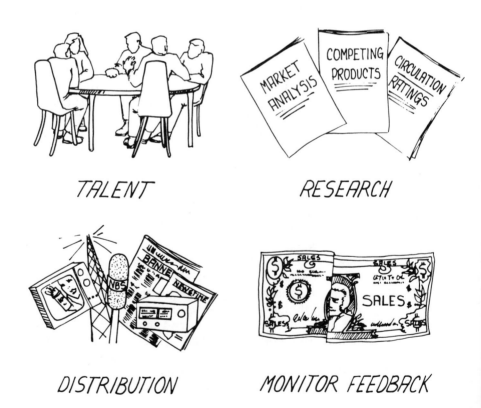

TALENT   RESEARCH

DISTRIBUTION   MONITOR FEEDBACK

a multi-million dollar company, a political figure, or a nonprofit organization. Basically, the agency performs three major tasks.

Research Functions

The first task is research. In order to distribute the message to the public successfully, the agency must first understand all that it can about the product. Imagine you are responsible for handling the advertising for a principal lumber company. The company wants to develop an advertising campaign for a new by-product it has developed. This by-product is small chips of bark which have previously been burned as waste. It is your job to plan the advertising campaign.

One of your first jobs is to research the product and the company. You must learn everything you possibly can about both. Your research must even take you close to the heart of the firm's inner operations. In order for you to make effective advertising judgments that may involve thousands of dollars, you must know how that firm ticks. Occasionally research may reveal certain questionable business operations, dealings that may force your agency to withdraw from handling the campaign. Handling a disreputable firm's advertising may leave your agency with a problem collecting money for your services, to say nothing of a lawsuit for fraudulent advertising and possible tangles with the Federal Trade Commission. This research into the company and its product is called *product research.*

Market research is the second function. This type of research aims at locating the potential market for the new product. You'll need to know if there are other products on the market that can successfully compete with your client's product. You'll want to know where the customers for the product can be found. You'll want to know the characteristics of your potential customers. Are they home owners? Are they apt to do their own gardening and yard work, or do they hire professional gardeners to do these tasks? Answers to these questions are part of market research.

Distribution

The second important task is *distribution.* Here you will decide what type of message you are going to create for the company and what media will be most helpful in sending this message to the public. Let's assume that your research into the company's background gives it a clean bill of health, and you decide to continue with the account. You have learned that the bark chips make a good bedding to place around shrubbery. Next, you conduct further research into a possible name for the bark chips. Your research strikes a positive note on the name "Barko!" The name is catchy, it is easily remembered, and it carries the substance of the product into the name.

Now comes the decision on how to tell the "Barko!" story to the public. It's time to call a meeting of the agency's department heads.

Account Executive:	The lumber company has decided to market the small wood chips which are waste material when bark is ground off the logs. The chips are a few inches long and come in all shapes. They'll bag them in fifty pound sacks and we're calling it "Barko!"
Research Director:	We've investigated the product and the market as thoroughly as possible. The bark chips are great for placing around shrubbery. We see the market as basically home owners who do their own gardening and yard work.
General Manager:	It's a good account all around. The lumber company has been in business for fifty years, and they have an excellent credit rating. Any ideas on how to tell the story?
Art Director:	I think some pictures toned with soft brown shades will tell the story best.
Production Director:	OK, but don't go too far; color television has more potential than brown. Let's consider using some bright yellows, oranges, and greens.
Art Director:	Since this stuff comes in all shapes and sizes, perhaps we could arrange a cartoon character around it.
General Manager:	That's cutting our budget close. Cartoon production is too expensive with this account.
Photographer:	We could shoot some sharp photography of sunlit patios with Barko around the shrubbery.
Copywriter:	That might work well. We could develop a series of commercials to stress seasonal outdoor decorating.
Media Buyer:	I envision running some ads in the syndicated section on gardening in the Sunday paper and tying in the theme to evening television and radio. Perhaps some billboards would also be helpful. In addition, I feel a brochure sent to all the gardening outlets in the state would be an excellent sales piece.

This conversation illustrates some of the numerous considerations involved in planning an advertising campaign. Notice how the development of the commercial message encompasses the creative talents of many people. Precisely because it would be too time-consuming and costly to develop this expertise within the lumber company, has its management hired the ad agency. Moreover, the people at the ad agency can look at the company's product objectively. They aren't so closely associated with the product or the company that they can't point out possible negative aspects of the product that should be considered.

Monitoring Feedback

The third important task of advertising is *monitoring feedback*. Although this may be accomplished in various ways and is not always included in the ad agency's contract, it can be an important part of the business-media relationship. Perhaps retailers receive complaints about Barkos. Perhaps there is a rival product and the public is confusing your product with its competition. By monitoring consumer feedback, a decision on whether or not to revise the message, the medium, and/or the target audience can be made.

The preceding paragraphs have provided us with a brief look at the operation of an ad agency. As the business of reaching the public with information about new products becomes increasingly complex, the work of ad agencies becomes more and more important. No longer can a firm make a decision merely to advertise in a storefront window or in the local newspaper. Complex multi-media buying decisions, the psychology of attitudes affecting styles and color combinations, and the ability to coordinate advertising messages across many different media demand talent—talent based on the ad agency's years of expertise. Most medium-sized cities and many small communities have ad agencies. Wherever creative talent can be mustered and enough clients found to use these services, an ad agency is likely to appear. Many large, diversified corporations supplying national and international markets are developing their own ad agencies right within the company. These *in-house* agencies serve much the same function as an independent ad agency except they deal exclusively with that company's products. Although there is some danger in being "too close" to the company and its line to treat them objectively, such dangers have not deterred the growth of in-house agencies.

public relations

Directly related to advertising is public relations. In fact, there is a very fine line that distinguishes them. Basically, where advertising is concerned with selling a product, public relations is concerned with creating a favorable image for the company that produces the product. As responsible consumers of mass communication, we need to be aware that many of the messages we receive via the mass media are concerned with public relations. The thin line between public relations and advertising is evident when a fast food chain sponsors a bike-a-thon for a national charity. In the charity ads, the food company's name and trademark are used in the same way that they are used to sell sandwiches, yet the message solicits participation in the bike-a-thon. What the company is trying to do is create a favorable impression for itself as well as interest the public in its product.

The Philosophy of PR

Why bother with public relations? Why not just concentrate on selling sandwiches? That may be satisfactory if the company's only goal is to sell sandwiches at their current locations. However, what if the chain wants to expand? Perhaps the next community in which it plans to build a restaurant has had bad experiences with a similar food chain. As the request for the company's restaurant comes before the zoning board, there is considerable negative reaction to the application. However, the company officials remind the board and the concerned citizens about their involvement in local charities with their national bike-a-thon. This public relations event may be just the touch needed to garner approval for the building application.

One of the major criticisms of public relations is that too often it's similar to shutting the barn door after the horse has escaped. Effective public relations programs should help *prevent* problems in image and public opinion before they occur, not after. Many colleges and universities learned this the hard way in the late 1960s when campus demonstrations broke out in opposition to the Vietnam War. For a number of years, higher education had placed emphasis on how the university served its students rather than on how it served its state or community. When campus demonstrations occurred, many citizens reacted against higher education because they believed that the only thing happening on campuses was disruption. The result was a serious cut in state budgets and alumni contributions, which directly affected the quality of higher education. Higher education wasn't prepared for the unrest, and most college public relations departments were unprepared to handle the crises. They frantically tried to sway the tide of public opinion in the other direction, but it was too late. This was a prime case of the horse having already escaped from the barn. After the unrest had quieted, colleges and universities seriously reevaluated their public relations efforts. They began to try to break down the "town-gown" barriers in their communities. Although effort has continued, the rebuilding process has been difficult for many schools whose images had been severely damaged. Had an effective public relations program been instituted before the campus unrest occurred, there is a good probability this loss of public support might largely have been averted.

Many public relations firms act as the voice for certain industries. Such national organizations as the American Gas Association work in cooperation with the entire industry to help identify critical issues concerning the industry and to gain public support for the industry through national campaigns. The Mortgage Bankers Association represents much of the banking industry and actually presents journalism awards for stories related to banking. The contest, along with publicizing the banking industry to the news media, also promotes special features, articles, and documentaries carrying the message of the financial world to the public.

The Publicity Function

Publicity is another important aspect of public relations. In most cases, publicity deals directly with the gatekeepers who control the flow of news. The forces directed toward such gatekeepers can be tremendous. These people are usually bombarded with telephone calls from press agents, piles of press releases on everything from new products to politicians, tickets to free dinners where a politician is appearing or a company is delivering its latest annual report, and countless other tactics from people and organizations all trying to receive free media exposure. If they successfully receive this free exposure, it is often more valuable than media exposure obtained through advertising campaigns. For example, a feature article of a new product in a national magazine may elicit a much greater reader response than an advertisement for the new product. Readers who see the product in the feature article are not resistant to its message as they may be to the message in an advertisement. If a politician makes a favorable impression on the evening news, the publicity can be much more credible than if he or she appears in a paid political advertisement.

Those whose job it is to obtain free publicity work very hard at it, sometimes with limited results. In many news rooms, personnel are so accustomed to press releases that they often don't bother to open certain mail. The letterhead is enough to tip them off. In most cases, the press releases are tossed away because the person trying to obtain free publicity has done one of two things. This person has probably first inundated the media with almost daily press releases. Rarely does a single subject or politician warrant that much publicity. After all, if you were a regular reader of a newspaper and saw that every issue had a story about a local congressman or congresswoman, you would begin to grow somewhat suspicious of the paper's credibility. Second, many press releases try to masquerade as news. The press release begins with a lead sentence such as might be used to introduce a major international event; the second paragraph reveals, however, that the politician is simply speaking to the ladies' aid society. The gatekeeper thus loses trust in the source of the press release and tends to shy away from future releases.

Publicity, when it is effective, can reap many rewards. One of the more successful publicity campaigns was carried off in Oregon where a teacher at a community college invented an "executive toy." This toy was made with a line of steel balls hung in a row on individual strings from a small wood frame about nine inches square. Using Newton's Third Law of Motion, which says that for every action there is an equal and opposite reaction, you could pull one of the steel balls back, let it go, and the steel ball at the other end of the line would bounce while all the other steel balls remained stationary. Beverly Green, president of Green/Associates Advertising, Inc., was responsible for successfully marketing the gadget through free publicity. The publicity campaign involved sending letters, press releases, and samples of the novel toy to newspapers, television stations, and magazines throughout the United States. The toy appeared in such publications as *Playboy, Newsweek, Boy's Life,* and *House Beautiful.* It also appeared on such national television shows as the *Today Show,* Johnny Carson's *Tonight Show,* the *Merv Griffin Show,* the *Joey Bishop Show,* and the *Steve Allen Show.* This media publicity brought the toy to the attention of millions of people, of whom 200,000 purchased their own by the end of the first year of production.

This is just one example of how free publicity was employed to market a product. The channels of mass communication are limited, so the competition is stiff. Yet when you can gain exposure on the media, it can have far reaching results.

summary

In Chapter 8, we have briefly examined the recording industry, advertising agencies, and public relations firms.

The recording industry makes available to radio stations the larger part of their programming. Radio, in turn, is the proving ground for most new records and tapes. The industry, at best a chancy business for the aspiring recording artist, has evolved from a simple function—that of publishing sheet music—to a multimillion-dollar business involving many talents and much technological knowhow.

Advertising agencies are responsible for many of the commercial messages in the mass media. The main asset of the advertising agency is talent. The creative talents of such people as the production director, research director, general manager, photographer, copywriter, media buyer, and account executive all combine in a team to call the attention of the public to a product or service. Along with talent, the ad agency is involved with research, distribution, and monitoring feedback.

Public relations firms are also concerned with calling the public's attention to a product or service, but their emphasis is primarily on communicating a positive image about that product or service.

opportunities for further learning

BURKE, JOHN D., *Advertising in the Marketplace*. New York: McGraw-Hill Book Company, 1973.

CANFIELD, BERTRAND R., and H. FRAZIER MOORE, *Public Relations: Principles, Cases and Problems*, 6th Ed. Homewood, Ill.: Richard D. Irwin, Inc., 1973.

CUTLIP, SCOTT M., and ALLEN H. CENTER, *Effective Public Relations*, 4th Ed. Englewood Cliffs, N.J.: Prentice-Hall, Inc., 1971.

DUNN, S. WATSON, and ARNOLD M. BARBAN, *Advertising: Its Role in Modern Marketing*, 3rd Ed. Hinsdale, Ill.: The Dryden Press, 1974.

KARSHNER, ROGER, *The Music Machine*. Los Angeles, Calif.: Nash Publishing Corporation, 1976.

SCHICKE, CHARLES A., *Revolution in Sound: A Biography of The Recording Industry*. Boston, Mass.: Little, Brown and Company, 1974.

advertising messages

CHAPTER NINE

It is an average morning for Sally. She awakes at six. When the clock radio snaps on, the sounds of the commercials echo "plus cold tablets . . .," "twice as fast as aspirin . . .," "mild for children . . .," "for bites, burns, and sunburn . . .," and countless others. She manages to sort out the toothpaste, grab a toothbrush, wash, and head to the kitchen for breakfast. Turning on the television, she is confronted with "vitamin enriched . . .," "flour crusts . . .," "dissolves instantly . . .," and "free prize inside. . . ." The next fifteen minutes also bring television commercials for two movies and a promotional announcement for an evening television western. She finishes breakfast and goes upstairs where she leafs through a woman's magazine to see "made in Italy . . .," "exercise sole . . .," "black patent . . .," "camel smooth . . .," and "buckle bracelet. . . ." After dressing she heads for work. Turning on to main street, the neon flashing billboards tell her of special carpets, beer, baseball, bars, and brooms; so it goes until she reaches the office where she reads the morning newspaper filled with more advertising.

Advertising messages fill our lives from the moment we awake.

164

They are disseminated through magazines, radio, television, newspapers, and billboards. Each and every one of us is faced with the same daily messages — messages which inform, persuade, and entertain. Our relationship to these messages varies depending on our value structures, attitudes, and desires. However, all of the advertising messages have two things in common. They are reaching us, and they are affecting us. As consumers of mass communication or as professionals working in mass communication, it's important to know and understand the appeals and the different types of advertising. That is the purpose of this chapter, to bring us closer to an awareness of advertising and how it affects us.

value appeals in advertising

As individuals, we possess certain characteristics that trigger different reactions to specific types of communication. One such group of characteristics are our values. Broad-based characteristics of a population, value structures are defined as "a normative, conceptual standard of the desirable that predispositionally influences individuals in choosing among personally perceived alternatives of behavior."[1] Values are usually a product of our early childhood development and are not easily changed. Since they form the basis for many of our decisions, appeals to our value structures are very common in mass communication.

Since values are culturally based, they can vary from one culture to another. Thus, advertising which takes advantage of one culture's preferences may prove ineffective or even offensive elsewhere. The concern over wholesale transmission of cultural values via international satellite is one example of resistance to mass advertising.

Most researchers have defined the range of values into six broad categories: *aesthetic, humanitarian, intellectual, materialistic, prestige,* and *religious.*[2] Looking at each of these values separately, we can recognize the value-oriented appeals found in advertising. Keep in mind, though, that personal value structures are complex and that decisions usually rest on weighted combinations of values. A single advertising message may also appeal to several values.

Aesthetic Value Appeals

Aesthetic appeals attempt to evoke a sense of beauty and grace in our environment (Figure 9–1). We tend to react positively to visual appeal in advertising. A promotion for a series of famous paintings or sculptures would probably be based mainly if not totally on aesthetic appeal. Beautiful scenery as part of a travel poster on the other hand could also appeal to aesthetic values.

Music is also a viable advertising medium that communicates feelings and emotions. Music can be combined with pictorial beauty to create an aesthetically pleasing format. For instance, the Grand Canyon Suite accompanied by scenes of sunset on snow-

Figure 9–1 Aesthetic value appeal. (Produced for Vail Associates, Inc. by Advantage Vail Photo by Peter Runyan.)

capped mountains provides a dimension of beauty and majesty that has significant appeal to people with even minimal aesthetic values. In most cases, the appeals to dominant aesthetic values are found in highly specialized publications. Magazines targeted toward artists or musicians will usually carry ads with aesthetic value appeals.

Humanitarian Value Appeals

Humanitarian value appeals are some of the most widely used in advertising, and these appeals can reach out across cultural boundaries. Civilized people have a natural concern for others, and it is this love and respect of people upon which humanitarian appeals are based. We have all seen the ads for CARE or Project Hope with the picture of the hungry, crying children staring at us (Figure 9–2).

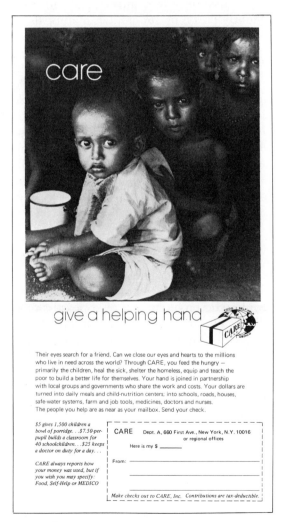

Figure 9.2 Humanitarian value appeal. (Photo courtesy of CARE.)

The predominant appeal in these instances is toward our humanitarian values.

Humanitarian value appeals are also frequently seen in ads directed to parents, especially when the product concerns their children. Pictures of children are common in ads for everything from cameras to health care. The young child lying in bed with a fever followed by the display of a cold remedy, and a child with a skinned knee followed by a display of an adhesive bandage are both humanitarian appeals.

Humanitarian appeals are also prevalent in ads showing groups of people sharing fun or fellowship, participating in non-prestige social gatherings such as picnics. The latter are much more subtle appeals than the ones of the starving child, but still involve the basic premise that people enjoy being with and caring about people. Commercials for greeting cards and long distance telephone service are also frequently based on humanitarian appeals.

Intellectual Value Appeals

Intellectual appeals are based on an individual's love and respect for knowledge. Knowledge is a product of our culture that occasionally becomes a predominant value, as, for instance, when a student devotes himself to scholarship or research. More often it is the basis for more dominant goals such as acquiring a job or prestige. Thus although the appeal to intellectual value is infrequently used, one can find examples in magazines geared to persons on above-average educational levels. For example, an ad for a set of encyclopedias or great books may employ the intellectual value technique.

Materialistic Value Appeals

Some of the most dominant and most frequent value appeals found in advertising are those directed to materialistic values. We are an acquiring people who enjoy having nice possessions and the money to purchase them. Our orientation into the materialistic mold begins from when we acquire our first toys and continues when we acquire an automobile, a house, and so on. Regardless of whether materialistic values are dominant, people usually make decisions based on their "money's worth." The materialistic appeal is therefore common, especially during times of economic recession. Ads which tend to lean predominantly toward the materialistic value structure include banks advertising their low interest rates, automobile dealers selling their luxury cars at a few hundred dollars savings, and home furnishing outlets offering dining room sets at bargain prices.

The finest and most modern home appliances, the best panelling for the recreation room, and the air conditioner for the bedroom are all excellent candidates for materialistic appeals.

Prestige Value Appeals

The prestige value is closely aligned with our desire to obtain some form of power and position among our peers. Typical appeals toward prestige values include those made by special schools claiming to help us win that promotion or conduct the most interesting conversation at a party. When an advertiser equates wearing a certain suit with leadership, he is appealing to our desire for prestige. The same appeal is also frequently used in children's advertising, for example, suggestions that a child should be the first on the block to own a new toy or the first in the neighborhood with a new bicycle. Many have expressed concern with the quality of children's advertising, however, and some organizations, notably consumer groups, have established codes against using appeals to the prestige value of children.

Religious Value Appeals

Appeals to religious values are not used as frequently in advertising as other value appeals. Although some preachers might disagree, it is difficult to relate consumer product demand to the worship of a supernatural being. Religious appeals are mostly used to persuade people to attend church or to make religion more relevant in their daily lives. Religious appeals are most strongly felt by those whose value orientation is predominantly religious; for example, as a group, the elderly tend more oriented toward religion than some younger generations (Figure 9–3). Those actively employed in church related professions or whose religious heritage is significant would also be more likely to react to religious value appeals. Such themes as brotherhood, worshipping together, caring for others, and similar "people-oriented" themes combine religious and humanitarian appeals.

appeals to basic needs

Everyone shares certain basic biological and psychological needs. The three primary ones are *food, shelter,* and *sex.* We need to eat to live, we need protection from the elements to survive, and each of us has a biological sex drive which has enabled the species to survive. The greater part of persuasive advertising across all media asserts its claim to satisfying these needs.

Food product accounts, for example, make up a sizeable portion of the income of many an ad agency. We are continually exposed to ads for food products, and it is no accident that among children, Ronald McDonald is the most recognizable character after Santa Claus. Breakfast cereals abound on Saturday morning television, and savory sauces precede, permeate, and parcel the evening news, conveniently scheduled when the majority of us are sitting down to a meal. Exhausted athletes quenching their thirst with the latest

"There's nothing I can do. I'm just one person."

Do you really think God is going to let you get away with that?

If you feel one person is too insignificant to help make the world a better place, then work together with others at your local church or synagogue. Example: in Montana, one congregation was disturbed by the lack of adequate housing for senior citizens in the area. Through its perseverance, a non-profit building with 111 homes is now a reality. There are lots of things you can do, too. The God we worship expects more from us than sympathy and good intentions.

Start treating your brothers and sisters like brothers and sisters.

RELIGION
IN AMERICAN LIFE

A Public Service of This Magazine & The Advertising Council Ad Council

Figure 9–3 Religious value appeal.

fruit drink, children running home from school to raid the refrigerator, and families barbecuing a sizzling steak on a backyard grill are all appeals to our basic need for food. One limitation on food as an advertising appeal is that its overall usefulness as a marketing strategy is mostly limited to just that—food. Culinary delights have, however, been used to attract customers to specific airlines or steamship cruises.

Another common appeal, and sometimes a controversial one, is sex appeal in advertising. It can be subtle, as in a commercial for eye glasses, or more direct, as in some advertisements in leading men's and women's magazines. All are based on the fact that people are sexually attracted to each other (Figure 9–4). Multi-million dollar industries have developed around cosmetics, hair coloring, elevator shoes, padded bras, toothpaste, panty hose, bikinis, cologne, perfume, eyelashes, and hard liquor, to name a few. Some of the most successful sex appeal themes have been used to market health foods and diet drinks.

The women's rights movement has had some strong criticism for sex-appeal advertising. In one state, protests arose over the use of a billboard advertisement in which a woman dressed in black velvet was used to sell hard liquor, likening its taste to the soft touch of velvet. On the whole, however, the attractiveness of the body remains a popular basis for advertising. One of the reasons is its almost universal application. Cultural differences do exist, however. What may be sexually appealing in one culture, may not be in another.

Shelter, like food, is somewhat limited and is usually directly related to building products or similar items. Often combined with materialistic values, such shelter-oriented ads as good investments in a home, long-lasting weather siding, leakproof shingles for the roof, or dual pane insulated windows are common. On occasion, motels and hotels have also used the shelter appeal on a theme of "coming in out of the storm."

It is important to remember that on few occasions are any of the appeals we've discussed used exclusively. For instance, as you sit in front of your television set or read the evening newspaper, the message that states that the new car is priced $500 cheaper also says it will add prestige to your life, will probably enhance your sex appeal, and has beauty and grace equivalent to a fine artistic masterpiece. Likewise, the appeal for your vote on the city bond issue will more than likely stress that your children's health and education are at stake, and you will save gasoline by not having to take your garbage to the city dump. As consumers of mass communication, you should become familiar with these various appeals and learn to identify them. With this knowledge, you'll be able to make more intelligent and critical judgements concerning the issues and products the appeals are designed to support.

types of advertising

Although the appeals just discussed form the persuasive base for advertising, there are many different types of ads in which these ap-

Figure 9–4 Sex appeal. (Ferber Strauss Glass Inc.)

peals are used. The most common types are *standard advertising* and *public service advertising*. In addition, contemporary social issues, the criticism of advertising mentioned earlier, and governmental regulations have induced new types of advertising. Among these are *social responsibility advertising, counter-advertising, corrective advertising, advocacy advertising,* and *image advertising.* Let's examine the different types of advertising in more detail.

Standard Advertising

Standard ads appear in all media and are financed by the company or organization which has products to sell or services to render. The motive is to sell and to create in the consumer a feeling of need and desire for a product or service. Decisions as to the type of message the ads will use, in what media they will be placed, and how often they will appear in the media are usually made by the manufacturer or distributor, sometimes in conjuction with an ad agency. Once these decisions are made, time or space is purchased and a contract is signed specifying such things as the number of times the ad will appear, when it will appear, and in the case of billboards, at what location. There is usually some type of tangible market feedback to judge the ads' effectiveness, such as the number of sales resulting directly from the ad. Standard advertising is the financial lifeblood of commercial mass media.

Public Service Advertising

Public service advertising supports nonprofit causes and organizations. Time or space for this type of advertising is provided free as a service to the public by the print or broadcast media. Most public service advertising is for the purpose of soliciting contributions of either time or money for the nonprofit enterprise. Contributions to such organizations as the Red Cross are received almost exclusively through public service advertising.

Federal regulations demand that a certain amount of time be devoted to public service programming. Public service announcements (PSAs), more evident in American broadcasting than anywhere else, run a regular schedule with the commercials. They usually last anywhere from a few seconds to five minutes, the most common lengths being thirty or sixty seconds.

Prime time on broadcasting networks devoted to PSAs is a valuable commodity worth many thousands of dollars. As a result, there is considerable competition among nonprofit organizations to obtain exposure for public service advertising. In any given week, a broadcasting station receives dozens of public service messages, and it is up to the station management to determine which ones to air. Therefore, nonprofit organizations such as the American Cancer Society, the Red Cross, and the United Way spend thousands of dollars annually to produce quality public service messages that can compete with the finest creative talents of ad agencies. To do less would seriously limit their chances for obtaining air time, since broadcasters concerned with the overall image of their station's programming have little interest in airing substandard PSAs. Many stations concerned with their community's development will make an effort to contact local nonprofit organizations for PSAs pointed at local community needs.

Public service advertising in the print media is concentrated mainly in those magazines that devote free space to nonprofit organizations. Although there is no legal requirement for the print media to do so, most magazines cooperate with the Advertising Council and contribute advertising space. Major outdoor companies also cooperate with nonprofit organizations and provide public service space. Outdoor companies, however, expend considerable effort in designing and pasting up the bulletin. Moreover, they must usually foot the rental for the property on which the bulletin is displayed.

Social Responsibility Advertising

A screech of tires, the sound of smashing glass, twisting metal, and the plea to "drive safely." This message adorns billboards and magazines and is the subject of radio and television messages which are especially plentiful during holiday seasons. The safe driving ads and others which admonish us to act responsibly belong to social responsibility advertising. These ads are usually sponsored by either a nonprofit organization, such as the National Safety Council, not linked to any one industry, or special public relations organizations representing a particular industry.

An example of the latter is the Distilled Spirits Council of the United States, Inc. The Council is the public information and research arm of the distilled spirits industry. A major campaign of the Council through its Licensed Beverage Industries division is to instill reponsibility in drinking (Figure 9–5). Its advertisements have a dual purpose: raising the public's consciousness about drinking, and informing the media that the industry is taking an active role in promoting a responsible attitude toward alcohol consumption. The major thrust of this campaign came just after cigarette commercials were banned on television. Although, because of the NAB Codes, advertisements for hard liquor seldom appear in broadcasting, there is nothing to prevent a major anti-drinking campaign from developing in a fashion similar to the anti-smoking campaign. Perhaps if the cigarette industry had provided a responsibility in smoking advertising campaign, cigarette ads would still be running on radio and television. The distilled spirits industry is thus applying the extremely effective public relations technique of combatting poor publicity before a significant image problem can arise.

There are many other types of social responsibility advertising besides the two we have already mentioned. Significant campaigns to use natural resources responsibly have become common, and land use planning, fire prevention, and wildlife management are just three examples. Energy conservation has also received wide exposure in ads sponsored by nonprofit industries and in some cases the energy companies themselves.

Counter-Advertising

One of the most controversial types of advertising is counter-advertising, advertising directed *against* a product or service. The use of counter-advertising reached public attention in 1972 when actors

Figure 9–5 Social responsibility advertising.

such as Burt Lancaster appeared in a series of commercials directed against such things as common household cold remedies and strip mining. Counter-ads directed against specific products are rarely seen on a national scale. Nevertheless, industry and public concern over such ads has become significant. Advocates of counter-advertising claim that standard advertising does not sufficiently inform the public to enable consumers to make intelligent buying decisions; counter-ads are therefore necessary to counteract some of the allegedly unwarranted claims found in standard advertising. Some familiar counter-ads are those which warn against abusive collection practices by credit agencies, the dangers of air and water pollution (Figure 9–6), and cigarette smoking.

The issue of cigarette counter-advertising surfaced in broadcasting in 1967. It was then that the FCC declared the Fairness Doctrine in relation to cigarette advertising, and stations were required to program counter-advertising to balance cigarette advertising.[3] Although the FCC said that the cigarette counter-ads were a unique case, and the courts upheld the claim,[4] within three years,

Figure 9–6 Counter advertising.

the courts ruled that other situations also warranted counter-advertising. Because there is no legal requirement, non-broadcast media are less likely to run counter-advertising. There is a general feeling among many advertising executives that to stress too much counter-advertising might prompt the tobacco industry to place their ad dollars elsewhere.

Counter-advertising is usually financed by public interest firms which donate time and money to a counter-advertising cause. One of the most active organizations in the early 1970s was the Stern Community Law Firm, founded by Philip Stern. The Stern Concern, as it was commonly called, was involved in counter-advertising against Bayer aspirin ads, water pollution, and harrassment by collection agencies. Another group called Friends of the Earth actually went to court to force New York City broadcasting stations to air counter-advertising against pollution. A small group of congressmen even recommended counter-advertising against the major oil companies' corporate image advertising. At one point, letters were sent to thousands of stations nationwide requesting they exercise their duty under the Fairness Doctrine and air counter-ads so that the public could see both sides of the energy crisis.

Obviously, there has been considerable resistance to counter-advertising by broadcasters. The National Association of Broadcasters as well as the Television Information Office, both professional groups representing the broadcasting industry, have opposed widespread requirements for stations to run counter-ads. The major television networks have actually turned down advertising which could have created demands for counter-ads. A specific instance concerned ads by the Phillips Petroleum Company. Phillips wanted to advertise how it contributed to the general welfare of society through taxes and other corporate involvement. ABC, NBC, and CBS all said "no," so Phillips placed the ads with individual stations instead.

A campaign against requiring broadcasters to air counter-ads was launched by the Television Information Office in a widely distributed copy of an address by Judge Lee Loevinger, a former justice of the Minnesota Supreme Court, a former member of the FCC, and now a Washington, D.C. attorney.[5] Loevinger stated a number of reasons why the FCC's proposal for required counter-advertising was not favorable. Among others, Loevinger's arguments included:

(1) There were logically fallacious reasons urging counter-advertising. Loevinger contended that although "the FTC states that not all ads raise the kind of issues or involve the kind of problems that make counter-ads appropriate, it also says that counter-advertising is necessitated by advertising that is silent about any negative aspects of

the product, and then asserts that this characteristic is inherent in all commercial advertising. Thus the FTC is itself inconsistent and contradictory in asserting both that its proposal is responsive to problems created by certain types of advertising and also that such problems are inherent in all advertising."

(2) Counter-advertising would result in the destruction of the economic foundation of broadcasting. It would drive many advertisers away from the medium, thus undermining the broadcaster's economic support.

(3) Income lost to counter-advertising would result in cutbacks in such programming areas as broadcast journalism.

(4) Counter-advertising is "unreasonably discriminatory against broadcasting." There is no indication that the FTC or other government agencies could require non-print media to carry counter-ads.

(5) New products would be hindered from entering the market. Advertising is the key means of informing the public about new products, but claims to novelty or improved operation would be controversial and elicit counter-advertising.

(6) The purpose of counter-advertising was to increase government power, in particular that of the FCC and FTC.

(7) "Counter-advertising is the antithesis of free speech."

The effectiveness of counter-advertising is still moot despite recent research efforts. The Bayer aspirin counter-ads apparently made Bayer users adopt a more cautious attitude toward the product, but the statistical figures were not significant.[6] There was no indication that in a real life situation attitudes would have changed significantly, that peer group decisions about the product might have contradicted the effectiveness of the ads, or that the decrease in favorable attitude would have remained over time.

Counter-advertising remains a concern of mass media. The interpretation of the Fairness Doctrine in broadcasting, the possibility of lawsuits against other media, and liability for broadcasting and printing unfounded claims in product advertisement are certainly factors media executives don't take lightly. At the very least, the issue of counter-advertising has made media management stop, consider, and scrutinize the content of advertising.

Advocacy Advertising

Closely related to counter-advertising is advocacy advertising. Whereas counter-advertising is normally directed at a particular objectionable product, a company producing such a product, or an industry responsible for creating a societal ill, advocacy advertising champions preventive action against illegal or illegitimate activities affecting the public welfare. Ads raising our awareness of heroin addiction, the rising crime rate, and impoverished conditions in the ghetto are all examples of advocacy advertising. Some advocacy advertising can be as controversial as counter-advertising. For example, a series of advocacy ads run in Chicago newspapers and sponsored by radio station WVON dealt with the subjects of heroin addiction, rape, and venereal disease. They were blunt and minced no words. One ad showed a black teenager next to a birthday cake with the headline, "For her 14th birthday she got a new dress, a stereo set, and syphilis" (Figure 9–7). The caption under the picture read:

> It happened so fast. She didn't know. He seemed so nice. He just wanted to talk. She didn't know. A day of pride and fun and dreams, shattered in a horrible, living nightmare. And for a little girl suddenly joy and childhood and innocence were forever lost. The Black Giant is working 24 hours a day to get the man who did it. Operation Crime Stop special alerts and bulletins frequently interrupt our regular programming. They cost us the time other stations use for jokes and jingles. But we want all the rapists and muggers and pushers behind bars. And until they are, Operation Crime Stop will continue, with on-air descriptions of what they look like, with exposés of how they work. What to watch out for. How to protect yourself and your family. The trust of our now million-plus listeners has now made us Chicago's Black Giant. We are doing everything we can to deserve that trust. Join us. If, together, we can save some children, we'll all feel a little bigger. When you are Chicago's Black Giant, you do more than just spin records. WVON-1450 AM.

This ad prompted a large listener response, which the station brought to the public's attention in a separate ad (Figure 9–8).

In most cases, advocacy ad campaigns are sponsored and paid for by an organization which wants to be associated with community involvement. The ads may or may not be directly connected to the sponsor's own business interest. The Distilled Spirits Council, for instance, which we learned has sponsored the responsibility in drinking ads, has also warned against the ills of moonshine liquor. Moonshine is, of course, not only illegal and harmful but can also cut into the profits of licensed distillers.

Advocacy advertising is on the increase. Although such advertising may not be popular, it does have a profound impact on the public and may often shock us into awareness of situations previously hushed by society.

Corrective Advertising

"Super bloopers make your feet run faster." "This vitamin cures all ills." "Thirst-quench has better nutrients than any other drink." Ex-

Figures 9–7 and 9–8 Advocacy advertising.

aggerated claims such as these are prime targets for corrective advertising, which are attempts, usually instigated by regulatory orders, to correct false or misleading advertising.

Many government agencies are involved in policing advertising claims, including the FCC, FTC, and the Food and Drug Administration, but the agency responsible for ordering corrective advertising is the FTC. The others assume more of a preventative role. The Food and Drug Administration, for instance, has established strict rules of ingredient disclosure, thus guarding against deceptive food and drug labeling. Similarly, the FCC strongly encourages radio and television station management to reject advertising that may be deceptive.

The classic case of corrective advertising occurred in 1971 when the FTC reached an agreement with the ITT Continental Baking Company to correct advertising that inferred that eating the company's Profile Bread would result in weight loss. According to the FTC, Profile Bread was no different from other breads except that the slices were thinner. The baking company was ordered to stop using weight loss as a pitch and to spend part of its advertising budget over a one-year period to tell the public their bread wasn't an effective weight reducer. The result was a television commercial with the script:

> I'd like to clear up any misunderstandings you may have about Profile Bread from it's advertising or even its name. Does Profile have fewer calories than other breads? No, Profile has about the same per ounce as other breads. To be exact, Profile has 7 fewer calories per slice. That's because it is sliced thinner. But eating Profile will not cause you to lose weight. . . .

In 1975, the FTC ordered the maker of Listerine mouthwash to start including in its advertising a statement to read, "Contrary to prior advertising, Listerine will not prevent colds or sore throats or lessen their severity." The company denied it had claimed the mouthwash was a cold cure and readied an appeal. Obviously, there are arguments for and against corrective advertising. Supporting arguments claim the ads are necessary to put the "bite" on companies who readily defy regulatory measures. In addition, they're necessary to inform the public that misleading claims do appear, and therefore the consumer should be more critical of advertising. Negative arguments say that years will have passed by the time the wheels of the enforcement process begin to turn and a misleading advertiser has been made to retract claims he has flaunted for his product. Others claim that people are attracted by the novelty of the corrective ads, which call their attention to the product rather than to the corrective message, and the regulatory purpose of the ad is therefore defeated.

Image Advertising

Image advertising grew out of the ecology and Watergate era of the mid-1970s, a manifestation of disenchantment with big business and the public's concern over the environment. For corporations, especially oil companies, image advertising became a second nature. It was part of their natural public relations function. They would go to great lengths to show how they were working to protect or reclaim the environment during drilling and exploration. Such scenes as waterfowl flying in front of an oil rig or the rays of a setting sun across reclaimed grassland were designed to create a favorable corporate image. Other image advertising was more subtle—sponsoring a highly acclaimed play or symphonic program on radio or television. These all served to elevate companies' "corporate images."

Again, you should remember that these various types of advertisements are often intertwined. The key to recognizing the various strategies and understanding their purposes is your active participation as a responsible consumer of mass communication.

presenting the message

There are many factors associated with the actual presentation of advertisements that can have a direct bearing on their effectiveness. These include language complexity and, in the case of broadcast commercials, rate of delivery.

Language Complexity

Research has shown that simple messages are better understood, liked, and retained than complex ones. The use of simple sentences and common words and the elimination of jargon all contribute to effective communication. The commercial filled with formidable words, long sentences, or unfamiliar phrases will only lose the interest of the reader or viewer.

Other language characteristics also affect communicability, especially in commercial messages. Dramatization of a message, for instance, will usually make us attend to it more closely. Personal pronouns such as "she," "he," or "you" will hold our attention more than indefinite words like "one's" or the "individual."

Rate of Delivery

In broadcast messages, the rate of delivery can greatly affect a message. Sometimes messages are deliberately read fast to gain attention. As an example, a commercial for the local dragway should be read considerably faster than one for a local funeral home. Research has shown that broadcast messages can be increased as fast as 180 words per minute (wpm) before recall of the message begins to drop. Of course, if this rate were continuous over a long period of time, such as during a thirty-minute newscast, it would be extremely difficult to concentrate on the message, and the listener's retention would again decrease.

Two additional processes have been employed to alter the amount of information that can be contained in a broadcast message. One is referred to as *compressed speech*. By using special machines, the recording of a voice can be accelerated without altering the tonal qualities, which in the past caused a high-pitched rapid delivery commonly called the "Donald Duck" effect. The object is to compress a given number of words into a shorter time span than normal delivery would permit. The advantage is the ability to say the same thing but take less time and therefore pay less money.

The other message-altering process, called *mnemonic joining*, is essentially the overlapping of portions of a sentence. For example, if you were producing a message and wanted to list the names of all bands that were appearing at a weekend rock concert, you might decide to employ mnemonic joining. Before the name of one rock band had been completely pronounced, a second announcer would start naming another rock band. Thus, during certain split seconds, the names of two rock bands would be heard simultaneously. The theory behind the use of mnemonic joining is that we are able to speed hear as we are able to speed read. Research has shown the mnemonic process, however, to have no advantage in recall when straight, concise dialogue is used. However, it does have possibilities for listings such as those in the rock band example.

Visual composition will also affect the way commercial messages are perceived. For example, the use of blank or *white space* will tend to gain our attention or cause us to scan the page for a message. White space can be used very effectively to enhance a short message. Some advertisers, however, balk at paying for white space when their actual message occupies, say, only the lower right hand corner of the page.

matching medium with message

Not all messages are equally effective in all media. Each medium and each message has certain characteristics that either make for a good relationship or dictate against the combination. These relationships between medium and message apply, of course, to all types of presentations. A review of each medium will make this clear.

Take television, for example. Suppose you are the media buyer for a toy company that manufactures "action" toys. To advertise the toys, you choose television. It has the ability to capture the bright colors and the movement of the toys. No other medium can successfully match that combination. On the other hand, suppose your toy company only sells by mail order. Obviously the buyer can't cut order forms out of the television screen the way he or she can with a print medium. Thus, your next decision is to investigate advertising in another medium.

Looking over the local newspaper, you decide your mail order ad would do well within its pages. After consulting the rate schedules, you purchase an ad in the Sunday comic section. This not only gives you the opportunity to display the toy's colors, but also to print the coupon readers can use to order the toy. On television, viewers could only write to the toy company and send money. But if they didn't remember or copy down the address when it appeared on the screen, they had no way to respond. With the newspaper, they can simply clip the coupon, add a check or money order, and receive delivery of the merchandise. However, newspaper advertising does have its disadvantages. For instance, there is no way to select a target audience. Except for purchasing space on the "family living" page, you cannot direct your advertisements toward a predominantly female audience.

Similar media-message characteristics are inherent in radio. What if you were selling a product whose greatest asset was its sound? A particular automobile manufacturer, Mazda, successfully developed a radio advertising campaign using the sound of the car's rotary engine transposed into music. The engine was expressed in a smooth-sounding hum while other automobiles' piston engines spewed a choppy, cranky sound. Radio was able to convey this sound appeal in a way that other media could not. Although television could reproduce the sound, the audio would be in competition with the video image of the commercial. And, of course, it would be impossible to achieve the desired effect with the print medium. Thus, although the message is important, matching the message with the proper medium can prove a paramount task in modern advertising.

indirect messages

Imagine you are watching an evening television thriller. On the screen, a fugitive dashes from behind the side of the building, firing two shots at a police car. From there he quickly climbs into the driver's seat of a new luxury automobile. He slams the door shut, starts the motor, and gasses it into a purr. The sun reflects on the front fender and glistens across the pin-striped side and chrome-trimmed fenders, fading into the color-coordinated vinyl top as the car speeds gracefully out of the driveway. From behind the bushes comes the star private detective who jumps into another car of the same model. Much like the fugitive's car, the detective's car shimmers in the evening sunlight, the sculptured fenders and sleek lines accented by the sequenced turn signal lights. As the camera zooms in, the car darts across the screen, and the spell of the sculptural design is broken only by an interior view of the detective picking up his two-way radio microphone from under a walnut-accented, leather-upholstered dashboard.

For us, the viewers, it has been another exciting chase scene of a favorite television adventure series. We relaxed in our easy chair as the commercial appeared, telling us about the fine lines and value of a new automobile that, by coincidence, happens to be the same model car the fugitive and the detective drive. But who wants to watch a commercial? We leave to raid the refrigerator. Interestingly enough, when it comes time for us to buy a new car, we seem to be attracted to this specific model of automobile. We're not sure why, but there's just something about this certain make of car that we like and will probably buy. Without realizing it, we have purchased the same type of car that the fugitive and the detective on our favorite television adventure drove. We have been influenced by a very subtle, indirect message.

Most messages are easy to recognize. For instance, we would not question the fact that a television commercial is placed there to persuade us. Similarly, we would not question the fact that the radio commercial and the newspaper or magazine ad are all examples of open, direct advertising. We see them and realize that someone is attempting to influence our attitudes about something. We may also be resistant to them. When someone with a briefcase appears on our front steps, we are immediately on the defensive. We don't want to be sold something we feel we are not ready to buy. Similarly, unless the commercial is entertaining, we may tend to avoid it or set up defense mechanisms to guard against messages we feel are intentionally trying to influence us.

What happens when we are not on our guard? We watched the adventure program because we were attracted to the plot, liked the stars, and wanted to relax. We let our defenses down. As a result, we were probably more impressed with the detective's and the fugitive's car than we would be with the commercials that openly attempted to sell the same automobile. As consumers of mass communication, it is important to be aware of all types of messages, not merely those we know are attempting to change our attitudes or influence our actions. In the case of the adventure program, the producers had an arrangement with an automobile manufacturer to furnish, free of charge, that make of car for the program.

Of course, our example with the car is only one type of subtle, intentional advertising. The entertainer who also has an interest in a clothing company named after him would find it difficult not to boost sales or set fashion trends every time he or she appeared in the limelight. An autobiography of a politician that appears in paperback just at the time he is running for election can lure a passerby to a bookrack with the same enticement of a television commercial or newspaper advertisement. In each case, the message may not be a blatant advertisement for the product, but it certainly captures the consumer's attention.

hidden messages

Depending on their visual format, certain commercial messages can be deliberately camouflaged as noncommercial messages. The Sunday newspaper which devotes a full page to articles about condominiums may also contain an advertisement for condominiums, designed to look exactly like another news story. Just as your defenses were down when watching the adventure program, your defenses may also be weak when pleasurably reading the Sunday paper. The tiny word "advertisement" that appears at the bottom of the article will be lost in the shuffle of bold headlines. A clever format has thus given the advertisement the added credibility of "news." Similarly, you may turn on your television set and watch an entire documentary on the fine record of the mayor of your city. Anchoring the documentary is an authoritative-looking journalist who guides the show from one film clip to another, noting the mayor's activities and accomplishments. Only if you wait until the very end of the program are you alerted to an announcement, almost too small to read, which tells you that you have been watching a paid political program.

acceptance of advertising

Studies by the American Association of Advertising Agencies (AAAA) show a general public acceptance of advertising. One report, authored by Rena Bartos, compared trends in public acceptance of advertising between 1964 and 1974; public perceptions were favorable to advertising that promoted genuinely better products and services. Some of those polled even held that advertising helps raise our standard of living. Interestingly enough, 88 percent of the people polled in the AAAA study thought that advertising was essential.

How we feel about advertising may be influenced by the quality of advertising in the area where we reside. It may also reflect the media to which we are most attuned and what buying habits we may have developed. For example, the AAAA study showed that our opinions about advertising are *primarily* influenced by the advertising we see on television. Naturally newspaper, radio, and magazine advertisements will also have their effect. Direct mail and billboards contribute the least to our opinions about advertising. The AAAA study also showed that the issues we are most concerned about are advertising's credibility, entertainment value, advertising as a social force, and consumer benefits (Figure 9–9). We are also concerned about the way in which it manipulates and motivates us, its clutter and intrusiveness, its content, and media support of advertising as an institution. Of these, our negative opinions center on its credibility, content, intrusiveness, and its ability to manipulate and motivate us.

Advertising has been criticized by some for turning us into a materialistic society, isolating the poor who cannot afford the majority of products splashed across billboards, the television screen, and countless other media. Advertising has also been held responsible for creating an artificial demand for products which we don't need and in some cases are actually harmful to us. Counter-advertising, corrective advertising, and social responsibility advertising have emerged from this concern to change the tide of mass persuasion more toward the public's welfare and away from commercial exploitation. Ad executives speaking on college campuses are fielding questions about why the agencies are continually producing ads which show women in their traditional roles as housewives and childbearers, thus supporting the status quo and perpetuating traditional role models for young children. These and many other considerations will remain important concerns. One thing is certain— advertising is a major force in our society. It is an important part of media content and has perhaps a greater effect on our lives than any

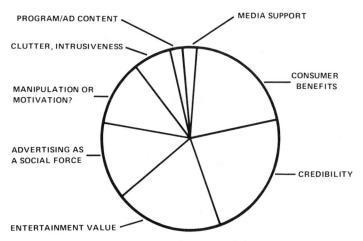

Figure 9–9 The extent to which opinion about each issue contributes to overall attitudes toward advertising.

other type of media message. For this reason, it is important to know as much as possible about all types of advertising messages.

summary

Advertising messages continually surround us. Our value structures, attitudes, and basic needs affect the way in which we perceive these messages. Our personal values are rooted in our culture and in our unique background, both of which largely determine our decision-making process. The value appeals found in advertising messages evoke our sense of beauty (aesthetic appeals); our concern and love for other people (the humanitarian appeal); or our desire for knowledge (the intellectual appeal). One of the most common appeals is that based on our desire for material things, or our tendency to place primary importance on money. Closely aligned with materialistic values are appeals to prestige or power values. Belief in a supernatural being is the basis for religious value appeals. Appeals to attitudes and basic needs are also common in advertising. Although we have for convenience sake discussed values, attitudes, and basic needs separately, we should remember that a single advertisement may and usually does contain several value appeals.

There are also many different types of advertising. Standard advertising, the most common, attempts to persuade or inform us to purchase certain products and services. Public service ads are those devised by nonprofit organizations to answer to a public need. Social responsibility ads seek to warn us against the dangers inherent in the excessive use of some product. Counter-advertising concentrates on warning consumers about alleged fraud or misrepresentation in advertising. Advocacy advertising warns against the dangers inherent in purchasing illegal products or in engaging in illicit activities. Corrective advertising is employed when an enforcement agency determines a previous ad has misrepresented a product. Image advertising stems from the ecology movement of the 1970s and operates much like public relations. As with advertising appeals, a single ad may combine several techniques.

Considerations such as the cost of the ad, the audience to be reached, and the nature of the product determine where an advertising message will appear. How messages are presented will also determine their effectiveness. Such factors as rate of delivery, language complexity, and visual composition play major roles. Overall, advertising is accepted as an important part of any economic system, and a large majority of the population feels it creates better products for society.

opportunities for further learning

CARDAMORE, TOM, *Advertising Agency and Studio Skills: A Guide to the Preparation of Art and Mechanicals for Reproduction.* New York: Watson-Guptill Publications, 1970.

NELSON, ROY PAUL, *The Design of Advertising.* Dubuque, Iowa: Wm. C. Brown Company Publishers, 1967.

NORINS, HANLEY, *The Compleat Copywriter.* New York: McGraw-Hill Book Company, 1966.

RIS, THOMAS F., *Promotional and Advertising Copywriter's Handbook.* Blue Ridge Summit, Pa.: Tab Books, 1971.

TURNBULL, ARTHUR R., *The Graphics of Communication: Typography, Layout, Design,* 2nd Ed. New York: Holt, Rinehart and Winston, Inc., 1968.

WRIGHT, JOHN S., DANIEL S. WARNER, and WILLIS L. WINTER, JR., *Advertising,* 2nd Ed. New York: McGraw-Hill Book Company, 1971.

mass media news:

the selection

and

treatment of stories

CHAPTER TEN

Chapter 1 discussed the role of the gatekeeper in mass communication. We learned that one of the functions of the gatekeeper is to expand the informational environment of the receiver. In other words, the gatekeeper disseminates information which the public would not normally receive. The gatekeeper also limits the information for the receiver. Obviously, gatekeepers cannot reproduce for the public each event they must cover. Thus, the information we receive from gatekeepers in the form of stories appearing in the mass media is abridged. To better understand the forces that act upon the gatekeeper and how we receive messages from mass media, let's spend a day with a reporter at a medium size newspaper.

experiences of the working reporter

Harry's day begins at seven. As the alarm buzzes, he turns on his radio to the local newscast, eats breakfast, and heads for work. At the newspaper, the editor assigns him to cover a drugstore robbery that has just occurred and to later stop by the police station. A photographer is also assigned to the story.

When Harry arrives at the drugstore, it's a mess. Windows are broken, the drug case has been smashed, and sizeable quantities of drugs are missing. Harry confronts one of the police detectives at the scene. The officer tells Harry that the missing drugs are narcotics which belong to a drug rehabilitation center. The police detective asks Harry not to release the story. He feels there is no opportunity to apprehend the thieves if word gets out that narcotics were stolen. Harry doesn't make any promises. He has, however, known the officer for a long time, and the detective has provided Harry with inside information on a number of major stories. He definitely doesn't want to lose the officer as a news source.

"Anything else I should be aware of?" Harry asks.

"No, not that I can think of," replies the detective.

Harry, continually taking notes, thanks the officer and leaves. It's a long drive to the police station. The short cut Harry usually takes is through one of the rougher parts of town. As he passes the rows of shanty apartment houses, he remembers the many times he has

"REMEMBER, HARRY—DON'T RELEASE THE STORY!!"

been there before, covering the seamier side of the city. He thinks the drug rehabilitation center was foolish to use that particular drugstore as a place to store narcotics. The drugstore has been robbed many times, it's located near a high crime area, and is frequented by people who have been in trouble with the law. In fact, much of the help comes from the adjacent high crime area. He ponders the thought and thinks about a possible angle for the story.

At the next intersection, Harry pulls off the street, walks into a tenement house, climbs the stairs to a small apartment on the top floor, and knocks. Inside lives Sam, an old acquaintance and one of Harry's most reliable leads since he first became a reporter. Sam had been arrested on a drug rap and served time. He could count on Sam to know what was happening on the street below.

"What's the story on the narcotics heist, Sam?" asks Harry.

Not wanting to get involved, Sam merely shakes his head sideways.

"Look, Sam, we're not fooling each other. No one is going to know where I got the information. No one even knows I am here."

"OK, Harry, but you've got to promise."

"I promise," says Harry and reminds Sam that he hasn't ever broken his trust before.

Sam then tells Harry that the narcotics have been transported out of the city, perhaps even out of the country.

"I talked to one of the guys involved in the holdup, but that's all the information I have," says Sam.

Harry takes notes, thanks Sam, and leaves.

Next he'll stop at the police station. There he checks the log of daily police activity and finds one of the community's most influential merchants has been arrested on a drunken driving charge. A check of the log also reveals a suicide. Harry copies the information, gets back in his car, and heads for the newspaper.

At the paper, activity picks up. Other reporters arrive from their "beats," and the afternoon edition takes shape. Harry starts to chat with the city editor just as the owner of the paper walks in. The owner mentions he heard on the radio about the downtown merchant who had been picked up for drunken driving. He also reminds the editor that the same merchant spent almost $25,000 in advertising with the newspaper last year. Harry notices the editor beginning to churn inside. Neither misses the owner's intimation to table the story.

Harry talks with some of his colleagues who have faced this problem before. One had actually been fired from a small town paper in a similar situation. Another reporter expresses the opinion that the editor can't sell his soul every time an issue like this arises.

Together they wonder for a moment what the editor will decide. He decides to run the story and face the consequences.

Just at that moment, the mail arrives. The editor, with a hectic day already in progress, drops a pile of letters on Harry's desk and asks him to sort through it. Much of the mail includes press releases, many of which will go in the waste basket. Inside one letter are two free tickets to a dinner at the electric company. Each is stamped with the words "complimentary." Harry puts the tickets into an envelope and sends them to the accounting office. There, checks will be drawn for the exact amount of the dinner tickets and sent to the electric company. He next skims a release about a list of science fair winners and suggests to the editor that it will make a good story. The editor agrees. Now he opens a letter to the editor objecting to Harry's treatment of a zoning case before the county planning commission. Harry reads the letter, goes to his file, and checks the story for accuracy. Everything seems to be in order, and the facts verify; but the reader objected to the amount of space given the various arguments in the case. Rereading the story, Harry realizes how the reader might feel the story had been mishandled. Later today he'll do a follow-up on the county planning commission's final report. He'll keep the letter in mind.

A check of the clock finds deadlines fast approaching. More decisions must be made on what stories will run and which ones will

wait for another issue or perhaps never be used. Harry estimates the amount of material he'll contribute to today's evening edition. Despite everything that's happened, it has been a slow day for copy. The editor decides against using the story about the suicide. The man took his life in private, and personal feelings about the incident tell him it just doesn't warrant news coverage. Although the obituary column will list the deceased, the suicide won't appear elsewhere in the paper. The editor comes by again, this time with a picture of the ransacked drugstore. This might lend enough to the story to put it on the front page. Checking with the other reporters around the office, Harry finds it's been a slow day for many of them. On most days, the drugstore robbery wouldn't have warranted front page coverage, but today was different. Also, Harry hadn't forgotten his conversation with Sam. The drugstore robbery could turn into a major scoop for Harry, and he is glad to see the story receiving attention.

Other deadlines are approaching. Across the news room the state editor checks facts on some rain damage which plagued the southern part of the state. The wire service story called it "devastating." The state editor calls the police department in the city where the flooding reportedly is the worst and learns that the only damage has been to some sewer systems in the city, but even that is minor. He then checks with the county sheriff in the same community and receives the same information. He next calls the wire service to see where they had received the story. The wire service editor said they had pieced it together with other flood damages from around the state. Now it's clear what happened. The wire service mentioned some of the devastation that occurred around the state and listed one particular community as being affected. True, the community was hit but little damage occurred. In the process of passing from the local reporter to the editor of the community newspaper, to the wire service editor, the story became distorted.

In the next room sit three student interns from the university. They have only been on the job three weeks, but the state editor feels he can trust their judgment on this one.

"Come in here," he calls. "Listen, I need to piece together this material on the rain damage. Each of you get on the phone to the three major cities downstate. Find out everything you can about what's happened and then check back with me. We'll get together in about fifteen minutes and make up a composite story."

The students go to work and return in fifteen minutes. For the next five minutes they sit with the state editor and discuss the elements of the story which will run in the evening edition. They piece together facts, make sure they check out, consider the use of key adjectives to describe the damage, and even select a picture received from the wire service. Meanwhile, Harry has finished his story about the drugstore robbery. However, he worries about the local television station getting the information about the narcotics transfer. If the station breaks the story on tonight's news, Harry's scoop will be lost.

That evening Harry watches as the television news makes only vague reference to the robbery and doesn't say anything about the narcotics transfer. Harry scooped them.

Harry will also have problems, however. Two weeks later, the police arrested a suspect in the drugstore robbery. A month later the deputy sheriff arrived with a subpoena for Harry to appear in

court. The prosecutor read Harry's story on the narcotics transfer, and the prosecutor and the police want to know where Harry has obtained the information. Harry thinks about Sam and the promise he made.

We'll learn more about what happens to Harry and his subpoena when we join him again in Chapter 17.

forces affecting the gatekeeper

Tracing a reporter's activities in and out of the news room has revealed many of the factors affecting the selection of messages in mass communication. Using our experiences with Harry, let's look at each of these factors in more detail.

Economics

With the exception of noncommercial media, such as campus radio stations or some campus newspapers, most media are commercial, profit-making businesses. Our context, of course, is the free world countries where the majority of media operate as free enterprises. We have already learned that private financing has a distinct advantage over government-financed media when it comes to news control. However, such media must still make a profit or go out of business.

Had Harry's scoop about the narcotics transfer needed further investigation, economics would again have entered the picture. The ability of the newspaper to afford freeing investigative reporters to cover the story would have had a direct bearing on the type and amount of information the public received. Labor costs and newsprint costs also affect the operation of the newspaper. Perhaps economic considerations might force Harry's newspaper to reduce the number of pages. Even if it does cut back, however, the number of advertising pages, the newspaper's bread and butter, will probably not be affected. News will be what suffers.

Economics can affect media messages elsewhere. Television stations can be very expensive to operate. Purchasing and maintaining electronic equipment as well as trained personnel can be costly. Like newspapers, television has certain basic operating costs. Engineers, directors, and producers all draw on the station's payroll. The evening anchorperson won't be trained to repair a $100,000 color camera. In television, when personnel cuts take place, the news department may be the first to go.

Radio is no different. In some cases, economics can play havoc with this medium. At many radio stations, one or two persons staff the entire news department. Eliminating one position may reduce the department's ability to cover news by fifty percent. Such economic considerations as permission to make long distance telephone calls and freedom from other on-air duties at the station can all affect how well a news team can gather and disseminate news to the public. If Harry's editor had been in charge of news at a small radio station operating at a low profit margin, his decision about whether to air the story about the downtown merchant might well have been negative.

Remember, economics can powerfully affect the type and content of the messages that we, consumers of mass media, receive.

Living with Regulation

Harry had a vivid taste of regulation when the deputy sheriff arrived to serve him with a subpoena. This incident might determine if Sam ever talks to Harry again, and consequently whether Sam's information is ever disseminated to the public.

Had Harry been working for the broadcast media instead of the print media, he would have felt the effects of regulation even more sharply. For example, if Harry had wanted to interview a political candidate about his views on crime, he would first have to be certain to use the interview as a bonafide news item, or else offer any other candidate running for that same office equal air time according to the FCC's Section 315.

Other regulations also affect messages in mass communication. Profanity on a radio broadcast may result in the station's being fined. What, for example, if the profanity is a direct quote of a public figure? Could the station or newspaper print or broadcast the message without fear of reprisals? Obviously, the answers to those questions are neither simple nor direct. Such questions do, however, give some insight into how regulations affect both the flow and content of news in society.

The Demand of Deadlines

Every reporter lives with deadlines. The ever-present deadline can make the difference between gaining an exclusive story or being "scooped" by a competitor, between being able to report all the facts or just some of them, between being able to use a story or being forced to hold it for lack of information. For a news reporter deadlines mean working under extreme pressure on a daily basis, pressure that forces him to spew forth his ideas, thoughts, and words at an often unsettling pace.

In the broadcast media, the pressure of deadlines is even more acute. For radio, which can air news almost simultaneously when it happens, deadlines literally come every minute. Of course, problems with accuracy arise when stories are broadcast too soon after a news event occurs. It takes time to gather news and prepare a story. Even when a story is reported live, there are many background details which cannot be reported without time and effort.

Consider the example of the state editor and his student interns. Harry's newspaper reported the flooding downstate. However, the information available at the time the newspaper went to press may have been limited. There may have been reports that two people were killed, yet subsequent reports increased the figure to four. With its later deadline, the television station could then report the correct figure in its evening newscast. Moreover, the next morning when Harry listened to the local radio station, the stories of death and destruction would have been much more accurate than either Harry's newspaper account or the television broadcast. Deadlines made the difference. They determine when information can be released, how much is available, and how accurate it is.

Deadlines and news reporting are always companions. To be a responsible consumer of news you need to know how they work together. When we read or hear news we assume accuracy. We must, however, be alert to certain cues which may help us gauge the degree of this accuracy. Such phrases as "at press time" and "at least one source" alert us to missing gaps in a story or missing links in a chain of information.

Personal and Professional Ethics

The incident of the newspaper owner approaching the city editor and informing him that the man arrested for drunken driving spent $25,000 in advertising would make many reporters quit immediately in disgust. Although economic concerns are undeniably important, the professional journalist cannot condone suppression of newsworthy information; his function is finding and publishing the truth. For the owner to have suggested compromising the newspaper's integrity for the sake of advertising would not only be considered poor journalism but prostitution of the press and a request to deliberately participate in a breach of ethics.

When Harry opened his mail, he found tickets to a publicity dinner. They were marked "complimentary," what journalists commonly call *freebies*. Freebies can range from tickets to a church supper to excursions to a foreign country, which are also called *junkets*. Harry's newspaper has a policy against accepting freebies. Therefore any freebie must be reported to management. If the function is important and requires paid admission, then the newspaper would purchase admission passes just like everyone else. The policy against freebies tries to prevent any opportunity, regardless of how small, for biased reporting. The paper wants its readership to receive objective news coverage and doesn't want freebies to endanger that objectivity.

The editor's decision not to print the story of the suicide involved a judgment based on personal ethics. For journalists, personal ethics may be the pivotal factor in deciding whether to withhold information or to satisfy the public's right to know. Following the Watergate scandal that saw Richard Nixon resign from the United States presidency, there was a series of televised discussions between major Washington correspondents during which information about the private lives of high public officials came to light. This information involved the officials' alleged association with everything from alcohol to illicit sex. Yet in discussion, the reporters said they had long been aware of such things but had made the decision not to make the information public. Again, such decisions were based on a code of personal ethics which discounted this alleged activity as having no definite effect on the officials' performance per se.

The author's own experiences in covering stories have often involved the personal ethics factor. On one occasion, two fugitives from a mental institution stole a car and headed for the state line. After the capture, the opportunity occurred to take pictures of them as they emerged from the squad car in police custody. However, the following day when it came time to use the story, a superior made the decision not to use the names of the two fugitives or their pictures. The case fell into the realm of crimes committed by suicidal and mentally ill persons. The story that reached the public only mentioned that a stolen car had been recovered and two escapees from the state correctional institution had been taken into custody.

About two months later, a similar incident forced another judgment of personal and professional ethics. On an early Sunday morning, the static on the police monitor was broken by a report of a sniper in a ravine shooting at police cars with a high-powered rifle. One officer whose car had been hit was keeping the man "pinned down" until assistance arrived. As the morning progressed, a number of other law enforcement officers arrived at the scene. It was determined that the sniper, who had escaped from the same state correctional hospital, had a high-powered rifle with a telescopic sight and ample ammunition. Unsuccessful attempts by law enforcement officials to entice the man to surrender prompted a decision that a group of officers, armed with rifles, form a human line and walk side by side toward the ravine, all the time requesting the man to surrender. Nightfall was rapidly approaching and many felt that in darkness it would be easy for the man to escape and threaten the lives of area residents. As the police line moved to a ridge above the ravine, the fugitive shot one of the officers in the stomach. Immediately, the line opened fire. The fugitive's body, riddled with holes, was a somewhat gruesome sight. Nevertheless, the same superior who had determined not to use the pictures or names of the fugitives who had stolen the car, made the decision to use pictures of the dead sniper as well as his name and all the details surrounding the event. Why that decision?

A number of personal and professional reasons were behind the decision. For one, the police officer died. In addition, the reporter's superior had been employed by a federal law enforcement agency before becoming a journalist. Moreover, the police officer had been a high-ranking official in one of the communities served by the news medium. The incident, unlike that of the stolen car, had occurred in broad daylight, and the standoff with police officers lasted almost eight hours. The activity also took place on the only main highway connecting two major communities. All traffic for an eight-hour period was either stopped or detoured. In short, it was an incident of which the public became very much aware, especially in a location where events of this magnitude were not that frequent. Thus, the story captured more attention than it might have, had the event occurred in a high crime area.

Similar personal and professional decisions are made every day by gatekeepers responsible for reporting news to the public. Ask yourself what decisions you might have made had you been the news executive. Would you have used the story with the pictures? Would you have used film of the event if it had been available?

Contending with Competition

Harry's distress over the possibility of the television reporter's getting his scoop story is typical of competition among the news media. This competition is inherent in a free press and usually fosters the reporting of more than one opinion or approach to a story. Competition can also nurture the growth of true investigative journalism. Media in competition will sometimes take the extra initiative to explore an issue in depth rather than be satisfied with superficial information.

Plain economics fosters competition in many areas. Larger markets, for instance, have the financial base to support more than one news medium; large metropolitan areas can even support more than one newspaper. Some smaller communities, however, face information control by a single news medium that may be biased on certain issues. In such cases, competition would have a positive effect on freeing the flow of information to the public. As we learned in Chapter 2, concentration of media control in joint newspaper, broadcasting ownerships has been curtailed by the actions of the FCC. In some localities, direct orders by the FCC have blocked concentration of media ownership by requiring the sale of some properties by multi-media owners.

Negative aspects of media competition surface particularly in the electronic media, where the ability to air news almost simultaneously as it occurs breeds frenzied competition. The result can be news distortion. For example, put yourself in the seat of a radio news cruiser that has just received a call to cover a labor dispute at a major industrial plant. Also enroute to the event is another news cruiser from a competing station. Both cruisers are equipped for live, on-the-scene broadcasts. Both of you, sensing the other's presence, begin live reports. You describe a group of men fighting, and report that it is the result of another flareup at the picket line. After the broadcast, you get out of the news cruiser to learn some details. You discover the fight you were reporting was actually a rough and tumble football game. You are shocked. Had you not been quite as concerned about the competitive edge, you would have taken the time to investigate all the details. Your actions were inexcusable to say nothing of being unprofessional and irresponsible. You may also have opened up yourself and your station to a libel suit. Except under extreme crisis conditions such as a natural disaster, the impression that listeners spend their time switching back and forth from one station to another just to see who airs the news first is a fallacy.

One of the nation's leading broadcast news consultants reacts negatively to the common practice among broadcast journalists of listening to the competition's newscasts. Such a practice, he contends, is a waste of time and effort since the listeners or viewers who are tuned to your station won't know what the competition is scooping you on in the first place. Certainly, a news medium that consistently airs or prints information days after an event occurs will lose credibility. Yet, the continual dissemination of misinformation due to hasty overreaction to competition will also lose credibility.

Competition in itself is beneficial and safeguards a free press. It must, however, be taken in its proper perspective so that both a free and *responsible* press is the end result.

News Value

The term news value is a relative term. It refers to the *value or importance of an event or the potential impact of an event in relation to other events or potential news stories.* For example, the news value of the story about the sniper who shot the police officer was very high. But it was high *in comparison* to other events which may have been happening simultaneously or had happened on previous occasions in the community. Note the words "in the community." The geographical sphere of influence of the message will also affect its value. Again, the story of the sniper had its highest value in the community where it occurred. Although it may have had enough value to be selected as news by a gatekeeper in a neighboring community, its relative value there would have been less. Similarly, Harry's story about the drugstore robbery would have more news value in the city where Harry's newspaper was published than in a community hundreds of miles away.

Another factor influencing news value is the number of people affected by an event. For example, the sniper's actions caused many hundreds of people to be stopped or detoured from their normal route of travel. The fact that a high-ranking police officer was shot affected everyone in the community where he worked. All the people affected by an event contribute indirectly to the news value of the story.

When Harry's editor decided to use the story about the science fair winners, he was making a judgment based on the news value of that story over other possible stories received from the press releases. The science fair winners were news because they attended local schools in the community served by the newspaper. Since the winners probably had parents, the activities of those children would be understood by parents everywhere. Thus, although science fair winners may not have seemed like an important story, it actually affected or could affect a large number of people. It was for this reason that the editor chose the story over others.

The News Hole

Directly related to news value is the news hole. To understand this concept, imagine a large auditorium full of students, each of whom wants to spend the day on a bussed field trip. But only one bus load can go. When the instructor looks over the auditorium everyone in the room tries to gain attention. Some shout. Others wave their hands and hold up signs. Others become the object of attention by sheer accident, such as having a sign fall on their heads. Still, only a small percentage will be able to make the trip since space is limited. Now liken the students to all the events in society competing for the attention of the gatekeepers in the media. Some events may deliberately try to gain attention, such as issuing a press release. Other events attract attention by accident, such as the downstate flooding. Certainly, many of the events to which Harry was exposed could have become news stories. However, the news hole Harry's editor had to work with was only so big. There were only so many pages to Harry's paper, just as there was only so much time allotted to the evening television newscast of Harry's competitor.

The size of the news hole is also determined by the number and news value of events which may have attracted the gatekeeper's attention. Had it been a busy news day at Harry's paper, the mere presence of so many stories might have filled the news hole to capacity, and there would have been no room for the story about the science fair winners. We the public are exposed to only a fraction of the information that *could* be reported to us. What we do receive is determined by the size of the news hole in relation to the number and value of the messages which vie for attention in the limited space or time at the gatekeeper's disposal.

Attention Factors

Many things besides newsworthiness draw our attention to messages in the media. Although certain stories in themselves often command our attention, others may need help in the form of visual or aural stimuli. The story of the drugstore robbery, for example, made the front page partly because the picture attracted attention to the story. Audio actualities on radio, and film or videotape on television all can attract attention to the newscast.

Headlines in a newspaper are another attention-getting factor, as are certain kinds of type. Front page layout may also focus attention on some stories rather than others. In fact, the entire design of a paper may bear a direct relationship to the attention it receives and, consequently, its circulation.

This concept can be better understood by examining the design of two competing newspapers, the *Philadelphia Bulletin* and the *Philadelphia Daily News*. The *Bulletin*'s primary means of sales is through subscription; that is, most people have the *Bulletin* delivered to their doorstep by home carriers. The *News*, on the other

LATE SPORTS, NEWS AND STOCKS

The Evening Bulletin

INDEPENDENT—LOCALLY OWNED — WITH SUNDAY MORNING EDITION — 4 EDITION

NEARLY EVERYBODY READS THE BULLETIN — D — WEDNESDAY, APRIL 16, 1975 — FIFTEEN CENTS

Good Evening

TONIGHT / TOMORROW

If you wondered, in only 4 years since 1874 (last one 1943) has the 1st half of April been colder. But it's changing. Fair tonight, low only 40. Sunny tomorrow, high 63. (Details on Page 45.)

Viet War Orphan Dies

Brought to Erie, Pa., from San Francisco Saturday night by the Catholic Social Services, a 3-month-old Vietnamese war orphan known only as "Baby John" died today before he found a new home in America. St. Vincent's Health Center in Erie said he weighed only 6 pounds, "simply couldn't retain any food." (Related story on Page 13).

• • •

The Environmental Protection Agency and the states were given broad discretion by the Supreme Court to permit some air pollution to continue beyond the deadline for national air quality standards. The 7-1 decision, overturning a lower court ruling on Georgia's plan, gives the EPA the right to OK variances granted by states to polluters as long as over-all compliance with standards is maintained.

• • •

Despite 9 days of exhausting negotiations, the 18-nation energy conference in Paris collapsed as oil producers and consumers remained in a deadlock. No provision was made for a higher-level session later. Industrial nations demanded that oil be the chief business of this one. Led by Algeria, the oil countries insisted that all raw materials (not just oil) sold by underdeveloped nations be considered.

$1,871 a Month for Ex-Speaker

Nice work if you can get it: The Pa. Employes Retirement Board disclosed that ex-House Speaker Kenneth Lee, 53, a Sullivan County lawyer and unsuccessful candidate for lieutenant-governor, will get a state pension of $1,871 a month for life. Top salary for Lee, who served 18 years, was $26,100 — or $2,175 a month.

• • •

Horrors! Pa. state Rep. Marvin Miller (R-Lancaster) made a stunning suggestion to the House—prohibit lobbyists from buying drinks, dinners or anything else for state officials. A stricken House rejected the mad proposal 155-26.

Ford Outlines GOP Comeback

Addressing his party's $1,000-a-plate dinner in Washington, President Ford promised Republican candidates he'll work as hard for their election as for his own in 1976 and declared the GOP can make a comeback by campaigning against ever-higher federal spending and huge budget deficits. Dinner ticket sales were 600 — an all-time low.

• • •

Closed when the board of education ran out of funds, public schools in East Haven, Conn., reopened under a court order directing city officials to borrow the $333,000 needed to operate them until June. The 2-day "vacation" was enjoyed by 5,700 pupils in the 8 schools.

First Lady's Secretary Ousted

Mrs. Nancy Howe is out as First Lady Betty Ford's personal assistant. Now on paid administrative leave, she'll be dropped from the White House payroll May 31, a spokeswoman announced. Her departure follows the suicide of her husband James and comes during a White House inquiry into who paid for a trip the Howes made to the Dominican Republic.

Howe — Landon

Stricken with a fainting spell at one of his radio stations, Alf M. Landon, 86, the Republican who was trounced in the 1936 presidential election by Franklin D. Roosevelt, was hospitalized in Topeka, Kan. His condition: "Satisfactory."

Unexpected 'Gifts'

In Raleigh, N.C., the U.S. mails brought unexpected "gifts" to 25 state senators. They received tightly-rolled marijuana cigarets in plain white envelopes in what appeared to be a lobbying attempt to persuade them to introduce legislation OKing the use of "pot." Attached to each cigaret was a piece of paper with the message: "Try it, you'll like it."

— — *Frank Brookhouser*

A Correction

The Bulletin reported Monday that April 25 is the last day for Philadelphians to register to vote in the May 20 primary. It's April 21. The Bulletin sincerely regrets the error.

The Evening Bulletin

129TH YEAR, NO. 1 • COPYRIGHT, 1975, BULLETIN CO., PHILADELPHIA, PA., 19101 • 215-662-7550

TODAY'S CONTENTS

Cambodia Calls for Cease-Fire; Offers to Surrender Powers

Saigon Loses A City

Bulletin Wire Services

Saigon — Tank-led North Vietnamese troops captured a provincial capital along the South China Sea today and Communist artillery briefly shut down South Vietnam's major air base.

Military sources said 5,000 North Vietnamese troops, backed by 40 tanks, overwhelmed outnumbered defenders at Phan Rang, a provincial capital 165 miles northeast of Saigon.

The three-pronged assault swept the city's military base, forcing the 2,500 government rangers in Phan Rang to flee on warships anchored off the coast.

The fall of Phan Rang, capital of Ninh Thuan Province, left the Communists in control of 18 of South Vietnam's 44 provinces and two-thirds of the nation's territory.

Military sources said North Vietnamese gunners bombarded Bien Hoa Air Base near Saigon with rockets and artillery today, halting air strikes against Communists advancing toward the South Vietnamese capital. The base reopened after six hours.

Military sources said the barrage destroyed at least four F-5 jet fighter-bombers.

There were no immediate reports on casualties at Bien Hoa, 14 miles northeast of Saigon. The base, the largest air installation in South Vietnam, houses three-quarters of the government's air force.

The Communists also stepped up pressure on the besieged provincial capital of Xuan Loc, considered by many military strategists as the key to the battle for Saigon.

Military sources said infantry overran a government outpost eight miles northwest of Xuan Loc.

But the reports said the government forces who have been battling the North Vietnamese at Xuan Loc for a week continued to hold the provincial capital 40 miles east of Saigon even though it has been leveled and is now isolated.

Bulletin Staff Photo by William Owens

Officers search woods near Colonial Park Apartments, Richardson st. and Route 13, Andalusia, Pa., for clues in killing of Bensalem Township policeman, James Armstrong.

Proposal Sent to Sihanouk

Bulletin Wire Services

Phnom Penh — The Cambodian government has called for a cease-fire and offered to surrender its power to Prince Norodom Sihanouk in Peking, the International Red Cross said this afternoon.

Sihanouk, ousted from power in Cambodia in 1970, is titular leader of the insurgents, who have taken over the Phnom Penh airport and are reported inside the capital.

There was no immediate official word from Sihanouk, but the Red Cross said it had reports that he refused to accept the offer.

Instead, Sihanouk advised members of the Supreme Council in Phnom Penh to leave the country, Alain Modoux, chief Red Cross information officer in Geneva, quoted the reports as saying.

Khmer Rouge Told

The Red Cross said its delegation in Phnom Penh received the proposal from the Cambodian government and immediately relayed it to Sihanouk.

It said the Phnom Penh administration proposed the cease-fire and transfer of power "in order to stop this fratricidal conflict."

Officials at Red Cross headquarters in Geneva said the Cambodian government proposal "amounted to an offer of surrender."

They said it was relayed to Khmer Rouge rebel forces now fighting inside Phnom Penh as well as to Sihanouk.

Await Reply

The 16-member Red Cross delegation based at the Royal Phnom Hotel in the Cambodian capital is standing by for a reply from Sihanouk, the officials said.

The Red Cross delegation,

Please Turn to Page 2, Col. 4

The Daily Chuckle

It is said that the world is run by those who are willing to sit until the end of the meeting.

Killer Grabbed His Gun

Officer Slain Fleeing Bandit

By CHARLES H. WALTON, 3D

Of The Bulletin Staff

The killer of a Bucks County, Pa., policeman apparently stole the officer's pistol and chased the unarmed man around a company parking lot yesterday, firing at him repeatedly.

The officer finally got back to his patrol car and, though badly wounded, made a desperate effort to reach a shotgun in a bracket in the front.

Patrolman James Armstrong, 28, of the Bensalem Township police, was found dead sprawled across the front seat. The shotgun, removed from its bracket but unfired, lay beside him.

His police dog, Shep, locked in the back, had been shot in the neck. The car itself was hit by bullets. The rear window was shattered.

Alarm Issued

Police issued an alarm for a man identified as Joseph M. Hennessey, 28, of the 9400 block of Kirkwood st. in the Academy Gardens section of Philadelphia.

Dorothy Pollock, district justice in Lower Southampton Township, last night issued a warrant charging Hennessey with murder.

Police said the FBI is cooperating in the investigation on the possibility that the suspect may have crossed into New Jersey.

Bensalem Police Chief Lawrence Michaels said identification cards of Hennessey were found near Armstrong's police car. He said a tan station wagon, identified as the getaway car, was traced to Hennessey.

Michaels said police also were investigating whether the killer had an accomplice. He said Armstrong's last radio message when he reported spotting the fugitive car was that a middle-aged man also was in the vehicle.

Revolver Missing

The killer was believed to be a man who had held up a gasoline service station earlier in Bristol Township.

Chief Michaels said that when Armstrong's body was found, the .357 Magnum revolver he carried was missing from his holster. The weapon was not found.

Apparently, however, Armstrong was shot with a .45-caliber automatic. There was no indication that any other weapon was fired during the shooting spree. Blood was found on the parking lot 20 feet from the patrol car, police said.

A woman witness told a reporter she saw a man brandishing a large pistol chasing another man around the parking lot at the rear of Color Craft Corp., a film processing firm, at Clairmont and Highland aves., near Bristol pike and Woodhaven road, Bensalem Township, Bucks County.

"At first, I thought it was some of the employes cutting up during lunch-time because they were running around the cars," the woman said. "The man fired about six shots at the officer."

She said she saw the policeman ducking behind parked

Please Turn to Page 3, Col. 1

Shapp Net Put At $2.8 Million

By DAVID RUNKEL

Of The Bulletin Staff

Governor Shapp disclosed today that his net worth increased nearly $200,000 last year and as of Dec. 31 stood at $2.8 million.

A conspiracy of silence shrouds conflicts of interest in the State Legislature, former PUC Commissioner Herbert S. Denenberg says in his series of articles whicH continues today on Page 5.

His net worth, however, is about one-third of what it was when he started his political career 10 years ago.

Shap made the disclosure in filing a new financial-reporting form. At the governor's request, all members of his cabinet and all but one of the top-ranked state employes appointed by the governor filed disclosures before yesterday's deadline.

The one exception was Louis J. Carter, a Public Utility Commission member who has filed disclosures in the past,

Please Turn to Page 4, Col. 1

Late Sports

RACING

1ST, GARDEN STATE

Carolina Kim	4.40	2.80	2.20
Quick Date		3.80	3.00
Positivo			4.40

2D, KEYSTONE

Jaunty Jolly	6.80	4.00	4.20
Mariquill		14.80	7.80
Hallowed Hill			4.80

Daily Double: (1-7) paid $43.80

Details in Sports Section

Firemen Halt Phila. Blaze After 36-Floor Climb

By JOHN J. GAFFNEY

Of The Bulletin Staff

The elevators wouldn't work. Electricity was cut off.

Smoke filled corridors and stairwells as 100 persons scrambled for their lives.

Firemen had to lug hoses and equipment up stairs as far as the 36th floor.

There were bad moments as a three-alarm fire that started in a basement utility room damaged Five Penn Center Plaza, a 36-story office tower at the northwest corner of 16th and Market sts. in center-city Philadelphia last night.

Three Injured

Two cleaning women and a fireman suffered minor injuries.

But all the occupants of the building escaped and none of the 80 exhausted firemen was seriously injured.

The fire was discovered just before 11.30 P. M. when maintenance workers, who were getting ready to finish their shift, noticed billows of smoke on the upper floors.

Robert Murphy, 38, the building superintendent, said a security guard sounded an inside alarm at 11.29 P. M.

Police said there were 100 persons in the building, about 50 of them on seven different floors working in computer rooms of the Colonial Penn Group Data Corp. There were also 44 maintenance workers and several security guards on various floors.

Mrs. Mildred Carson, 63, of 1526 Adams st. in the city's Frankford section, a cleaning woman, said she was on the 27th floor when she first

Please Turn to Page 6, Col. 1

GM Cars Rust From Lack of Whale Oil

Detroit — (AP) — A 1971 law protecting sperm whales has led to transmission problems for at least 5,500 General Motors car owners and a $2.2 million repair bill for GM, the company says.

When the whales were put on the endangered species list, GM was forced to find a substitute for the whale oil used in rust-resistant automatic transmission fluid. The new fluid, first used in 1973 models, wasn't rustproof.

GM said yesterday the potential problem could affect 3.3 million of the cars built during the 1973 and 1974 model years, and 1975 models built before last November, when the transmission fluid was changed. So far, 5,500 of those car owners have reported transmission problems due to rust.

GM said it would pay for repairs, estimated at $400 a car, even if the normal 12-month, 12,000-mile warranty has expired.

John C. Bates, GM service director, said the new formula fluid was tested for 8.9 million miles before it was used in mass production, and no problems were found.

Last summer, however, reports of problems started to come in from some Pontiac owners. By fall, owners of Chevrolets, Buicks, Oldsmobiles and Cadillacs also reported transmission troubles.

The other auto companies say they have not encountered similar transmission problems. They also stopped using whale oil several years ago.

Figure 10–1 Notice how the appearance of the two front pages differ. The *Philadelphia Daily News* is designed to attract attention at the point of purchase. (Reprinted by permission of the Evening and Sunday Bulletin. © 1975 Philadelphia Daily News.)

hand, is sold mostly through newsstands. Thus, in order to attract the attention of potential buyers as they pass the newsstand, the *News* has adopted a design much different, both in physical characteristics and in front page appearance, from that of the *Bulletin* (see Figure 10–1). For example, the visual material on the front page of the *News* is much more intense and is designed to catch immediate notice—attention strong enough to result in a sale. Were both the *News* and the *Bulletin* sold primarily at the newsstand, the

205

Bulletin might change its visual format to attract more attention. The physical composition of the *News,* a tabloid, also makes it attractive to the "mobile" buyer. Most of the people who buy the *News* are commuters. They ride the mass transit system of Philadelphia and must carry their paper with them. In most cases, they read it while holding the paper in one hand and supporting themselves on the subway hanger with the other. This is a considerably different atmosphere from that of the *Bulletin* reader, who may sit at home in an easy chair with both hands free to turn the pages. Thus, the format of the *News* is compact and manageable for easy reading.

Peer Group Pressure

In our introductory story, the owner of the newspaper walked into the news room and suggested it might be better not to run the story about the businessman arrested for drunken driving. The other reporters felt the story should be used. Had the editor asked, he undoubtedly would have received enthusiastic support for his decision. Much more active peer group pressures can influence the actions of journalists through special publications that have a watchdog effect on the press. Some cities have magazines called "journalism reviews." They regularly comment on and criticize the activities of the press. A journalist who constantly reports inaccuracies and who may have associations which lose credibility for the other members of the press, may be shunned by other members of the profession. This is not to suggest that taking a different stand on issues is grounds for an informal censure—however, other actions can be.

For example, some reporters may actually carry police credentials and have arrest powers. Although such action may create inroads to various situations, it can also obscure the real function of the press and consequently give all media a general lack of credibility. Law enforcement officials may also lose their credibility when they carry press credentials to do undercover work. There are few professional associations that can successfully monitor such activities, except perhaps peer groups in the same community. When the various media do patrol one another, results have proved encouraging.

One effective means of peer group pressure is the increasing number of local newspaper columnists who keep an eye on the broadcast press through regular columns about radio and television. Items which have appeared in newspaper columns include analyses of internal hiring practices and broadcast employee qualifications. Some broadcasting stations have also aired programs critical of the work of newspaper journalists. Such peer group pressures among media personnel can make gatekeepers take a serious look at their work and the implications it has for the public.

Lack of peer group pressure can have just the opposite effect. This condition, which exists especially in small communities, shows up in a kind of narrow-minded reporting of the issues that influence their public. Consider the life of a newspaper reporter in a small town where there is no local radio or local television station. Also imagine the reporter has no one else on the staff to assist with news gathering and reporting. What happens? Stated succinctly, he can get into a rut, and the public suffers. Day in and day out, the reporter sees the same people and reports the same news, but at no time has the opportunity to have his work scrutinized. He can get the basic facts correct, but his stories reflect a narrow line of thought that pervades his limited number of news sources. Isolation and lack of peer group pressure have thus resulted in a daily diet of limited reporting.

Perhaps the reporter develops what is commonly called a "police complex," where the only real news the community receives comes from the police blotter and the traffic fatality list. The other issues affecting the community go unnoticed and unchecked. This kind of reporting could permit a slow takeover of corrupt government—it might even seem with the tacit approval of the press.

The Effects of Time

It was almost thirteen years after the assassination of President John Kennedy that the press as a whole began a serious inquiry into the events which took the life of the president in Dallas, Texas, in November of 1963. Shortly after the assassination, there was a mammoth amount of reporting which dealt with all the alleged facts of the assassination and dismissed any possibility of political motivation playing a role. The Warren Commission issued its report, and the press duly publicized its existence. A rash of books criticized the findings of the Warren Commission, but after a few years they were relegated to the back shelf. Then, after the wounds of emotion had begun to heal, a better climate seemed to encourage objective investigation. The first efforts came slowly, with a few widely scattered programs on the assassination showing the film of Kennedy being shot. Finally, however, the inquiry gained momentum which even resulted in network news coverage.

Time is a force which affects the ability of the press to gain perspective on an event. The Kennedy assassination is just one example. Others include the reporting of campus unrest in the late 1960s. When the first signs of unrest were reported, for instance, there was an almost unanimous negative public reaction to the work of the media. For the press, it was a new issue that many reporters saw from the perspective of an "outsider" whose only time spent on a college campus was at Saturday football games. After that first spring of academic troubles had proved the subject of much heat but little light, the summer gave the press a breather to gain a proper perspective on what had actually happened on the campuses and to review their coverage techniques. The following year saw much less criticism of the way in which the press reported the campus troubles, for journalists now had a deeper insight into the real issues surrounding the trouble and avoided reporting only statistical figures such as the number of people arrested or estimates of property damage.

Reacting to Feedback

Harry's letter from the reader reacting to the coverage of the zoning case was a form of feedback. Unsolicited feedback in mass communication is not that plentiful, and as a result, what is received can affect decision making. Harry will now keep the letter in mind as he prepares the follow-up story about the zoning commission. He is keenly aware of the possibility of getting into a rut and losing touch with his readers in the daily routine of the job. Thus, letters and other feedback to the news department demand serious consideration. At some newspapers, there may even be an ombudsman whose sole responsibility it is to review feedback from the readership.

Reaction to this feedback may prompt moderate changes such as a new emphasis in the coverage of a particular series of events. On the other hand, it may influence editorial comment or even impel special feature articles. You should never discount the impact of reader or viewer feedback. Your own letter to the editor or the head of a major broadcasting complex can be a key indicator to personnel on what the public is thinking and why. One letter indicates to management that there are many other people who undoubtedly feel the same way but just didn't take the time to write. One letter may be all it takes to prompt a reporter to question a news source, check an additional source, or conduct an in-depth interview that reveals a serious problem affecting the community. We'll learn much more about feedback to mass media later in this book.

summary

Many factors work in relation to each other to influence the selection and treatment of mass media news. These include (1) economics, which refers to the profit-loss structure of media operating as part of a free enterprise system; (2) regulations legislated by local, state, and federal governments to control the operation of the media and to ensure freedom of the press; (3) deadlines, which limit the time in which a gatekeeper can collect news before it is necessary to disseminate it; (4) personal and professional ethics, those forces upon which gatekeepers often base decisions in selecting information to become news; (5) competition, the safeguard of a free press in a democracy; (6) news value, a term signifying the importance of one event in relation to other events; (7) the news hole, an expression meaning the total amount of available space or time in which to present messages in order of decreasing value; (8) attention factors, visual or aural stimuli that enhance a story; (9) peer group pressure, those decisions which are influenced by colleagues; (10) the effects of time, the objectivity one gains with the passage of time; and (11) reaction to feedback, the communication received from the audience.

opportunities for further learning

BERNSTEIN, CARL, and BOB WOODWARD, *All the President's Men.* New York: Simon and Schuster, 1974.

CIRINO, ROBERT, *Power to Persuade: Mass Media and the News.* New York: Bantam Pathfinder Editions, 1974.

HOHENBERG, JOHN, *The Professional Journalist*, 3rd Ed. New York: Holt, Rinehart and Winston, Inc., 1973.

HULTENG, JOHN L., and ROY PAUL NELSON, *Fourth Estate: An Informal Appraisal of the News & Opinion Media.* New York: Harper & Row, 1971.

KENNEDY, BRUCE M., *Community Journalism: A Way of Life.* Ames, Iowa: Iowa State University Press, 1974.

LEROY, DAVID J., and CHRISTOPHER STERLING, Eds., *Mass News.* Englewood Cliffs, N. J.: Prentice-Hall, Inc., 1973.

MARBUT, F. B., *News From the Capital: The Story of Washington Reporting.* Carbondale, Ill.: Southern Illinois University Press, 1971.

MEYER, PHILLIP, *Precision Journalism.* Bloomington, Ind.: Indiana University Press, 1973.

NIMMO, DAN D., *Newsgathering in Washington.* New York: Atherton Press, 1964.

processing the news:

everyday events

and

crisis conditions

CHAPTER ELEVEN

Up to this point, our discussion has centered on those factors which affect the selection of the news prior to its dissemination. Now our attention will turn to what happens to news once dissemination begins.

the gatekeeper chain

When the flooding broke out downstate, the state editor at Harry's newspaper looked at the wire service and saw a report of "devastating" destruction. Wanting to confirm the report, he solicited the help of the university interns at his station who contacted police and sheriff departments in the communities hit by the flooding. The interns found conditions were less severe than the wire service reported. After checking, Harry discovered that the story had passed through many different editors and, in the process, had become distorted, similar to what happens in the elementary school game of "rumor." In this game, the teacher would whisper something to one student in the room, and then that student would whisper it to another student. By the time it reached the last student, who would then repeat it aloud, the message was entirely different from what the teacher had intended. Although the distortion of news messages from first to last gatekeeper may not be as extensive, the same thing can and does happen in the flow of mass media news.

To understand this process, it is necessary to examine the concept of the *gatekeeper chain.* A gatekeeper chain exists when more than one gatekeeper processes the same news story with a *limited amount of feedback* from the other gatekeepers in the chain. Let's examine the flow of information in reporting the wire service story at Harry's newspaper (Figure 11–1). Imagine that you are a newspaper reporter assigned to cover the story about the flood, the first gatekeeper, or G_1. You dutifully travel to the scene and take notes on what you see. Returning to the office, you report your observations. The city desk reporter (G_2) may rewrite your story to read:

> The Clearwater River overflowed its banks today near the downtown section of Pineville. First reports are that two persons sustained minor injuries and three homes were destroyed.

The city editor (G_3) then reads the story and changes it to:

> Flash flooding hit Pineville today as the Clearwater River overflowed its banks, destroying homes and injuring residents in the area.

Now the story goes to a major wire service bureau in the state. The bureau receives a continual inflow of information from all over the region and uses this information to prepare a report for its newspaper subscribers, including Harry's paper. At the wire service, a reporter (G_4) works to collate all the information about flood damage. Now the story reads:

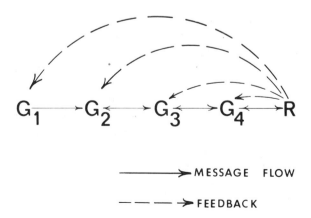

————————➤ MESSAGE   FLOW

— — — — ➤ FEEDBACK

Figure 11–1 Gatekeeper chain.

> Flash floods swept over the state today doing millions of dollars in damages and injuring more than 100 persons. Pineville and other cities were hit by the sudden storms.

Obviously, the story that reached Harry's newspaper was entirely different from the one you originally reported from the scene at Pineville. Nevertheless, word for word, there had been millions of dollars in damages, more than 100 persons had been injured, and Pineville was one of the communities which had been hit. On the other hand, a person who read the wire service description and had relatives in Pineville could easily have been left with the impression that the town had been swept off the map. Rearrangement of the factual material, minor changes made in the story by the various gatekeepers, and the merging facts at the wire service all led to a misleading story. It was at this point that the editor called in the student interns to verify the facts.

the gatekeeper group

Let's join the state editor and the student interns as they prepare the final copy on the devastating flood.

Editor: OK, what have you been able to pick up?

Melinda: Well, it wasn't too bad at Pineville, just some homes lost.

Bill: I checked with the sheriff, and he said the two injuries were to children.

Editor: Were they hurt very badly?

Bill: No, but the family dog drowned and a ten-year-old girl almost drowned trying to save it.

Melinda: That might be good to note. Stories like this can become too impersonal.

Editor: Good idea, Melinda; I wouldn't have thought of that. Guess I've been on the beat too long.

Bill: I'll write up a draft, and then Harry can check it over.

Melinda: OK, I'll see if there's an update.

The conversation between the state editor, Melinda, and Bill was an example of the operation of a *gatekeeper group* (Figure 11–2). Gatekeeper groups can operate at any point within a gatekeeper chain. The advantage such groups have is that they permit interaction to take place between gatekeepers. Interpersonal communication between members of the group results in greater accuracy simply because the information can be processed before it is dis-

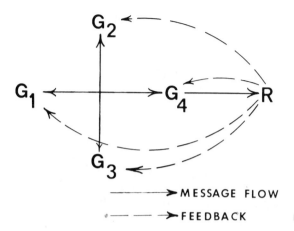

G_2

G_1

G_4

R

G_3

———————➤ MESSAGE FLOW

●— — — —➤ FEEDBACK

Figure 11–2 Gatekeeper group.

seminated to the public. The message here was clarified, changed, rewritten, and evaluated by each member of the group.

New developments in electronic journalism have eliminated certain uses of the gatekeeper group. For instance, a television news correspondent in a foreign country may send a filmed report via satellite to a news bureau in New York. From there, the report may be transmitted to a regional distribution center and then retransmitted to subscribing stations. Unlike Harry's newspaper, the filmed report remains relatively unchanged from the time it was originally prepared. The only real distortion might be technical "noise," such as visual or audio interference. However, this would not change the content of the report.

news value

Just as news value affects the selection of news, it also affects the processing of news. A news item of high value will be disseminated more frequently than a news item of low value. For instance, a radio station news director may decide that a high value news item should air on every newscast between 6:00 a.m. and 12:00 noon. The same news director, although rewriting the story, may also decide it is significant enough to be the lead story in each of these newscasts. Similarly, the editor of the local newspaper may decide the story is significant enough to use in both the morning and evening editions of the newspaper and even place it on the front page of both editions. When he positions the story at the top of the front page and uses bold face type to attract reader attention to the headline, he is again underlining this story's importance.

Media Attention

The value of a news event will also affect the number of media which are attuned to it. For example, a major international development will not only be the subject of intensive coverage by newspapers, radio, magazines, and television but may even be debated in pamphlets, books, and on film. As time elapses, of course, the number of media still publicizing the event will decrease, just as its intensity as a news item decreases. A political assassination might well be the subject of a week of news reports on virtually every wire service, radio and television station, newspaper, and news magazine worldwide. After a month's time, however, the only media doing follow-up stories about the event might be news magazines in the home country.

Distortion

News distortion can also result from varying degrees of news value. It is especially important to recognize that news events of high value often border on the chaotic. The flooding that Harry's newspaper reported might have caused a breakdown in the communication system, and people might not have known what was actually taking place. Information available shortly after the flash flood would thus have been mostly rumor. With the passage of time and decrease in value of a news item, it is possible to report from an improved perspective and with greater accuracy. We have already seen how varying deadlines affect news flow. For example, because the deadline at Harry's newspaper was fast approaching, the editor almost published the story about the flood directly as it came across the wire service rather than waiting to have the facts verified. Now add to the pressure of a deadline the distortion inherent in news of high value, and it is easy to see how errors in judgment can be transmitted to errors in news reporting.

news diffusion

Closely related to news value is *news diffusion*—the process by which news is disseminated to the receiving public. To understand news diffusion, let's see what happens when the evening edition of Harry's newspaper reaches the street. An executive of a fertilizer company buys a copy of the paper at a newsstand, reads the story about the flood, and is alarmed about the reported damage to farms owned by a number of his customers in the heart of the flood region. He goes back to the office and immediately tells his colleagues about the flooding. They in turn tell other colleagues, and within a ten-minute period, almost the entire office is clustered around the radio to hear news updates on the flooding.

The experience of the fertilizer company executive illustrates what happens when news of high value reaches the public. In this case, the news was disseminated through interpersonal communication much faster than through the mass media. Also, those who heard about the event through interpersonal communication then turned to mass media to gain additional information. Moreover, within a relatively short time it had reached many other people who were also affected by the event. To recapitulate, when the news of high value enters a social system, (1) it diffuses very rapidly; (2) much of the diffusion process is through interpersonal communication; (3) there is a tendency to search out mass media to learn more about the event; (4) a large number of people affected by the event became aware of it very rapidly.

Now, let's consider what might occur when news is of low value. Let's assume the executive purchased the newspaper as usual, but this edition contained a story about an economic upturn in agricultural industries. When he returns to the office, the sales manager walks in, and the executive tells her about the economic forecast he has just read. She replies with a quick "that sounds good," and continues with her work. About half an hour later, another colleague goes out for a coffee break, returns with the same edition of the newspaper, and reads about the predicted economic upturn. He mentions it to the executive who says he has already seen the item. About this time, some members of the sales force stop by the office to ask about new accounts. The sales force leaves, and there is no mention about the item in the newspaper. Meanwhile, the radio plays softly in a corner of the office. Now ask yourself, what is different about the diffusion of news in this case?

First, we can see that although the economic forecast affected the employees of the fertilizer company, it was not of immediate concern to them as was the news of the flooding. Second, the diffusion process was less through interpersonal communication and more through individual purchases of the evening newspaper. Third, no one hurried to gather round the radio to hear the latest updates. As the radio continued to play background music, many people in the office remained completely unaware of the news. Comparing the diffusion patterns of the two events, we see that both interpersonal and mass communication played their parts in the diffusion process, but that these varied depending on the value of the event.

Many other factors will affect news diffusion: the time of day an event occurs; when an item is released by the media; to what audience and through what medium it is first released; and the education, age, sex, and other demographic characteristics of the audience, to mention a few.

media credibility

Ever since the ancient Greeks noted that a message delivered by one spokesman had more impact than the same message delivered by a different spokesman, the concept of "ethos" or credibility has been accorded much attention. Research into interpersonal communication has investigated how the source of a message can affect its reception, a concept referred to as *source credibility*. We know, for instance, that the leader of a nation will have more credibility when talking about foreign policy than the factory worker expounding his preferences to a hometown audience. The factory worker, on the other hand, may have more credibility than the national leader when the subject is factory production. Besides the effects of message and source upon the ultimate reception of a message, we must also reckon with the role of different media. Their contribution to a story's believability is called *media credibility*.

Research has suggested some general trends about media credibility, trends that do not necessarily remain constant but do reflect the public's perception of the news media. For example, in the 1930s when radio first appeared as a medium, it quickly jumped ahead of newspapers as the most credible news source. Whether it was really more credible or contained fewer inaccuracies than newspapers is debatable. Yet the public clearly preferred hearing the news over the radio, and there were several reasons for this. First, the medium was new. Then the dimension of sound added a realism to mass communication that was reflected, for one thing in Franklin D. Roosevelt's increased political stature. His "fireside chats" were not only novel but also instrumental in cementing a closer bond between the people and the president of the United States.

On Halloween night in 1938, radio's credibility as a mass medium was vividly demonstrated when actor Orson Welles broadcast his famous radio drama, *The War of the Worlds*. Its theme was a takeover by spaceships from another planet of the East Coast of the United States. Despite repeated announcements that the play was merely a radio drama, Welles succeeded in producing mass panic among thousands of listeners, who actually waited in fear for the Martians to swallow their community. Even today's highly refined television techniques cannot command this same blind belief.

Since the 1930s, research has followed the public's changing perceptions of media credibility. We know, for example, that newspapers have regained much of the overall credibility that they lost to radio in the 1930s and early 40s. We have also seen television surge ahead as today's most credible medium. However, we should be cautious about assuming that messages received via other types of mass communication are therefore less credible. Television's enormous credibility is attributable not only to the tremendous impact it has on our lives. Another factor is that there are two dimensions to television—sight and sound. People also spend more time with television than with any other medium.

However, it is also important to consider each message and source separately in judging media credibility. For example, few members of the financial community would contest the fact that the *Wall Street Journal* covers economic news more credibly than any television station. However, if you were to ask a rodeo rider which medium he considered more credible for rodeo news, *Western Horseman* or his favorite television station, *Western Horseman* would undoubtedly be the winner.

Certain characteristics inherent in different media lend themselves to different types of messages. The ability of television to capture motion and color of major sporting events is unequaled by any other medium. A detailed contour map necessary to understand a complex story on the environment can, on the other hand, hardly be reproduced on a television screen.

mass media and crisis reporting

Xenia, Ohio, awoke to a typical spring morning on that April 3, 1974, as people watching NBC's *Today Show* heard the following national weather report:

> Scattered severe thunderstorms are expected today and tonight over a large area in the center of the country. Our sky-warn bulletin area reaches from northeast Texas and southeast Missouri, across Arkansas, Tennessee, Kentucky, Illinois, Indiana, Ohio, and West Virginia into western Virginia and North Carolina to northeastern South Carolina and Georgia on through the northern parts of Alabama, Mississippi, and Louisiana. Tornado watches will already have been out this morning until 9:00 Central Time from northeast Texas and southeast Missouri on across the southeastern part of Arkansas into western Tennessee, northwest Mississippi, and Upper Louisiana. The weather pattern is very active.

At 4:40 p.m., that active weather pattern triggered a tornado which ripped a path of savage destruction through the very heart of Xenia. With winds up to 300 miles per hour swathing across the countryside at 50 miles per hour, the 1000 yards-wide funnel obliterated buildings, killed 35 people, and eliminated more than 1500 homes in a little more than ten minutes. The only blessing was that the children had gone home. If it had struck earlier, more than 1000 of them could have been killed in their classrooms. The town collapsed into a state of combined panic and shock. Sirens wailed as fire, police, and ambulance crews worked through the night.

What happened in Xenia has happened to other communities hit by similar disasters. Be they earthquakes, floods, tornados, fires, or war, they cause a tremendous disruption in the social system they affect. The panic and confusion following the brunt of the disaster is an attempt to regain stability. The mass media assume many roles during these crisis conditions. They are faced with processing and disseminating information while under considerable stress, and shoulder a major responsibility for helping the system regain its stability. To understand this process, let's look at how people react during a crisis.

Personal Reactions to Crisis

When a crisis strikes, people and social systems display several stages of reaction. Research has shown that, although the degree of reaction will depend on the severity of the crisis, the overall stages are fairly consistent.[1]

The first stage is, understandably, *fear*. Physical and emotional tension mounts and, in some cases, leads to overt expression of that fear. When you know that the tornado is roaring your way, that the flood is going to burst the dam, or that the bombs are dropping, you react. The natural tendency to avoid injury by taking cover can bring out either the best or the worst in people. For even though our interpersonal relationships may by quite strong under normal conditions, these same relationships may yield to our instinct for self-preservation. This is not to suggest that every mother will abandon her child or every man his wife, but these things can happen. At the end of the Vietnam War when fear of the approaching North Vietnamese troops sent refugees scrambling to board evacuating aircraft, soldiers actually shoved their wives and children off loading ramps so that they could save their own necks. Similar *antisocial behavior* patterns can exist. If a disaster shelter fills up during an air raid, you may be just as apt to close the door on your best friend as you would on a complete stranger, especially if it meant the difference between your staying inside the shelter or being shut out. A general atmosphere of *nonrational behavior* will also exist. People won't think straight. The rational processes which might determine proper decision making under normal conditions will be absent. A stunned resident of a ravaged city may walk aimlessly among live power lines knocked down by a storm; another person may drink polluted street water.

A crisis will also change the normal channels of interpersonal communication which exist under non-crisis conditions. You may not care whom you seek out for information vital to your personal safety. The drive to return your life to normality may not preclude your asking help from a total stranger or even your worst enemy. People who had been in the April, 1974, Ohio tornados commented on this communicative openness. One witness likened this general exchange of information to the formation of a "tribal culture." There was a sense of group cohesion with persons one never knew before the tornado struck.

Using Media During Crises

In both warning a community of an impending crisis and returning it to stability, mass media play important roles. This does not mean, however, that broadcasting a warning over a local radio station will automatically send people scurrying for cover. How a person reacts to a warning from the media depends on his or her previous experience with a crisis. For instance, the community that has already experienced the ravages of a tornado will be much more apt to react to a tornado warning than a community that has never been hit. Persons who have never been through the experience commonly assume that disaster can never strike their community. A survey in Louisville, Kentucky, after tornadoes whipped through that region in 1974 found that 59 percent of the people who were surveyed said they would have to see a funnel before they headed for shelter.[2] On the other hand, when I interviewed a Michigan resident whose community saw twelve people killed by a tornado, he said people in his community react very quickly. "Whenever the slightest indication occurs, either cloudy skies or a media bulletin, they take precautionary measures."

In the Midwest a truck carrying a cannister of toxic war gas stopped at a truck stop near an interstate highway, and the driver discovered the cannister was leaking. Ten witnesses at the truck stop seemed to be overcome from the fumes and were whisked to the hospital. The remaining truck stop occupants as well as residents of a nearby motel quickly evacuated the area. Yet just a few miles away in a nearby community, life went on as usual despite constant warnings on local radio that the wind was blowing the dangerous fumes in the community's direction. Interestingly enough, another resident almost twenty miles away heard about the gas and wanted to leave the area immediately. Her reaction was based on previous experience. She had lived in the West where there had been a well-publicized case of livestock deaths due to military testing of war gas. She had also seen the movie *Rage* starring George C. Scott. The picture portrays a sheep rancher and his son who are accidentally and fatally exposed to military nerve gas. This combination was enough to prompt her desire to drive in the opposite direction of the truck stop, even though she already lived twenty miles from it.

Despite some people's reluctance to rely upon mass media for warnings, their attitudes change dramatically once the disaster hits. It is then that media become vital sources of information. After the Xenia, Ohio, tornado, for example, the local newspaper stayed at its presses, constantly printing updated editions listing the names of people killed or injured in the devastation, information about emergency care facilities, and damage estimates. It won a Pulitzer Prize for its efforts. People in crisis situations are insatiable for news, and those who experienced the Xenia tornadoes reported they bought as many newspapers as they could "get their hands on." The local radio station also provided tremendous assistance during the post-crisis period.

The desire to obtain information seems to destroy all regular media habits. One resident told the author he "scanned the broadcast spectrum" for information, abandoning his customary loyalty to a single station. Another resident close to the destruction told of actually walking around the house with a transistor radio up to his ear while simultaneously keeping the television turned on full volume in another room. And when the radio station changed from news to music, he would immediately change stations to catch another newscast. Other people, too anxious to wait for the media reports, telephoned the media directly for information.

Media Reaction to Crises

Not only is the community shaken out of its routine—changes occur inside the media as well. As can readily be surmised, conditions are far from normal. The work load becomes tremendous, and schedules are carried out under high tension. The media become a clearing house for information, both incoming and outgoing. Far more information processing takes place than under non-crisis conditions. A radio station, for example, may typically schedule a newscast once every hour. During a crisis, however, that same radio station may switch its format to continuous all-news programming in order to serve its stricken community. The station's staff may also change roles in a crisis. The program and music directors may completely disregard their regular duties to aid the news staff. In addition, the news director will usually assume charge of all on-air programming.

Problems arising from these abnormal conditions vary. Two university professors, Galen Rarick, Dean of the School of Journalism at the University of Oregon, and James Harless of the School of Journalism at The Ohio State University, investigated what happens to local radio stations and their personnel during a natural disaster. Under a grant from the National Association of Broadcasters, they investigated the operations of stations which had faced one of three different types of disasters—flood, blizzard, or tornado. They found a major problem facing station personnel during a disaster was transportation. They found that four-wheel drive vehicles were almost indispensable. Without four-wheel drive, tire chains had to be used for many hours at a time, causing tires to "overheat and pop" and leaving personnel stranded and unable to provide needed information to their community. Rarick and Harless also found that if reporters had two-way radios installed in their vehicles, they wouldn't have to waste time searching for a telephone to relay their reports. Station personnel also felt walkie-talkies would be beneficial, and, for stations that can afford it, auxiliary power and transmitting equipment. Management agreed that "if you are off-the-air, you are nothing."

In investigating the role of the station staff, the two professors discovered that at many stations, the staff was willing to work to the point of exhaustion. There were no interpersonal problems among the staff—they pulled together. Yet there were difficulties in the staff's ability to gather and process the news during the crisis. One newsman who wasn't accustomed to carrying a press pass had a hard time gaining access into an area that had been sealed off to prevent looting. Rarick and Harless also found that news personnel had to be careful of whom they used as news sources. One "newsman found the public no more than 80 percent accurate in reporting details" of a snowstorm. In the case of the tornado, people were so "frightened and shocked" after it hit that they couldn't remember what happened. Government agencies may be reliable sources for accurate information, but their helpfulness varies from town to town. A classic case cites a local official who couldn't even find the key to the courthouse! Rarick and Harless recommend that stations processing news and information during a crisis be prepared in advance. News personnel should have at their fingertips the names of the best news sources, and the station should become an integral part of its community disaster plan.

THE XENIA DAILY GAZETTE

93rd Year, No. 115   ★   Xenia, Ohio, Thursday, April 4, 1974   ★   8 Pages—15 Cents

Xenia digging out from day of horror

THE XENIA DAILY GAZETTE **3**
Commemorative Edition
April 3, 1975

By JACK JORDAN and RANDY BLACKABY

Splintered Xenia houses show force of giant funnel. (AP)

A bright sun late this morning reflected on the tornado-spawned miseries of Xenia, literally laying bare a community's soul still in shock but rallying back from its worst-ever tragedy — more than 1,000 injured, and the death toll now mounting steadily — already 32 known fatalities.

Man was tackling the massive destruction wrought by tornado winds that roared through the city, generally from southwest through downtown and out northeast, with 85 per cent destruction. Its noise was more awesome than any freight train — and its destructive might actually bounced a freight around like a toy, adding to the cutoff of emergency equipment.

There was ample noise again today, as workmen began cleaning up and searching through wreckage for additional victims. But Xenia's tremendous tornado left a city and environment reeling, certainly for days, but likely months and even years. Xenia had nothing to compare it with, not since founding in 1803.

Many of the dead were children. Five persons were reported killed at the A & W root beer stand, 62 Dayton Ave. Bodies were gathered from several areas and taken to the root beer stand for transportation to other facilities.

One woman, severely injured, was pregnant, and having her child when the storm hit. Officers found her dead, and her baby still fighting for survival.

Parents were roaming the streets, especially in the Arrowhead subdivision, looking for children and mates. Husbands were returning home from work, and trying to find what was once home and family — some of them without luck.

Few areas of the city escaped the devastation. South Hill and the extreme north end were notable exceptions to the tornado's wrath.

The escape of the north side from the severity suffered by the rest of the city is one of the few blessings the community could count today — it

spared Greene Memorial Hospital.

THE DOWNTOWN business district sustained varying degrees of damage. Some businesses were leveled to a point where identification could be made only by familiarity with the location and memories.

For example, all that could be found of what was once the Mr. Donut Shop on N. Allison Avenue were the stools, standing alone like mushrooms, with the building nowhere in sight.

Across the street, the Kroehler Mfg. Co. exemplified the terrific impact. A tractor-trailer rig was blown approximately 100 yards onto the roof of the Community Lanes Bowling Alley across the street.

To the east, the wreckage of the Penn-Central freight train gained most attention. It had been lifted from the tracks and thrown into the Kroger Store parking lot and onto a nearby used car lot. Several fatalities are said connected with this. The Kroger store was obliterated.

North from the center of town, James Super Valu store, 52 E. Market St., was destroyed, and almost all of the older homes on N. Detroit Street were in ruins all the way to Ankeney Mill Road.

Little was left of Xenia High School, as the mighty winds heaved school buses into the structure. Central Junior High School sustained heavy damage, but nothing like the high school.

Police reported six schools were destroyed,

but they were not named.

If the disaster had occurred a couple of hours earlier, students would have been in the buildings. Marshall Drive residences were reduced to lowly piles of broken lumber and Stadium Heights suffered much the same.

But undoubtedly the greatest destruction was in the Arrowhead subdivision where block after block of small brick homes was flattened in an area about halfway between Bellbrook Avenue and W. Second Street. In many instances it was almost impossible to determine houses ever existed.

Many were said injured at Wilberforce and one man was reported killed, although confirmation has not been received.

AID ARRIVED quickly from surrounding cities and counties, and it wasn't long before squads and police units from as far away as Columbus, Piqua, Troy and Wilmington arrived.

Dayton police raced to the aid of Greene County authorities, roping off streets and routing looters.

In fact, the response to the disaster was of so great a magnitude the influx created mass confusion for a couple of hours in communications and coordination systems.

Medical aid arrived from many of the same areas which supplied police and rescue help. The Disaster Canteen from the Columbus Red Cross chapter set up shop at the court house, dispensing free coffee and box lunches.

Bodies still being found

The grim death count continued to rise all morning as ambulances brought the fatalities to the OSSO Home Armory, serving as a temporary morgue.

Last night a temporary morgue was set up in the new wing at Greene Memorial Hospital, where county Coroner Justin Krause and sheriff's detectives fingerprinted and tagged 21 bodies.

The bodies were then transported to the Montgomery County morgue. There the victims were photographed for later identification.

This morning the morgue was moved and the same process continued until about 28 bodies had been transferred to Montgomery County.

Officials said all bodies will now be kept at the OSSO Armory and identification will be made there by relatives.

The number of dead was expected to rise considerably as the day progresses since more bodies have been found today in the rubble. A child victim died last night at Children's Medical Center. Theresa Cross, 2, daughter of Mrs. Charlene Cross, 795 Doral Drive, died of injuries about 10 p.m.

GMH officials gave definite identification on

another victim, Dorothy Rowland, but with no age or address.

Gazette's little late

Your Daily Gazette, a little late today, was being delivered in as near normal a manner as possible.

Stories were gathered by the Gazette's news staff and sent to Middletown by messenger and telephone, where type was set and pages prepared for the eight-page newspaper. Some pages will be readily identifiable as being from the Middletown Journal, a sister newspaper of the Daily Gazette in the Chew Newspapers organization.

The paper, printed on The Journal's presses, then was brought back to Xenia for distribution at two points — bundles at King's Plaza on the south edge and single-copy distribution at Gilliger IGA on the north side.

Efforts were being made to reach as many carriers as possible to get copies to our customers.

GIGANTIC TASK AHEAD
Shock is slow in wearing off

By Jack Jordan
Daily Gazette Editor

Xenians, grateful to be alive, took a look at their beloved city estimated to be at least half devastated, and began the gargantuan task of putting together a community again.

Xenians bereaved by dead or missing relatives and friends were coming back from their shock and trying to keep busy today.

The massive tornado left a lifetime imprint on those who experienced the terror. The casualties will mount over the next several days, it is believed.

Hundreds of millions of dollars' damage is more comprehensible to Xenians than the appearance. This city wouldn't have looked any worse if a major battle in a war had raged through its confines.

This city never has known adversity of this magnitude; few communities have.

Digging out, patching up, rebuilding and shaping a new face downtown and in residential areas and shopping districts will require years.

Ohio's Gov. John J. Gilligan, here several hours last night, pledged whatever state assistance is available immediately; certainly massive assistance efforts will come from federal disaster

agencies.

Aside from the many Xenians killed or injured, the tornado didn't discriminate. It leveled new brick homes on slabs and it literally tore asunder big old homes that had stood for a half century and more.

Xenia High School was demolished, so was Warner Junior High and the city's other intermediate building, Central Junior High, were windowless and perhaps structurally damaged. Only grade schools in untouched residential areas remained.

This community of commuters, not known as an industrial center, lost much of its West Side industry — from the Kroehler Mfg. Co.'s furniture plant on through brand new plants such as Tremac Corp., left in ruins.

Downtown business was shattered; many buildings will have to come the rest of the way down. Fringe shopping centers were eliminated, particularly Kennedy Korners in the West Side.

The Daily Gazette, for the first time in its 106-year history, was printed today outside its own plant — by the sister operation, the Middletown Journal. The Gazette's downtown plant, battered and scarred, can return to vital communication

operations once gas-fired metal furnaces are safe to function.

The Greene County Museum and Historical Complex, at the north end of the downtown district, is in ruins but Greene County's Carnegie District Library two blocks away seemed to have escaped the brunt .

St. Brigid Catholic Church, the city's largest denomination, was rubble; badly damaged were other churches, notably the Church of the Nazarene at the swath's entrance into the city.

As observers last night, we witnessed the chaos of law enforcement, safety and rescue units come from all over the state to seek out the injured, move in on the "sick" who appear swiftly to loot, and then establishment of some semblance of order.

This morning the chains of command were beginning to shape up, admittedly for a concentrated effort to gain control and apply priorities.

It was heartening. It was sound, sensible leadership headed by City Manager Bob Stewart. There is no other course than to comply and cooperate.

Only in that way will Xenia come alive again.

The front page of the Xenia, Ohio, *Daily Gazette* headlining the tornado disaster. The newspaper won a Pulitzer Prize for its reporting efforts.

Special Reporting Problems – Civil Unrest

Not all crises result from natural disasters. In recent years, civil unrest has turned many an event into a crisis situation. Covering this crisis requires just as many skills, if not more, than covering a natural disaster; just as many pitfalls can hamper a news team's efforts in disseminating the information to the public.

A reporter assigned to cover an incident of civil unrest should be sure to guard against being "used" by the participants. Bright lights, television cameras, and microphones inspire some people to theatrical performances. Staged protests designed to attract media attention still occur and, unfortunately, the press has been all too eager to capitalize on these incidents. Irresponsible journalists added fuel to the fire of academic and social unrest during the decade of the 1960s when they eagerly pounced on campuses in the middle of a demonstration and interviewed anyone from a nonstudent to the lowest flunky on the academic ladder. The techniques used to report unrest at an industrial plant on a New Mexico Indian reservation evoked similar complaints. Instead of interviewing the local Indian workers, the press was criticized for accepting outsiders as representative spokesmen for the regular employees.

Reporting inaccurate information is especially hazardous in covering civil unrest. Take the problem of estimating crowd size. A group of three thousand people marching down the middle of a community may be interpreted in a number of different ways. Under the pressure of deadlines or in the haste of doing a "live" minicam report, you might refer to the group as "organized protestors numbering in the thousands." Does the comment "scores of angry tribesmen" accurately describe between ten and twenty Indian workers who are occupying an industrial plant?

Public officials can also take advantage of a reporter's situation. Realizing the limitations imposed by deadlines, these people sometimes supply information that distorts the truth. During the tense period when school bussing was instituted, one group of school officials succeeded in convincing the press there was really a larger percentage of children attending school than were actually in the classroom by reporting lower total enrollment figures. The press, under pressure, didn't have time to verify the facts and bought the distorted version.

Information Flow

Reviewing these examples, we can begin to theorize what occurs during these crises. First come the problems of *distortion* and *time*.

When deadlines, pressures, varied news sources, and tremendous information-processing demands merge, distortion has ample opportunity to prevail.

The greatest opportunity for news distortion exists immediately after the crisis takes place. For example, in the case of the tornado which struck Xenia, Ohio, the major distortion occurred within the twenty-four hour period immediately after the disaster. Some conflicting accounts are bound to exist because not all gatekeepers have the same information at the same time. As a result, updated information is constantly being released to the public. For example, the estimate of the number of people killed in the Xenia tornado varied because newspapers in different time zones went to press at different hours of the day. When any given newspaper went to press, it may or may not have had the same estimate of casualties as did other newspapers. Two days following the tornado, April 5th, the *Chicago Tribune* reported "at least 25 persons died," at Xenia. The San Francisco *Examiner* reported "32 known dead," and *The Times* of London reported that 30 people "are known to have died in Xenia."

The number of media attuned to a crisis will also vary. During a crisis or immediately afterward, that is, at the height of the distortion period, many media will carry information about it. Again, using our example of the Xenia tornado, we see that for about two days after the tornado hit, many news media carried information about the event, including newspapers, wire services, and radio and television stations. With the exception of the Xenia media, in the immediate weeks and months after the event, only news magazines were bannering the story. About six months later, NBC produced a documentary entitled *Tornado*, which was shown during prime-time television. Approximately eighteen months after the event a Cincinnati, Ohio, newspaper reporter, Polk Lafoon IV, published a book on the subject. The media attention habits discussed here are typical, yet coverage patterns will vary, depending on the incident. Furthermore, certain factors may refocus the attention of the media upon an event long after it has been forgotten. The news that a government committee has been appointed to reopen the case of a political assassin, the discovery that a dam which had burst and drowned a city had been reported weakening months before the break, and the news that a new earthquake detection device has been invented all can stimulate media to feature news about a past crisis.

The rules which govern the processing of news under normal circumstances are often suspended during a crisis. As consumers or practicing professionals an awareness of this new set of rules is necessary in order to react appropriately to events—whether you're at the scene of the action or sitting at home trying to piece together news of the event.

summary

This chapter dealt with the processing of news. Two forces that have a significant effect on news processing are the gatekeeper group and the gatekeeper chain. The gatekeeper chain allows for little interpersonal communication between gatekeepers and consequently fosters a greater opportunity for distortion. The gatekeeper group, on the other hand, permits gatekeepers to check and recheck each other's decisions and therefore lessens the opportunity for distortion. News value also plays an important part in news processing. News of high value will be aired by more media and may be diffused more frequently than news of low value.

Closely related to the intensity factor is news diffusion. News of high value will be diffused faster than news of little value. As in processing, rapid diffusion will increase the possibilities for distortion. In high intensity situations we're more apt to communicate and to receive important news by word of mouth than from mass media.

The medium which disseminates the news can also affect how we perceive it. Because society is so attuned to television, it is generally accorded more credibility than other mass media in the face of conflicting news reports. Media credibility is, however, not an absolute, but a relative term; each medium has its own forte, lending it superior credibility for a particular message and source.

When a crisis takes place various abnormal conditions exist within the media. There is a heightened demand for information by the public. People seek out media to tell them what is happening as part of the adjustment process that will eventually help them return to normal. Within the media, personnel may be called upon to put forth superhuman efforts; special equipment may be needed; and reporters may experience unusual difficulty in both gaining access to information and deriving factual accounts from reliable sources.

opportunities for further learning

CANTRIL, HADLEY, *The Invasion From Mars: A Study in the Psychology of Panic.* Princeton University Press, 1940.

DENNIS, EVERETT E., and WILLIAM L. RIVERS, *Other Voices: The New Journalism in America.* San Francisco, Calif.: Canfield Press, 1974.

McCombs, Maxwell, Donald Lewis Shaw, and David Grey, *Handbook of Reporting Methods*. Boston: Houghton Mifflin Company, 1976.

Quarantelli, E. L., *The Disaster Research Center Simulation Studies of Organizational Behavior Under Stress*. Columbus, Ohio: Ohio State University Disaster Research Center, 1969.

Taylor, James Bentley, Louis A. Zurcher, and William H. Key, *Tornado: A Community Responds to Disaster*. Seattle, Wash.: University of Washington Press, 1970.

Turner, Ralph H., and Lewis M. Killian, *Collective Behavior*. Englewood, Cliffs, N.J.: Prentice-Hall, Inc., 1957.

producing

televised messages

CHAPTER TWELVE

The fast-moving, polished scenes of a television thriller, the mellow transition between moods of an afternoon drama, and the flawless spontaneity of a prime-time situation comedy appear so effortless that it is easy to lose oneself in the plot without ever being aware of the specific actions, the rehearsed lines, or the pre-planned movements of each actor. By the time a television program reaches us, it has gone through a rigorous process of production, editing, and direction that involves the labors of many people, both in front of and behind the cameras. It may consist of the news team and backup crews all pulling together to bring you the events of your community in thirty or sixty minutes of televised perfection. It may be the production crew of a network program creating a film for later viewing on network television or future syndication. Whatever the message, whatever the medium, the production of messages is a complex, artistic, and exacting process. It takes talent, coordination, cooperation, leadership, stamina, intelligence, and the ability to give and to follow directions.

During our lifetime, many of us will be part of this exacting process. We may be the guest on a television interview show, the newsmaker in our local government, the extension agent preparing a television program on nutrition, the educator using instructional media in the classroom, or the business executive preparing a major presentation for distribution to other employees through a closed circuit television or teleconferencing system. Whatever our role, an understanding of the "behind the scenes" activities that make the production of television messages possible can prove invaluable. Our treatment here will be general and basic; for those whose interest we may peak, texts are available that treat these concepts in detail. Specialized courses will also give you a better understanding of the processes involved in producing televised messages. We'll begin with a look inside a television studio.

inside the television studio

A television studio is a complex array of monitors, cameras, communication systems, switches, and lights. Basically, it serves one main function—to capture and transmit picture and sound.

Structural Components

The studios of most television stations consist of much of the same physical properties as found in small theaters constructed for live plays. *Lights* supply the proper illumination for the cameras to capture the action, *sets* provide the scenery or backdrop for the picture, and *props* lend a more realistic effect to the action. In the typical television studio, the amount of scenery and props depends on the amount of locally originated programming. Studios that produce many of their own programs may have all sorts of sets and combinations of sets. These may be suspended from the ceiling and brought down when a particular show is ready for airing, or they may be on rollers so they can be wheeled back and forth in front of an area where they serve as a backdrop. There are even fixed position sets that form part of the studio walls.

Some studios have at their disposal "special effects" scenery such as a rear screen that serves as an easily changed backdrop. Made from a semi-opaque plastic material, rear screens are usually about eight feet square and have a slide or motion picture projector positioned behind them. A projected image then shines through from behind the screen. The advantage to such a device is that the announcer can sit in front of the screen without casting a shadow on it. Other special effects may be achieved by *special effects gener-*

ators that can create such visual scenery as moving messages or weather patterns, satellite and radar pictures, and multiple split-screen techniques.

Studio size depends on the size of the market which the station serves and also on the combined station and studio. If, for example, the station is affiliated with a major network that produces much of its own programming for network distribution, then the studio will be large and well equipped. Space can run as high as 3,000 square feet and more.

Separate from the *main studio* area is the *television control room* (Figure 12–1), which becomes a sort of command post when a program is being produced or is on the air. Other support areas for the control room and studio usually include an *audio production room,* an *engineering shop,* a *darkroom,* a *film and videotape editing room, film storage area,* and *transmitter room.*

Electronic Components

Located within the station complex are key electronic components which are an integral part of the production process. One of the most important components is the set of *television cameras.* They can vary in size from hand-held miniatures costing a few thousand

Figure 12–1 Television control center. (WRTV-TV.)

dollars, to full-scale studio color cameras which cost well over $100,000. Most stations are equipped with a minimum of two studio cameras. The number of supplementary cameras for remote broadcasting purposes may equal the number of news personnel employed by the station. In some major stations, transport systems for both cameras and their operators may include vans, airplanes, or even marine craft. The cameras are connected, either directly through *cables* or indirectly through *microwave* hookup, to the station's control room.

The *master control console* is the heart of the control room operation. Here video images from various cameras can be *mixed* to yield a composite "on air" image, which can then be *dissolved* to an image produced by another camera, or even transformed into special effects such as *split-screen* images. Positioning one picture on top of another one, called *supering,* is another capability of the master control console.

Groups of control switches called *banks* or *busses* are central to this complex functioning. One group may be used to control a coordinated camera unit; another grouping may control the audio portion of the program, and a third, the videotape recorders or film and slide chains. *Film* and *slide chains* are motion picture and slide projectors, the lenses of which are directed into the lens of a specially fixed television camera, which in turn transmits the image of the film or slide over the air. The film chain can thus be used to show major motion pictures or feature documentaries, or to supplement news programming. Programs employing slide or film chains can be supplemented with videotape and audio recorders that are also controlled from the master control console. Another vital component to any production is an *intra-studio communication system* necessary to provide communication between the control room and the studio. A system of head phones with two-way communication capabilities similar to those used by a telephone operator fulfills this function.

Human Components

One of the most important people in the operation of the television studio is the producer. As Zettl states:

> The television producer is the organizer of a show. He frequently creates show ideas and then prepares the necessary material for on-the-air production. He takes care of all financial matters, contracts, and material clearances. He knows what technical facilities are available and what the potentials and limitations of these facilities are. The producer coordinates rehearsal and performance schedules and sees to it that his

show receives the necessary publicity and promotion. The specific duties of the television producer naturally change with each different show idea. Sometimes a show has to be developed from scratch; at other times the television producer may receive a television script in which most of the production details have already been worked out.[1]

Working with the producer and his or her alter ego is the *director*. On the director's shoulders falls the creative responsibility for the complete production. The director is an artist, a professional capable of fusing color and sound, characterization, and electronic mastery into a composite of technical excellence. The subtle meaning behind the actor's slightest movement, the inflection in his voice, the movement of a camera to reflect and capture a mood and emotion are all part of the director's repertoire. As the show progresses, the director intertwines the components of the production in much the same way that an artist blends paints on a palette. Once production commences, the director becomes the key individual who not only commands the respect of his entire crew but also helps them to learn, develop, and perform as professionals.

The director, however, functions only thanks to the help of such support personnel as the *floor manager*, who communicates the commands of the director to the performers; *camera operators;* and the *technical director*, sometimes called the *switcher*, who is responsible for the delicate operation of the master control console. The technical director coordinates the video and audio controls, switching from one camera to another and from one microphone to another, all at the director's command. In some smaller television stations, one person may assume the combined roles of producer, director, and switcher. The overall coordination of every member of the production team is evidenced in the finished product. Every member of the team must pull his or her load with expertise and cooperation. It is this ability to integrate creativity with technical knowhow that produces a quality program.

The end of production work does not necessarily mean that the show is ready for airing. The show may need editing, or portions of it may even need to be reproduced. Especially with television commercials there is the need to mesh specific information into a limited time span of sixty or thirty seconds, a task requiring precision.

Other types of programming may not require extensive editing. Evening news programs, for example, are almost always programmed live except for prerecorded film or videotape inserts. Thus the studio crew is working alongside journalists and anchormen as the program is aired. Because the same basic format is duplicated daily, pre-program planning by the crew is minimal compared to that required for other types of programming.

behind the scenes of a major television production

So far we have concentrated on the components of a typical local television studio. However, much of what we see on television, especially prime-time television, is not produced at the local studio or on videotape, but on film before a live audience. Many such programs are regular features that make up a predominant share of the network television schedule. Some may be produced by the networks themselves—for example, special news documentaries. Others, produced by independent companies, emerge from essentially the same processes used to produce in-studio programming but usually evolve over a longer period of time. They may be filmed instead of videotaped and may require much larger casts than those appearing on the local television news program.

To gain some insight into the production processes used on such shows, let's pay a visit to one of America's more popular television productions, the *Mary Tyler Moore Show*, produced by MTM Enterprises.[2] The show involves a week-long production process and is filmed rather than videotaped, as are many other programs, e.g., *All in the Family*. Three cameras are used to record three copies of the final performance, which are then edited into the master film ready for airing. We begin our week at the CBS Studio Center in Studio City, California.

The Week Begins

It is mid-morning, and the production manager, producer, story consultant, director, assistant director, script supervisor, art director, set decorator, property master, and the men's and women's costumers are meeting to discuss the present and upcoming weeks' episodes of the *Mary Tyler Moore Show*. The department heads are reviewing the present week's script page by page, considering all the technical aspects of the show: the timing of the episode, time lapses between the sequences, wardrobe changes, props, unusual lighting, additional sets, actors, extras, and a guest star. This is the way the entire production process begins, week after week, for six months.

By the time the morning production meeting ends, the action has moved to Stage Two where members of the cast are reading through the script for the first time.

This week's show, written by Ed Weinberger, will be the 93rd of the series. It is about the "Teddy Awards," the local awards in Minneapolis, and the campaign by Ted Knight to win best newscaster award. The show centers around the awards banquet, the presentation of the award to Knight, the problems of the news team in coping with his ego, and the climactic appearance of a guest star at the end of the program.

The first run-through of the script begins. Seated around one long table, the cast reads through the script as the script supervisor times the sequences and the producers listen for line interpretation, pace, and comedy. This formative period not only forces the actors to develop their characterizations fully, but also allows the producers to see which parts of the show will work for them and which will need rewriting. Much of the success of the show lies in the ability of the cast to take a simple line, develop it, produce an action or a look, and reach the audience as believable characters. They work as a team, where everyone has ideas and everyone contributes.

Once through the morning activities, they break for a two-hour lunch. It's now 2:30 p.m., and the cast is back to begin the staging of Act One. Any additional sets needed for the show have already been pre-constructed and assembled on the stage.

During the afternoon's rehearsal, the director, Jay Sandrich, works with the movements and actions of the actors on the set. At this point he is more concerned with their position and placement than with their lines. Because of the constant revision of the script, the concentration on lines will come much later this week. In fact, before this afternoon is over, six new pages of revision will have been sent down from the producers' offices. It's now 4:30 p.m., and the first day of the rehearsal is finished.

Tuesday morning brings still more blue pages (revisions to the white page script). This second day of rehearsal continues the step-by-step process of staging the show whereby each sequence is blocked, reblocked, and rerun. Director Sandrich spends the morning reworking the staging of Act One with the revisions and trying to remove the trouble spots. After an hour lunch break, the cast returns to stage Act Two.

The Major Revisions Begin

It's Wednesday morning. A 10:00 a.m. call for the stars finds them with the director progressing through the entire script. As usual, there are more pages of revision, but nothing that will upset the major staging of the previous two days. The day moves along smoothly, and at 3:15 p.m., the cast has been through the complete staging of the show. At this time, "the jury"—the executive producers, producer, and story consultant—are called down from their offices to view the complete run-through. Meanwhile, the cast has been studying and working together on their lines. Although it is not required, most of the run-through is done without scripts. It is now that we begin to appreciate the producers' talent and creativity in adding that final touch. Perhaps it is merely a change in diction or in gesture, but their sense for comedy often makes the difference between a good show and a great one!

After the Wednesday afternoon run-through, the producers and story consultant now return to the offices of MTM Enterprises to work on the final version of the script. They'll stay until 10:00 p.m. doing a complete revision. Sometimes the "brain session" involves only minor adjustments. More often, however, they rewrite entire sequences. The revised script is now sent to an all-night script service which types, duplicates, and delivers it to the studio by Thursday morning.

It's 9:00 a.m. Thursday morning, and the cameras are brought in. This is the beginning of a long, tedious day of blocking (planning the position) the three cameras used to film the series. First, the cast runs through the sequence minus the cameras. This gives the camera operators a rough idea of the work before them. Then stand-ins arrive, and the director works in a stop-and-go fashion with the three cameras, assistant director, camera coordinator, and directors of photography and lighting. Once the floor is marked off with colored tape to represent the territories of cameras A, B, and C, the actors arrive to do the sequence. As the lines are delivered and the actions carried out, the camera coordinator directs the camera movements via headphones to the three people on each camera—the camera operator, the first assistant operator, and the dolly grip.

Still the three cameras seem to be moving about the set in orchestrated chaos. The director can't allow them to obtrude upon the comedy or to move about at random, because the sets are lighted from all four sides, and one camera can easily throw a shadow the others will pick up. The director supervises the shooting of a master camera and two close-up cameras. With these he must regulate the actors' movements so that they don't interfere with each other's close-up, yet remain within optimal range for the master shot. This particular week, Sandrich solved this problem by using the zoom lens on camera B to obtain another needed close-up.

On Thursday afternoon, Sequence D, the banquet room scene at the Teddy Awards, poses a particular problem because of the number of people involved. Three cameras aren't enough to transmit the facial expressions of the seven principals seated at a round table. In order to capture these reactions on film, a staged reaction will have to be done after the audience leaves on Friday night. The director will also do a reverse shot at that time to provide the viewer with a different angle and the illusion of a large banquet hall.

At 4:00 p.m., while the slow camera blocking process continues, important decisions are being made in the film cutting room. The film editor and associate producer are busy working on the film from the previous week's show. Both the director and the writer are on hand to view the rough cut. There is one problem to be solved—the show runs 190 feet of film too much. It must be cut to the 24 minutes and 30 seconds running time for television. But what to cut? The associate producer wants to take a deep cut, but the writer objects to losing a good line. With precision and creativity, the film is run and rerun until all the editing has been completed. Returning to the set meanwhile, the entire show has been blocked by 6:30 p.m., and only one day remains in the filming process. The assistant director has called the fifteen extra persons needed for the banquet scene and will have Friday afternoon to work with them. With a noon call for Friday, the cast and crew break; the actors will go home and study their scripts, while the director relaxes because his work is primarily over.

At noon on Friday, everyone is ready to begin the run-through, complete with cameras, from the beginning of the script. The run-through not only helps gell the script for the actors, but also pinpoints the camera moves and accustoms the cast to the three "monstrosities" staring them in the face as they enact the scenes.

This week, there has been an aura of excitement on the set as the cast anxiously awaits the Friday afternoon arrival of their special guest star from New York. In order to ensure the element of surprise for the television audience, the producers have asked everyone to keep the star's name a secret until the show is actually being filmed. Various columnists and photographers have been invited to be in the live audience. At 3:30 p.m., the special guest star walks onto the set with the executive producer and the producer. In order to orient him to the scene, he'll run it through once with the stand-in playing the role. This will enable him to observe the staging. Then the entire cast will rehearse the sequence three times with the guest star and prepare for the final run-through or dress rehearsal.

The dress rehearsal complete with cameras, cast, and props runs smoothly and takes a little over an hour. Even when it is finished, there are lines, especially in the last scene, that the producers aren't happy with. As the cast and crew break for dinner at 5:30 p.m. the producers, director, and assistant director meet to iron out the minor difficulties.

The cast and crew eat dinner at the studio commissary and then return to the stage for makeup, wardrobe, and preparation for the show. By 6:00 p.m., there is a long line of people outside Stage

Two waiting to see the show. Our studio seats three hundred, and, as usual, there is a standing-room-only situation. Sandrich says that as a director specializing in comedy, he loves doing the show before three cameras and a live audience. To him, it's like staging a new thirty-minute play every Friday night with nearly five full days of rehearsal to work with the actors and writers on perfecting each scene.

The Live Production

By 7:00 p.m. Friday, a full studio audience is ushered in for the final filming of the show. Technicians begin to check out cameras, microphones, and lights. The audio person and camera coordinator settle into the sound booth. As final preparations for the filming are being made, Lorenzo Music comes out and begins warming up the audience. Suddenly the live music stops, and all is quiet. John Chulay, the assistant director, gives the first direction to roll the cameras. Within seconds, the word "speed" is being announced from the control booth, and a calm, steady "action" follows. The filming has begun. It is 7:35 p.m.

Both camera operators and actors have their moves memorized, and the show switches from Ted Baxter's dressing room, to Mary's apartment, to the news room without much difficulty. A forgotten or misread line will be redone in the "pick-up" after the audience leaves. Although at first a bit reserved, the audience now begins to warm up and provides good reactions. No mention has been made of the surprise guest star — in fact, the audience has no idea there is going to be a special guest. In the last scene, Mary and Murray are talking in the newsroom and Ted is on the phone. Murray sees someone in the hall outside the office and becomes excited, and then so does Mary. Suddenly, without any warning, Walter Cronkite walks in, and the audience roars with applause. Cronkite flew out especially to appear on the *Mary Tyler Moore Show* because he likes it so much, and everyone on the show is overwhelmed by his presence.

By 9:30 p.m., the audience leaves the studio. Pick-ups are now filmed and scenes and parts of scenes reenacted to correct minor errors in dialogue, actor movement, and camera shots. Then at 10:25 p.m., soundtracks with Ted Knight and Valerie Harper are recorded. In reviewing the rough cuts, the associate producer found some of the lines weren't recorded clearly. This requires the actors to redeliver their lines to the boom microphone. Finally at 10:45 p.m., the studio work is completed. Actors and crews are released, and sets are already being disassembled for the next week. We've

ended one week of production for the *Mary Tyler Moore Show.* At 10:00 a.m. on Monday, the entire process will begin again, while this show enters its final stage in the film cutting room.

observations

Our visit to the *Mary Tyler Moore Show* has given us some insight into the interaction of people, cameras, and control processes that also operate but on a smaller scale in the local television station.

The raw form of the program, from which its entire planning and development takes place, is the script. However, what is on paper may not always put the actors at their ease. For this reason the script remains flexible and open to the creative talents of the actors. The interrelationship between director and actor, and sometimes between director and writers, becomes a true team approach. The actors' knowledge of their own capabilities, personalities, and the roles they portray, are all tremendously important in judging where a line should be changed or deleted, where words should be added, or where action and movement should be redirected. Movements and gestures of Mary Tyler Moore may be changed so that the true character she portrays can come through in the final staging. Dialogue of Ted Baxter that does not reflect an ego-filled personality may be changed to better accentuate the character of the self-centered television journalist. Working with new talent is also a must. Just as local stations may recruit people from the immediate community, so do the major networks. Temperament, tolerance, and willingness to be compatible with others become key prerequisites. Fortunately for this particular show, there is a close association among the staff offstage as well as on. Each is secure in his or her own professional role, having been award-winning performers in their own right.

The show's production must also fully understand the nature of its viewing audience. It is, and will continue to be, syndicated for family viewing. In recognition of this fact, for example, jokes which might reflect negatively upon certain segments of a national audience are carefully avoided. There is a trust and loyalty which develops between an audience and a program. To breach this trust with programming content that offends or insults can cost a show its audience and eventually result in its cancellation. In addition, because the star of this show is a woman, care is taken to understand the woman audience. Mary's needs, interests, and professional and personal roles must be kept in perspective. Many of the episodes are written by women, and a woman story consultant, Treva Silverman, has been employed as a further check in this sensitive area.

Besides its national viewing audience, the production needs to be aware of the studio audience, for it is the studio audience which gives the emotional cues to the viewing audience. A live studio audience that reacts favorably to lines and actions will add immeasurably to the final production. Such legitimate reaction, as opposed to the "dubbed in" variety is a contagious experience. A live audience also keeps the actors in tune with the direct feedback from the show. The result is a production already tested and found to be an enjoyable experience for those who have seen it.

The equipment component of the program is also a factor to be reckoned with and accepted. The director's skill and expertise in the film medium is taken into consideration from the very start of the planning. Ever present in the director's mind is the perspective of what the actions will look like in their final form when they reach the cutting room and eventually the living rooms of millions of people. The actors must also contend with the equipment component. Although they are well adjusted to the presence of cameras, the actual confrontation during filming remains a unique experience. The operation of the equipment becomes just as critical and just as much of a creative force as the work of the director and actors. When people and machines are functioning smoothly, each in its own role, the final product is an artistic and professional program.

producing instructional television programs

One of the most rapidly developing areas of mass communication is the field of instructional television programming. Instructional television (ITV) began in the early 1950s and then, after a spurt of widespread interest among educators, reached a plateau in the 1960s. There were two major reasons for the decline. First, there was a general fear among teachers that ITV would eventually supplant them in the classroom. Second, the medium had developed so rapidly that there was little opportunity to evaluate its effectiveness in the classroom.

Now that time has permitted us to evaluate the medium, we can forecast an era of eager acceptance, not only in education but in business and industry as well. In fact, many major corporations have their own fully equipped television studios to produce ITV programs for use inside the company or syndication to other corporations for information and training sessions. Governments around the globe are beginning to see ITV as a means of informing the masses about such things as good nutrition or skills needed on particular jobs. Moreover, with the development of cable and two-way cable systems, instructional media are becoming a major force in society. School systems, even in remote areas, will be equipped with some type of instructional television facility. In the future, satellite communication will make ITV available to virtually every school system or corporate facility that wants it, regardless of the location.

In our lifetime, ITV will affect every one of us. The next generation will, in all probability, grow up in school systems where ITV programming will play a dominant role in their educational experience. Already college graduates are frequently involved in management training programs, portions of which are taught by ITV. You yourself may even become an instructional media specialist responsible for developing and producing ITV programming to educate large numbers of people.

To be an informed participant or consumer of ITV, we should understand something about the production and development of ITV programming. You will note in the preceding paragraphs, for instance, that the term *production* has been used synonymously with *development*. This is because production is actually a developmental process that involves various steps or stages.[3] We will take a cursory look at these various stages. As in all areas of technology today, specialization has necessitated that each stage have its own expertise. However, it is equally important to understand the overall process of development. For example, imagine you have been appointed the ITV coordinator of a local school system and are responsible for producing all its ITV programming. Your latest assignment is an ITV program on the subject of the newspaper industry to be used as a teaching aid by high school journalism instructors. What do you do?

Program Planning

Your first step is to make certain that no one else has produced an ITV program on the newspaper industry equivalent to the one you have in mind. If such a program is already available, you will want to seriously consider whether your treatment will contribute new material or a new outlook.

If you decide to go ahead, the next step will be to gain an understanding of the needs of journalism students and teachers. After all, if the program is not something the students will benefit from, and if the teachers are less than enthusiastic about using it, then your efforts may be wasted. You must also consult with experts in the field; in this case, you will want to consult two sources. One will be journalism teachers. By involving those who will use the program when it's completed, you give them a say about the content of the program and make it relevant for their curriculum. The other source you'll want to consult are experts from the newspaper industry. Working with professionals will help to assure that the information you include is factually correct. The journalism department at a nearby college or university may also prove helpful.

Next you'll want to check with key people who will be involved in the production process. If your school system is a major producer of ITV programming, then you will undoubtedly have contacts with professionals in television production. These will include television engineers, technicians, and even actors. You will also need to determine the type of programming format you intend to use. Will you employ a traditional format with a teacher in front of the camera or will you include an interview with a local newspaper executive? Perhaps your final program will be a major documentary on the newspaper industry. All of these factors should be taken into consideration.

Another important task will be to review the literature dealing with your topic. In reviewing articles in journals and other scholarly publications, you may discover key facts to include in your program — quotes from authoritative sources in the field of newspaper publishing as well as predictions on what the industry will be like ten years from now. Finally, a survey of both textbooks and general reading material should find your program taking final shape in your mind; the important elements begin to take on meaning in relation to one another and the various approaches to teaching the subject gradually solidify.

Identifying Goals

Your next critical step is the identification of *goals* you want to accomplish with the program. This involves two phases. First, you should be aware of the ability and previous knowledge of the students to whom you are directing the program. If your program is designed for use at the high school level, for instance, but your material and methods "talk down" to the students, your work will have little value. Second, once you have determined the students' abilities, you'll want to draw up a general list of concepts they should know after having seen the program—for example, the major steps involved in publishing a newspaper, the tasks of key personnel at the paper, how a reporter covers a story, and how the final product is distributed. Once you draw up the list, you'll want to be consistent in carrying it out.

Planning Evaluation

Now that you have established your program's goals, you will want to find a way to measure your success in conveying those ideas. You should consult experts in the field of tests and measurements; perhaps the educational testing bureau of your school can even assign expert personnel to help you. You will want to work with them in developing a set of questions which will be administered to students participating in the program. These tests should determine if you, and the ITV program, have achieved your objectives.

Producing the Program

Now the excitement builds. You have cleared all the hurdles in the planning stage. Now you can begin preparing the script, getting ideas onto paper and then revising them again and again until the script generally meets the approval of all involved. It is also at this point that a decision on the length of the program is made. You will ask yourself whether a one-hour program or a series of shorter programs will be more effective. Keep in mind the attention span of the projected audience and how many times the lesson may have to be repeated before satisfactory learning takes place.

Certain ideas may simply not be practical. The director may veto

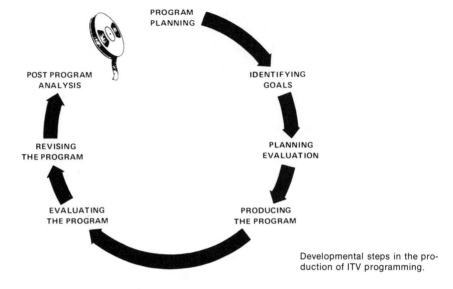

Developmental steps in the production of ITV programming.

a certain idea because it is technically impossible, or the engineer may suggest a better way to approach a scene in view of certain technical limitations. Finally, after all the discussions and rewrites have yielded an acceptable script, actual production begins. Even now certain segments of the program that looked good on paper may prove impractical and have to be revised.

Throughout the production, you must be careful to involve everyone in the process. After all, the excitement is now reaching its peak and everyone wants to play a part in the production, either on or off camera. To exclude key people will not only bruise egos but may affect the morale of the entire production crew. Your diplomatic skill will often be the keystone that cements everyone's efforts under high stress. When the program is completed, however, the reward will be worth the effort.

Evaluating and Revising the Program

You have completed production. The important question now is, How successful were you in achieving your goals? The evaluative tests designed to determine this success will now be administered to a control group of students. You will probably want a group of independent persons to serve as the evaluation team, since it might be difficult for you and the production staff to be totally objective in your judgments. After all, your own creative talents have come to bear on the entire production.

If the evaluation reveals that certain goals weren't reached, you may need to institute minor, or even major, revisions. Perhaps the mere change of a few lines may achieve the desired effect. On the other hand, the entire organization of the program may be faulty. Regardless of what is involved, problem areas must be identified so that revisions can be made. They should not be looked upon as failures.

Post-Program Analysis

Once the program has been finalized, a review of the entire production process will prove instructive. Since you'll more than likely be involved in producing other ITV programs, it will be useful to recall each step in the production process while the program is still fresh in everyone's mind. Perhaps you'll decide to change your organizational framework or research methods for your next ITV production. Or maybe you'll find ways to cut costs. All of these considerations should come to light during the post-program analysis.

In conclusion, producing an ITV program is a deliberate step-by-step process that involves many people. As in network production, a total cooperative effort among on- and offstage personnel is required to coordinate the human and the technical aspects of the production. Only through an understanding of this cooperative developmental effort can you be a responsible consumer or producer of ITV program.

summary

The studio, with its structural components, is the raw plant from which emerge finished televised messages. Such accessories as sets, props, and special effects equipment contribute visual and auditory realism to the production. Television studios usually cover an area of 3,000 square feet or more. They consist, along with the main studio area, of a control room, audio production room, an engineering shop, a darkroom, a film and videotape editing room, a film storage area, and transmitter room. Electronic components include television cameras, cables, master control console with its banks or busses, and an intra-studio communication system. Microwave equipment may aid in remote broadcasting. The human components of the studio are the director, producer, camera operators, engineer, floor manager, and technical director, also called the switcher.

Major network television productions, especially those in syndication, use film rather than videotape for live productions. Our example, the *Mary Tyler Moore Show*, begins a week-long process of program development with a Monday morning production meeting and ends with a Friday evening filming before a live audience. The important qualities that assure long-term success in such a venture include the ability of the cast (1) to work together as professionals, (2) to accept criticism and adjust to changes ordered by the director, (3) to remain aware of the audience—both studio and viewing—and (4) to work in the presence of the electronic components of the production process.

Instructional television programs are becoming increasingly commonplace in school systems and corporations everywhere. The production process used in the development of an ITV program is much more refined and exacting than that for commercial programming. Whatever type of televised program is being produced, its success will depend on the cooperative efforts of many talented people working together as a unified team.

opportunities for further learning

GORDON, GEORGE N., *Classroom Television.* New York: Hastings House, 1970.

KUHNS, WILLIAM, *Exploring Television.* Chicago, Ill.: Loyola University Press, 1971.

ORINGEL, ROBERT S., *Audio Control Handbook for Radio and Television Broadcasting,* 4th. Ed. New York: Hastings House Publishers, 1972.

STASHEFF, EDWARD, AND RUDY BRETZ, *The Television Program: Its Direction and Production,* 4th Ed. New York: Hill and Wang, 1968.

ZETTL, HERBERT, *Television Production Handbook,* 2nd Ed. Belmont, Calif.: Wadsworth Publishing Company, Inc., 1970

the concept
of the
mass audience

CHAPTER THIRTEEN

We have already learned how advanced technology makes it possible to reach millions of people through a single medium with a single message. Thanks to the era of electronic journalism, audiences can be simultaneously exposed to sound, motion, and color. Through the use of satellites, television programs can be beamed across continents, and audiences in America and Asia can share in Olympic games being played in Europe or South America. The purpose of this chapter and of Chapter 14 is to examine the concept of the mass audience, to gain some understanding of its component parts, and to determine how it perceives messages from the mass media.

the audience as receivers of mass communication

Early theories held that the mass audience was an unidentifiable group of people, having separate life styles, who were *individually* affected by the various mass media with which they came in contact. Reaction to mass media was thus seen as an individual rather than a collective experience. This theoretical approach to understanding the role of the media and their audience was termed the "hypodermic needle" approach.[1] Two assumptions that can easily result from such an approach are that (1) a person receives information directly from the mass media and not through an intermediary, and (2) that reaction is individual, not based on how other people might influence us.

Subsequent research in sociology and related disciplines restructured these theories, introducing the concept of various *subgroups* within the mass audience. This concept of a "mass within a mass" provided new insights into how we, as members of a mass audience, both receive information from the mass media and react to that information. For example, we can receive information directly by watching television, listening to the radio, reading a newspaper, leafing through a magazine, or some other form of direct contact with the media. On the other hand, some of our knowledge is derived from other people who have been exposed to the media and have, in turn, relayed the message to us. In a sense, these people who relay the message to us play the role of gatekeeper. And, just as the gatekeeper working in the media both expands and restricts our informational environment, so the person delivering an interpersonal communication may both expand and restrict our informational environment.

To make this concept more relevant, let's return to our example of the fertilizer executive who had just returned to the office. Along with digesting the material about the downstate flooding, he also skimmed the financial page of the newspaper. On the steps outside the office, he meets the office manager. During the course of their conversation, the executive tells the office manager about the flooding and also mentions the good news about an economic upturn. The executive suggests that the office manager consider purchasing agribusiness stocks as an excellent personal investment. The office manager mulls over the advice of the executive. She has heard about a number of the agribusiness stocks and feels they might make a good investment. However, until now, she has never been influenced to the point of buying. Her conversation with the executive has changed all that. She values his advice. He has made many successful investments in the stock market. She also knows that he reads a large number of financial magazines, the financial page of the local newspaper, and specialized economic publications that offer tips on potential investments. Based on the executive's advice she decides to purchase the agribusiness stocks.

Opinion Leaders and the Two-Step Flow

The above example has illustrated two important concepts in under-standing the mass audience—the *two-step flow* and *opinion leaders.* First, let's examine the two-step flow. This theory was posited by three researchers, Paul Lazarsfeld, Bernard Berelson, and Hazel Gaudet, who studied the 1940 U. S. presidential campaign.[2] In the process of interviewing people about the election, they found that much of the voters' information received about the campaign came from other people. This concept has been expanded upon since that time, but the primary hypothesis remains essentially the same— much of the information disseminated by mass media comes to the individual's attention second hand from people who relay their in-terpretation of it. The case of the executive reading the financial news in the newspaper and then suggesting that the office manager buy stock was an example of the two-step flow.

In addition, the executive *influenced* the office manager's opinion on the stocks—he was an opinion leader. This concept, which also evolved from the research of Lazarsfeld, Berelson, and Gaudet,[3] hy-pothesizes that relayers of information from mass media can also in-fluence the attitudes and/or decisions of the receivers. Since the pioneering research on both concepts was completed almost three decades ago, the theories have undergone significant testing. To re-view the results of all of this research would be impossible here and is not the purpose of this text. However, a look at some of the interpersonal relationships that exist when we receive information and are influenced by the media and/or other people can give us more insight into this theoretical framework.

We are all acquainted with someone we respect for his or her opinions on world affairs. This other person is usually very much at-tuned to the mass media and may read more than one newspaper per day, some news magazines, and also listen to a number of radio and television news presentations. We may thus tend to rely on this person's judgments about world affairs. Type of medium may also determine how and with what influence an opinion leader func-tions. For example, some opinion leaders are attuned to more spe-cialized media which give them an authoritative stance on specific subjects. You, as students, are in class to learn about mass commu-nication. You rely on your instructor to provide you with recent and authoritative information. Your instructor, because of his or her in-terest in mass communication, most likely reads scholarly journals dealing with the subject, journalism reviews, and radio-television columns in the local newspaper, and probably watches television programs dealing with issues surrounding mass media in society. Because your instructor is so attuned to the mass media, especially when it concerns his or her area of expertise, you rely on this person as an opinion leader.

Now imagine for a moment that you cut class and you miss a lecture in which the instructor relates new research findings that he or she read about in a scholarly journal. You know you probably will be penalized when it comes time for an examination, so you borrow another student's class notes. When you choose the student, you pick someone you feel took good notes and could relay to you an accurate interpretation of the instructor's remarks. You were again seeking someone who, for you, would be an opinion leader. Notice that more than one person was involved in relaying information to you from the mass media—in this case, the scholarly journal. Both the instructor and your fellow student became opinion leaders. Thus, *although this process is still referred to as the two-step flow, it may involve more than just one relay person.*

In addition to the indirect communication we receive via the two-step flow, we may turn directly to the media either to receive more information, to reinforce an opinion presented to us by an opinion leader, or to form our own opinions. For instance, assume that the information about new research published in the scholarly journal seems strange to you. You feel that despite the authoritative posture of both your teacher and your friend, you just can't accept it as valid. Instead, you decide to refer to the journal and read the article yourself. In this case, you use media as a *check and reinforcement* for the information you received from the opinion leader. What actually occurred was an interrelationship between the media and the opinion leader, an interrelationship which ultimately determined how you were informed and influenced by media content.

First Exposure and Media Credibility

Certain persuasion theory research suggests that whatever information we receive first may have a greater tendency to influence us than subsequent information. This is especially true if we perceive this *first exposure* source as credible. Thus, if you first see a politician on television and are positively influenced by this individual, then you might be hard to convince otherwise. Similarly, if a respected friend is the first to tell you that a politician is corrupt, chances are that you may be impervious to any information you may receive later from other sources.

The *credibility* of the medium itself also influences how we perceive messages. For instance, if your first exposure to a politician is on a TV newscast and television is a particularly credible medium for you, you may react positively toward that individual. Perhaps your community puts a high value on television as a source of news, and the newscast features a commentator you respect. Over time this commentator has brought you accurate and up-to-date news. All these things put together may cement your favorable impression of the politician which someone else cannot change. In this particular situation, the mass media had the edge on interpersonal communication as an opinion leader.

Ego Involvement

Your reactions are also influenced by how *ego-involved* you are with the issues to which you're exposed. In other words, whether you were influenced at all either by the media or the opinion leader would have depended on how closely you were involved with the issue. Let's look at this concept in more detail because research has shown that it affects our reaction to media messages of all types.[4]

The author had an opportunity to participate in a three-day meeting with the top executives of a well-known oil company. During the course of discussions with representatives of management and their public relations personnel, the subject of corporate image came up. The oil company was very much concerned about its image in light of high gasoline prices and the energy crisis. One official expressed disillusionment about any real possibility of molding public opinion, since one attempt by the company to do so had failed. He stated that the company had "tried to warn the consumers about these gas shortages three years ago, but it didn't have any effect." Management had, in fact, run a series of ads warning of possible gasoline shortages and the need to conserve natural resources. The problem was, however, that at the time the ads ran, the public wasn't ego-involved in the issue. Gasoline was about 30c per gallon, there was no shortage, and people were oblivious to such things as conserving gasoline, buying smaller cars, forming car pools, or any of the other activities and issues that evolved from the energy crisis. In fact, there is little evidence to assume that the public was even aware of these ads.

Realizing that its campaign was fruitless, the company eventually cancelled its advertising. Then, the oil embargo rudely awakened the nation to its energy problems. Suddenly the public became *very* ego-involved with the issue, but it was too late. The image of the oil company had plummeted to a new low. There was a scramble to see what could be done to improve the corporate image.

Along with other oil companies, this corporation hired a large and prestigious public relations firm to conduct a corporate image study which revealed some serious problems. When one of America's best known advertising agencies was approached to try to help the firm out of its image doldrums, the ad agency said that the company's image had been irreparably damaged. Obviously, the oil company wasn't totally at fault, yet its warnings to the public were ill timed.

There is another side to the oil company's problem that directly applies to our discussion, namely the role of mass media in forming the corporate image. For, what contributed to the poor image of the oil company was the fact that during the first months of the gas shortage and high gasoline prices, the oil companies were enjoying tremendous profits. The average motorist just couldn't understand why, when there was a shortage and the oil companies weren't selling as much gasoline, the companies could be making such a big profit, unless it was the extra money the consumer had to pay for gas at the pump. To counteract this surmise, the oil company shifted its emphasis away from gasoline and oil products all together and instead developed a series of advertisements focusing on the fine attributes of its employees. The advertisements stressed how concerned those employees were about the welfare of their communities and fellow citizens and how they participated in a number of local charities and civic volunteer groups. Although this effort didn't lessen the burden of high gasoline prices, it did attempt to convince the public that the oil company wasn't impersonal, uncaring, and greedy. Thus the company turned to its advantage the fact that gasoline was a highly ego-involved issue and began to develop a corporate image that was the complete antithesis of a profit-hungry bureaucracy.

Mass media play a tremendously important role in creating ego-involved issues because of their power to disseminate information rapidly and to large segments of the population. When the gas shortage occurred, the media created an ego-involved issue almost overnight by reporting the stark contrast between energy shortage and oil company profits. In addition, the mass media became in effect the sole source of information on this issue for the public. The only opinion leader to successfully challenge our views about oil company profits might have been a close friend or relative in the oil business. This person probably would have had access to information from personal experience and/or exposure to specialized publications which may have revealed little known aspects of the energy shortage.

spheres of influence

Now that we are familiar with the concept of opinion leaders, we should investigate how they operate within different *spheres of influence*. It is only in this *social context of the mass audience* that we can observe the true effects of media on society.

First, let's examine a typical sphere of influence—you and your closest friends at school. Let's imagine that you have a group of about five fellow students with whom you spend considerable time. One afternoon, you all enter into a discussion about the upcoming school elections. You personally don't know for whom to vote. One member of the group, we'll call him Pete, has regularly read the school newspaper in detail. He is well versed on all of the candidates and proceeds to explain why he will vote in a certain way. Your group decides Pete is right, and you tacitly agree to follow his example. Obviously Pete is an opinion leader in the sphere of influence covering school politics. He is also the one who is most attuned to the mass media, in this case the school newspaper. The information he read was communicated to the rest of the group through the process of the two-step flow.

Now let's assume that after the discussion about the school election, your group decides it wants to go see a movie. Neither you nor your friends have seen any of the movies playing at local theaters. However, one member of your group is an avid movie fan. Her name is Carol, and she devotedly reads every film review she can. She subscribes to magazines dealing with film, reads the arts section of the local newspapers, and is the first to tune to a television or radio talk show in which a motion picture producer or director is a guest. You and your friends naturally turn to Carol for advice on which movie to see. She recommends a science fiction thriller and tells your group all about the great reviews it has received. She also says she has seen the producer interviewed many times, and based on what she knows, he is a veritable genius. You and your friends decide to heed Carol's advice and see the science fiction thriller. Here, again, an opinion leader is relied upon in the decision-making process. And again the opinion leader is more attuned to the mass media than other people—in this case to film magazines, reviews, and radio and television interviews.

Overlap between spheres of influence and opinion leaders is common. For instance, perhaps your friend Pete, along with being well versed in school politics, also took a keen interest in film, and Pete's opinion was just as respected as Carol's. Then Pete would serve two spheres of influence.

audience demographics

With a mass audience, it is often difficult to locate certain segments of the population to which specific mass media messages are to be directed. For example, a successful advertising campaign for a Rolls Royce must first locate an audience whose income level is high enough to afford it. As a result, media planners must rely on demographics as a means of categorizing the population. *Demographic characteristics are the basic statistical data concerning such things as age, sex, education level, income, and ethnic background.* They are used more often than any other method to pinpoint a certain mass audience and thus to determine such things as how much an advertiser will be charged for airing a commercial during a particular television program at a specified time. Demographics can be applied to local media that serve a given geographic area as well as to national media. For instance, your local radio station reaches a specific portion of the total community listeners, which is again identifiable as a group because of its demographic characteristics. If you were to walk into the manager's office at the local station and ask him what the characteristics of his station's audience are, he might reply, "We reach the upper-income, middle-aged male." Further investigation might reveal that his station programs a lot of play-by-play sports which attract this type of audience. Similarly, if you were to walk into the office of a network executive and ask what type of audience her network prime-time programming reaches on Wednesday nights, she might say, "the middle-income individual whose median age is thirty-four." In each case, both media executives identified their audience based on demographic characteristics.

Now for the purpose of comparison, let's examine what would take place if you walked into the office of a media manager who was responsible for publishing a magazine called *Skiers, Ltd.* The publisher would certainly be able to tell you the demographic characteristics of her audience. However, this would not be the only important quality of the audience. Of equal importance would be their interest in skiing. They would be joined, not so much because of their demographic characteristics, but because they liked to ski. Advertisers, although wanting to know the average income of the audience, would be mainly interested in them because of this skiing interest. It would be an ideal place to advertise ski apparel, ski equipment, and ski resorts. On the other hand, if an advertiser wanted to reach an audience predominantly in their mid-twenties all hobbies or other interests aside, he would want to find another mass medium that would accurately reflect this demographic feature. Perhaps network television or radio might be a much better medium in this instance. We'll learn more about the process of reaching specific audiences, called *target audiences,* in the next chapter.

In perspective, as a result of certain demographic characteristics, media specialists and researchers have become very proficient in determining media habits of the mass audience. Although new research techniques are being developed to supplement audience demographics, the older method still remains the foundation for categorizing the mass audience.

audience psychographics

One of the new research frontiers that scrutinizes the mass audience is called psychographics. It attempts to define and distinguish a variety of psychological characteristics of the mass audience, traits that are more complex, more difficult to pinpoint, yet in some ways more predictable of media attention habits than demographics. Let's look at some of these characteristics and see how they apply to our study of mass communication.

Preference Theory

Preference theory as applied to the mass television audience predicts viewer behavior based on specific programming concepts. An Ohio State University professor, Robert Monaghan, joined by three other researchers, Joseph T. Plummer of Leo Burnett, U. S. A., and university professors, David L. Rarick and Dwight A. Williams, developed four basic categories to express viewer preference.[5] These four basic preference elements, *reality, value, complexity,* and *seriousness,* can be further broken down into subelements. Theoretically, a program can contain any combination of the four basic preferences. Combining these elements to correspond to certain program orientations, researchers identified two hypothetical types of viewers: (1) those who prefer programs high on nostalgic human interest, "realistic science," and "light humor and music"; and (2) those who prefer "reality-oriented adventure programs having dramatic conflict between good and evil."

The concept of preference theory and its application to and integration with other research methodologies is, of course, preliminary and should be regarded as just one framework for analyzing the mass audience. To help understand the concept, think of your own preferences and ask yourself if the programs you watch fit into the basic categories discussed here. Also ask yourself if you are typical of either group of viewers discussed above. Stop and speculate for a moment. If your assignment were to plan the fall schedule of a major television network, what types of programs based on the above categories of viewer preferences would you choose?

Program Clusters

Closely related to preference theory is the theory that as members of a mass audience, we are attuned to certain program groups or clusters.[6] Much of this research and that on life style analysis, which appears later in the chapter, has been done at Leo Burnett, U. S. A. by Dr. Joseph Plummer. Although the cluster concept may occasionally overlap with program types postulated by preference theory, it actually admits of many more types of programs, and these clusters actually help to mold viewer preferences. As an illustration, assume that you are a fan of televised professional football games. You might then become a fan of televised college football games, and these enjoyable experiences may persuade you to tune in other sports programs. If your preference is for situation comedies and you regularly watch the *Mary Tyler Moore Show*, you may eventually become a devotee of *Rhoda* or the *Bob Newhart Show*. How can such information be interpreted into usable data for practical application? Stop for a moment and examine your viewing habits. Do you find that you are watching certain television programs which are very similar in content? Do you make a concerted effort to arrange your schedule so you can watch certain television programs? If your answers are "yes," then you may have certain group preferences for media attention. This theory can apply to print media as well, for if you enjoy reading a certain type of magazine, you may find yourself purchasing additional similar magazines.

Attitudes and Opinions

We have already learned that attitudes and opinions are closely related. They become important qualities for media planners and fall into the realm of psychographics. They come into play when the traditional demographic characteristics are not sufficient to plan media content. For instance, age and income may very well help to determine attitudes about welfare payments. However, if these were the only characteristics you took into consideration when planning a media persuasion campaign to revise the welfare system, you would have little success. Many other characteristics of the mass audience help determine attitudes toward welfare, and it becomes imperative for the media planner to look directly at those attitudes, disregarding, for the moment, demographic characteristics.

After sampling audience attitudes, you may discover that unfavorable attitudes about the current welfare system are held by middle-income people. Based on psychographic information about these individuals, you plan your media campaign to reach them. Had you just assumed that the attitudes of all income groups were alike, your media campaign would have been needlessly costly. Moreover, had you merely assumed that certain attitudes about welfare followed directly from membership in specific age and income groups instead of dutifully investigating these attitudes, your media campaign would have failed miserably. Based on the information you have received, you may also discover that you'll need to use different media to reach these middle-income individuals. Perhaps they watch more television than other income groups or read certain consumer magazines. Your media campaign will then have the greatest chances for success if advertisements are placed in these media.

life style analysis

Life style analysis assumes that our lives fall into certain patterns, termed life styles, and these life styles are closely related to the type of television programming to which we may be attracted.[7] For example, you, as a college student, may have a very disciplined life style. You may arise every morning at seven, eat breakfast by eight, and attend your first class at nine. Between ten and noon, you study in the library. The afternoon and evening hours of your day are just as disciplined and organized as your morning hours. Other characteristics of your life style may be reflected in your attitudes toward, for example, your clothes. Perhaps you dress conservatively, wearing a dark grey or blue suit for "dress-up dinners." The car you drive is also an inconspicuous economy model. In accordance with this life style, you have certain preferences for specific media and media content. For example, typical television programs you watch might be the evening news, interviews with political figures, or documentaries. You might also subscribe to several news magazines, and if you read the newspaper daily, you will almost always turn to the pages which carry national and international news as opposed to sports. Your movie preferences probably lean toward biographical films about famous men and women in real life situations.

On the other hand, your personality may be just the opposite of our conservative acquaintance. You lead a carefree life style, enjoy stylish clothes, would rather read the comics than the front page, and prefer a motion picture filled with romance and fantasy. You couldn't care less about news magazines but would prefer to leaf casually through your favorite fashion magazine or enjoy a good fiction novel. Obviously, both your life style and the type and content of media you are exposed to differ greatly from the preferences of our friend who likes dark blue suits. Of course, the two examples mentioned here are extremes. Perhaps you fall somewhere in between. Wherever you find yourself, life style analysis suggests that your life style is a possible predictor of your media preferences.

selective exposure

Do we tend to tune in to media messages when we believe the messages will present a view that supports our preconceived attitudes? Asked another way, do we *selectively expose* ourselves to media messages that we perceive as supporting our beliefs about something and thus *avoid* communication that will *conflict* with our preconceived ideas? Answers to these questions center around the concept of "selective exposure"—a concept that is not clearly defined in research literature. Theoretical basis for the concept of selective exposure has been reviewed by Sears and Freedman, who conclude that the research on the concept is not unequivocal.[8] Although we may not randomly expose ourselves to media content, the reasons for this non-random exposure may not wholly lie in our seeking out consistent information with our own attitudes. In some cases, we may actually expose ourselves to information *because* we disagree with this information and want to scrutinize it more closely.

Consider a fund raising event that took place in South Dakota. Senator Charles Percy appeared on television as the featured speaker at this Republican dinner in the eastern part of the state. His speech was covered by the local television station. A research study by the author investigated the viewing habits of one small community served by the television station. Results of the research showed that, for all practical purposes, the great majority of the viewers were Republicans. We might conclude that these Republicans were already favorably disposed to Senator Percy and therefore tuned in to watch his speech. Thus, we might claim that they selectively exposed themselves to this communication because they felt Percy's remarks would be consistent with their own political beliefs. On the other hand, we might look deeper into the psychological basis of viewer habits and ask why did some Democrats view the speech. Did they have a desire to tune in deliberately to media content which was perceived as being inconsistent with their own ideas so that they might subject this to close scrutiny? Although it could be argued that they also selectively exposed themselves to the media, they did so for different reasons than the Republicans did. In considering the fact that we may very well selectively expose ourselves to varying types of media content based on predisposed attitudes, the basis and type of these predispositions are important in considering the concept of selective exposure. Stop and consider your own media attention habits. Do you selectively expose yourself to certain types of media messages? Why?

diffusion of innovations

As consumers of mass communication, we are constantly exposed to material that both informs and persuades: information about new discoveries in technology, products designed to make our life easier, inventions, and other innovative procedures. The role played by mass communication in convincing us of the worthiness and benefits of various innovations has been under research and investigation for some time.[9] There are *no concise formulas* to express the role of mass communication in convincing us to acquire these products, because each of us is unique, as is each product and each individual situation. But some general trends are discernible and can aid in our understanding of this process.

Steps to Acquiring Innovations

To understand the process, imagine you are considering purchasing a new portable electric typewriter. Your old manual typewriter just doesn't work well anymore and you *need* a new one. While reading a magazine, you happen to stumble across an ad for such a typewriter, and the ad catches your eye. The new electric portable has a cartridge ribbon system, which means you don't have to change ribbons, and also has a separate cartridge from which to make erasures. There are keys for Greek letters, an automatic carriage return, and many other features. You glance at all the features the ad presents and then flip to another article in the magazine. The next day you happen to be watching television, and a commercial appears which shows the typewriter you first became *aware* of while reading the magazine. Now you are really *interested*. There it is in living color with all of its new features. You then decide to discuss the machine with some of your friends who also have similar portable electric typewriters. While you're discussing it, you're constantly *evaluating* its features. Next, you make a trip to the office supply store and investigate the typewriter further. There you encounter the sales clerk who explains the features to you and asks you if you would like to borrow the typewriter on a *trial* basis until you make up your mind. You think that idea is great, bring the typewriter back to your room, and begin using it in your school work. Finally, after about two weeks of trying it out, you decide you like the typewriter and *acquire* it. Of course you could have decided to reject the typewriter in favor of a different model.

The process which led up to your decision to buy the typewriter involved several steps. First, you had a *need* to purchase the typewriter. Your old typewriter just wasn't satisfactory. Second, you be-

came *aware* of the new typewriter. Your accidental encounter with it in the magazine alerted you to its many features. Your second exposure to the typewriter, this time on the television commercial, created an *interest* sufficient to the point of discussing it with your fellow students. These discussions helped you *evaluate* the typewriter in comparison to your old one and others on the market. Then you made the decision to go one step further. You made arrangements at the office supply store to take the typewriter on a *trial* basis. After the trial period, you then decided to *acquire* the typewriter.

Although our example used a particular sequencing in the step-by-step process, this is not the only arrangement possible. For instance, you might evaluate the typewriter only after you have had it on a trial basis. You might acquire the typewriter after a long trial and evaluation process, then a month later reject it and go back to using your old one. Also, although the example here concerned typewriters, keep in mind that a similar step-by-step process takes place when we decide to acquire any new product. Perhaps it's a farmer in Southeast Asia learning of a new fertilizer, a teenager reacting to a new record, or a business person deciding to adopt a new accounting procedure. Whatever the case, there are certain steps to the acceptance of a new innovation, and mass communication is part of the process.

Persuasion Strategy

The media themselves often capitalize on the steps a potential buyer goes through in acquiring a new product. For instance, you may have seen a television commercial that compared features of the new typewriter model with those of older manual typewriters. That same television commercial may have "role played" the other steps in the acquisition process. Perhaps it began with a setting much like your room at school. There, seated around the desk, were three students discussing the merits of the new typewriter. The conversation went like this:

First Student: Gee, I have always thought about buying the new cartridge typewriter. I really need one for my school work. (need, awareness, and interest)

Second Student: I did and it's terrific. I compared all of its features with those of others on the market and decided it was the best. (evaluation)

Third Student: I'm using one now on a trial basis and plan to buy it. (trial)

Fourth Student: Well, in that case, it sounds like a great deal. I'll go to the local office supply store and buy one. (acquire)

This role playing technique enabled the television commercial to involve the viewer in a way that simulates his own behavior. Whatever the method, however, in our mass media society, we are accustomed to receiving information about innovation. We are constantly informed, via mass communication, of scores of new products and inventions that purport to make our lives easier. We tend to trust science and technology to produce goods and services that will benefit us and usually exhibit minimal resistance to trying them. In some cases, mass media have even used new technology as a sales pitch. Just think of all the products that appeared after the first manned space expeditions. The themes, "used by the astronauts," "a new discovery from the Apollo missions" or "developed by the space program" abounded.

Although Americans may react positively to these innovations, such is not the case in other areas of the world, especially in underdeveloped countries. Here it is not only cultural resistance to new innovations that is operative, but also a tendency to resist certain types of media. A tribal chief in Liberia may not be persuaded to try a new farming method simply because he sees its apparent benefits on television. Here again, the role of the two-step flow and the opinion leader come into play. Thus before an innovation is accepted, it may sometimes be necessary to publicize it both through interpersonal communication and the media at each step along the way.

researching the mass audience

What we know about the characteristics of the mass audience and its relationship with mass media is the result of about four decades of research, a short span of time when we consider how long, for example, the print media have been with us. There is still much to learn about the mass audience and many starting points for new research. For instance, in Chapter 1 we learned that there were three basic types of communication — intrapersonal, interpersonal, and mass communication. Research in each of these three areas has proceeded from a different theoretical base. In intrapersonal communication, highly controlled laboratory experiments have employed such apparatus as electrodes and galvanic skin response to measure brain waves and other electrochemical impulses in the body. Interpersonal communication research has been mostly under closely controlled laboratory conditions, frequently in the college class-room. In many cases, this research has consisted of students receiving some type of message and then being tested for attitude change. Mass communication research, on the other hand, has mostly consisted of field or survey research, in which a sample population responds either to a questionnaire or a home interview.

When students of communication have tried to structure a theoretical base for all types of communication from these three very different types of data, results have been less than ideal. Psychologist Carl Hovland, in discussing the subject of attitude change, summarized the differences in results obtained through research using experimental and survey methodologies.[10] Among these differences were such things as the length of the message used to test attitude change, the influence of experimenters, the difference in interpersonal reaction, and the elapsed time after exposure to the message. These differences, among others, reflect some of the difficulties in researching the mass audience.

Imagine you are a researcher hired to test viewers' reactions to a new television commercial for a certain brand of soap. You arrange for a group of people not currently using that brand of soap to gather in a classroom, sit quietly, and watch the commercial. You then elicit their opinions about new soap. Their answers suggest they have changed their opinion about their current brand of soap and will try the new one. You are excited; your commercial works. But does it? You select a community in your area, purchase time on a local television station, and wait for sales to go up. But they don't. What happened?

To answer the question, review some of the carefully controlled conditions of your "laboratory." Recall first that your group watched the entire commercial from start to finish. But what happened outside the laboratory? Many people only saw part of the commercial. They may have headed for the refrigerator at the very instant the commercial appeared. This limited exposure naturally affected their reaction to the commercial. Second, when your group entered the classroom setting, they perceived your wishes and reacted accordingly. This influence was not present in the home environment. Third, you also asked your group to sit quietly. They weren't permitted to talk to each other. Yet when viewers saw the commercial in their home environment, the situation was entirely different. They could interact freely, and their reactions may have been exactly opposite to those expressed in the classroom. Perhaps one member of the family told the rest that the brand of soap featured in the commercial wasn't any good, and the rest of the family believed her. When you showed the commercial in the classroom, you tested for attitude change immediately after the airing. But after waiting a few weeks to compile the results of your mass communication campaign, you discovered what you couldn't find out from the interpersonal, classroom setting—that after a few weeks, people's preferences for soap returned to what they had been before the commercial.

Of course, there are many other factors that come into play, all making the results of your research misleading. These four conditions are just some of the ones that make researching the mass audience a difficult process. Although you wanted to obtain as truthful and as valid results from your research as possible, moving research out of the laboratory made it possible for many unknown variables to interfere with the results.

the functional use of media

For the most part, our discussion of the mass communication audience has been in the context of how the media influences the audience or how the mass audience reacts to the media content. Our study has been primarily one-sided, and we have so far failed to consider the interactive qualities of our media-audience relationship. We have been asking the question, "What do the media do *to* people?" instead of "What do people do *with* media?" This same myopic approach was noted by well-known media researcher and scholar Elihu Katz, who stressed that much media research proceeded from a "bookkeeping" outlook indicative of the first question, rather than to a "functional" or "uses and gratification" approach, which would be indicative of the second question.[11] Let's look at this "functional" concept in more detail so that we can gain an awareness of how the mass audience interrelates with the mass media.

Film: Highbrow, Middlebrow, and Lowbrow Audiences

One of the ways we can study this concept is through film audiences. The motion picture has become an established medium of mass communication. Over the past fifty years, it has touched on virtually every segment of society, has dealt with every subject, and has reached every audience. And yet for these audiences, it has had many different meanings and has performed many different functions.

Louis M. Savary and J. Paul Carrico, writing about motion pictures and their audiences, divide the film audience into three distinct groups—*highbrows, middlebrows,* and *lowbrows.*[12] For each audience, film performs a different function and has a different meaning. For example, the highbrows look at the medium as an artistic expression and derive intellectual satisfaction from a well executed film. They may attend a movie more than once, not necessarily because they like the plot or the actors, but because they want to study the work of a famous director or review the camera techniques. For the lowbrow audience, the experience is entirely different; perhaps it's an excuse to get out or an escape from life's daily routine. Between these two groups are the middlebrows, somewhat knowledgeable in what a good motion picture consists of and able at least to differentiate between a really good and a really bad film.

Savary and Carrico typify the current audience for films as belonging to none of the three types previously mentioned. Still predominantly in their late teen and young adult years, they are more sophisticated than past generations. Having taken courses in film, they have a much deeper understanding of the medium and its social implications. Savary and Carrico have labelled this knowledgeable generation the "postbrow" or "no-brow" audience.

Television Soap Opera: Compensation, Fulfillment, and Advice

The film audience is, of course, not the only audience which can be approached in a functional manner. For example, our society is all witness to the loyalty and involvement that the midday television audience has with soap operas. What functional relationship does this audience have with this type of program? If the role of the audience for similar radio programming is an indication, we can expect at least three bases for this functional relationship—"compensation through identification; vicarious wish fulfillment; and sources of advice for appropriate role playing."[13]

Consider the area of *compensation through identification.* As members of society, we assume certain roles and must make decisions based on these roles. Naturally, we seek to receive approval or recognition for what we do. Direct approval comes from someone telling us we are doing the right thing. Indirect approval comes from our knowledge or assumption that others are doing the same things we are. The soap opera thus provides a form of indirect approval. The person watching sees other people experiencing the same relationships, trials, and tribulations that he or she experiences. It may be meeting a new neighbor, having a love affair, splurging for a new coat, or whatever. The important thing is that there are, even though only portrayed on the television screen, people living similar lives and having experiences similar to one's own.

The person who views soap opera as a means of *wish fulfillment* is in a different functional relationship to the medium from the first viewer. This individual is only wishing that those things taking place on the screen were happening to her or him, not actually experiencing them. In this situation, the audience uses the program as a fantasy to imagine what the lives of other people are like. Perhaps their environment is unpleasant, drab, or routine, and they have neither the ability nor the real desire to change their life style. Yet simply by exposing themselves to the soap opera, these viewers participate in a fanciful interlude that serves its purpose for them.

Anyone who has ever watched any soap opera will notice the development of a series of plots and subplots that represent human relations problems to be solved, for example, an in-law spending too much time at her married child's home, a member of the family suffering from alcoholism, or a neighbor with marital problems. The viewer is faced with the question of how to deal with these situations. The soap opera provides the answers. This type of viewer is seeking *advice* on what role he or she should play in his or her own life when faced with similar situations.

The Agenda-Setting Function

With the advent of sophisticated means of measuring the relationship between mass media and media audience has come the development of preliminary theoretical concepts, which posit that media not only inform us but they influence us about what is important to be informed about.[14] In other words the media create an *agenda* for our thoughts and influence us as to what's important. For example, if the media in a local community provide considerable coverage of a local bond issue the residents of the community may very well perceive the bond issue as being of great importance to the community, even if it isn't. The media coverage of issues in a political campaign may help us to perceive certain issues as being more important than others and consequently influence our decisions about candidates based on how they address themselves to these issues. Major research on the agenda-setting function of the mass media is now being conducted at a number of universities. There are some problems associated with this research. One of the most troublesome is the monitoring of all media that affect an individual and then determining how they actually do affect the person. For instance, a major market may have upwards of fifty different media channels bombarding a population. Keeping track of all of these media messages is an awesome task. By first determining which media are important to certain population groups and then concentrating on these media, the control of intervening variables has permitted at least a preliminary theoretical base for the agenda-setting function.

The Broad Context of Functional Use

The uses and gratification, or functional, relationships described here are only a few of the many ways a person attuned to the various mass media can interact with them. It is, however, in the context of the mass audience that the importance of these functional relationships lie and on this level that they will affect societal development. For instance, if you personally need a new dress and can't find one you like in the store, you may order one from a catalogue. The catalogue, a medium directed to a specialized audience, had a very identifiable use—to order merchandise—and each individual purchaser's decision will affect only that person. On the other hand, the content of television and film affects millions. Yet we have seen that the process of researching the mass audience is a difficult one. When we do begin to understand more about our functional relationship to the mass media, we will undoubtedly have a far greater insight into how we use media, instead of how media use us.

This functional emphasis for future research is important. Some of the criticism of media has been that media give us exactly what we want to consume, and as we consume, media managers and planners provide us with more of the same. If we are, in the broader sense of an entire society, interrelating with media in a functional sense, then we need to know more about this relationship. We need to know such things as how media affect our political system, how our attitudes and values are formed, and what role media play in this formation. Answers to these questions will evolve from more than just a "bookkeeping" approach to mass media research. Perhaps as students of mass communication, you can help find these answers.

summary

Although technology permits us to reach a mass audience of millions of people simultaneously, mass communication must also be concerned with reaching many specialized audiences. People receive and are influenced by messages conveyed directly by mass media or indirectly through interpersonal communication. When information from the mass media is disseminated via face-to-face communication, the process is known as the two-step flow. Individuals who are attuned to mass media and who pass information to other people, influencing their opinions in the process, are known as opinion leaders. How we react to messages disseminated via mass media may be determined by how ego-involved we are with the issues with which the messages deal.

Our spheres of influence will also help to determine how we react to messages from mass media. Typical spheres of influence include our family, friends, and co-workers. Opinion leaders can have an influence in more than one sphere of influence.

Demographics and psychographics are two important tools that media planners use to analyze the mass audience and to make decisions about the content of media. Demographic characteristics include such things as age, sex, income, and education of the mass audience. Psychographics attempts to break down the mass audience in terms of such traits as media preferences, audience perception of media content, and public attitudes and opinions. Our life styles are another important determinant of the media content to which we will be exposed. A study of this subject has revealed that we not only selectively expose ourselves to media content in accordance with acquired preferences, but also that media content itself helps to develop these preferences.

Mass media are also instrumental in the diffusion of new innovations. Although varying in emphasis and order there are primarily six steps involved in this process—need, awareness, interest, evaluation, trial, and acquisition or rejection. This same six-step process is also used as a basis for media persuasion strategies.

Many variables can become involved in researching the mass audience. As a result, it has made it difficult to develop a theoretical base for studying the audiences of mass communication and providing a link with research in intrapersonal and interpersonal communication. This has been especially true in research on the functional uses of media. As a student of mass communication, perhaps you can help, through research, to make this theoretical base stronger.

opportunities for further learning

CHANEY, DAVID, *Processes of Mass Communication*. London: The Macmillan Press Ltd., 1972.

LIEBERT, ROBERT M. et al., *The Early Window: Effects of Television on Children and Youth*. New York: Pergamon Press, 1973.

ROGERS, EVERETT M., and F. FLOYD SHOEMAKER, *Communication of Innovations: A Cross Cultural Approach*, 2nd Ed. New York: Free Press, 1971.

SCHRAMM, WILBUR, and DONALD F. ROBERTS, Eds., *The Process and Effects of Mass Communication*, 2nd Ed. Urbana, Ill.: University of Illinois Press, 1971.

SHERIF, CAROLYN W., MUZAFER SHERIF, and ROGER E. NEBERGALL, *Attitude and Attitude Change: The Social Judgment—Involvement Approach*. Philadelphia, Pa.: W. B. Saunders Company, 1965.

target audiences

CHAPTER FOURTEEN

Mass media are directed toward many specialized audiences. For example, such network television programming as professional and collegiate football games draw a higher income and more proportionately male audience than other types of programming. Afternoon soap operas are directed toward a predominantly female audience; Saturday cartoon fare is directed toward children. The purpose of this chapter is to look more closely at some of these specialized audiences, called *target audiences—any group of people who have a common bond consisting of demographic or psychographic characteristics, or a combination of both.* They could be comprised of farmers, teenagers, or people with a specific ethnic origin. We'll examine several of these audiences as well as the channels, or media, used to communicate with them. As you read Chapter 14, *keep in mind that all audiences overlap,* and the term "target audience" is used merely as a tool to define some arbitrary categories, not to exclude one audience from another.

the black audience

The civil rights movement of the 1960s focused new attention on black people. Blacks became recognized as a major force in society, one which media planners realized was not receiving the attention it deserved. Slowly but steadily, black personalities and ideas began to penetrate the media. Today, black writers have developed popular syndicated features, black journalists regularly appear on the evening news, black personalities sell products in print or broadcast advertisements just like their white counterparts, and black cartoon characters are chuckling their way to popularity. Network radio has also realized the importance of the black audience with Mutual leading the way in 1971 by forming the Mutual Black Network. This was a broadcasting first. The programming was news directed toward the black audience, with stories selected for their appeal to the black community. For stations that had been attempting unsuccessfully to reach the black community, the Mutual Black Network was a big boost. Previously a radio station might have directed its musical programming toward the black audience, but its network was still geared to the white audience. The result was schizophrenic programming which had only limited appeal. Now stations could coordinate their total message to the black audience.

Yet television and radio were not the only media to program for black audiences. The recording industry developed a major emphasis on soul music primarily for blacks, and it quickly became popular with whites. Black recording stars emerged, soul hits peaked the charts, and black recording companies and labels became profitable business ventures. As we learned in Chapter 4, films also geared for this specialized audience with black film stars and films oriented toward blacks. The black press began to flourish with newspapers and magazines directed toward black audiences. Take, for example, *Ebony* magazine. Started as a medium providing blacks with a medium to communicate black success stories, *Ebony* gives the black audience a magazine specifically directed toward contemporary achievements. Carried within its pages are articles about blacks, articles written by blacks, and advertisements which feature blacks.

Even black advertising agencies have developed to assist clients in reaching black audiences. These black ad agencies are also acutely aware of the media attention habits of blacks. For instance, blacks are light magazine readers.[1] Blacks are, however, heavily attuned to television. For example, an A. C. Nielsen study examined the television viewing habits of blacks in five major markets — Chicago; Detroit; Washington, D.C.; Philadelphia; and Cleveland. The study found that black households were more attuned to television than households generally. The study also found that television programs featuring blacks were more popular in black households than total (blacks plus other) households (Figure 14–1).

Black Culture and Product Purchase

Media began to realize that blacks had a unique culture of which most media content was not indicative. For one thing, blacks had somewhat different status symbols than whites. Kevin A. Wall, president of the New York based Black Creative Group, noted in *Advertising Age*,[2] for example, that credit is more important to blacks "and they will tend to use it more. It increases their confidence when they shop with responsible retailers." He also noted that blacks are venturing into new shopping areas, "often preferring higher status stores than whites of comparable means. . . ." The buying habits of blacks and the material goods acquired are also different from those of whites. For example, WIGO radio in Atlanta cites a Brand Rating Index study which shows that appliance purchase expectations during a twelve-month period revealed that blacks were 50 percent more apt to purchase a gas stove than whites, 31 percent more apt to purchase a console television set than whites. Especially interesting is the profile of the black housewife. This profile reveals a media audience which is not responsive to the traditional products and media appeals directed to the larger mass audience. For example, Kevin Wall notes among other traits

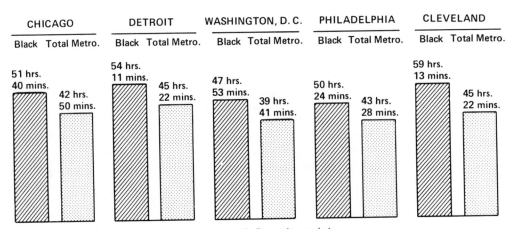

Figure 14–1 Television viewing trends among blacks in five major markets.

that the black housewife is not as interested in women's liberation as the white housewife and that she does not try to save time in the kitchen where "she puts more of herself into meals, and she expresses herself more through tastes she creates, rather than those directly out of a box."[3] This fact alone signaled a need for new focus upon the habits of the black consumer.

Revising Black Audience Data

With the greater emphasis on reaching the black audience, market research now sought to determine how blacks were consuming their new media. A study of the black press indicated that much of the market research on traditional circulation trends was invalid. Black newspapers have more readers per copy than general circulation newspapers among the general public. Thus, to try and use standard sources as a measure of circulation and a basis for charging advertising rates was not economically sound. Also, it was clear that traditional measures of sampling the reaction of the black audience to black media had to be changed. For instance, it is not valid to take a random sample of telephone numbers from a metropolitan phone book and expect to reach the black audience in the same way whites can be reached, because there may not be as many phones per household within a given area among blacks. Research also shows that blacks are not particularly responsive to direct-mail advertising and do not respond in traditional ways to gimmicks, such as the "cents-off" merchandising schemes.

There was also a need to revise demographic data, which had in the past shown a traditional black poverty class. A true black middle class was emerging to match the white middle class. Added to this was the discovery of a "motivated-achiever" group of blacks who wanted to get ahead and were responsive to motivational appeals unique to their culture. Certain brand preferences began to develop along with categories of consumer goods. For example, such things as cosmetics, clothing, housing, entertainment, home furnishing, and automobiles experienced tremendous growth in sales among blacks.[4]

Spanish-culture audiences

Along with calling attention to the black audience, the civil rights movement also propelled into public consciousness other minority audiences, among them those based on the Spanish culture. The predominant Spanish-culture audiences in America are the Mexican-Americans (Chicanos), Puerto Ricans, and Cubans. Like the black audience, the Spanish-culture audience is considered a primary target audience. These people represent a major population force in the United States, especially in the metropolitan areas of New York, Los Angeles, Miami, and the larger Texas cities, where they also have considerable economic power.

Spanish-language newspapers and magazines have been common fare for many years. However, it has been radio and television that have made the major inroads in appealing to this audience and in providing advertisers and programmers with a medium to reach and hold the attention of this previously inaccessible group. In markets where there is a large proportion of Spanish-culture inhabitants, many stations air television programs specially designed to appeal to this audience. The Spanish International Network, for example, serves television stations in major Southwest and West Coast cities. In addition, advertisers no longer neglected stations programming predominantly to the Spanish-culture audience. The interest in minorities has placed a new emphasis on these new "channels" of communication, and advertisers discovered that, like blacks, Spanish-speaking audiences had many unique cultural identities. Research into characteristics of Spanish-culture audiences found that they preferred Spanish-language programs even though they had no difficulty understanding English. It also revealed that Spanish-culture audiences were apt to develop stronger loyalties to advertised products than Anglo-American viewers and tended to be more receptive to promotional campaigns. In addition, in Spanish surnamed households, "85 percent of all respondents name a Spanish program as their favorite television show."[5]

Spanish Advertising

Advertisers have begun to apply what sociologists have known for a long time, that people have pride in their cultural identity. A bulletin displaying nothing but the product and its brand name might ordinarily be effective, but to convince and motivate Spanish-speaking consumers, a message written in Spanish increases the attention and identity with the advertisement. As a result, many outdoor bulletins for brand name products in Spanish neighborhoods carry the accompanying message in Spanish. The same is true of advertisements in other media (Figure 14–2).

Carrascolendas

Attention to the Spanish-culture audiences also surfaced in the area of educational television programming. Realizing that there were

Figure 14-2 Spanish language advertising reaches a target audience while retaining cultural heritage. (OMAR.)

some unique educational problems associated with teaching Mexican-American children, a major effort was made to initiate bilingual education through instructional television. Researchers at the University of Texas developed a program called *Carrascolendas* that achieved national attention and became a major syndicated award-winning ITV program on public broadcasting stations throughout the United States. Research showed the program to be an effective teaching aid and focused new attention upon the use of educational television in teaching minorities.

The Spanish-culture and black audiences are only two minority audiences receiving special attention by mass media. In San Francisco, for instance, various media gear part of their programming toward the city's large oriental population. In fact, radio stations which announce in Chinese and the major Chinese-language newspapers comprise a very strong political and economic force among these groups. In areas of the Southwest and upper Midwest, the American Indian audience is drawing the attention of the media. In communities surrounding Indian reservations, for example, certain radio stations program special music and news for this audience.

the college student audience

It's a big moment. You're a college freshman, arriving on campus to look over the buildings and the people who will be a major part of your life. In a way, you cease being a private citizen and enter a new world. You will have new friends, new surroundings, new opportunities, and new experiences. Along with all of these changes, you will also have a completely different association with mass media than you had at home. Let's look at some of the ways mass media will affect your life in college environment.

Media Isolation

To start with, you will be far more isolated from events occurring outside the college community than you were at home. When you lived with your parents, more than likely your media habits were very much like theirs. This probably included watching the regular evening television news programs, reading or at least glancing at your hometown newspaper, and reading some of the magazines to which your family subscribed. As a college student, however, you will probably not be exposed to national media to anywhere near the degree you were in the past. Because of group living arrangements and different life styles, you will not necessarily be a regular viewer of the evening television newscast. You may not even read a daily newspaper unless it happens to be assigned in class. Unless your campus is located in a major metropolitan area where you can still receive your hometown radio station, you will most likely attune yourself to other radio stations. In general, radio will predominate over television as a mass medium in your life, and music will be its primary appeal.

The news you wish to hear will concentrate on campus activities unless, of course, there is a major international development, and even that may pass unnoticed.[6] A research study on news diffusion at a major midwestern university found that even after twenty-four hours had passed an attempt on the life of a candidate for the United States presidency went unnoticed by almost fifteen percent of the students. When the head of the Federal Bureau of Investigation died, almost twenty percent of the student body didn't know of his death twenty-four hours later, and only a few percent became aware of it in the ensuing two days of the survey. Similar results were discovered for such events as the death of a leading international ruler and a major emergency during the manned space flights. What it all points to is the isolation from national and international news that occurs among the college population. Basically, access to media and the luxury of time to consume media messages have dwindled.

The Role of Campus Media

It is important to understand the role campus media will play within this environment. These media will function within the college community in much the same way as the press does in our larger society. The administration of the college will be in the same perspective as the government in Washington is to the national media. If for some reason a scandal develops in the college or university administration and is reported in the campus press, the reaction of the student body can be much the same as that evoked by a major national scandal. The campus press may become just as alarmed at the elimination of a budget for a new curriculum as the national press would be if the government eliminated the budget for the entire department of Health, Education, and Welfare. The pressure the campus press can place on the college or university administration may also be just as great as that placed on the White House or Congress by the national press. This is assuming that the campus medium is itself credible. In many colleges where campus media go unadvised and over time lose their credibility among students and faculty, then whatever is reported will either go unread or will not be taken seriously.

More than likely, you will also become a major consumer of instructional media. You may take part in classes which are primarily based on "self-paced" learning. In these classes, you will sit at a media console and operate a videotape recorder that will play an ITV program for you. If you don't feel you learned everything from the ITV program the first time you saw it, you will be able to play it back and review the material. You may also find your instructors bringing major network television programs into the classroom. A documentary produced by one of the major networks may be an excellent teaching and learning aid, and your instructor will include it as a supplement to class lectures. In addition, you may be exposed to instructional radio programs which will be used much in the same way as ITV programs. You may even be a part of a radio or television audience that earns college credit and takes a complete college course via instructional radio or television aired over the campus station or a local public broadcasting station.

Reaching the Student Audience

Now place yourself in the role of a media manager whose responsibility it is to reach a college student audience. Overall, your job would be extremely difficult. The audience would be isolated from most of the mass media, and even your decisions about products the college student consumer would use may be skewed by students' reactions to peer group decisions. Clothing purchases would not necessarily be determined by the clothing sales advertised on the local radio or television station or even the local newspaper. College students purchase most of their clothing before they even arrive on campus. In addition, college students purchase toiletries at the local drugstore near campus; not because they read an ad about the drugstore products, but because it's convenient. Although some students may own a car, many others do not, and traveling around town to take advantage of bargains is difficult. So what do you, as a media manager, do? You might use the campus newspaper as one medium of communication. In most cases, the campus radio and television station would be prohibited from accepting advertising because they're normally noncommercial educational stations. National magazines popular among college students would be another way of reaching the college audience, although you would also be paying to reach a large segment of the non-college population.

Suppose you are an advertising manager for a politician running for office in a district that contains a large college student population. You must specifically reach this audience and direct a specialized message to them. Some of the techniques used in such successful campaigns have been both ingenious and subtle. For instance, one advertising agency used direct mail to reach the student audience. The agency carefully avoided making the direct-mail literature look too polished and thus prevented the students from perceiving it as a product of the "establishment." The direct-mail piece was therefore run on a ditto machine instead of being professionally printed. A few billboards near the campus were another important addition to the campaign. Although many students didn't drive, they did walk, and the strategically located billboards near the campus were one of the few means of reaching the students.

By its very nature, the college student audience will continue to be extremely selective in its exposure to mass media. Likewise, from the standpoint of advertising, many of the traditional channels to this audience are not available for commercial messages or are highly inefficient from a cost standpoint. Take the time to examine your own campus community and determine how you would reach this audience if you were a media planner.

the young adult audience

This audience is one of the most sought-after by commercial mass media everywhere. It is a highly acquisitive audience, purchasing everything from coffee pots to homes. It is also impressionable to commercial messages since its buying preferences are not yet fixed. Young adults in the age range of eighteen to thirty-four years of age encompass the great majority of our population, including such sub-groups as college students.

The young adult audience is the lifeblood of the film industry since this group attends more motion pictures than any other age group and is a trend setter for the entire industry. Young adults also constitute the mainstay of the paperback book market and are the primary determiners of other media content as well. Unlike older audiences, which tend to be attuned to media content based on life styles, young adults are not as apt to adhere to any given pattern and therefore are more selective in the media they consume. They have a mobile life style, giving them the opportunity to pick and choose their media. If they don't like the evening prime-time television fare, they are apt to shut the set off and go to the movies, attend a sports event, read a magazine, or participate in some other activity. They will not, as the older audience, remain glued to the television screen regardless of the program.

Radio can reach this audience as does its mentor, the recording industry. However, some radio stations that direct themselves toward this audience with a special type of musical programming find it difficult to hold their listenership with changing trends in music. With today's strong influx of country-western music onto the traditional rock charts, some tough decisions face program directors. Should they program some of the new country-rock and stay with the trends or hold firm to the traditional rock music and exclude country? To ignore the country influence may send many of their young adult listeners to other stations, but to include it would mean duplicating the music of some country-western stations. Whatever decision the program director makes, his audience will be less clearly defined than in the past, and that will surely have an effect on everything from ratings to revenues. A magazine editor who finds she is losing her audience faces the same predicament. Should the decision be made to try and accommodate the new audience or go after the one that's lost? What would you do?

When it split according to the four network concept, ABC radio placed heavy emphasis on the young adult audience with the formation of its Contemporary and Entertainment Networks. Mutual followed suit with its Mutual Progressive Network. In most every community of moderate size, there is a radio station that caters to the young adult audience. In many communities, broadcasters will gladly relinquish their share of the general listenership if they are able to capture the majority of the young adult audience. For, in dollars of advertising, it is more valuable than any other single group of people.

the occupations

A person's job is one of his or her most important possessions. This being so, our occupational roles often determine our life styles and consequently our media attention habits. Consider, for example, blue collar workers whose office is the factory. Their day, unlike other peoples', may have varied starts. Their shift may start at seven in the morning and go until four in the afternoon, or they may work one of the night shifts from eleven until seven in the morning. They will commute to work, listen to the car radio, and be influenced by peer groups, specifically fellow workers. The most important organization to them may be the labor union. Although other news is certainly of concern, news of labor, economics, plant layoffs, and similar information will be of keen interest to them no matter where it occurs.

If you were a news director at a radio station in a sizeable blue-collar community, you would carefully take this audience into consideration. For example, you might schedule three major newscasts in a twenty-four hour period to reach this audience when it changed shifts at the local plant. You might make the factory and its operation as regular a part of your beat as other community institutions such as the police department and education. When any news about organized labor reached you, you would air it immediately. If you were program director at this same station, you might feel this audience was important enough to program their type of music. After all, factory workers might comprise a majority of your audience when the rest of the city is fast asleep.

Perhaps the audience we are concerned about is not the factory worker but the farmer. Imagine you are the media buyer for a large fertilizer company and are preparing to purchase radio commercials on one of two local radio stations. Will you choose the station which has the most listeners? Perhaps not. Instead of the number of listeners a radio station can deliver, you need to know the number of *acres* the station can deliver. For instance, if 1000 listeners of a station happen to be farmers, and these farmers own 75 percent of the acreage in the listening area, then this station is far more valuable to you than the one with the most listeners. You would also be concerned with the station's programming. Weather forecasts are extremely important to the farmer as are special farm programs. Trade magazines would also be helpful in reaching this audience.

If you were the news director at the radio station serving this audience, you would also be concerned with the farmers' needs. You would be vitally conscious of weather news and would give it far more attention than your city counterparts. You would also be on the alert for such things as storm warnings, livestock reports, and grain features. You might even subscribe to special wire services that carry weather news or farm news. These could very well be a major and regular part of your newscast if your station did not air a special farm show. Even with such a program, you would find it valuable to repeat agricultural forecasts in your news presentation to reach this target audience.

Occupational audiences, when they do exist, are very important. They are audiences which are usually rather cohesive, with common bonds, such as union memberships. They also constitute a key to program planning where life styles determine media attention habits. The employees of a factory, for example, who get off work at 3:00 a.m. can comprise a loyal audience for an early morning radio newscast.

the woman audience

The women's movement opened the eyes of the media to a female audience in a state of transition from the traditional sterotype of the housewife to an emphasis on the professional, career woman. We began to read magazines, hear songs, see films, and witness television programs all reflecting women's new image as a partner and collaborator with men in all spheres of life.

Cosmo to Foxy Lady

One of the prime examples of a successful publication geared toward this "newly discovered" audience is *Cosmopolitan.* Helen

The working woman, a target audience gaining more and more attention.

Gurley Brown, who authored the book *Sex and the Single Girl,* took over the reins of the publication and began to structure its content and image toward the young woman who believed in having the freedom to make her own choices. The magazine slowly began to deal with issues which before had been taboo in almost any magazine except sex magazines. Freely discussed were such topics as women in careers, money management for women, sexual life styles, and many others that directly appealed to the liberated female (or the woman who thinks she is liberated) and/or the man and woman who want to know what the liberated female is thinking about. The front cover of the publication adopted a theme of high-fashion clothing on a well exposed and well endowed woman's chest. Although that didn't necessarily express any theme of the women's movement, it was an eye-catcher and helped the over-the-counter sales of the magazine. The magazine became in some ways the female counterpart to *Playboy*; one issue even included a centerfold. Gradually, however, other more strictly sex magazines such as *Playgirl* and *Foxy Lady* cornered their share of the market.

Other women's magazines advocating special themes sprang up, including *Ms.*, *Women Sports*, and *New Woman*, to name a few. The women's movement also had its effect on such traditionally conservative magazines as *Redbook*, which gradually shifted their emphasis toward a more liberated standpoint.

Television and the Recordings

Television began to portray women in roles traditionally relegated to men. Women doctors, judges, police officers, and lawyers became common, although the stereotyped role of the housewife endured in television commercials. A notable exception was the Campbell Soup's commercial with the line, "I've got a working wife."

Other media as well as support industries began to respond to the women's movement. The recording industry projected women's role as a major social force in such recordings as *I Am Woman*. The other side of the coin, the plight of women in the subordinate role of "follower" and servant, was expressed in such songs as *Only Women Bleed*.

Ms., Miss, or Mrs.

Even journalism had much to contend with in accurately reflecting a new title of "Ms." when covering a story. One editor of a major paper summed up the use of Ms. by saying it was mostly common sense. If you were aware a person did not like the title Ms., then you didn't use it. If the person was a senior citizen, then usually the term Miss or Mrs. was more appropriate. Many women in the news found themselves referred to by their last names on second reference just as their male counterparts were. A resolution passed by the 7,000 member Women in Communication, Inc., called on the wire services to "eliminate the use of courtesy or social titles for newsmakers who happen to be female or extend such usage to newsmakers who happen to be male, and . . . to adopt the practice of identifying all newsmakers by gender and marital status directly and only when pertinent to the story. . . ."

The Homemaker

Despite the career orientation facet of the women's movement and its ramifications in all types of media, there still remains a major segment of the population who fill the traditional and significant role of housewife and homemaker. They continue to be the buyers of most of the country's household goods, foodstuffs, and housewares. Magazines such as *Ladies Home Journal, House Beautiful,* and *Better Homes and Gardens* serve a large homemaker audience. A quick look at the television fare on any weekday reveals the predominance of game shows and soap operas, programs that have drawn some of the largest female audiences of any media. A perusal of the products advertised on daytime commercials also indicates that media advertisers are keenly aware of the housewife's role as home manager.

the elderly

It has only been since about 1970 that serious and detailed study has been given to the relationship of the elderly to mass media. The fruits of those labors, both in scholarly circles and within media organizations, have finally recognized the traditional stereotype of the elderly as just that. For, as a group, the elderly are not necessarily a depressed, socially isolated burden on society. The media, however, have not paid serious attention to this group of people, one reason being simply that they did not represent the affluent middle-aged consumers of society and were therefore neglected by media whose main concern was reaching the affluent.

Media Portrayal of the Elderly

Their portrayal in the mass media was characterized by such spoofs as the *Over The Hill Gang* on the late night television movie or public service announcements asking for "young" volunteers to work with the "old" people in society.

Aronoff examined the portrayal of the elderly in prime-time television and found a relationship between the way the media portrayed its characters and the age of those characters[7] (Figure 14–3 and 14–4). The research reported that the older a male character was, the more he was apt to be portrayed as a "bad guy" (Figure 14–3). The older a female character was, the more apt she was to be portrayed in a role which implied failure (Figure 14–4). There is evidence to indicate some minor changes in these trends. The elderly are beginning to be portrayed as authoritative figures dispensing "wisdom"

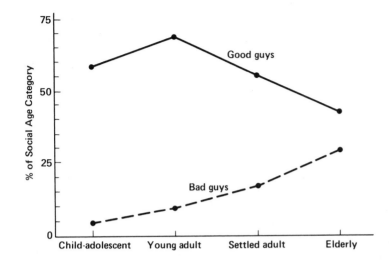

Figure 14–3 Frequency of "good guys" and "bad guys" among social age categories for major male non-cartoon characters.

on a subject. Not atypical is the commercial for Sominex, a substance advertised as helping people to fall asleep. The commercial shows two generations portrayed by a mother and daughter both having trouble "falling asleep at night." The daughter learned about the product because her mother told her how effective it was. There has also been an effort to call attention to the plight and "portrayed plight" of the elderly, especially in radio and television fare. One organization which actively supports fair treatment of the elderly in media is the Gray Panthers. In 1975, they appeared before the Television Code Review Board of the National Association of Broadcasters to lobby for a change in the NAB Television Code

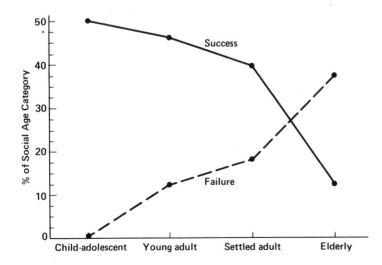

Figure 14–4 Frequency distribution of success and failure among major non-cartoon female characters.

which would alert broadcasters to be sensitive to portrayal of the aged. Whereas the Code had previously alerted the broadcasters to material dealing with sex, race, creed, religion, or ethnic background, the word *age* has now been added. The Board itself said the inclusion was directed not only toward the elderly but to all ages.

Special Features and Functional Uses

Scholarly research has made a systematic investigation of the ways in which the elderly use media.[8] Many newspapers are now beginning to carry special syndicated features as well as local news and special sections devoted to the elderly. The content of these publications varies greatly, but most express common themes centering around activities for the elderly and programs in which the elderly are participating. Also prevalent are special consumer tips for the elderly, such as advice on money management and nutrition as well as medical information. More publications are now directed exclusively toward the elderly, such as the magazine *Retirement Living*. Many are official journals of organizations whose membership consists primarily of the elderly. Such publications also provide an avenue for advertisers to reach this target audience at what is usually a more efficient cost per thousand than through other media.

There are also many functional uses of media for the elderly. For instance, soap operas permit the elderly to identify with characters with whom, because of their own life style, they have little real contact. Such identity can help reduce the feeling of "isolation" that often occurs when one lives alone.[9]

The real groundwork for a beneficial relationship between the elderly and the media will be laid when media content reflects the true characteristics of this audience and portrays them realistically rather than stereotypically. There are untapped frontiers available for cable television to truly "involve" the elderly with media. Such things as special broadcast seminars permitting two-way interaction among shut-ins can help alleviate the loneliness that some elderly persons face and can actually stimulate a "neighborly" environment for them, thus creating new and vital interpersonal relationships.

international comparisons

Our discussion of target audiences has centered on audiences indigenous to the United States. These groupings however, are not universal, since each culture consumes media, manages media, and plans media content in ways that are considerably different from those of every other population. A comparison by A. C. Nielsen between Japanese and American audiences illustrates these differences.[10] Of course, we can only speculate as to whether the life styles of the two nations contribute to their television viewing habits, or whether the type of television programming influences their life styles. Surprisingly, the hours of television usage per household are greater for Japanese than for Americans. Nielsen research shows just under six hours of television usage per household in the United States, but well over six hours for the Japanese city of Tokyo and over six and one-half hours for Osaka. There is also less seasonal variation in television usage in Japan than in the United States. Whereas average winter viewing in the United States is almost twenty-nine percent higher than summer viewing, in Japan the difference is nineteen percent, based on Monday through Friday daytime viewing and all evening viewings. Another notable difference between television viewing habits of Japanese and American audiences occurs over the course of a daily schedule.[11] Comparing data gathered in New York and Tokyo, researchers found the peak viewing times in Japan to be 8:00 a.m., noon, and approximately 8 o'clock evening. In the United States, on the other hand, television viewing in the morning proves to be rather low, especially at 8:00 a.m., but gradually increases to prime-time levels between 8:00 p.m. and 9:00 p.m., although peak levels never equal those in Japan (Figure 14–5).

The type of programming that appeals to Japanese audiences is also different from American audiences' preferences. Here again, as with all other differences between the two audiences, the question becomes, Is this because the programming determines interests or because the interests have determined programming? A look at top-rated Japanese television programs shows three news programs in the top ten slots, whereas in the United States, no news programs are in the top ten. The common theme of several popular television shows that attract and are directed toward the Japanese housewife is that of the "beautiful heroine suffering through life, abused by an intolerable husband. Misery upon misery is her fortune,"[12] until extricated by her hero.

Such differences open up new opportunities to study the role of media in society. Project yourself for a moment into the future and imagine you are a media planner at a time when satellite communication beams programming from your television network to both Japanese and American audiences. How would you attract audiences across cultural boundaries? How would you compensate for the different life styles and different programming tastes of the Jap-

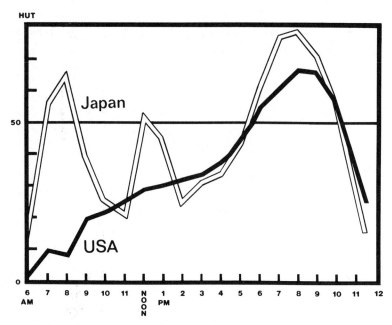

Figure 14-5 Comparison of peak viewing times in Japan and the United States.

anese? What decisions would allow you to compete for the mass audience of both nations? What would some of the social consequences of this type of media arrangement be, and would they ultimately prove harmful or beneficial?

summary

Target audiences are defined as "any group of people who have a common bond, that bond being demographic or psychographic characteristics, or a combination of both." The increase in specialized media has made target audiences more important for both media planners and advertisers. No longer does the concept of the mass audience conjure up an unidentified group of people, a faceless crowd with no common characteristics. Specialized audiences require specialized messages, and media planners are taking these target audiences seriously. More and more media content is portraying the unique cultural and linguistic heritage of such minority groups as blacks and Spanish-speaking Americans. People's occupations are another example of target audiences. To reach them the media have developed many kinds of special presentations. Trade magazines, for instance, direct their content toward such target groups as farmers, truck drivers, and dentists. The women's movement has also been instrumental in mobilizing an important target audience, one that is changing, diversified, and individual. A target audience that has been overlooked for many years by the media is the elderly. Common misconceptions about the elderly's role in society are currently being broken down and portrayed more positively by media. International comparisons between the United States and Japan show different media habits which reflects the fact that target audiences differ in composition and in media habits from one culture to another.

opportunities for further learning

Canadian Broadcasting Corporation, *What the Canadian Public Thinks of the CBC*. Ottawa, Ontario: Canadian Broadcasting Corporation, 1963.

GARNETT, BERNARD E., *How Soulful is "Soul" Radio?* Nashville, Tenn.: Race Relations Information Center, 1970.

GREENBERG, BRADLEY S., and BRENDA DERVIN, with the assistance of JOSEPH R. DOMINICK and JOHN BOWES, *Use of the Mass Media by the Urban Poor*. New York: Praeger Publishers, 1970.

KATO, HIDETOSHI, Ed., *Japanese Research on Mass Communication: Selected Abstracts*. Honolulu, Hawaii: The University Press of Hawaii, 1974.

LOPEZ, RONALD W. and others, *The Role and Functions of Spanish-Language-Only Television in Los Angeles*. Claremont, Calif.: Claremont University Center, Center for Urban and Regional Studies, 1973.

MURRAY, JAMES P., *To Find an Image: Black Films From Uncle Tom to Superfly*. Indianapolis, Ind.: Bobbs-Merrill Co., 1973.

WOLSELEY, ROLAND E., *The Black Press, U. S. A.* Ames, Iowa: The Iowa State University Press, 1971.

feedback:

the print media

CHAPTER FIFTEEN

In Chapter 1, our communication models displayed feedback as a principal component of the communication process. This chapter and Chapter 16 examine this concept in more detail. The role of feedback in mass communication cannot be overemphasized. One of the most important factors upon which media professionals make decisions, is something that is constantly being monitored, whether it be letters to the editor, the latest television ratings, an evaluation of an educational radio program, or box office receipts from a new motion picture. Feedback determines how media function and respond to the mass audience they serve.

As members of a mass audience, we are constantly taking part in the feedback process. When we purchase a product that we have seen advertised in our favorite magazine, we give the manufacturer of the product and the advertising agency that created the ad an indication of the success of their persuasion effort. When we clip a coupon from a magazine, we become part of the feedback data on such information as the effectiveness of the circulation of the magazine and, in some cases, what age and sex of reader is most likely to respond to the offer. If we take part in a radio listening survey, we may provide feedback data on the listening habits of thousands or millions of people.

The importance of feedback has translated into a multimillion dollar business. For example, the A. C. Nielsen Company, which provides a number of feedback services to media corporations, does approximately $150 million in annual business. Other major corporations involved in similar activities also do annual business in the multimillion dollar category. Let's now examine the different types of feedback in the print media, their functions, and how they affect media decision making.

letters to the editor

Some of the most loyal readership of any portion of the editorial page belongs to letters to the editor. This important feedback to the print media reflects a wide range of opinion, spurs people to react, and initiates a good deal of thought among newspaper editors. Surveys on the number of letters editors receive, their impact and use vary.[1] At the *New York Times*, for example, approximately 40,000 letters are received annually of which about seven percent are printed.

The number of letters published by a local newspaper can tend to reflect the number it receives. If a newspaper publishes your letter, you are naturally going to be more responsive about writing another. Certain cultural indicators can also reflect how active the public is in writing letters to the editor. Newspapers in New England, for instance, tend to receive more letters to the editor than do newspapers in other sections of the country. It's hypothesized that the heritage of the old New England town meeting may be responsible for such profuse feedback.[2]

Letters editors receive usually originate from people acting on their own behalf or on behalf of an organization. The characteristics of the typical letter writer are different from those of the typical citizen in the community. The person who writes letters to the editor will usually be older than the norm of the community, will in many cases be a professional person, and will be more conservative. He or she will also be better educated than the average citizen, will usually have a higher average income, and may be apt to voice his public concern on more than one occasion. Usually, a letter writer will be well versed on the major issues affecting the community and will be able to understand and communicate these issues. Such persons resemble the opinion leaders we discussed in Chapter 14.

In some cases, groups may organize a barrage of letters to a substantial segment of the press, under the guise that these letters are spontaneous responses from individual citizens. Actually, of course, such letters represent an organized persuasion campaign to sway public opinion via the letters to the editor column. It has been suggested that in a democratic society, letters to the editor serve as a "safety valve for the political system as much as it functions as an instrument of persuasion" and that another function "of letters to the editor in a democratic society is that of catharsis" which "gives the irate, the antagonist, the displeased a chance to speak out and be heard."[3]

readership surveys

The operation of a modern newspaper is a complex process. It demands the decisions of skilled people assisted by reliable research data and information affecting every part of the newspaper's operation. New technology, competition from other publications as well as the broadcast media, and increased labor and printing costs all demand carefully thought out operational decisions. One of the most important sources of information for these decisions is feedback from newspaper readers. To continually monitor this feedback, most major newspapers regularly conduct readership surveys, *detailed analyses of the newspaper's audience*. Assume you are sitting in the publisher's chair and have to make decisions about the operation of a modern newspaper in a major city. You would need specific types of feedback on which to base your decisions.

Demographics

Demographic feedback basically consists of data regarding the *age, sex, education,* and *income* of your readers. It is valuable in helping you to make management decisions. For example, if the readership survey shows a major portion of your readership is between eighteen and twenty-two years of age and there is a large university in your newspaper's coverage area, you might assume that the newspaper reaches that university. This information could prove useful to advertisers who want to use your medium to reach the college students. If the survey reveals a significant portion of your readership owns homes in a given price range, are employed, and reside in a certain section of the city, then you might decide to permit advertisers to purchase space in just those issues reaching this specialized target audience. Demographic information can also be obtained for specific regions in the coverage area, regions which coincide with your specialized distribution system. Areas with high income or highly educated readers are target audiences for specific types of advertising. With this demographic information in hand, the newspaper's sales department can approach advertisers and explain exactly the type of audience the specific editions of your newspaper will reach and how it can be an effective sales medium.

Life Style Analysis

In Chapter 13, we learned how life style analysis was used to predict the television viewing habits and preferences of the mass television audience. Life style analysis also becomes important to newspaper publishers, but in a different way. With newspapers, life style analysis is not so much concerned with the types of newspaper content the reader will prefer, but more with how and where the reader is exposed to the newspaper. This information is important both from a sales and from a use standpoint. For instance, we learned in Chapter 11 how different front page formats of two Philadelphia newspapers were the result of their respective readers' purchasing habits. One was primarily purchased from a newsstand, the other by subscription. Because a large segment of the Philadelphia population commutes to work on mass transit systems, the newspaper sold at the newsstand designed its format for this reader's on-the-go life style.

A reader's life style can also determine the time of day that he or she reads the newspaper. Suppose your readership survey indicates that one section of the city contains many factory workers who work a 7:00 a.m. to 3:00 p.m. shift. These people arrive home at about 3:30 p.m. and want to relax and read their newspaper by 4:00 p.m. If the newspaper constantly arrives after 6:00 p.m., that impact is lost. They probably will have already watched the evening news on television and will have little hesitancy about cancelling their subscription. Keeping this life style information in mind, you can make arrangements for these people to be the first to receive the newspaper when it comes off the press. If delivery trucks start loading the papers at 3:00 p.m., shipments to that section of the city can be the first loaded and the first to arrive at their destination. Thus, through feedback about the life style of your readers, you have been able to improve your service to them.

Distribution

Life style analysis has also made its mark on newspaper distribution. Just as the television viewer may change channels or turn the set off if the picture is fuzzy, the newspaper reader may cancel a subscription if the newspaper arrives at a different time every day.

An efficient, well-monitored distribution system is therefore vital to your newspaper's operation. Most newspapers have a separate circulation department to handle any eventuality in this area.

Just as your readers' life styles determine when they read the newspaper, so does the distribution of the newspaper help determine their life styles. Many a family sets the alarm clock for Sunday morning, basing that decision on how long it takes to eat breakfast *and* read the newspaper before planning other activities. The business person who must leave for work without reading the morning paper may feel as out of sorts as the person who awakes to find the cupboard bare of coffee. Wherever possible, the distribution system of your newspaper should be designed to meet the needs and habits of the audience it serves.

Community Attitudes

Few newspaper publishers would argue the fact that a newspaper is more than just an instrument to spew out news and advertisements. It is a major social force in a community. It serves the community and at the same time reflects it. Newspapers, although not public relations sheets, are usually managed by concerned citizens who are interested in seeing the community prosper along with the newspaper. Psychographics, as part of a readership survey, ascertain the attitudes of residents toward their community. Such information is important in a variety of functions, such as determining editorial policy and news content. Broadcasters, by law, are required to monitor the attitudes of the public and identify those issues which are of concern to residents. Although newspaper publishers are not required to do so, many take readership surveys, in the course of which they may discover, e.g., a dislike for the sprawling, unchecked, industrial development within the community. Such information provides an excellent basis for a series of news stories or perhaps an editorial that might spur the community's planning commission into action.

Pricing

The cost of newsprint, labor, distribution, and technology have made operating the modern newspaper an expensive enterprise. To offset these costs, a newspaper has two major sources of income— advertising and circulation. The two vary directly: The larger the readership, the more a newspaper can charge for advertising, because the advertisements will reach a greater number of people. When it does become necessary to raise the circulation price, some serious soul searching takes place, since a price increase could cut circulation so significantly that advertising rates would also have to be reduced. To ease this soul searching, readership surveys can determine whether or not a sampling of readers feels the newspaper is worth the price. But before you initiate the rate increase, you will have to take into account such other factors as competitively priced local newspapers. Will you be able to maintain a competitive circulation if you institute a price increase? Data gathered during the readership survey will certainly help you make this decision.

Credibility

The days have vanished when newspapers were the only news source for a community. Today they compete with radio, television, and magazines, among others. Yet newspapers are primarily a news medium, and to be successful, they must be a credible news medium in the eyes of their readers. A radio or television station may have an abhorrent news department, yet be a successful enterprise since it rests on the laurels of its entertainment programming. Newspapers do not enjoy this luxury. Thus, a continual monitoring is important to determine how the newspaper compares in credibility with other media in the same community.

If research data show a decline in news credibility, then the publisher will need to determine why this is taking place. On the other hand, if readers consider the general reporting of the newspaper accurate, then they demonstrate faith in the publication. Of course, a newspaper's reputation on the editorial page may tend to be reflected in its news coverage. For example, people who feel a newspaper is Republican oriented may tend to perceive the news coverage of political issues biased, regardless of how objective the reporting may be. Knowing about these perceptions is the first step in correcting them.

Sectional Usage

Every section of a newspaper is important to its overall content. Therefore, feedback on the effectiveness of these various sections can keep a link from weakening the entire chain. For example, a loss in readership of the sports page calls for action. Perhaps a layout change, a new column, or a syndicated feature will draw readers back to this section of the paper. Perhaps the coverage of more women's sports will increase readership. Your readership survey should be able to pinpoint the trouble spots.

Special features are also important to monitor. There are numerous syndicated items that a newspaper can carry, but no newspaper can carry them all. Therefore, you need to obtain feedback on which features are really attracting and holding your readership and which ones are just receiving casual attention. Determining which features to use in newspapers is much the same as programming music on a popular radio station. The slightest change can affect the attention and loyalty of the audience. Readers consume a newspaper because of a combination of factors. Over time, a series of small, almost unnoticed changes can begin gradually to change readers' opinions until they cancel a subscription. Trying to detect these changes in use and preference patterns when they are in the formative stages is very difficult. But the key is to identify them before they become too deeply rooted that the circulation begins to suffer or other media evolve as more useful and preferred than the local newspaper.

Advertising Involvement

Newspaper readers can become involved with the medium. In some ways they can become even more involved than with the broadcast media. It's difficult to carry a television commercial with you to the grocery store, but taking along the grocery ad from the local newspaper is common practice. This type of involvement is important to recognize and identify. Specific knowledge about it can be communicated to your advertisers, especially those who want their advertisements to elicit particular behavior from the reader, such as sending in a coupon.

Feedback about this involvement is also relatively easy to gather. Newspaper coupons redeemed at a local restaurant are a definite numerical indicator of the success of the ad. Similarly, the number of people who respond to a classified ad is an indicator of how involved readers are with this section of the paper. Monitoring this type of feedback tracks the heart of the economic lifeblood of your newspaper. It's an important indicator of your newspaper's ability to reach an audience and that audience's reaction to your newspaper's advertising content.

accepting feedback: the role of the ombudsman

In several European countries, an *ombudsman* is a public servant who serves as an intermediary between the public and public officials. When citizens have a formal complaint, they can take it to the ombudsman who represents their grievances. At a typical newspaper, ombudsmen serve much the same purpose. Their role is to accept feedback from readers on any issue, from suggestions for feature stories to complaints about news coverage.

From the public's standpoint, the presence of an ombudsman permits an opportunity for feedback to the newspaper which would otherwise not be possible. The press carries with it a charisma that seems impenetrable to the average citizen. The old cliche, "power of the press," leaves many a person feeling helpless about even communicating with the fourth estate, let alone complaining to it. With the presence of an ombudsman, however, the public at least has the feeling that someone will listen. There is a name or an address to contact. Even the mere presence of such a person lessens the public's apprehensions about communicating with the press.

How an ombudsman reacts to feedback depends on the severity of the complaint or the issue at hand. It also may depend on the support the ombudsman receives within the newspaper itself. If the ombudsman is little more than a figurehead for the public's view with little influence among the newspaper staff, then his or her effectiveness is minimal. On the other hand, where the ombudsman has considerable influence, he or she can use feedback from the public to influence everyone from the beat reporters to the editorial staff. Ideally, the ombudsman is the person with a finger on the pulse of the community. Thus, his or her input into decisions about the content of the paper should be regarded seriously. The use of an ombudsman has become more common in recent years with new attention focused on the fourth estate. Attacks on the press from national political figures, especially during the Nixon administration, gave many newspapers a new awareness of their image in the community. One way to monitor this image and break down some of the negative attitudes about inaccessibility of the press was to begin employing ombudsmen.

reader profiles

The demise of such popular mass circulation magazines as *Life* and *Look* created a revolution in the magazine publishing industry. No longer could magazines compete for the mass audience that television was dominating, and advertisers refused to pay the high prices that mass circulation magazines were asking. The result prompted the development of the specialty publication, directing itself to a well-defined, target audience. We have already encountered several of these magazines that are designed to appeal to groups of people with common interests. Such interests and the ability to identify them is the key to the specialty magazine's success. *Reader profiles* are the tools used to ascertain both the demographic and psychographic characteristics of specialized magazines' audiences.

Reader profiles are detailed surveys from a sample of the magazine's readership obtained via subscription lists and followed up by direct-mail questionnaires. For example, a leading woman's magazine designed to attract the young, "with it" female reader might ask basic demographic information such as age, sex, education, and income. More detailed questions might solicit such information as the size school the person attends, the amount of money she spends on clothes and cosmetics, the number of dates she goes out on per week, and the number of movies and concerts she attends. Additional detailed information might search out her attitudes on women's liberation, women's rights, sex, politics, and men. From these data, the magazine develops a comprehensive, detailed profile of the typical reader.

The uses of the reader profile are many. For instance, the attitudes of the readers are an asset in determining the editorial line the magazine takes. It can also help to decide what feature articles to include in future issues. For example, if a reader profile determined that a magazine's audience was comprised of readers who believed strongly in women's rights, then it would be foolish for the magazine to espouse an editorial policy against these views. Similarly, if the reader profile revealed attitudes favoring traditional marriages, it would be foolish to include feature articles on nontraditional or other quasi-marital arrangements. In addition to its purely editorial functions, the profile permits magazines to compile information about readers' buying habits and life styles and furnish these data to prospective advertisers and advertising agencies. In this case, the reader profile actually becomes the sales prospectus for the magazine.

Reader profiles are also important in determining the advertising rates the magazine will charge. For example, a circulation of three million readers with incomes of less than $10,000 per year may not be nearly as enticing to a prospective advertiser as a readership of one million with incomes of more than $50,000 per year, especially if the product being advertised is an expensive one. Thus, the advertising rate for the magazine with the three million circulation may be far less than one would have assumed.

Another important function of reader profiles is determining changes in the audience. As we learned in Chapter 4, when this occurs, publishers must make some major decisions. If, for instance, readers' attitudes have become more conservative, the publishers must ask themselves if the shift has occurred because of an actual change in opinions of the readership or because the magazine has lost liberal subscribers. Assume the latter is the case. Then the publisher must ask if it is better to accommodate the new-found audience or recover the lost one. The decision is tough, yet without reader profiles supplying this information, a publication has no means of telling what audience it is reaching or if it has any reader loyalty among that audience. This information is essential if any specialized publication is to succeed.

reader service cards

For an advertiser, there are many different ways to determine the effectiveness of an ad. One, the reader service card gives readers an opportunity to request additional literature and information about an advertiser's products. One of the most direct forms of feedback in which a reader can participate, it opens up communication directly with the advertiser and is a reflection of the ability of the publication to produce advertising results. Reader service cards usually appear in the form of postcard inserts near the back of magazines and consist of a series of numbers which the reader can circle (Figure 15–1). Each number on the card corresponds to an advertisement within the magazine. In some cases, the reader service card may direct you to send a small remittance for either literature or small sample of the merchandise.

Assume you are reading a specialty magazine on stereo music. Inside the magazine are advertisements for many different types of stereo record players, cassette tape players, and other similar mer-

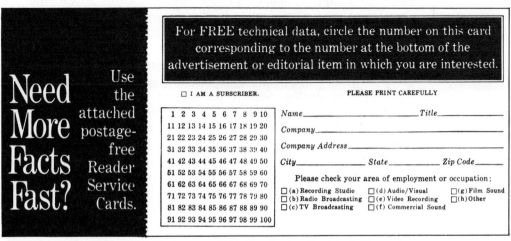

Figure 15–1 Reader service card. (© Sagamore Publishing Co., Inc. Reprinted with permission.)

chandise. As you read an advertisement for a particular brand of cassette tape player, you notice at the bottom of the advertisement the words, "Circle number 38 on the Reader Service Card." Your interest prompts you to do so, and then mail the card to the address printed on the reverse side, a central clearing house for reader service cards. The information on your reader service card is fed into the central clearing house's computer, and at the end of the month, the company whose advertisement corresponded to number 38 on the reader service card will receive a list of names and addresses of all potential buyers. The company will then send you promotional literature describing the cassette tape player that appeared in the ad. They may also refer you to their closest retail outlet and, very occasionally, even give your name to that outlet.

The value of a reader service card is considerable. By reflecting the circulation and effectiveness of the publication, it provides some of the most meaningful feedback that an advertiser and publication can receive. When a publication agrees to include a reader service card, it puts itself on the line to deliver an audience to the advertiser. After all, if no one sends in a reader card, then the company will probably look elsewhere to place its ad. But when people do take the time and energy to send in a card, it usually means they are actively involved in the publication, read it carefully, and take it seriously. Reader service cards are also rather effective as far as recall of the advertisement is concerned. Since these subscribers are not casual readers, buyer motivation and, eventually, sales results can be much greater than those from a normal print advertisement or even a television or radio commercial.

Studies have traced the dollar sales volume from reader service cards to be approximately $50 for every $1.00 in advertising. Not atypical of reader service card sales figures are those compiled by Hudson Home Publications of Los Altos, California. The Hudson Home Publications Research Department in cooperation with A. C. Nielsen researched the market effectiveness of ads appearing in Hudson Home Publications which elicited reader service cards. Two types of audiences were researched, the home consumer and the trade or business that responded. Research showed, for instance, that a four-color, one-half page ad for ceramic tile produced 1,001 replies; a four-color, one page ad for paneling produced 1,143 inquiries. The traceable sales and specifications (construction bids, etc.) for the ceramic tile ad was $20,466 and $132,909 for the paneling ad. Thus, reader service cards, while enabling publisher and advertiser to tabulate the number of readers who actively responded to the advertisement, can also show, in economic terms, how profitable an ad is.

feedback in direct mail

Our discussion of reader service cards and reader profiles has shown us two important areas of feedback to the magazine industry—advertising effectiveness and the characteristics of the magazine audience. Both of these types of feedback come into play in direct mail. As you'll recall from Chapter 4, direct mail caters to a specialized audience that can be reached through mailing lists and other selective procedures. There are few "unknown" members of the direct-mail audience.

Feedback in direct mail is primarily concerned with three factors: (1) the number of responses to direct-mail literature; (2) learning the characteristics of the direct-mail consumer; and (3) testing the effectiveness of direct-mail literature.

Response to Direct Mail

The most important information and the true test of the effectiveness of direct mail is the number of responses a piece of direct-mail literature receives. For example, suppose as one part of your fund-raising campaign for a political candidate you decide to use direct mail. You have selected a list of people from the same political party as the candidate, have carefully designed the literature, have invested the creative talents of an advertising agency, and have spent a considerable amount for printing, and an even larger amount for postage. Now you await the results of your efforts.

As the mail begins to come in, you realize that the contributions you are receiving are sizeable, and you will probably take in enough money to meet the expenses incurred in designing, printing, and mailing the literature. You also realize that some of the return envelopes contain much more money than others. In fact, as you examine the contributions, you begin to see a pattern developing. There seems to be a group of contributions in the "more than $100" category and another group in the "$2.00 to $5.00" range. Naturally, you would like to receive more of the $100+ contributions. You begin to plan another direct-mail campaign to reach more of these big contributors. This leads us to the next important area of feedback, discovering the characteristics of the direct-mail consumer.

Consumer Characteristics

The process of researching the characteristics of the direct-mail consumer is much the same as that used to develop the reader profile.

First, you design a questionnaire that can be computer coded so that respondents' answers can be fed into a computer for fast, easy data analysis. Your questionnaire is very detailed and solicits such information as age, income, home ownership, number of children, and place of employment. In our example, you select a sample of people in the $100+ range and send them the questionnaire. You then analyze the data from the returned questionnaires.

The data tell you the large contributor is a home owner and that he or she earns an average annual income in excess of $40,000. There seems to be no indication that contributors' occupations have anything to do with how much they contribute. There are lawyers, accountants, small business people, and a variety of other occupations. You also discover that many of the contributors are not of the political party of your candidate. You discover your candidate has a hidden area of strength with people outside his own political party.

Testing the Effectiveness of Direct Mail

You now plan a special piece of literature to reach the person who will make large contributions to your candidate. You will use the list of party members living in the zip coded area of high-income home owners of one specific test area. Knowing that some of the large contributors were members of the opposing party, you decide to send half of your mailing to party members and half to people who are not on your party member list. A few days later, the contributions begin to come in. They are primarily in the $100 category, and you realize there is no difference in the number or amount of contributions between the two political groups. Your direct mailing has given you some very worthwhile information. Your campaign is a success. Moreover, the information you attained will make your future direct mailings much easier.

Your direct-mail campaign to obtain contributions for a political candidate employed three types of feedback—the response from the reader in the form of contributions, the characteristics of the direct-mail audience which you researched through questionnaires, and testing your hypotheses about the direct-mail audience on a test area. All improved the effectiveness of the campaign and all were interrelated.

clipping bureaus

Imagine you have been appointed director of public information for an international association. Your primary responsibility centers around obtaining as much publicity for the association's annual convention as possible. Your planning and work begin months in advance with locating a list of all the news media in the convention city. You prepare a press kit with background information on the convention and the association. The association is comprised of educators and scholars, so a partial list of interesting research papers is also included in the press kit. A month or so before the convention takes place, you hold a news conference in the convention city and explain to the news media all the details of the convention, suggesting things for them to cover. Not only local radio and TV journalists, but also newspaper and specialty magazine publishers are invited to attend. Finally, the convention time arrives, and various reporters show up to cover the proceedings.

At the conclusion of the convention, it now becomes your responsibility to give an account of your performance to the officers of the association. Everyone has seen the reporters, but the executive directors need some tangible evidence that your efforts at publicity were received and used by the news media. You solve your problem by contracting with a *clipping bureau* to peruse publications that may have carried news about the convention, to clip all such stories, and then furnish you with these clippings as tangible feedback of your "job well done."

Before you select the clipping bureau, you'll want to determine what range of publications you want clipped. In our example, you'll not only want newspapers clipped, but also articles from those specialty publications who sent reporters to your press conference. The next thing you have to determine is the extent of the clippings. Besides all of the news stories about the convention, you'll also want clippings of any advertisements you placed. Perhaps exhibitors at your convention placed advertisements in various publications to the effect that people could visit their booth at your convention. Again, you'll want clippings of these ads. If other associations held conventions at the same time your association met, you may also want to know how these organizations fared, both in terms of publicity and advertisements. You may even want to subscribe to the clipping bureau's *scrapbook service* in which the bureau mounts all of the clippings it collects in an attractive scrapbook ready for you to present to the officers of the association. Also, since your association is international, you'll want to be sure foreign language publications are scrutinized. For all of this work, you will be charged either a flat fee or on a cost per item basis, which means you'll pay a certain amount for every item clipped.

Clipping bureaus can provide feedback on the success of any public information or public relations effort. Any company which goes to the expense of making a concerted public relations effort wants to know how successful it was. If the individual, public relations firm, or advertising agency it hires can't produce any evidence of results, then chances are the company will take its account elsewhere. Thus, monitoring the press and providing feedback to clients is an important function provided by the clipping bureau.

action lines

In Chapter 14, we discussed the audience's relationship to mass media as a "functional" process whereby there were certain *uses* and *gratifications* which result from our involvement with media. In the past decade, there has been an increase in the use of an instrument of feedback to newspapers and magazines which involves the individual functionally with the media. The instrument is commonly referred to as an *action line*, and it appears in the form of readers' letters to the newspaper or magazine complaining about a problem with some product, service, or company. The publication then helps the readers try to solve their problems. A company that will not honor a warranty or a mail-order product that never arrived are typical problems received by action lines.

The company contacted by an action line representative can receive either good or bad publicity, depending upon how it handles the reader's problem. Because of this publicity aspect, action lines are usually quite effective in problem-solving devices. Naturally, when companies are out of business or have fled town, there is little an action line can do.

From a theoretical standpoint, action lines also serve another function for the users of mass media. Although they are concerned with helping a specific individual, the published replies actually serve an entire readership. Thus, the service goes beyond a one-to-one functional relationship to a mass functional relationship. In addition, the issues dealt with by action line usually relate directly to our everyday lives, often more so than other news content of the publication, and give us specific responses to direct inquiries. Action line therefore serves a more personal and involved interactive process than many other forms of media content.

advice columns

Our discussion of feedback to the print media would not be complete without including the subject of advice columns. These presentations range from local columns to nationally syndicated features. Advice columns have increased in scope to include everything from sex problems to automobile repairs. Women's features such as Dr. Joyce Brothers, Ann Landers, and Dear Abby are some of the more familiar. We have already touched upon these columns in our earlier discussion of syndication, but you should keep in mind that they are also a form of feedback to the media. Advice columns operate as does action line, to give the individual a functional relationship to the media, which often becomes mass communication to a national audience. Although many are commercial enterprises in their own right, they constantly elicit feedback from the mass audience.

summary

Feedback to the media is an important monitoring process for media managers and planners. Among various types of feedback to the print media, one of the most common is letters to the editor. Such letters reflect a wide segment of public opinion and are usually the result of spontaneous reactions to media content. In some cases, however, letters to the editor serve as an organized persuasive device coordinated by certain groups of people. Readership surveys are another important source of feedback to the newspaper industry. These surveys measure demographic characteristics of the audience that help identify subgroups of people as regular readers. Other information solicited from the surveys includes life style analysis on how and when readers are exposed to the newspaper, community attitudes that help mold a newspaper as an effective social force, public reactions to increases in subscription prices, how the newspaper is perceived as a news source, how the readers use and perceive different sections of the paper, how involved they are with newspaper advertising, and the effectiveness of the newspaper's distribution. In recent years, many newspapers have started to employ ombudsmen to handle reader feedback on everything from the quality of news coverage to the reliability of delivery service. How effective the ombudsmen are is determined by how well the staff responds to their suggestions.

A common feedback device for magazines is the reader profile. It is important in determining the changing attitudes of the magazine audience and how the magazine should alter its content to respond to these attitudes. Certain trade publications use reader service cards, which permit the reader to circle a number on a postcard insert and receive additional information about advertised products. Feedback in direct mail concerns itself with three basic characteristics. These include the effectiveness of the direct-mail piece in soliciting reader response, the characteristics of the direct-mail audience, and the testing of revised direct-mail literature. For people and businesses involved in public relations and advertising, clipping bureaus are an important source of feedback. Such bureaus monitor the print media and clip articles, advertisements, and similar items dealing with a specific theme. Special features of the print media that encourage audience feedback and help to provide many functional relationships with the media include action lines and advice columns. Consumer complaints about products, services, and companies are topics handled by the action line reporter; the social and moral climate of the mass audience finds expression in the advice column.

opportunities for further learning

Doig, Ivan, and Carol Doig, *News, A Consumers Guide.* Englewood Cliffs, N.J.: Prentice-Hall, Inc., 1972.

Howe, Quincy, *The News and How to Understand It.* New York: Greenwood Press, 1968.

Rivers, William L., William B. Blankenberg, Kenneth Stark, and Earl Reeves, *Backtalk: Press Councils in America.* San Francisco, Calif.: Canfield Press, 1972.

feedback:

the electronic media

CHAPTER SIXTEEN

Like print media, electronic media are also attuned to feedback, much of it taking the form of letters from the public. Other forms of feedback, such as the broadcast ratings, are indigenous to the electronic media and serve as the basis for many decisions affecting broadcast media content. You the consumer should be aware of feedback to the electronic media and of your role as initiator in the feedback process.

letters from the broadcast audience

On the average, broadcasters do not receive as much mail from the public as publishers, mainly because of time constraints in airing that mail. It would be difficult to free sufficient air time to read letters to broadcast stations and such a decision could seriously hamper a radio station's music format or a television network's programming of entertainment shows. In addition, a broadcaster can't physically add extra minutes to the time in a broadcast day the way a newspaper can add pages to the next edition. Thus, where there is no forum to publicly air the letters, actual letter writing tends to drop off. Moreover, people are not in the habit of writing broadcast media the way they are the print media. Letters to the editor have been a traditional way of life in America since long before broadcasting arrived. Letters to the broadcast media are more recent and not as common. There are also regulatory constraints on indiscriminately airing letters, such as the Fairness Doctrine.

This does not mean that letters to the broadcast media aren't encouraged. The CBS program *60 Minutes* concludes with excerpts from viewers' letters, and many local stations are encouraging listener and viewer opinions with "speak out" or "ask the manager" programs. Another means of "publishing" viewer and listener feedback uses a recording device attached to the station telephone. Viewers or listeners are then requested to call the number and have their opinions recorded for later airing as part of special programming or news features. Any audience reaction is encouraged by the FCC, and even those opinions and letters which are not aired are kept in broadcast stations' "public files," which any individual is entitled to see during regular business hours.

Although it is not easy to stereotype the person who writes a letter to the broadcasting industry, he or she does project certain general characteristics. As with letters to the editor, the broadcast letter writers tend to be active in their community. They could very well be the "opinion leaders" we discussed in Chapter 13. A research study investigated the characteristics of people who responded to a network news program showing the execution of a suspected enemy soldier in Southeast Asia. A total of ninety letters were analyzed, and it was found that "the writers were politically active compared with the general population. Sixty-nine percent were members of at least one voluntary organization, 10 percent had initiated a petition for some campaign or cause, 16 percent had solicited for such a petition, and 64 percent had signed a petition."[1] Thirty-three percent of the letter writers said they worked on the campaign of a political candidate (as opposed to 7 percent for the general population). "Of the respondents, 24 percent said they were frequently 'asked their opinion' on the Vietnam War; 51 percent said they frequently 'offered' it. Nearly one-third (32 percent) had written a broadcaster at least one time in the past year, . . . 30 percent had written a newspaper editor, and 15 percent had written to the FCC."[2]

Some people assume that writing a letter to the media is a waste of time. Such is not the case. Most broadcasters, local and network, appreciate feedback from the mass audience and welcome the opportunity to initiate and/or respond to a dialogue with their audience. They therefore take the time to seriously evaluate every letter that is received.

broadcast ratings

They have been criticized for being inaccurate, biased, unreliable, and phoney. They have been accused of canceling quality programs, determining network policy, and influencing everything we see and hear on the broadcast media. In addition, they have been perceived as being a subsidiary of the television network and cooperating with sponsors. All of these misperceptions are just that, misperceptions. The broadcast ratings are the services which tell how many people are viewing or listening to what, when, and how often. Some of the most familiar services include the Nielsen Television Index, Arbitron, and Pulse. The rating services have nothing to do with the networks and are not responsible for canceling programs. They have also proven themselves as being, for the most part, very reliable and producing some of the most accurate and sophisticated audience research data available anywhere. But they are by no means perfect. Along with the major rating services, which are well controlled and professionally responsible, are minor ratings services which fall prey to some of the methodological pitfalls that make criticism of the broadcast ratings legitimate. It is important to learn how ratings work, what function they have, and how reliable they actually are.

The Role of Broadcast Ratings

Broadcast rating services are businesses whose services are subscribed to in much the same way that media subscribe to syndicated material. The product the rating service sells is feedback, feedback about the size and composition of the audience attuned to specific media. For instance, if you were operating a commercial television station in a major city, you would want to know how many people watched your station in comparison with other stations. Detailed demographic information would also be important. You would want the rating service to discover how many women aged 18 to 49, the major purchasing group for advertisers' products, watch your station. Similar information would be important for the male audience and the teenage audience, both of which are important to various advertisers. Similarly, you would want to know *when* these audiences tuned in your station. You would also want answers to other questions, such as, Did a particular program command a larger share of the audience than some others? What share of the audience did your newscast capture as compared with competing television stations? Again, all of this information is important because advertisers need to know what audience their commercials are reaching in order to purchase air time wisely.

Advertisers also want to compare the cost of reaching these people. By combining the information found in the ratings with the station's rate card, an advertiser might discover that the cost of reaching 1000 people (cost per thousand) via your television station is less than the cost per thousand on another television station. If it could also be substantiated that your television station reached a significant portion of an audience that the competing station missed, the advertiser will probably be convinced that an investment in your station will maximize his profits.

You may find that certain programs need to be rearranged or even cancelled because of limited viewership. Notice the word *you*. As a media executive, it is you making the decision to cancel or reschedule a program, not the rating service. Many a viewer, laboring under this misconception, has complained to the rating services about the cancellation of a favorite television program. Similar criticism has been unjustifiably cast on rating services when radio personalities have been dismissed because they didn't attract enough listeners.

Although broadcast managers for the most part accept the larger rating services as being accurate and reliable, the public does not. A lack of understanding of the methodologies used causes considerable skepticism. Personal preference is also a powerful emotion, and all of the mathematical formulas in the world will not convince a devoted viewer that a favorite television program has been cancelled because few people watched. The reply from the skeptic may be, "That's impossible; *all* my friends and the people at work watch that program *every* week!" This enthusiasm may be misinformed in two ways. First, *within that sphere of influence*, perhaps everyone does watch the program. Second, perhaps because a few people watch the program and talk about it at lunch, the other friends don't want to be left out and they also watch. However, neither "standard" represents an accurate indicator of how the rest of the viewing audience feels about the program. What *is* behind the development of a broadcast rating?

The Making of a Rating

A typical skeptic of the ratings might also claim there is absolutely no way that a small group of people selected to tell what television programs *they* watch or what radio stations *they* listen to can possibly determine what thousands or millions of other people are watching or listening. The skeptic is criticizing the procedure used by the rating services called *sampling*. Sampling means examining a small portion of something to estimate what the larger portion is like. You know, for example, that if you buy a box of chocolate chip cookies and eat one cookie from the box, chances are very great that all the other cookies in the box will taste the same. This same principle applies to the rating services. It isn't necessary to survey every home in the United States with a television set, called a *television household,* or every home using television, referred to as *households using television* (HUT), to determine such things as how many color television sets are in use or how many people are watching a particular program.[3]

You may ask, "Well, then, if I can eat one cookie and tell what the other cookies in the box taste like, why can't I ask everyone who lives on my street what they're watching on television tonight and that will tell me what the rest of the country is watching?" You might be able to, but the chance for *sampling error* would be great, not because you made a mistake or asked the wrong questions but because you did not obtain a *random sample* of the entire population you wanted to measure. It would be much the same as buying a box of assorted cookies instead of a box of chocolate chip

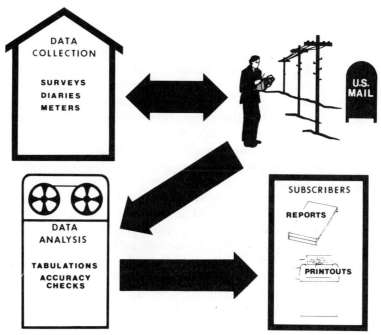

The process of broadcast ratings.

cookies. Then if you ate one cookie from the box of assorted cookies, you wouldn't be able to tell what the rest of the cookies in the box tasted like. The same principle applies to the television preferences of all the nation's viewers versus the people who live on your street. To determine the taste of the remainder of the cookies in the assortment, you need to eat more than just one cookie, but you wouldn't have to eat the entire box. When you select a sufficient random sample of cookies, you are assuring yourself that every cookie in the box has *an equal chance of being selected.* In this procedure the entire box of cookies is known as the *universe* or alternatively, with broadcast ratings, as the *sample area, metro area,* or *rating area.*

To select a random sample from the universe of assorted cookies, for example, you might assign each cookie a number, and then using a list of random numbers, choose a group of cookies to taste. The group you chose would most probably represent the different tastes. Similarly, the rating services use a random sample of the national population, approximately 1200 viewers, to give an accurate reading of what the national audience is watching. Although that figure might seem unusually small, results are accurate within a few percentage points (attributable to sampling error). Mathematicians centuries ago proved that a truly random sample is all that is needed to tell the characteristics of a larger population. Moreover, once a certain number of persons is chosen for the random sample, increasing this number won't significantly change the outcome. In other words, a random sample of 1500 or even 15,000 viewers wouldn't change the results to any great degree.

By using a random sample of the population of the United States, the rating services are able to project what the entire national population is watching. This final figure is call a *projection* and represents, within the margin of sampling error attributable to a certain size random sample and universe, the approximate number of people who are tuned to a given radio station or watching a particular television program.

Projections are interpreted in a variety of ways, one of them being *cume,* meaning "cumulative audience," the number of different persons or households which watch or listen to a given station or program during a certain time period. If individuals are being counted, then the projection is referred to as *cume persons;* for households it is referred to as *cume households.* Overall, you would want to know what *share* of the audience your station or your various programs captured. This measure, usually termed a *rating,* is a percentage of the total number of households or persons tuned to a station during a given time period. A final measure of some importance is *frequency,* or how often the viewer tunes in a given station.

Now that you are familiar with some of the basic information that a rating service provides and how the data are interpreted, let's look at the actual data-gathering process.

Gathering Data

Some of the most critical steps in determining a television rating occur during the data-gathering process. After the random sample has been chosen, it becomes necessary to secure the cooperation of people who will be willing to provide the information the rating service is trying to collect. There are many reasons people are hesitant to cooperate with a rating service. They may simply be resistant to a stranger's knocking on the door or calling them on the telephone to request their help. Other prospective candidates may not be home or may have moved. To overcome these obstacles field representatives employed by the major rating services are highly trained in everything from persistence to interpersonal relations, training that has paid off in a high cooperation rate of approximately eighty percent.[4] One interesting research finding has shown that the person who watches educational television is more likely to cooperate with a rating service.[5] Thus, a rating service that only used "easy cooperators" as a data base could find its results skewed toward educational television programs. This fact leads us to conclude that, although a high cooperation rate is important, in order to secure fairly accurate ratings, precaution must be taken to use persistence with some persons selected by the random sampling procedure.

Differences in personality among interviewers is also an important consideration. You know that you can react differently to the same question asked by different people. The tone in their voice, their articulation, and their inflections all influence your interpretation of the question asked. When many different people gather data, these same variables can distort the results of the survey. A very minor rewording of the question can also obstruct results. Rating services, therefore, conduct sophisticated training sessions to make sure their interviewers are asking the same questions in the same way.

In addition to personal and telephone interviews, rating services frequently use two other methods of collecting data. In one method, the *diary* (Figure 16–1), the viewer or listener keeps a record of the programs and stations he or she tuned to at periodic intervals during a given week. This schedule is then sent back to the survey company which tabulates the results of all diaries submitted. In some cases, a small monetary incentive is included with the diary, usually a quarter or half dollar. The other method, commonly referred to as the *meter method,* is employed extensively by A. C.

Figure 16–1. The diary is a common method of obtaining data in broadcast ratings. (Courtesy American Research Bureau.)

Nielsen. Nielsen secures the cooperation of a household to install on the television set a small, inconspicuous monitoring trademarked device called an Audimeter (Figure 16–2), which is connected through a telephone system to Nielsen's central computer. The computer automatically dials each monitoring device at specific intervals and records the readings. The monitoring device tells what channel is on at virtually any time of the day and also if more than one set is in use in the household. Diaries also supplement the Nielsen data gathering process. Although each system has its merits and demerits, research has tended to show little difference in the reliability of data from either one.[6]

Despite the precautions taken by the rating services to provide accurate and reliable data, there is still no fool-proof method of predicting a radio or television audience. Thus, the services are not immune to criticism. There are still skeptics who feel the services

Figure 16-2. The A. C. Nielsen Audimeter constantly monitors television viewing habits. (A. C. Nielsen Company.)

don't accurately project a valid listenership or viewership. Certainly some specialized audiences are extremely difficult to monitor, even with the best data gathering methods. For example, in communities where there is a large transient audience consisting of such groups as college students, tourists, and commuters, the projections may not as accurately reflect the true listenership or viewership as they do for stable population centers.

Research methods often fail to account for minorities and the poor as well. If a rating service uses the telephone book to obtain a random sample, for instance, it can miss a large segment of low income families. Similarly, the less-educated may find the diary procedure too cumbersome and may therefore provide inaccurate information which can skew the final results. Another variable is presented by the case of some persons who watch television but are more proficient in a language other than English. This language barrier may result in misinterpretation of both questions and answers.

Monitoring the Rating Services

In the 1960s, television evolved into the most dominant communicative force in history. It also became apparent that much of its programming was determined by the ratings. Concern over the accuracy of the ratings and their impact on national programming prompted congressional hearings on the subject in 1963. The publicity of the hearings clearly brought to the industry's attention the need for some systematic self-regulatory body to assure confidence in broadcast ratings and avoid government regulation. Thus, the National Association of Broadcasters and other professional associations joined together to form the Broadcast Rating Council (BRC). The Council's main role was to provide the industry and the rating services with an increased element of credibility to assure advertisers that radio and television were in fact reaching the audiences they said they were reaching. The charter of the Council states:

> to secure for the broadcasting industry and related users audience measurement services that are valid, reliable, effective and viable; to evolve and determine minimum criteria and standards for broadcast audience measurement services; to establish and administer a system of accreditation for broadcast audience measurement services; to provide and administer an audit system designed to insure users that broadcast audience measurements are conducted in conformance with the criteria, standards and procedures developed.

Since its beginning, the Council has acted as watchdog over the rating services, with its power based on its ability to affix or revoke its seal of approval on the rating services and their surveys. The Council coordinates a major auditing process of rating service practices, paid for by the rating services themselves. These audits involve all phases of the rating process from the development of sample design, to the gathering of data, through data processing, to published reports. The audits are unannounced and vary from one geographic region to another. In return for the Council's accreditation, the accredited services agree to: (1) provide information to the BRC; (2) operate under substantial compliance with BRC criteria; and (3) conduct their services as they represent them to their subscribers and the BRC.

Overall, the Council has been successful. It has effectively adjusted its procedures over the years to accommodate the rating services' more sophisticated data gathering and processing. Above all it has enjoyed the acceptance of the major rating services. This independent monitoring agency that allows members to employ self-regulation remains a much more satisfactory alternative than government or industry influence or control.

The ratings services will continue to be a major source of feedback for the broadcasting industry. However, technological advancements will undoubtedly affect their operation. Special exterior monitoring devices for keeping track of a household's television viewing habits from outside the home may improve accuracy. A device to monitor radio station listening from automobiles passing on a freeway will also be a big boost to rating accuracy and will inevitably institute a review of the methodologies currently in use. CATV is also influencing the rating services. Special compensations are now made for CATV homes since they have greater access to television and presumably furnish researchers with more data. Two-way cable systems hooked into central computers are capable of monitoring television viewing habits for every cable subscriber. Such systems in use on a national scale would have the potential of monitoring many thousands of television households which, in a local market, could come close to accounting for 100 percent of the television households.

surveying station image

As readership surveys are designed to monitor opinions about the print media, station image research serves the same function for the broadcast media. If you were a manager of a radio station whose ratings were consistently slipping, you would want to know why, and you would want to base any changes in programming on specific findings of an in-depth survey indicating the public's perceptions toward your station. Perhaps you feel that your news programming is your weak spot, so you hire an independent research firm to investigate such things as the public's perceptions of your overall news programming, how listeners perceive the qualifications of your news personnel, how well they can identify the names of your personnel, and how credible they feel your news reports are.

Applying the Results

The completed survey shows some interesting results. First, you discover that the public perceives your local news as quite credible but your national news as slipshod. Listeners also rate the competing station's news personnel as better qualified. In addition, the public can only identify two of the five people you employ in your news department.

Armed with this information, you now begin to rectify these sore spots. You decide to affiliate with a major network and relieve your local news team from reporting any national news. Whereas before the survey you had three of your news personnel working outside the studio, you now bring these "less recognizable" journalists into the studio and make each responsible for at least one major newscast per day. You also decide to purchase some ads in the local newspaper and run a series of "station profiles" detailing the background of your news department staff.

Six months later, you decide to contract for another survey, identical to the first. You learn that your decisions were wise. Results show that the public perceives your station's national news coverage to be very credible; the addition of the network helped considerably. Results also indicate that the public is able to recognize every member of your news department and feels they are very qualified. Your decisions also begin to pay off when the next rating survey is released; your station has moved ahead of its nearest competitor. All of these improvements in image are directly attributable to your initial survey, for without it you could not have determined *why* your ratings were falling.

Reliability of Station Image Surveys

The same methodological considerations that yield reliability in ratings also apply to surveys of station image. Again, one must be careful to gather a true random sample of the population and to ask questions which elicit the specific information you are trying to obtain. The manner in which questions are posed becomes even more critical than with rating surveys, since the questions are often more subtle. For example, a rating survey may simply ask when, where, and at what time you listen to a particular radio station. The station image survey, however, may ask why you listen or what your impressions of a particular station are in comparison to other stations. Since there is more involved than a simple "yes" or "no" answer, the interviewers must be carefully trained in voice inflection, expression, and other vocal qualities to avoid influencing the respondent's answer. When open-ended questions are asked, such as "Explain why you like radio station WAZY?" there's a need to tabulate the many varied responses so that a meaningful pattern emerges. Station image surveys, like ratings, can prove extremely beneficial to broadcasters. They can ascertain much about how we, the public, feel about a given medium and what qualities a station possesses that makes us one of its listeners or viewers.

ascertainment of community needs

As we learned earlier, the broadcasting spectrum is limited. There is simply not room on the airways for everyone who wants to operate a broadcasting station. As a result, the federal government, through the FCC, controls the frequencies used by broadcasters and legally requires them to operate in the public "interest, convenience, and necessity." This means that broadcasters are *privileged* to operate a broadcasting station and use the airways—they do not have a *right* to do so. Thus they must continue to be responsive to the needs of the community and audience they serve.

The FCC requires most broadcasting stations regularly to identify the needs of their community and develop programming in accordance with these needs. The theory behind the required ascertainment procedures is that the licensee represents all those persons in the community who don't have a license, and the licensee's programming should therefore be responsible to all their various needs and interests.

Suppose you were manager of a television station. Periodically you would have to survey a representative sample of "community leaders" to obtain their impressions of the issues confronting the community. Such leaders, as stated in the FCC license renewal Form 303, consist of "leaders in community life—public officials, educators, religious, the entertainment media, agriculture, business, labor, professional and eleemosynary organizations [those supported by charitable contributions], and others who bespeak the interests which make up the community." Once you obtained these opinions, you would need to plan your programming accordingly. We'll assume that four major issues confronting your community are urban renewal, relocating the railroads because of constant traffic snarls, the quality of the water, and law enforcement. It now becomes your responsibility to develop programming which will inform your audience about these issues.

You decide to call a meeting of your programming and news departments to discuss the findings. A number of programming decisions result. The news department decides to produce a series of documentaries to inform the public about urban renewal. A special series of "town-meetings-of-the-air" will also be aired to present the issues surrounding the relocation of the railroads. To be held in a public auditorium and broadcast live, these meetings will bring the public together with railroad officials to discuss relocation. The news department will also highlight the key elements of the meeting on the regularly scheduled news programs. As to the water problem, your station already airs a weekly community issues program but has never invited anyone from the city water commission to be on it. This oversight will now be corrected, and a special "pollution alert" will be added to the daily weather forecast to tell people when the river is unsafe for swimming. The station is already involved in treating the subject of law enforcement. A special investigative documentary is being produced to be aired a few months from now and will deal with police pay and merit promotion systems.

By monitoring the feedback from public officials and leaders and then developing programming to meet community needs, you are acting in accordance with FCC regulations. However, in order to be certain you are reflecting the real issues, you should also systematically monitor the general public, using the random sample technique. Perhaps the issues confronting the people are somewhat different from those expressed by community leaders. Only by obtaining a composite picture of the situation can a station manager make meaningful decisions.

the affiliate and the commercial networks

Although the rating services are by far the primary form of feedback, networks also consult with their affiliate stations. Affiliates make their opinions known to network management through a group of delegates, normally comprised of certain station managers of the network's affiliate stations. If local stations have complaints or opinions they wish expressed to the network, they tell their delegates who in turn meet with the network's management. Although no network will act on isolated complaints, when affiliate feedback becomes substantial about an issue and is well represented geographically and demographically, then the networks will make efforts to remedy the situation.

Another method of feedback to commercial networks is provided through the *clearance ratio*. If a network plans to broadcast material of questionable taste, it will notify all the affiliates well in advance of the forthcoming program and then air it via closed circuit to all network stations for their perusal. If enough of the stations decide they don't want to air the program, then the network realizes it will suffer from the low ratings the program will undoubtedly receive. It is then up to the network to decide: (1) if it is wise to air the program at all; (2) to reschedule it for another time period; (3) to permit local affiliates to videotape the program, then air it at a later hour; (4) to cancel the program entirely.

How do the affiliates in turn make their programming decisions? They do so by being responsive to the feedback they receive from their viewing audience. A careful monitoring of this feedback can enable broadcast management to determine what is suitable or unsuitable for local audience consumption. However, communicating to local broadcast management what their preferences are becomes the public's responsibility. Only when individuals take time to communicate their reactions to the local broadcaster can the local broadcaster, in turn, relay that feedback to the networks.

feedback to public broadcasting

Public broadcasting is different from commercial broadcasting in many of its operations. For example, whereas commercial broadcasting is primarily concerned with feedback from the major audience rating services and has little direct contact with its mass audience, public broadcasting uses several different methods of feedback and *is* in direct contact with its audience. It has to be. The commercial broadcasting audience *indirectly* supports the medium through purchasing advertised products, but the audience for public broadcasting *directly* supports the medium through contributing, serving on station advisory committees, and organizing fund-raising drives. This "public participatory awareness" is the foundation upon which public broadcasting operates and thrives. As a result, public broadcasting monitors, gathers, and analyzes feedback from various audiences perhaps more than any other medium. We'll now examine this process in more detail.

Assume that you are a national executive with the Public Broadcasting Service and are responsible for planning network programming for the next season. Precisely because the *public's* input into your decision is so important, you will garner your data in a number of ways, leaning heavily on feedback from PBS affiliate stations.

Feedback from Affiliate Stations

Since the affiliate stations will eventually air the programming, and since they are directly accountable and responsive to their local audiences, their input to your planning is critical. They are close to

The PBS interconnection system linking a national network of public broadcasting stations.

the pulse of their community and will be the ones who will most directly benefit or suffer from your final decisions.

The role of *station managers* in this process should not be underestimated. They have the knowledge, through constant interaction with their staff, of the types of programs their local audiences like or dislike. They are also cognizant of the budget limitations of their stations, what types of programs stimulate "participatory awareness," and how their own operating schedules will need to be adapted in order to accommodate PBS programming.

Another important link in your feedback process is the station *program manager.* This person's duties are to select the programs for airing, schedule their air time, and oversee the production and direction of locally produced programs. Program managers, like station managers, will also regularly monitor audience feedback to determine what the audience is viewing. Since they know how this audience feedback affects local scheduling and programming, you, as a PBS executive, should monitor their opinions more frequently than those of the station managers. In fact, you should solicit feedback from the program managers on a quarterly basis and then after each poll, call a group of eight to twelve program managers together to evaluate the national responses from these quarterly polls.

You can also monitor feedback on scheduling through *weekly carriage reports.* These are prepared by the local stations to give the network an idea of how PBS-originated programs fit into local stations' schedules. For instance, if these reports show that there are two popular scheduling times for a given program, then the program may be sent twice at different times during the week to accommodate the affiliate stations.

Feedback from the Audience

You'll want to review the letters that your own office receives and those received by affiliates. Legitimate criticism or praise that emanates from those letters can greatly affect future programming.

Other data will result from special studies or even from the commercial rating services. When public television programming does show up on a commercial rating survey, you'll want to determine why. Is it a particular program that has captured the rating service's attention? What type of audience is watching the program? Is the program locally produced, and if so, is its programming concept suitable for national distribution? Still other questions feedback might answer are: When do people turn to public television and for what purpose? For instance, a federal agency may fund a research project to determine the uses children have for a particular PBS program. You'll want to review this research and decide whether it might function as a model for other new programming concepts. All of these direct audience inputs can help you be much more responsive to your audience.

Outside Observers

The Public Broadcasting System also regularly employs special observers to give their opinions on specific types of programs. These experts in their own field provide the network with post-program analyses that can be important in gaining a perspective on present programs and planning future ones. Many individual stations, through their advisory councils, also have expert "observers" who regularly provide feedback to program management.

Feedback from Other Media

In recent years, there has been an increase in the number of newspapers, magazines, and radio and television stations which employ media critics. Public broadcasting has quite often been singled out to receive these reviewers' praise or criticism. Most public broadcasting stations keep a scrapbook for both reviews and general news coverage of their own station or the public broadcasting concept. A perusal of this information will help to determine what the media critics are writing and the mass public reading about PBS programming. You, as a program planner, may be able to spot trends in the critics' reviews and locate certain types of programs which are especially praised or criticized.

The Station Program Cooperative

When it was first introduced, some media critics referred to the Station Program Cooperative (SPC) as an innovative idea in program selection. It utilizes direct feedback in the form of financial commitment from affiliate stations to determine which programs will make up approximately one-third of the programming distributed by PBS.[7] Essentially, the SPC operates in the following manner. As the person responsible for determining what program will be funded under the SPC system, you will first develop a set of national program needs using all of the feedback information mentioned above. Based on these needs, you will solicit proposals from program producers. From this information, you will then prepare a catalogue of the program proposals for use by the individual public broadcasting system's licensees in planning their next season's programming.

This selection process by the individual licensees initiates a total, direct feedback procedure which eventually determines which program will be funded and which program will be dropped from further consideration. The first step in this feedback process is a *bidding round* in which the licensees indicate their interest in specific programs. At this point there is no financial commitment on the part of the licensee. From this information, the SPC official then determines which programs are the top contenders for selection by affiliate stations. After a second bidding round, during which the stations begin to commit themselves financially, some programs are tentatively accepted and others are dropped from the list. The final step, a *purchase round*, reveals stations making final commitments and programs being selected.

Feedback is one of the most important steps in the decision-making process of a public broadcasting station. Public broadcasting, by its very nature, must monitor much more detailed feedback at every level on the management chain. The interests of the local audience become feedback to the affiliates, and these data are in turn utilized by the PBS network. PBS programming is generally the result of a much more "participatory" process than occurs with most other forms of mass communication, a type of feedback in which you as a consumer can become personally involved.

filing a complaint

As a consumer of the broadcast media, you have every right to express your opinions to the industry without waiting to be contacted in a community ascertainment survey. For example, let's examine a hypothetical complaint you decide to file with a broadcaster. Imagine you represent a group of people who are lobbying for a large section of your city to be made into a park. Your group is convinced, after carefully monitoring a local television station, that the station has not made any concerted effort to cover and report the issues surrounding the proposed park, even though it has been a subject of long discussion at city council meetings, and letters to the editor have appeared in the local papers. You decide to write a letter. Your first thought is to write directly to the FCC; this would be a mistake. Since your group feels that the local station is the culprit, then it is that station which you should contact first to try and resolve your differences.

Once you have decided to write the manager and complain, you'll want to do it *promptly*. Waiting six months until the issue has ceased to exist will be of little value to you or the broadcaster.

You'll also want to be *specific* and explain the exact issues which you represent. Don't fill your letter with unrelated information. Also, include your name and address so that the manager can get in touch with you. In our example, we'll assume you have contacted the station manager. The two of you meet and discuss the problem. As a result, the manager agrees to schedule a special program in which your group and people who oppose the park will discuss the issue. As a concerned citizen, you have taken part in the feedback process and have opened up a responsible dialogue with a broadcaster. In this case, you represented a legitimate issue which was of concern to a large segment of your community.

Complaints to the FCC

If for some reason you wish to complain to a local station but wish to remain anonymous, you can contact the FCC directly. Or, if for some reason you are not satisfied with the action taken by the commercial broadcaster to resolve your complaint, you can contact the FCC. When this procedure is used, the *Broadcast Procedural Manual* of the FCC outlines specific guidelines which you should follow. The *Manual* states:

> Submit your complaint promptly after the event to which it relates. Include at least the following information in your letter of complaint: The full name and address of the complainant. The call letters and location of the station. The name of any program to which the complaint relates and the date and time of its broadcast. A statement of what the station has done or failed to do which causes you to file a complaint. Be as specific as possible: Furnish names, dates, places and other details. A statement setting forth what you want the station and/or the Commission to do. A copy of any previous correspondence between you and the station concerning the subject of the complaint. Try to appreciate that the person reviewing your complaint must make rapid judgments regarding the gravity of the matters related and the action to be taken. There are a number of simple things you can do to make his job easier and to aid your own cause: State the facts fully and at the beginning. Subject to fully stating the facts, be as brief as possible. If the facts are self-explanatory, avoid argument; let the facts speak for themselves. Avoid repetition or exaggeration. If you think a specific law or regulation has been violated, tell us what it is. If possible, use a typewriter, but if you do write by hand, take special pains to write legibly.

These guidelines are to make both the job of the FCC easier and to process your complaint more efficiently. If you do file a complaint to the FCC, you will be one of almost 25,000 people who do so every year. With this volume of feedback to assimilate, it is easy to see why step-by-step guidelines are a necessity. It is also easy to see why the best method is first to contact the local station and try and resolve the issue at that level.

It's wise to learn something about broadcast regulations before filing such a complaint. Some of the public is under the impression that the FCC has the power to demand certain programs be aired or taken off the air. *It does not.* Also, some of the public is under the mistaken impression that news programming is fair game for complaints. Although anyone is entitled to file a complaint about the operation of a broadcast station's news department, there are some rather strong safeguards assuring freedom of the press which in many ways exempt the news department from any control, including that of station management.

Despite the precautions to be taken by the complainant, the person who contributes responsible feedback to the media furthers the democratic process in a free society. The commercial broadcasting industry, because its licensees have the "privilege" of operating a station, is particularly sensitive to feedback from its audience and is prepared to react to this in a responsible manner.

electronic response indicators

They called her "Big Annie", and she was developed in 1937 by Dr. Frank Stanton of CBS and Dr. Paul Lazarsfeld, a well-known social scientist. It was one of the first electronic response indicators (ERI) used to register audience feedback, in this case reaction to radio shows. While listening to a radio show, a listener would have the opportunity to push one of three buttons representing "like," "dislike," and "neutral." After the program was over, the listener would explain his or her reaction to an interviewer. The concept was a new alternative to the more traditional surveys and attitude questionnaires.

Although Big Annie did not become the backbone of corporate decisions at CBS, she did spark the media's interest in electronic feedback, interest that resulted in modern devices operating on the same principle. One such instrument was invented by a professor of broadcast communication at the University of Oregon, Dr. Elwood Kretsinger. Kretsinger's electronic response indicator is called a "Chi Square Meter." Again, it simultaneously records an individual's responses to whatever he or she happens to be watching or listening to. Comparisons of responses among different individuals or groups are made using a statistical test called the chi square, thus the name Chi Square Meter.

Commercial Development and Application of ERIs

The popularity of ERIs as a method of analyzing feedback and audience response has been significant enough for a number of commercial firms to begin manufacturing the systems on a wide scale. These commercial systems are usually installed in a large auditorium with an ERI attached to every seat or desk in the auditorium. Each component has five buttons that can be programmed to indicate anything from an answer to a five-part, multiple-choice question, to expressing one of five such attitude responses as "strongly agree," "agree," "neutral," "disagree," and "strongly disagree." (Figure 16–3). The entire room of ERIs can be interfaced with a computer and can register the continual response of the entire room, sections of the room, or work statistical comparisons between various groups of people.

Recall the example we used in Chapter 12, to illustrate the production of an instructional television program on newspaper publishing. Assume you have produced the program and now want to test its effectiveness. You arrange for a high school journalism class to use a room equipped with ERIs and, at periodic intervals in the program, ask the class to respond to a series of questions prepared

Figure 16–3. An electronic response indicator permits instant feedback and the analysis of reactions to varied messages. (Instructional Industries, Inc.; JW/University of Texas News Service/Frank Armstrong.)

to evaluate your program's effectiveness. When the program is over, a computer printout tells you how the class scored on every question. Those questions the students missed may indicate that you need to revise one or more sections of the program. If you had not been using ERIs, you could have waited until the program was over and simply given them a paper-pencil test to evaluate what they had learned. However, you would then have had to score the tests and work the statistical computations by hand or wait until they could be done by computer.

Now suppose you are a producer assigned to develop an educational television program to teach history to a group of foreign students. You want to determine if the examples you used in preparing the program were meaningful to those students. Thus, after producing your program, using an ERI system, you have a group of students react to the program in "agree-disagree" responses. You may find that at one point in the program a particular example offended the foreign students. From this feedback, you will want to revise this section of the program and cut the offensive segment. These are just two examples of the way in which the ERI system can operate.

Similar electronic response systems monitor feedback from new television programs and from advertising campaigns in rather innovative settings. There are systems installed in mobile vans which can stop outside a grocery store and solicit shoppers to enter the van. Inside, customers watch a television commercial and have their reactions to the commercial tested. Then the operators watch the shoppers enter the grocery store and directly monitor sales of the product. ERIs which measure galvanic skin responses are also being used to measure audience reaction to everything from television programs to popular records. A device called a psychogalvanometer is used by a California firm to test reactions to commercials by measuring the sweat glands in the index and middle fingers of the right hand every couple of seconds. A similar system operated by another California firm monitors reactions to records it is considering for production.

Advantages and Disadvantages of ERIs

Electronic response indicators have basically two advantages over older evaluative methods. First, they are fast, especially when interfaced with a computer. What formerly took hours of work and computation can now be calculated almost instantaneously. Second, ERIs can measure detailed aspects of audience reaction, thus yielding much more sophisticated data bases. When decision makers can monitor audience reaction every few seconds, they have a more useful account of how an audience is reacting to a message.

The main disadvantage of such systems is the limited number of responses that can be monitored at any one time. Whereas a major rating service can obtain feedback from an audience large enough to predict national trends, most electronic response systems are designed for a group no larger than can be accommodated in a small auditorium. This limitation is not, however, a technological weakness. Electronic response systems that connect the home to a computer, much the same as the two-way cable system, already make possible the measurement of large audiences. Perhaps as resistance to this type of technology wanes, future feedback techniques will not only measure how many people were watching a television program but also tabulate their opinions of that program on a second-to-second basis.

feedback in the recording industry

It's Monday morning, and every disc jockey, radio program director, recording company executive, artist, composer, and everyone who has anything to do with the music industry is literally consuming every word of the *Billboard* chart published in *Billboard* magazine. There is even a *Billboard Hotline* that gives a three-day lead on the regular *Billboard* charts, arriving on Friday instead of Monday. These charts pinpoint the top hits everywhere. They can literally make or break a star or mean millions of dollars of profit, almost overnight. As we learned earlier, there are charts for a multitude of music types, including those which tell the international position of hit recordings from throughout the world. Record charts, feedback to the recording industry, compile all sorts of data, including record sales, the amount of air play disc jockeys are giving hit recordings, the number of times a certain song is punched to play in juke boxes across the country, and the savvy of industry experts. Their importance to this mass media support industry cannot be overemphasized.

The Billboard Charts

The typical *Billboard* chart lists ten important pieces of information which, when surveyed over time, can indicate how well a particular performer or group is doing, how well a particular recording company is faring, and the prospects for a record becoming a hit (Figure 16–4). For instance, assume the hit song you are keeping track of is "Sunset," recorded by Mary Doe. It might appear on the chart as follows:

6 7 5 SUNSET
Mary Doe, Apple 1201 (Capitol) (Tre-Hollis, BMI)

Billboard SPECIAL SURVEY for Week Ending 8 23 75
(Published Every Two Weeks)

Billboard Jazz LPs

This Week	Last Report	Weeks on Chart	TITLE Artist, Label & Number (Distributing Label)
1	1	25	**MISTER MAGIC** Grover Washington Jr. Kudu KU 20 S1 (Motown)
2	3	7	**THE CHICAGO THEME** Hubert Laws. CTI 6058 S1 (Motown)
3	4	18	**TWO** Bob James. CTI 6057 S1 (Motown)
4	2	20	**EXPANSIONS** Lonnie Liston Smith & The Cosmic Echoes. Flying Dutchman BDL1 0934 (RCA)
5	11	5	**LIQUID LOVE** Freddie Hubbard. Columbia PC 33556
6	10	16	**DISCOTHEQUE** Herbie Mann. Atlantic SD 1670
7	13	20	**NO MYSTERY** Return To Forever Featuring Chick Corea. Polydor PD 6512
8	8	20	**STEPPING INTO TOMORROW** Donald Byrd. Blue Note BN LA368 G (United Artists)
9	6	11	**TALE SPINNIN'** Weather Report. Columbia PC 33417
10	14	9	**A TEAR TO SMILE** Roy Ayers Ubiquity. Polydor PD 6046
11	7	35	**SUN GODDESS** Ramsey Lewis. Columbia KC 33194
12	5	11	**THE BRECKER BROTHERS** Arista AL 4037
13	16	18	**IN THE POCKET** Stanley Turrentine. Fantasy F 9478
14	25	3	**BECK** Joe Beck. Kudu KU 21 S1 (Motown)
15	23	40	**BAD BENSON** George Benson. CTI 6045 S1 (Motown)
16	18	9	**BASIE JAM** Count Basie & His Orchestra. Pablo 2310 718 (RCA)
17	9	18	**CHASE THE CLOUDS AWAY** Chuck Mangione. A&M SP 4518
18	28	5	**PHENIX** Cannonball Adderley. Fantasy F 79004
19	19	20	**I NEED SOME MONEY** Eddie Harris. Atlantic SD 1669
20	NEW ENTRY		**ESTHER PHILLIPS w/BECK** Kudu KU 23 S1 (Motown)
21	12	9	**SHABAZZ** Billy Cobham. Atlantic SD 18139
22	32	3	**SATURDAY NIGHT SPECIAL** Norman Connors. Buddah BDS 5643
23	31	3	**LEVEL ONE** The Eleventh House Featuring Larry Coryell. Arista AL 4052
24	21	5	**COME GET TO THIS** Nancy Wilson. Capitol ST 11386
25	15	44	**PIECES OF DREAMS** Stanley Turrentine. Fantasy F 9465
26	24	11	**NATIVE DANCER** Wayne Shorter. Columbia PC 33418
27	22	16	**THE AURA WILL PREVAIL** George Duke. BASF/MPS MC 25613
28	17	7	**PHOEBE SNOW** Shelter SR 2109 (MCA)
29	30	3	**EL JUICIO (The Judgement)** Keith Jarrett. Atlantic SD 1673
30	NEW ENTRY		**WHY CAN'T WE BE FRIENDS?** War. United Artists UA LA441 G
31	NEW ENTRY		**SOLO CONCERTS/BREMEN, LAUSANNE** Keith Jarrett. ECM3 1035 37 (Polydor)
32	NEW ENTRY		**I AM MUSIC** Carmen McRae. Blue Note BN LA462 (United Artists)
33	NEW ENTRY		**TIMELESS** John Abercrombie. ECM 1047 (Polydor)
34	NEW ENTRY		**SUNBURST** Eddie Henderson. Blue Note BN LA464 (United Artists)
35	40	3	**CRISSCRAFT** Sonny Criss. Muse MR 5068
36	20	20	**WHO IS THIS BITCH, ANYWAY?** Marlena Shaw. Blue Note BN LA397 G (United Artists)
37	27	7	**PURE DESMOND** Paul Desmond. CTI 6059 S1 (Motown)
38	38	3	**10 YEARS HENCE** Yusef Lateef. Atlantic SD 2 1001
39	39	3	**CORNBREAD, EARL AND ME/SOUNDTRACK** Blackbyrds. Fantasy F 9483
40	NEW ENTRY		**THE CASE OF THE 3 SIDED DREAM IN AUDIO COLOR** Rahssan Roland Kirk. Atlantic SD 1674

Figure 16-4. A *Billboard* chart listing the position of jazz recordings based on various industry and public-demand data. (Courtesy *Billboard.*)

The first two numbers on the chart indicate the record's standing for the current and the previous week, respectively. In our example, "Sunset" has moved up from seventh place to sixth place. This information immediately tells you that the recording is becoming more popular or is "climbing the charts." As program director at a radio station that is airing "Sunset" you might, on the basis of this listing, increase the frequency of air play of the song, for example, from one to two air plays every hour. You might also give it some additional buildup such as your own station's "pick hit of the week." All of these decisions, which may seem little more than radio "jargon," are daily judgments that can actually be reflected in profits or losses of hundreds or thousand of dollars. For the slightest change in a radio station's programming can provoke you, the listener, to switch stations or change your listening pattern entirely. When your decision is translated into rating shares which then affect advertising dollars, you can see how this "jargon" becomes very expensive indeed.

The third important number on our listing represents the number of weeks the song has been on the charts, in our example, five weeks. This information denotes how fast the song climbed to its present position. The remainder of the information tells the name of the song; the label and number, which in our example is Apple 1201 and very important if you must order it; the distributor's label, which in our example is Capitol; the publisher of the song, which for "Sunset" is a company called Tre-Hollis; and the licensee, which is BMI.

All of this information is digested, evaluated, cursed, praised, and promoted. Although the charts may seem somewhat removed from the mainstream of mass media and our own involvement with media in society, keep in mind that our feedback, in terms of record sales and station preferences, actually composes these charts.

Playlists

Another form of feedback to the recording industry is the radio station's *playlist* (Figure 16–5). Playlists are similar to the *Billboard* charts except that they are published by individual radio stations and reflect the popularity of songs in that station's immediate listening area. They are usually found in most record stores posted in a conspicuous place next to the record display racks. Many times they contain supplementary information, such as the latest "gossip" on station air personalities. They are distributed by direct mail and are a major piece of promotional literature for many radio stations. Playlists are also an excellent way for stations to assure themselves of obtaining free records for air play. In fact, when the energy crisis

WLS MUSICRADIO 89
WLS MUSICRADIO 89
WLS MUSICRADIO 89

FRED WINSTON

PLAYS

THE BEST MUSIC

IN CHICAGO

6AM — 10AM

LW	TW	WEEK ENDING NOVEMBER 1, 1975	VOL. 16, NO. 4
1	1	Bad Blood	Neil Sedaka
6	2	Island Girl	Elton John
2	3	Dance With Me	Orleans
7	4	I'm Sorry	John Denver
3	5	Fame	David Bowie
4	6	Ballroom Blitz	Sweet
10	7	Lyin Eyes	Eagles
13	8	They Just Can't Stop It (Games People Play)	Spinners
xx	9	Miracles	Jefferson Starship
5	10	Mr. Jaws	Dickie Goodman
8	11	Get Down Tonight	KC & The Sunshine Band
14	12	Heat Wave	Linda Ronstadt
xx	13	Rocky	Austin Roberts
11	14	Ain't No Way To Treat A Lady	Helen Reddy
xx	15	S. O. S.	Abba
		Rhinestone Cowboy	Glen Campbell
		Who Loves You	Four Seasons
		Fallin In Love	Hamilton, Joe Frank & Reynolds
		It Only Takes A Minute	Tavares
		Run Joey Run	David Geddes
		At Seventeen	Janis Ian
		Jive Talkin	Bee Gees
		Someone Saved My Life Tonight	Elton John
		Love Will Keep Us Together	Captain And Tennille
		Tush	Z Z Top
		Could It Be Magic	Barry Manilow

MUSICRADIO LP'S & TAPES

LW	TW		
1	1	Wish You Were Here	Pink Floyd
3	2	Red Octopus	Jefferson Starship
5	3	Windsong	John Denver
2	4	Capt. Fantastic & The Brown Dirt Cowboy	Elton John
4	5	One Of These Nights	Eagles
6	6	Toys In The Attic	Aerosmith
10	7	Born To Run	Bruce Springsteen
9	8	Fandango	Z Z Top
xx	9	Win, Lose Or Draw	Allman Brothers Band
7	10	The Heat Is On	Isley Brothers

The WLS Musicradio Surveys represent the station's estimate of current and potential music popularity as reflected in such measures as record sales, juke box play, audience interviews, listener requests, and national charts. Last week's and this week's positions are listed under LW and TW respectively.

Figure 16–5. A radio station playlist is an important part of feedback to the recording industry.

created a shortage of the petroleum products used to make records, some recording companies informed campus radio stations that they couldn't afford to send them any more free promotional records unless they received playlists in return. Along with retail record outlets in any market, station playlists are usually mailed to major recording companies, record distribution companies, certain artists and performers, and other radio stations. Just as the recording industry scans the *Billboard* charts, it also reviews playlists, especially those of major radio stations. In essence, being first on the playlist of some of the larger radio stations in the United States is equal in importance to a first on the *Billboard* charts.

Syndicated Charts and Playlists

In addition to station playlists and the *Billboard* charts, there are other charts and services used by the industry to gauge the success of its products. Some private individuals, primarily authoritative and knowledgeable program directors or disc jockeys, compose their own syndicated record charts and playlists. Such charts and playlists are usually detailed and can even reflect the rise of an obscure recording in a small market, thus indicating how it might do nationally. Just as news departments like to scoop their competitors, so programming departments try equally hard to discover new recordings that are destined to be major hits. Thus, such special services, charts, and playlists will continue to be important feedback devices to the recording industry.

summary

As with the print media, feedback to the broadcast media also plays an important part in media decision making. Letters from listeners and viewers constitute one type of feedback. Although not as plentiful as those received by the print media, letters often come from politically active individuals who serve as opinion leaders in their own community. The paramount form of feedback to the broadcast media, however, is from the rating services. Although the services' projections have been criticized as being invalid, efforts to perfect both data gathering and data processing have considerably improved their reliability. Station image surveys are also important and can provide much more detailed information than the rating services. Most local radio and television stations are required to gather feedback from their own communities. The process is commonly referred to as needs and desires surveys and is designed to identify issues and problems of common concern to the community.

The broadcasting networks are also attuned to feedback from individuals and from local affiliates. Commercial networks mostly base their program selection on data gathered by the rating services. They do, however, respond to feedback from representative groups of delegates affiliated with networks. The Public Broadcasting System uses an elaborate method of gathering and monitoring feedback which includes perusal of letters received by affiliate stations, communication between PBS and station managers and program directors, and a bidding process whereby the licensees of public broadcasting stations have a very direct say in what types of programs will be seen on the PBS network. Members of the community, on occasion, also have reason to complain to local broadcasters. This process usually opens up a responsible dialogue between the broadcasters and the complainant.

More sophisticated feedback is reflected in the development by broadcasting research of such devices as electronic response indicators. These instruments measure individual, up-to-the-minute reactions to various types of radio and television programming. A major support industry of broadcasting, the recording industry, uses charts and playlists as important sources of feedback.

opportunities for further learning

A Study of the Consistency of Local Market Television Ratings. Westfield, N.J.: Statistical Research, Inc., 1970.

American Research Bureau, *The Influence of Non-Cooperation in the Diary Method of Television Audience Measurement.* Beltsville, Md.: American Research Bureau, 1963.

GUIMARY, DONALD L., *Citizens Groups in Broadcasting.* New York: Praeger Publishers, 1975.

JENNINGS, RALPH MERWIN, and PAMELA RICHARD, *How To Protect Your Rights in Television and Radio.* New York: Office of Communication, United Church of Christ, 1974.

JOHNSON, NICHOLAS, *How to Talk Back to Your Television Set.* Boston, Mass.: Little, Brown and Company, 1967.

MONTGOMERY, ROBERT F., *Open Letter from a Television Viewer.* New York: J. H. Heineman, 1968.

NIELSEN, ARTHUR CHARLES, *Greater Prosperity Through Marketing Research: The First 40 Years of A. C. Nielsen Company.* New York: Newcomen Society in North America, 1964.

media business

CHAPTER SEVENTEEN

In 1959, professors Edmund Landau and John Davenport stated, "Some of the major problems of the mass media today are centered in the economic area. . . ."[1] Their statement still holds true. For in our free enterprise system, mass media reflect the economic forces which affect all of us. Competition for advertising dollars or government subsidies, starting new businesses or rejuvenating old ones, all hinge on money and management decisions. This chapter takes us inside mass media and views it as a business. In the pages that follow, we'll explore profit and loss in the newspaper industry, broadcasting as an investment, and the birth of a magazine. We'll look at book publishing, the financing of motion pictures, the insides of outdoor, recording industry economics, and the operations of ad agencies. *Although our experiences in each medium will be different, keep in mind that many concepts apply across the media.* For example, some of the concerns in buying a broadcasting property are similar to those in purchasing a magazine. In addition, the risks of financing a major motion picture are in many ways similar to those inherent in extending credit to a major recording artist. Let's begin with the newspaper industry.

profit and loss in the newspaper industry

Most of America's newspapers are old, established enterprises and social institutions in the communities they serve. So well established are they that starting a successful newspaper in today's economy is extremely difficult. Not only is the cost of getting started immense, but also the attraction of a loyal readership from some other well-established newspaper usually proves an insurmountable obstacle. Newspaper readers are simply not the fickle dial switchers of radio and television. Even if a new paper does manage to gain a circulation foothold, this doesn't mean that it will automatically gain the respect of the advertising community. And that respect is vital for success. There are still other factors involved in a newspaper's fiscal hot seat. Let's examine the most important ones—newsprint, labor, new technology, and advertising.

Newsprint: Cost and Supply

Newsprint, the paper upon which newspapers are printed, has reached record consumption. A research study by the Bureau of Business Research and Service at the University of Wisconsin estimates newsprint consumption for 1980 will peak 13,100,000 tons, an increase of about six million from 1959.[2] But increase is only part of the story—cost of newsprint has also jumped because the supply has not kept up with the demand. There are many reasons for this economic disparity. One is the profit margins of paper manufacturers and suppliers. In the past, these merchants have proposed various cost-per-ton price increases. The newspaper industry justifiably complained loudly and effectively postponed rate increases for some time. Gradually, however, economic factors in the paper manufacturing and supply segments of the industry became depressed. And with reduced profits, the manufacturers and suppliers couldn't expand and increase production. Finally, about 1971, everything came to a head. The gap between supply and demand began to close. The manufacturers and suppliers increased prices. The energy crisis crunched, and labor disputes developed which affected everything from lumberjacks to shippers. Supplies dwindled. Costs soared. For the average newspaper, the cost of newsprint increased about 80 percent just between 1971 and 1976.

As Canadian supplies began to dwindle, the United States' suppliers had to make up the difference.[3] Newsprint production figures reveal that U. S. suppliers increased their output 73.3 percent between 1963 and 1973, whereas supply from Canada increased only 15.6 percent during the same period. The North Central states, with production up 1,151 percent, carried most of the burden. To cut shipping weight and make the same tonnage result in more paper, the industry is experimenting with new ways to retain paper strength while making it lighter. Breakage, however, is a big problem. The lighter stock cannot withstand the stress of high-speed presses. Moreover, very thin newsprint causes a "see through" effect which makes the finished newspaper difficult to read.

To cut costs, some newspapers cut the size of their pages. One of the most drastic reductions was that of the *Christian Science Monitor*, which switched to a tabloid format half the size of past editions. *Monitor* subscription prices also rose. Other newspapers cut pages and cancelled features. Even a reduction in margins saved thousands of dollars, depending on the size of the newspaper.

Living with Labor and New Technology

As we learned in Chapter 2, new technology has heaped unique economic problems upon the industry. New techniques in printing mean new equipment, new expenses, and new personnel to learn the trade. Where labor unions are involved, technology can be forced to creep at a snail's pace when the unions try to protect jobs. Threatened strikes are common when skilled workers are fired because technology has made their jobs obsolete. When such strikes do occur, the result has been serious damage to the newspaper. Strikers have been accused of smashing presses to stop a newspaper from being printed by scab (non-union) employees. This action may have several consequences: the newspaper may either shut down, print the editions elsewhere, bow to union demands, or a combination of all three. Personnel costs for the average newspaper now run between 50 and 60 percent of the total operating expenses. When labor costs approach the latter figure, cuts in other areas generally need to be made. For at this point, profit margins shrink, and the expense of new technology can become prohibitive.

Newspaper Advertising

Before the impact of television, the fall of every year was a boom time for newspapers. It was new car time, and to announce their new models, the major auto manufacturers would purchase advertising in newspapers of every size. For the smaller newspaper, it was big and important money. Yet in the last ten years, the small newspaper has seen the auto makers' money vanish. Such has been the way of most national advertisers' media buying habits. They've concentrated their purchases on the larger metropolitan dailies and television, while withdrawing their national advertising from smaller newspapers. Newspaper advertising in general, however, is increasing. Estimated expenditures for 1980 are $9.8 billion.[4] The major share of that figure is attributed to local newspaper advertising, estimated at $8.3 billion. That's up from $4 billion in 1960 for total advertising and about $3 billion in 1960 for local newspaper advertising, an increase of more than 100 percent in both categories. National advertising expenditures have not enjoyed similar gains. While 1980 estimates are for $1.5 billion, that's an increase of only slightly more than $.5 billion dollars from 1960 expenditures. Comparably, national advertising on television has soared.

Despite the increase in advertising expenditures, some forecasters offer only cautious optimism about the future of the newspaper industry.[5] Not that an immediate danger of depression looms, but the industry must realize it is living in an era of rapidly changing social and economic conditions. In Chapter 5, we studied the theoretical development posited by Maisel that would link our existence in a post-industrial society with an increase in specialized media. Already, such general magazines as *Look* and *Life* have folded. With the advent of new technology and changing life styles, will we change the way we "consume" today's typical newspaper? Will our life style changes also evolve more rapidly than the newspaper industry can compensate for them? The ability of a newspaper to survive will thus depend on freeing itself from tradition, facing the reality of competing media, and understanding the changes which might have to be made.

the birth of a magazine

Although there are many magazines that commence publication and then fold after a few issues, overall, magazine publishing has enjoyed steady growth. What are the formulas for success? To discover them, place yourself in the publisher's chair. Let's assume you and your friends decide to start a city magazine for your community (Figure 17–1).

Staffing and Backing

First you'll need some capital. You may have money of your own to invest, or you may have to borrow. One thing is certain, you'll work on credit. The amount you can raise will determine how much talent you can hire to get the enterprise off the ground. You might consider hiring some professional illustrators, writers, graphic and

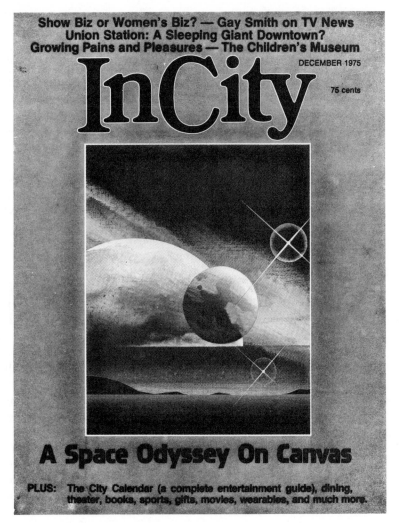

Show Biz or Women's Biz? — Gay Smith on TV News
Union Station: A Sleeping Giant Downtown?
Growing Pains and Pleasures — The Children's Museum

InCity

DECEMBER 1975

75 cents

A Space Odyssey On Canvas

PLUS: The City Calendar (a complete entertainment guide), dining, theater, books, sports, gifts, movies, wearables, and much more.

Figure 17–1. A city magazine—one of many that serve metropolitan areas everywhere.

design consultants, the best photographers, and other professionals. You realize, however, that you'll need to pay these people some rather high salaries. You look at the amount of financial backing you have and decide that although you could hire these top quality professionals, if your magazine didn't manage overnight success, you might have to fire them after the first issue or go bankrupt. Neither alternative is very satisfactory.

Thus, instead of hiring highly paid people to start, you rely on talented people who are just starting their careers as writers, illustrators, and in other creative endeavors. You decide their work is of good quality, and you won't need to solve tough problems that necessitate seasoned veterans. For instance, you will be carrying stories about local personalities, the media, and dining establishments in your city. These will be more essay-journalism pieces as opposed to in-depth stories that larger, national magazines might carry. These actions permit your initial investment to last until the magazine can establish itself and begin to receive substantial income from advertising.

Advertising and Subscription Rates

The first step in obtaining advertising income is to establish an advertising rate schedule which tells potential advertisers how much you'll charge them to advertise in your magazine. This will usually be broken up into various categories. For instance, you will have lower rates for black and white advertisements and higher rates for expensive color processes. You'll charge one rate if the advertiser wants his or her ad to run in only one issue, but offer a discount for longer running ads. Your rates will also vary depending on the size of the ad. For example, a full-page black and white ad will have a certain price, while smaller black and white ads may be broken down into two-thirds, one-half, one-third, one-fourth, or even one twenty-fourth of a page (Figure 17–2). You will also want to discount advertising placed by ad agencies, and offer an additional discount if payment is made within ten days after the advertiser receives the bill. A standard 15 percent discount is given to agencies, and we'll assume you decide to discount another 5 percent for prompt payment. The discount for prompt payment is considerable, but you need cash coming into your business as soon as possible.

The rates you finally decide upon will be a combination of two factors—what the market will bear and what competing publications are charging. For instance, you learn that a magazine similar to yours is published by the chamber of commerce in your city. Thus, you decide to undercut its advertising rates by a few dollars to make a buy in your magazine more attractive. Circulation will also influence later advertising rates, but for now this can only be estimated. One thing you definitely decide not to do, and that is to guarantee a certain circulation to each advertiser on a contractual basis. For if you didn't meet the agreed circulation, you would have to refund a portion of their advertising dollars; that could be financially crippling.

The subscription rate also rests upon many of the same factors as does the advertising rate. How much will you be able to charge for

InCity Magazine

Advertising Rates

	Space	1x	3x	6x	12x
	Full page	$375	365	350	325
	2/3 page	275	265	255	235
BLACK	1/2 page	225	215	210	190
AND	1/3 page	150	145	140	130
	1/4 page	125	120	115	105
WHITE	1/6 page	80	77	74	68
	1/12 page	50	48	46	42
	1/24 page	35	34	32	30

Frequency discounts apply to space used in a 12 month period.

Black and one color: $85 extra   4-color process: $150 extra

2nd cover	425	415
3rd cover	400	390
4th cover (4-color process only)	450	440

Figure 17–2. Advertising rates for a city magazine.

your magazine and still sell copies? A low price may garner sales but won't yield a profit. On the other hand, a higher price will keep people from buying your magazine, circulation will be low, and advertising rates must necessarily fall. Realizing that your decisions can be critical, you finally decide on a subscription rate that is slightly lower than your nearest competitor's but still profitable.

Finding a Distributor

Another important economic consideration is how to distribute your magazine. There are many different choices available. You could completely disregard subscription and newsstand sales and instead concentrate on giving your magazine away free to hotels, motels, and commuter airlines that fly in and out of your city. These businesses cater to the very people who would read your magazine to find out where to wine and dine. The only income you would realize, however, is from advertising, and you don't feel you can afford this arrangement.

So, you decide to make a business deal with one of your city's major magazine distributors. The distributor has access to most of the newsstands in the city and the surrounding counties. He will charge you a percentage of the retail cost of the magazine, and the retail establishment where the magazine is sold will take another percentage. The distributor informs you, however, that he can't guarantee all the business establishments on his route since your magazine will first have to be approved by certain businesses' board of directors. For example, the drugstore chain that wants only "wholesome family" reading material on its shelves will exclude your magazine until it sees some of your first issues.

Research

Although it will be fairly difficult to assess the potential readership for your magazine before it is published, you still want to base some of your decisions on more than just conjecture. You check into the census data for your city and determine the average income of the audience you intend to reach. You check readership data for other magazines to determine what types of people read city magazines and what assumptions you can make about the *pass-a-round-rate* — the number of people who read a given magazine in addition to the person who buys it. You also investigate the possibilities of securing a mailing list in order to send direct-mail literature to potential subscribers.

Production and Promotion

Finally, you begin the actual production work. You allow about two weeks each for writing and photography, printing, and distribution. This means that you are going to be paying salaries long before the first issue hits the streets. You find a good printer, one who can produce superior color material. When you discover her rates are too high, you arrange a *trade-out* with her. In this arrangement, the printer will receive advertising in your magazine in exchange for printing it. You feel the trade-out is beneficial because you need to limit your cash outflow as much as possible. Other decisions you make include how often to publish, what type styles to use, what the magazine's format will be, what paper stock to use, how long the articles should be, and similar decisions associated with the actual production and appearance of the magazine. You also want to notify your potential readership that your magazine will soon be available. So you schedule a major promotional campaign to begin one week before the magazine drapes the newsstands. The promotional campaign will include television commercials, radio commercials, and billboard advertisements. Here again, you work tradeouts wherever possible, exchanging advertising in your magazine for commercial time or space in other media.

You also decide to form an *in-house* advertising agency within your company. This agency will operate in the same way as a regular advertising agency, except that it will be exclusively concerned with handling advertising for your magazine. The advantage for you is that you will be able to receive an advertising agency discount on advertising you buy to promote your magazine. Your additional promotional ventures will include distributing free copies, sending press releases to the business page of your local newspaper, and perhaps appearing as a guest on a local television or radio talk show.

Analyzing Sales

At last your magazine hits the newsstands, and you wait anxiously to see how and if it's accepted. The anticipation is almost unbearable. When the results finally do come in, you are puzzled by some developments, surprised or even disappointed by others. In some areas of your city, the magazine is floundering. In others, it is cleaned off the shelves. You discover the slow-sales area consists of older families in the high-income brackets. Since many of the articles in your first issue catered to a younger audience, with information on discotheques and fast-food restaurants, your appeal to older, high-income residents was minimal. You decide that your next issue will feature information about concerts and theater for this audience.

You also discover that the area where sales are highest is near a college campus. You decide to increase distribution to this area and reduce distribution to the slow-sales areas, at least until you can build an acceptance for your magazine. Now it's on to your next issue, with more planning, more work, and more decisions.

An established magazine, of course, faces many of the same economic issues confronted by our new magazine. Decisions about advertising, subscription rates, distribution, research, production, promotion, and sales analysis preside over every issue published. Balancing revenue against expenses is a task definitely not limited to neophytes, especially in the communications industry. Salary scales will fluctuate depending on the people and the talent working for you, costs will increase, and readership will change. Although city magazines such as our example are capturing a growing share of the magazine market, many have also gone bankrupt or have merged with other publications. There are no proven rules for success. One issue may break sales records, another may flop. A cover design may attract people's attention, and a subsequent attempt to copy it on the next issue may fail miserably. The key is to find an audience, provide them with something they want to read, and manage to juggle finances to weather the bad issues with the good. It is an exciting business and one in which the economic and creative guidelines fuse and split with each issue.

investing in broadcasting

What began in the humble surroundings of an experimental telegraph in the late 1800s is now a billion-dollar business. Radio, television, and cable have enjoyed fruitful returns, and the income from all three has steadily increased. But figures are best left to annual reports and government summaries. Instead, let's venture into the world of the electronic media and concern ourselves with what makes the industry tick. Imagine that you have just been named an executive for a major corporation. Assume the corporation has been making considerable profits and now wants to invest some of these profits in a broadcasting or CATV enterprise. You have been hired to investigate these investment possibilities. Keep in mind that although we're talking about broadcasting and cable, many of the principles discussed here apply to other media as well.

Learning What's For Sale

Your first stop would be to find out what properties are for sale. Two ways of learning this are via the industry grapevine and through *media brokers*. The former operates as an informal communication channel among media executives. At any given time, knowledgeable media executives know what stations or cable systems are for sale or which ones an owner would consider selling if a fair price were offered. Media brokers are in the business of selling media properties in much the same way that real estate brokers sell houses. A good contact with a media broker is the quickest way to put you in touch with those people who have properties to sell.

Analyzing the Market

Once you learn what properties are available, you'll want to investigate fully each station's market. This market analysis will include such standard economic factors, among others, as the rate of industrial growth, average income of the population, and the population's demographic characteristics, all of which should help you decide for or against this particular investment. For instance, you might determine that it is basically an impoverished area, yielding only a slight profit, and not at all lucrative as a long-term investment.

Another important consideration is the competing media in the market. Assume you are considering the purchase of a radio station. All of the economic factors look favorable, but there are simply too many other radio stations in the market to make your investment profitable. Although you might be able to keep the station in the black, there simply wouldn't be enough advertising dollars to permit long-term growth. The competing media might also be in a much better financial situation than your company, which is just starting to make investments. For example, perhaps you find a radio station with a market that meets all of your criteria. Your prospective station is not the top station in the market but one which you feel can be improved. With an expenditure of $50,000 for promotion and new equipment, you feel you can make it the leading radio station. You have, however, failed to take into consideration the owners of the other stations. You discover one is owned by a major network. Now the network-owned station has almost unlimited financial resources. It hasn't bothered to spend money for promotion and improvements before because it didn't have any real competition. You provided the competition, but instead of matching your promotion dollars, the network sinks a quarter of a million dollars into its station. They not only remain number one, but you have exhausted your financial reserves and wind up slipping to an even lower position in the market. You didn't investigate the competition thoroughly enough, and financial disaster is the result.

On another note, let's assume you invested in a radio station but didn't research the station's past record of performance in the community. You purchase the station and find it impossible to make it profitable. Had you researched its history, you would have found that other owners couldn't make the station succeed either. If you had looked even closer, you might have discovered that a former owner financed the purchase of the station through a lending institution that had a reputation for lending money to *speculators*. These are persons who buy a media property and hold it for a short time while hypoing (heavily promoting) it to increase sales and then sell it for a profit. In the future you'll steer clear of investments such as these. Your company wants to own broadcasting properties that have a long-term growth potential, ones that will not only make an operating profit, but also increase in value over the years.

Perhaps you find a station which looks like a good investment except for internal snafus. You find that a large share of the annual billings — money billed advertisers for commercials aired on the station—is not real monies but rather trade-outs. Such trade-outs may be in the form of cars for the sales personnel or other fringe benefits not paid in cash. The owner has determined his selling price based on the annual billing of the station plus the trade-outs. You aren't interested in trade-outs since you plan to operate on a strictly cash flow basis. You make the owner an offer based on the annual billings *less* the trade-outs. Since the station hasn't made much of a profit, the owner decides to sell.

Television—The Network Dominates

Although many of the guidelines you followed as investment officer for your company in researching the radio station market apply to television as well, this field offers some new ground rules. You discover, for instance, that the network with which a television station is affiliated is one of the most important factors in determining how well the station does financially. With radio, the network provides only a small percentage of the total programming. You thus would have the opportunity to make many changes in this area if you desired. With television, however, almost all of its programming originates from the network. In fact, network reimbursements constitute a major part of any television station's income. Local commercial sales would be determined by how well your station was doing in the ratings, and that would again be primarily determined by network programs. If the network has a good season, then the station could realize a considerable income. If the network's shows consistently drag the ratings, then your financial picture would suffer.

Like radio, competition is a major factor, but comes this time in the form of cable. Perhaps you decide to construct a new television station in a market that presently has only one. All of the economic factors look positive—there are few radio stations and only one newspaper. But wait. There is also a well-developed cable system. The cable system imports a large selection of signals from other areas, enabling subscribers to receive all of the networks' fare plus independent and public television programs. Although you could build your television station, your programming would duplicate much of what the cable system already provides, and you probably wouldn't be able to capture enough of the audience to make your investment profitable.

Cable—Medium in Transition

In order for your investment survey to be complete, you also need to investigate cable. One of the first things you discover about cable is that it's a *capital intensive* enterprise; that is, *its maximum costs occur immediately.* With radio and in some ways with television, this does not necessarily happen. You could conceivably start a station with used equipment and a low-paid, inexperienced staff. With cable, however, that luxury is not present. The entire system has to be constructed before you can even begin to realize an income on your investment. Your capital outlays include a major antenna system, skilled technicians to install the cable system, and a complete repair and maintenance operation. The type of equipment you use and the cable you install have to meet FCC specifications, which means that you have to purchase high-quality cable and, in all probability, install a system with two-way capabilities.

Perhaps your prospective community already has direct home antenna reception of all the major network programs as well as those of independent and public television stations. You might be able to install your cable system in this instance, but few people would subscribe to it. You would probably have to increase the rates just to make ends meet. Yet if you increased them, people would drop their cable service, and you would lose even more money.

Instead of building a new cable system, you investigate the possibility of purchasing an already existing one. In doing so, you want to know how much *saturation* the system has achieved, or *what percentage of the total households are subscribers.* If the saturation is already high, you won't be able to expand the system. Thus, as a long-term investment, except perhaps for a tax shelter, it wouldn't pay off. Check also to ascertain that the existing cable system meets current FCC specifications. If it doesn't, your company may have to spend big money just to boost the equipment to FCC standards. Perhaps local politics are also going to enter into the situation. A system you are considering purchasing has had some serious tangles with the city council. Consequently, the council threatens to put such stringent controls on the cable system that operating it will be a hassle. All of these factors must be taken into consideration.

There is, you discover, a very positive side to the cable picture. Although your prospective system has a heavy saturation, it is also equipped for two-way cable operation. You decide it might be a good investment because in five or ten years when public resistance to new technology softens, you'll be able to provide subsidiary service to the community. People will be able to do their banking at home by using your two-way cable as well as enjoy many other conveniences.

Preoperative Projections

Whatever decision your company makes, future investment costs will be charted carefully. On these charts will appear such pre-

☑ *ANALYZE THE MARKET*

☑ *INVESTIGATE THE PROPERTY*

☑ *LOOK AT OPERATING PROFITS*

☑ *PONDER LONG TERM GROWTH*

☑ *CONSIDER THE COMPETITION*

☑ *PROJECT PRE-OPERATING COSTS*

MEDIA INVESTOR'S CHECKLIST

operative expenses as brokerage fees negotiated between you and the seller, attorneys' fees, and licensing fees to the FCC. Accountants will play a vital role in the sale or construction of a station or cable system, and market research will help you project future income. You'll also need to consider the initial "bank rolling" expenditure which will keep your investment in the black during the first few years of operation. What will be your promotion or improvement costs? You will compile all this information into a portfolio to present to your company's board of directors. They'll review the pros and cons of each aspect of the purchase and come to an investment decision.

book publishing

The energy crisis has taken its toll on book-publishing expenditures as it has on the cost of operating other media. Unlike radio and television, however, which can broadcast their messages over the airwaves, the book-publishing industry must transport its messages by truck, ship, train, and sometimes plane. Each of these sources of transportation will naturally continue to increase its rates as the cost of fuel continues to rise. When a book leaves the warehouse, many people handle it and many vehicles transport it. The labor costs of loading books onto trucks, the cost of purchasing the trucks to haul them, the cost of gasoline to run the trucks, the salaries paid to drivers, the cost of labor to unload the books, and the increased rental costs to display them in a bookstore or wherever else they're sold have all skyrocketed. This has triggered everything from bankruptcy and consolidation in the industry to instant success stories. Let's look at some of the economic forces at work in book publishing.

As have other print media, so have book publishers in recent years faced soaring paper costs. The chief villain is, of course, the inflated cost of energy and natural resources necessary to manufacture paper. In many cases, the market for books will simply not bear the essential price hikes to completely offset these paper costs. As a result, the difference has appeared in shrinking profit columns. This does not mean that book publishing is about to vanish from the American scene. It can, however, translate into lean years for stockholders until prices level off, for paper can represent as much as one-half the expense of publishing a book.

New Ventures: New Income

In a positive light, the paperback book industry is booming. This prosperity can be directly attributed to several factors. For one thing, although still expensive, it is much cheaper to ship paperback books than hardcover books. Paperbacks take up less space and weight, which trims their distribution costs. In addition, the industry is branching out into new, profitable areas. For instance, Bantam Books has developed a new gift book division. In a major commitment to this type of publication, Bantam hired Ian Ballantine the founder of Ballantine Books, out of retirement to head the new division, called Peacock Press. The Peacock Press publishes gift books with excellent reproduction of quality art prints (Figure 17–3). Retailing for a fraction of the cost of competing publications, these specialty items have literally stolen the market. Paperback originals by established authors are also increasing the potential of this upcoming offshoot of the industry. Many publishers will first publish a book in hardback, and then after sales have peaked, issue a paperback edition at a much lower cost. Paperback sales then capitalize on the publicity generated by the hardback edition. The paperback industry, however, not content to rest on its laurels, is reversing this technique and now contracts with authors to publish original editions in paperback. It thus reaps all the advantages of an original while also taking advantage of the paperback's low production and distribution costs. Pyramid Book's Bicentennial series by author John Jakes is one example that set publishing records.

Book printing processes have also improved. The high-quality printing possible with photo offset methods permits books with quality illustrations to be produced at a greatly reduced price from that of previous years. In an age in which books as a medium compete with color television, technology plays a vital role in making a book appealing to a buyer, both aesthetically and in terms of cost. Books about scenic areas of the United States, for example, can now

Figure 17–3. High quality printing processes have helped produce a consumer demand for gift books. (Covers of titles published by Peacock Press/Bantam Books. © Bantam Books, Inc. 1975.)

splurge with profuse photographs of these regions. Before advanced printing processes, it would have been impossible even to print such lavishly illustrated works, let alone find an audience willing to pay the high prices for them.

Direct mail as a distribution and sales method is also coming into its own for many publishers. Where specialized audiences and mailing lists to reach these audiences are available, direct mail has expanded many sales and profit horizons.

Even unusual undertakings can become profitable with imagination, research, and a little luck. Ballantine Books, for example, published a packet of blueprints for the "Starship Enterprise" from the popular *Star Trek* television series. More than a half million packets were sold. Publishing "sets" of books or reissuing books in gift covers has also proved successful. A popular book may beget sequels, and after five or so have been published, a gift box arrangement of an entire set can lure new readers and new buyers to bookstore shelves. Even the illustrations can turn into popular collection pieces. Norman Rockwell's paintings, which for many years decked the covers of the *Saturday Evening Post*, have been published and republished in collector's editions. Other special collections of circus stories, Christmas stories, Easter stories, recipes, and numerous other items have proved interesting reading and profitable book publishing ventures.

Production and Distribution: Cost Increases

Some publishers predict that future economic constraints on distribution will generate growth in regional publishing—books appealing to a particular region. As a regional book publisher, you wouldn't seek out manuscripts with appeal to a national readership but rather to a specific regional market. For example, instead of publishing a book about farming, you might instead publish one about farming in New England or in the Midwest. Similarly, instead of publishing an all-American cookbook, you might accept a manuscript about Southwest cooking. Although the market for regional books is more limited, sales density can be higher because of generally greater interest. Most important, distribution costs drop as the publisher concentrates on a specific region, say the East Coast. Many major publishing companies have already developed regional distribution systems, and some smaller companies are exclusively regional. One of the more successful regional presses is the Caxton Press of Caldwell, Idaho. Its primary distribution area, the Northwest, is also the focal point of its readership. Other publishers maintain similar regionalism within their published titles. The University of Tennessee Press, for instance, concentrates on books which deal with the heritage and people of that region of the country. Its list of titles also includes books on the Civil War.

Making Management Decisions

The manager of any publishing enterprise must constantly monitor the industry's cost factors. Besides production and distribution costs, the industry has such fundamental cost factors as sales and advertising. Here, the key is to attract and keep enthusiastic and dedicated people who have the discipline to work well without much supervision and who enjoy working on a commission basis. These people keep your firm in business. But as with every other cost, the expenses incurred by your sales staff are increasing. In any publishing venture, there are only so many excess dollars to go around after basic publishing expenditures. Thus, at some point you must decide if you can raise the commission paid to your sales staff without raising the price of the book. Other management decisions will also affect your profit. Knowing your book's market is crucial, because the larger the number of volumes that you print, the smaller the cost per copy. However, it costs just as much to print books that don't sell! One key to success in a new venture is not to overrun the initial printing, i.e., to avoid a situation of unsold books being returned to you from bookstores. For, again, distribution costs apply to sold as well as unsold books. In addition, plan for unexpected costs that might develop before the book reaches the bookstores, such as a truckers' strike that would necessitate shipping some books by air freight. All of the above factors could dramatically change the economic picture of your publishing venture.

financing the movies

Some called it the *Sound of Music* syndrome, this era of spectaculars in which Hollywood felt the only way to assure itself of successful films was to spend big money. But it was at this time that expenses and reality clashed and sent the executives of some of the largest motion picture companies to the banks, not to deposit money but to borrow it. It is from this point in time, the late 1960s, that we'll begin our look at contemporary economics of the motion picture industry.

The Industry in Financial Transition

Sharp financial business managers haven't always sat behind the desks of the motion picture corporations. Before television, creative geniuses or movie barons, as they were known, ruled the movie kingdom, and there was nothing that couldn't be sacrificed for the sake of creativity. If a picture went over its budget in adding the necessary glamour to suit the director's whim, over it went. The difference between then and now was that money seemed to stretch further in those days.

Television, however, brought competition, competition that required new management and new thinking within the industry. The film industry entered a transitional period that brought management with keen financial minds, people who could talk the language of accountants and bankers. Although creative talent was and continues to be the backbone of the industry, "dollars and cents" people began to make the final decisions.

At the same time, money became scarce and financial risks became much greater. In the later 1960s the industry also entered the era of the motion picture spectacular. The *Sound of Music* was a typical example of a picture that went all out with script, stars, and financial backing in the $20-million-dollar range. Fortunately, it was extremely successful at the box office. Such movies created a theory in the motion picture industry that big scripts, big stars, and big money automatically meant big box office receipts.

To obtain big money, the industry approached leading financial institutions to secure loans. Banks, however, were not used to lending money under the risks that were common in the motion picture industry. So the industry had to prove to the banks that there were responsible management and financial safeguards in any given film enterprise. One of the banks' primary concerns was budget over-runs. To counter this concern, film companies had to show that even though a director or producer might have a tremendous desire to shoot a special scene for a special effect, he would not do so unless he could maintain his budget. For the financial luxury of waiting thirty days for the weather to clear to achieve the proper lighting and scenery was not something upon which banks looked favorably. In order to further appease the banks, the industry also rearranged its contractual agreements with actors and actresses. The rule had been to guarantee a star a certain amount of money before the picture ever went into production, regardless of how well the movie did at the box office. Instead, film companies now began to offer the stars a percentage of the box office receipts.

Some banks did give credit to some of the larger film makers on the basis of past film successes. For instance, the typical film company may produce twenty-five films in a year, five of which may prove quite successful; another five may be financial disasters, however, and the rest may come somewhere near the break-even point. On balance, then, the company's profit record seems a reasonable credit risk. Film companies could also offer the banks collateral in the form of *in-the-can* films — movies which had already been run in movie theaters but whose income was still assured from re-releases and release to television. This was the type of collateral that appealed to banks. The fallacy, however, was in the formula. Big money didn't necessarily mean big profits. Three New York banks found that out after they arranged a credit line of over $70 million to one major company for four movies, only one of which was profitable. In fact, some of the most popular bank-financed titles, such as *Hello Dolly*, didn't live up to their financial expectations. As a result, some banks decided to reconsider the odds and backed out of the movie financing business.

Low Budgets and Big Profits

The old fairytale solution, though, the happy ending, was in sight. For, while some of the big-budget movies were bombing at the box office, some low-budget pictures, those in the three- to five-million-dollar range, were on the upswing. Two which turned the heads of the industry were *M.A.S.H.* and *Butch Cassidy and the Sundance Kid.* Paul Newman and Robert Redford helped the latter considerably. It meant a new formula was possible, one with only one of the formerly essential ingredients—big stars. In some cases, even big stars weren't always necessary, as Tom Laughlin proved in *Billy Jack.* Then almost as fast as spectaculars appeared on the scene, they disappeared. Today, movies in the seven-million-dollar range are permitting many producers and directors to experiment with their creative talents without endangering the financial structure of a movie company. This development has also allowed individual investors to get back into the movie financing business. People and organizations with a few million dollars to lend can reap tremendous profits if the movie is a success, yet they won't place their own corporate structure on the line in case of failure. This attitude has also given rise to more creative production flexibility, for if too tight a financial rein is placed on a production, creativity can suffer as well as quality. Today's producers have found that they can produce pictures of exceptional quality on reduced budgets, and the public is willing to accept them, sometimes even more eagerly than films of the "spectacular era" of the *Sound of Music.*

inside outdoor

One of the oldest media, outdoor advertising has managed to survive from the time of the Egyptian temples through wars, depressions, and inflation. Since the influx of automobiles and the construction of superhighways in the twentieth century, it has undergone fundamental changes. To better understand these, let's examine the income and expenses of a typical outdoor company and look at some of the issues which affect the industry's economy.

Income

Outdoor's income comes from the rental of strategically placed bulletins upon which a message can be affixed and viewed by pedestrians and passersby in cars, buses, trains, even planes. Approaches to airport runways often sprout bulletins either greeting newcomers or welcoming returning residents. Strategically placed bulletins are the key to a successful outdoor business, because if you were managing a company or an advertising agency and wanted to purchase outdoor advertising space, your main concerns would be (1) how many people would see your ad, and (2) the characteristics of this audience. The rent charged for any bulletin is determined by two things—the number of people who see the bulletin and the size and complexity of the bulletin. To determine how many people see the bulletin, traffic patterns become important. Three measures are taken into consideration in these patterns—the potential number of pedestrians who will see the bulletin, the number of automobiles that will pass by it, and the number of gross mass transportation passengers (people riding on buses or mass transit systems) to whom it is accessible. From these data, usually compiled by state and municipal governments, the outdoor company can determine the value of the space on its bulletins.

If you were an account executive for an outdoor company, you would carry with you to show to advertisers combinations of display arrangements available for their advertisements. One of the most common would be the rotary plan. Here an advertiser would perhaps purchase three bulletins, each with a different message, and then those messages would be rotated among the bulletins. It would mean that if an advertiser purchased bulletins 1, 2, and 3, then at the end of, say a three-month period, the message appearing on the first bulletin would be rotated to the second, the message on the second rotated to the third, and the message on the third rotated to the first. At the end of another three months, the rotation process would continue. In this manner, all three messages would reach the maximum number of viewers in the heaviest traveled areas.

Much of the outdoor companies' income derives from advertising agencies. To attract their business, outdoor's commission rate to agencies is the highest offered by any medium, running approximately 16-2/3 percent. The higher commission actually originates from a time when market data on the effectiveness of outdoor was not as exact as it was for the broadcast media (ratings) and print media (circulation). Thus, outdoor companies offered this higher commission as an incentive to ad agencies for taking more of a "chance" with a client's money.

Expenses

Outdoor companies maintain bulletins along highways, in smaller towns outside the major metropolitan areas, or wherever else they deem it profitable to locate a bulletin. Some outdoor companies charge advertisers an additional travel fee for servicing bulletins located outside the metropolitan area.

For the outdoor company, expenses are sometimes high and can increase without warning. One of the primary cash outflows is leases for land and space upon which to build bulletins. In some cases, a farmer's field will be a low-cost, long-term lease windfall to the outdoor company. In others, the cost of locating a bulletin on top of a downtown building may be almost prohibitive. Other costs are associated with the actual construction and maintenance of the bulletins. For example, bulletins come in many shapes and sizes. The simplest to construct is the standard, rectangular, unlighted bulletin. To this basic model can be added lights or *embellishments,* special cut-out designs which protrude beyond the basic rectangular shape. If an advertiser wants something more elaborate, outdoor companies offer a series of *louvers,* panels which rotate automatically and produce as many as three different messages, each appearing for about ten seconds at a time. With environmental concern running high, a hastily supported base of old utility poles may not satisfy city planners who expect modern metal supports and miniparks under the bulletins, all of which are maintained at the expense of the outdoor company. Elaborate bulletins will run well into the many thousands of dollars. Along with construction and maintenance, there is also the cost of paying everything from taxes to light bills, not to mention the increased costs of labor and materials. As the job becomes more and more expensive, the advertisers' rent for the bulletin must go up, and when it reaches a certain point, many advertisers stop and consider other media.

The construction process of an outdoor bulletin can involve many hours of in-shop production. (Naegele Outdoor Co.)

Economic Issues

There are many economic issues facing the outdoor companies — regulation being the most serious. Everyone from the federal government to local pressure groups has managed to put the economic squeeze on the industry. In some communities, public pressure groups have been responsible for completely eliminating bulletins. In other areas, regulations have made banks leery of advancing money for projects which they feel will be ruled illegal in a few years. Where there has been adequate enforcement of legislation prohibiting bulletins within so many yards of the highways, outdoor companies have had to construct larger bulletins simply to have them seen. This has effectively prevented many smaller companies from using outdoor advertising because they simply can't afford to switch from low-cost, smaller bulletins to larger ones.

Although regulations and similar financial constraints placed a serious burden on the industry, it has managed to bounce back, survive, and sometimes prosper. Many outdoor companies are capitalizing on the applauded mini-park bulletin concept, even if it is expensive. Others have gone through major staff reductions, especially after the Highway Beautification Act of 1965, and are now recuperating from this period by constructing fewer but large bulletins away from the highway and realizing more advertising dollars from those which are rented. It should be mentioned that, although the federal government passed laws regulating the industry, it failed to enforce these laws effectively. As a result, state and local governments have reached new and more cooperative agreements with the outdoor industry. Moreover, foresighted city planners involved in the construction of new shopping and residential areas have taken the need for outdoor advertising into consideration. They are beginning to include space for outdoor bulletins just as is provided for park benches, lighting, and other accessories to a construction project. Similarly, business leaders are realizing that it is sometimes easier to attract business if you can advertise your goods and services to people who are approaching the shopping malls in the prime mood to shop. Outdoor bulletins are the answer. With these cooperative efforts, the outdoor industry will continue as an important advertising medium.

the recording industry

The road to a hit record is becoming more expensive, affected by everything from price wars among record distributors to shortages of vinyl, the material used to manufacture records. In between is the consumer, whose fickle buying antics send many a recording artist into unemployment and promoters back to the drawing board. Records to the average consumer are a luxury, and the industry tends to sway with the economy. When the economy is up, record sales are up; when the economy is down, then record sales either drop or the consumers change their buying habits. For instance, singles may outsell albums simply because they are cheaper, and people wanting a certain hit sound may not want to spend the extra money for added sounds. The industry is also interrelated. Artists, through their contracts with recording companies, are not as flexible in the marketplace as artists in some other media. Whereas an author may easily fluctuate between different publishing companies, a recording artist is usually signed to one company and remains there until his or her contract runs out or is bought out by another company. The companies themselves are also involved in related areas of the industry, such as distribution, retail sales, and promotion. As a result, the entire industry is affected by its component parts, many of which may be controlled by a single corporation. Expenses lie primarily in two areas—promotion and distribution.

Promotion

There are rare occasions when a record simply makes it big on its own without the recording company's launching a major promotional campaign. The cost of these promotional campaigns and all of their various aspects can be in the millions of dollars. For example, recording companies have purchased a substantial number of commercials to introduce new artists. They've also paid fees for performers to appear on prime-time television programs and purchased blocks of tickets at rock concerts to give away to fans. Large record companies will also join with promoters to stage concerts and disco-dance fests featuring major rock stars. All these promotion efforts have a single goal: to give the artists ample exposure and thus attract attention to their recordings.

Another heavy expense involves keeping an artist or rock group soluble until they have the chance for a major hit record and can foot their own expenses. The recording industry is much like a crowded airport with planes flying in a holding pattern. With only so much room for planes to land at any one time, the rest have to stay airborne until they have the opportunity to land. Similarly, many recording artists are kept in business until there is an opportunity for them to penetrate the market; public demand dictates that only so many of them can be popular at any one time. All recording companies make major investments in talent, some of which never pay off.

It also costs money to achieve air play for the record. The costs of sending the records to radio stations throughout the country are continually mounting. These mailing costs, in addition to the soaring costs of petroleum-related vinyl, have prompted some companies to stop sending free records to college radio stations. This procedure can backfire for the companies, however. When Warner Brothers announced in 1975 that it would stop sending free records to college radio stations as a cost-cutting measure, a number of college stations staged a boycott and refused to play records that carried the Warner Brothers' label. A few weeks later, Warner changed its mind. What had started out as a budget-saving measure ended up costing the company money in lost air play.

Distribution

The distribution system for records is quite similar to that for books. Many of the same cost factors are also present. Transportation is one. Shipping of recording discs and cassettes is done by truck, and increased fuel prices affect the distributors' and eventually the consumers' costs. The distributor must also estimate the demand for the recording to avoid the costly process of returning unsold recordings. On top of this, price wars have complicated the distributors' woes. Record retail outlets are very much like gas stations. They buy from wholesalers but can also discount their merchandise. A market which has not only price but also time limitations placed upon it can suffer considerable loss from such tactics. A popular recording artist, for example, will have a hit on the charts for a limited time only. It is during this period that the public will purchase his record. Signs with "big tape discounts" and "cut-rate prices" abound, and consumers invariably find that shopping around does pay. Although the record companies have called for some cooperation in these matters, the FCC has been strongly against interfering, stating that recording companies must compete in a free market.

Overall, the recording industry has shown the ability to weather most of the economic storms it's faced—partly because it also has a system of royalty agreements suited to such different outlets as bands, jukeboxes, radio stations, and airline music systems, to name a few.

Along with price wars, the recording industry must also contend with the sellers of *pirated tapes*—illegally recorded music sold in violation of copyright agreements and contractual agreements with artists. The pirate companies have been the target of the industry and the justice department. Although there have been some major crackdowns, the practice continues. Pirate operations will record songs of popular artists directly from a broadcast or from other recordings and then sell the tapes at a big discount. Profits are considerable, since the pirate companies pay neither royalty fees nor the cost of distribution. Most are operated on a regional or even local basis with few outlets, thus eliminating most middleman fees. All that is needed is duplicating equipment and a retail outlet to sell the merchandise. From there, it's mostly profit. The fines for the offenders, however, are stiff, and a jail sentence can be an accompaniment.

economics of ad agencies

Two arguments can be heard by agency personnel whenever they gather. One executive will claim his or her agency is doing great because the economy is doing great. Another will claim that because the economy is in bad shape, businesses are advertising more, and thus the agency is doing well. Both arguments have merit and reflect some of the concerns of being in a business which is "in the middle."

Ad Agency Income

An ad agency's product is talent. This talent is responsible for creating and distributing advertising on behalf of a client who pays the ad agency to handle the client's advertising needs. Much of the income an agency receives comes from discounts it receives from media. Most discounts, which are in effect agency commissions, are approximately 15 percent. With the exception of newspapers, which generally still refrain from giving agency discounts, this percentage is fairly standard across all media. By the way of illustration, assume you're advertising "Barkos," the product we learned about in Chapter 9, and your ad agency is going to spend the sum of $10,000 to advertise Barkos in a gardening magazine. You contact the gardening magazine and purchase a $10,000 full-color insert. After the ad runs, the gardening magazine bills your ad agency for $8,500 ($10,000 minus 15 percent). Your ad agency pays that bill and then bills the company that manufactures Barkos for $10,000. When the manufacturer pays his account, your agency has received $1,500 income in the transaction. Of course, the agency's costs must come out of the $1,500, so that this is by no means clear profit. The American Association of Advertising Agencies estimates that in a typical large agency, media commissions represent about 75 percent of the agency's income. In smaller agencies, the percentage drops to as low as 55 percent. The reason for this difference is that large agencies usually cater to large markets where a thirty-second radio commercial may cost $250. Fifteen percent of $250 makes a nice commission. But smaller agencies in markets where $10 buys a thirty-second spot simply cannot exist on the commission alone. They must have other income.

Other income can be realized through an agency's own percentage charges. For instance, an agency may have a printing job to complete for a client. The printer allows the agency a 20 percent discount on the job to attract and keep the agency's business. We'll assume the non-discount rate for the printing job is $500. With the 20 percent discount, the agency is billed only $400 ($500 minus 20 percent). The agency then bills the client for $475, keeping $75 as a commission. Although the client still pays a fee over and above what the agency is charged, the client is still receiving the service at less cost ($25 less) than if he or she had placed the printing order directly with the printing company.

Some ad agencies have even entered into special arrangements with manufacturers whereby they not only handle a company's advertising, but also process orders for goods and services provided or sold by that company. For instance, an ad agency might handle the advertising for a new cooking utensil. In the media campaign, the agency purchases ads in leading homemaker magazines and issues press releases to media outlets that might give the new product free publicity. The agency then processes the orders for the new product and takes a commission on the gross sales, such as $5.00 on each utensil sold. These arrangements are not a general practice with all ad agencies, but they have proven a successful business venture for smaller agencies which have a limited market in which to secure accounts. Other income has been realized by agencies conducting executive workshops, sales training seminars, and other activities.

Within the agencies, there are many different arrangements for commissions and income. Any agency-client relationship, of course, rests on an agreement that is mutually satisfactory. Some agencies, for instance, provide different classes of service in accordance with clients, needs, wishes, and, most importantly, budgets. More experienced personnel and those with proven creative abilities may be enlisted to serve clients wanting the best service possible. Newer personnel may be engaged for lower quality, less expensive projects. Some large accounts from which the agency receives a major share of its income will receive top-of-the-line service simply because of the importance of retaining such a lucrative account. Different services within the agency can also affect the final cost to the client. For example, additional use of the secretarial force does not raise the cost of the total package anywhere near as much as extra hours of an art director's talent.

The Public Relations Function

Agencies involved in extensive public relations work will command a larger proportion of their clients' dollars than agencies primarily concerned with placing media buys. Public relations services for a client involve such things as meeting with media representatives on behalf of the client, sending press releases to media, visiting trade fairs, organizing promotional luncheons, and so on. Whenever such activities are involved, there's less outflow of cash for media buys and more retained within the agency. The actual amount of these "services" can account for as much as 50 percent of an agency's income.

Future Costs of Making Impressions

One factor that will largely determine the income of ad agencies in the future is the actual cost of advertising—placing a message with a particular medium to reach a target audience. Let's examine how one medium, television, will require more of the ad dollar to reach a target audience, women, between now and 1985. This future perspective was offered at a meeting of the Association of National Advertisers by Andrew Kershaw, Chairman of Ogilvy & Mather, Inc., Advertising Agency.[6] It illustrates how the cost of reaching women is increasing, but that the impressions—the number of times a person is reached by an ad—are decreasing. Figure 17–4 shows that in 1965, a $5-million ad budget spent on daytime network television would have reached all women, 18 years old and over, 96 times that year. However, that same ad budget in 1985 will reach that same audience only 24 times. The cost of keeping up with the 1965 impressions also becomes substantial. Figure 17–5 illustrates how the increase will be almost 300 percent for daytime network television. In other words, in 1985 it will be necessary to spend $20 million in daytime network television to make the same 96 impressions per woman that $5 million bought in 1965. Similar cost effectiveness is felt in nighttime network television. It will be necessary to spend $14.6 million in nighttime network television advertising in 1985 to make the same 38 impressions per woman that $5 million purchased in 1965. An expenditure of $5 million in nighttime network television in 1985 would make only 13 impressions per 100 women.

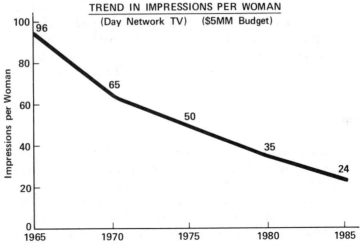

Figure 17-4. Trends in ad impressions per women.

Kershaw points out that "advertising budgets are not going to grow at that rate." He also points out that "research budgets are not going to grow at that rate." Kershaw's prediction for the future?—a necessity for more effective advertising and, in the case of television, shorter commercials. The talents of the ad agency seem to be assured of an even more receptive market.

The Agency's Position

The agencies themselves, however, are in the unique position of remaining flexible and still making money despite increasing costs. There are two important reasons for this. One is the fact that the ad agency takes its commission on the overall purchase price of the ad-

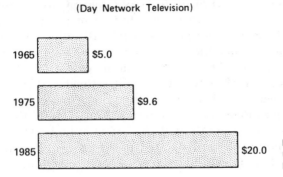

Figure 17-5. Millions of dollars needed to maintain 1965 impressions per women.

vertising. If the cost of purchasing advertising time increases, then the agency's commission increases proportionately. Second, in a highly competitive market that takes advertising glamour for granted, most businesses find themselves willing to spend gigantic sums if only they obtain the most for their advertising dollars.

the cb boom

Some years ago, when the FCC allocated a special frequency for two-way radio communication use by businesses, it could not foresee the phenomenal surge of popularity the concept of citizens' band (CB) radio would have in the mid 1970s. It was then, at the height of the energy crisis, that the speed limit of 55 miles per hour would put CB radios in the cab of long-haul truckers, who would use the radios to avoid speed traps and spot police officers, called "smokies." When the public attention to the idea of outsmarting the law became first a novelty, and then a major communication service between people, the FCC released the restriction that the CB radio frequencies could only be used for business purposes. It became a national hobby, as anyone who could afford the cost of a CB radio and an FCC license (although the latter wasn't always obtained), could go on the air. It has become a communication link between people leaping onto the scene years ahead of the wired city. CB now carries reports between motorists and those at home on every topic from country music, to traffic conditions, to smokey reports—all with a special jargon plus regional dialect.

There are easily started arguments on whether CB is a true form of mass communication. Nevertheless, it has had its impact on such things as radio-listening habits, and it is for that reason that the subject is briefly dealt with here. Although there hasn't been considerable data on exactly how much the CB penetration has siphoned off the car-radio listening audience, some preliminary figures have caused some concern in industry circles. Current estimates are that there is only a 5 percent penetration of the potential CB market.[7] But that accounts for approximately 10 million CB rigs in use and an estimated decline of 12 percent in auto listening. It is predicted that by 1981 the penetration will reach 24 percent market saturation, and thus the 12 percent estimated decline in auto listening estimate may become much higher. Those figures also translate into major monetary expenditures. The value of the 5 million units estimated to be in use in 1976 is $500 million. The 24 percent saturation predicted for 1981 will mean 28.5 million units worth $3.5 billion. This means big sales for retail electronic distributors and other retail outlets such as record stores, which also deal in consumer electronics. As students aware of this one facet of media business, keep abreast of the developments in the concept of citizens' band radio and how it will affect our communicative society.

summary

Fiscal concerns weigh heavily on all mass media, as part of our free enterprise system. This chapter has explored the realm of media businesses via a sampling of "happenings" within these businesses. The newspaper industry, for example, has been faced with increased costs for labor and newsprint. While overall income from advertising expenditures has increased, the industry still needs the flexibility to adjust prosperously to rapidly changing social and economic conditions. Magazine publishing, on the other hand, depends upon reaching a specialized audience. Therefore, a good distribution system, combined with good promotion and moderate expenses, will permit a new magazine to remain soluble until it can establish itself. Looking to other media, broadcasting is big business that sees a considerable amount of ownership change. Individual broadcasting properties, that is, radio and television stations and cable systems, are sometimes good investments, but the prospective buyer should carefully investigate all the factors which affect their success in their respective markets. A new line of "gift books" and new marketing techniques have kept the book publishing industry lucrative. Despite increased paper and printing costs, the industry has maintained a steady growth, especially in the area of paperback books.

Chapter 17 has also examined the financial outlook for the motion picture industry, outdoor, the recording industry, and ad agencies. The era of the high-priced movie spectacular is gone. Gone also is the need for major bank financing, lending agreements for such productions as *Patton, Tora Tora Tora*, or the *Sound of Music* that had approached the $20 million range. Following the damper put upon the industry by the passage of the 1965 Highway Beautification Act, outdoor has bounced back as a viable advertising medium. Profits in the recording industry fluctuate as the up-and downswings of the economy affect the average consumer. Luxury items, records and tapes clearly reflect the pinch of any recessionary period. Recently, pirate recording companies and price wars have caused the industry to examine how much both practices are affecting industry profits. Ad agencies' profits, on the other hand, have easily kept pace with the increasing costs of media space and advertising expenditures. The impact of citizens' band radio has also meant a major growth factor in the area of consumer electronics, and indications are that it may also affect auto-radio listening habits.

opportunities for further learning

ARGYRIS, CHRIS, *Behind the Front Page.* San Francisco, Calif.: Jossey-Bass Publishers, 1974.

DAVIS, CLIVE, with JAMES WILLWERTH, *Inside the Record Business.* New York: Morrow, 1975.

HOFFER, JAY, *Managing Today's Radio Station.* Summit Hill, Pa.: Tab Books, 1971.

HURST, WALTER E., and WILLIAM STORM HALE, *The Record Industry Book: How to Make Money in the Record Industry,* 2nd Ed. Hollywood, Calif.: Seven Arts Press, 1974.

OWEN, BRUCE M., *Television Economics.* Lexington, Mass.: Lexington Books, 1974.

media control

in the

twentieth century

CHAPTER EIGHTEEN

As we learned in Chapter 1, colonial newspapers were more political instruments than free agents. Colonial printers were far from independent of the Crown-appointed governors who controlled their government printing subsidies and consequently the content of their newspapers. John Peter Zenger had paved the way for the concept of a free press in America, but it took the Revolutionary War and the Constitution to assure it. The First Amendment to that document has been the backbone of that assurance, stating: "Congress shall make no laws respecting an establishment of religion, or prohibiting the free exercise thereof; or abridging the freedom of speech, or of the press. ..." There was of course, no way that the founding fathers could have imagined a time when communication satellites would roam the earth and cable television would deliver the morning newspaper. Not until after the Civil War did our government realize a need for more definite legislation to regulate the first of these new technological advancements. Careful and mindful of the Constitution, Congress began to formulate legislation which would restrict neither free speech nor a free press but would ensure

the safety of those who ventured onto the oceans in pursuit of foreign and domestic commerce.

early radio legislation

The Wireless Ship Act of 1910 was the first piece of legislation to
deal directly with the new "wireless" communication that later became known as radio. Basically, the law made it illegal for any
"ocean-going steamer" carrying more than 50 persons to leave a
United States port for a trip of more than 200 miles without ship-to-
ship and ship-to-shore communication equipment operated by a
trained technician. Enforcement of this regulation was the duty of
the Secretary of Commerce and Labor, who had the authority to arrest the "master" of any ship violating the order; the courts were
authorized to slap a maximum $5000 fine on the "master" for that
violation. The Act signified three things: (1) it provided an impetus
for the beginnings of the radio industry; (2) it was visible evidence
that Congress was recognizing the tremendous potential of the new
medium; (3) it sparked research and development of wireless communication for improving long-distance radio service.

It wasn't long after the 1910 Act, however, that Congress realized
it would be necessary to keep track of who owned and controlled
the two-way communication equipment so that the President of the
United States could gain control of it during wartime, should that
become necessary. Thus it was that two years later Congress passed
a second piece of legislation, the Radio Act of 1912. In the 1912
Act, Congress effectively legislated that anyone operating a radio
transmitter had first to have a license; that the only persons who
could obtain a license were citizens of the United States and Puerto
Rico or corporations chartered in either the United States or Puerto
Rico; that the owners and location of the equipment be identified;
and that there be some estimate of the distance over which the
transmitter could send. The Act also provided for separation between the frequencies of stations to eliminate interference, but it
left these decisions more up to the owners of the transmitters than to
the government. Yet the 1912 Act really had no practical way of
controlling the development of commercial broadcasting for mass
public consumption, for there was far more to radio than shipping
and commerce. Experimental stations began testing the air waves.
The 1920s arrived with KDKA broadcasting the Harding-Cox election and WGN carrying Chicago Cubs and White Sox baseball, Big
Ten Football, and the Indy 500. Radio was suddenly everywhere.
There was also the realization that with an audience of this size,

broadcasters could charge for messages sent over the air waves. Excitement and turmoil within the industry were mounting. A T & T tried to preempt the operation of the new medium.[1] That attempt didn't even get off the ground, though, because the new medium was already too far developed. To fight off competition, stations began to operate with higher and higher power.

Within a short while, it became apparent that something had to be done to bring things back under control. Congress therefore passed the Radio Act of 1927, in which was recognized for the first time the need for broadcasting to be in "the public interest, convenience, and necessity." Legislators also paid heed, both legal and political, to the fact that the airways, unlike the print media, were limited in their capacity to transmit messages at any one point in time. Only so much of the electromagnetic spectrum could be efficiently used for broadcasting; this scarce resource thus needed to be controlled. The 1927 legislation also established the first governmental body to control broadcasting—the Federal Radio Commission—a five-member group appointed by the president. The Act of 1927 contained some significant legislation that still applies to broadcasting today. It established a system of call letters for radio stations, a systematic method of license renewal and equipment modification, and qualifications for station operators. It also gave government the power to revoke licenses, to provide for inspection of station apparatus, and to assign frequency and power limits to stations, while retaining the regulatory provisions of the 1912 legislation, concerning communication for ships at sea.

The Radio Act of 1927 remained in force until 1934 when Congress, on the recommendation of President Franklin D. Roosevelt, passed the Communications Act of 1934. This Act identified broadcasting as a separate entity apart from both the "utility" or "power" concept and apart from "transportation." The Act replaced the Federal Radio Commission with the Federal Communications Commission and became the main piece of legislation, as later amended, under which the American system of broadcasting now operates.

the federal communications commission

Of all governmental agencies, it is second to none in its direct and profound effect on the lives of virtually everyone. The FCC is, whether directly or indirectly, the governmental body responsible for regulating relatively all of the messages millions of people see and hear every day through the broadcast media. Although the Commission has no broad power to censor the content of broadcasting, it does have the power to be sure those who are involved in broadcasting are responsible and take into consideration the public "interest, convenience, and necessity." With one sweep of the regulatory hand or even the suggestion of a major policy statement, it can affect the content of prime-time television, give networks second thoughts about children's television programming, afford a politician equal air time, and affect the daily operation of every local broadcasting operation in the country, which in turn affects each citizen.

Organizational Structure and Effectiveness

The Commission consists of seven FCC Commissioners appointed by the president with the advice and consent of the Senate. In recent years their appointment has come under close scrutiny in confirmation hearings, a sign of the importance of mass communication in our society in general and the control of that communication in particular. The Communications Act prohibits the Commissioners from having any conflicting interests while serving on the Commission; it also sets their terms for seven years and limits to four the number from any one political party.

There are arguments on both sides of the fence as to how effective the FCC is. On the one hand, the Commission has been criticized for taking too lax a role in broadcast programming regulation and allowing the networks, the broadcasting industry, and the politicians the upper hand. Others have argued that although the FCC

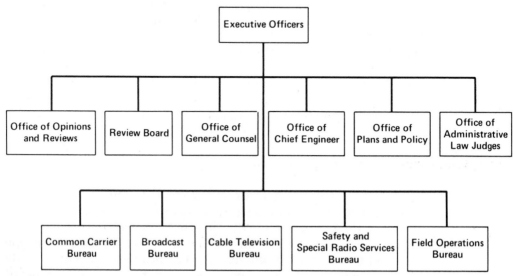

Figure 18–1. The organization of the Federal Communications Commission. (Adapted from the 1974 FCC annual report.)

is in fact a regulatory agency, it can very easily come into conflict with the First Amendment to the Constitution. Over the years, the Commission has increased in size to more than 2,000 employees, a development indicative of the typical trend toward government bureaucracy. However, the FCC does patrol the operation of thousands of commercial broadcasting stations and many times that number of two-way radio stations operated by citizens, local governments, and municipalities. The surge of interest in citizens' band radio has also increased the Commission's workload considerably.

As with any governmental agency, many Commission actions and decisions take their cue from developments within the industry. This is because in order to regulate an industry effectively and fairly one first needs to know how that industry ticks. To obtain this feedback, the FCC initiates a system of "opinion filings" in which broadcasters file with the Commission their opinions on pending rules and regulations. The FCC, in turn, weighs these opinions, because significant industry opposition to a proposed regulation might result in more law suits than compliance once it's passed. Many of the decisions the FCC makes are not popular with the industry, and many shouldn't be. But the Commission is caught between regulating an industry that must operate in the public interest and being the instrument of a political process that is ultimately accountable to the Congress. The Commission can even face pressures from the industry directed at members of Congress. Comments from broadcasters are not ignored in Congress, and a high level of criticism against any governmental agency can cause everything from investigative inquiries to budget hassles.

Policing the Industry

Despite the pros and cons of FCC regulation, the average broadcaster views the Commission as a very visible "police" force, for the Commission has had very few qualms about enforcing its power. A network of FCC field offices sends out inspectors to make periodic unannounced visits to stations to scrutinize various aspects of station operation. They check logs to determine if commercial messages are recorded as aired and billed to the sponsor; they check the station's public file to see if documents are in order; they inspect equipment; they monitor the programming of the station. Any perusal of the back pages of *Broadcasting* will document the violations and penalty fines resulting from these inspections. At license renewal time, each station makes a complete accounting to the FCC of its operating procedures and promises of service to the community. The toughest reprimand ever meted out by the FCC came on January 30, 1975, when the Commission denied license renewals to stations owned by media executive Don Burden. Stations WIFE AM and FM in Indianapolis, Indiana; KOIL AM and FM in Omaha, Nebraska; and KISN AM in Portland, Oregon, all were denied license renewals. The FCC claimed there had been attempts to slant the news in favor of Senators Vance Hartke of Indiana and Mark Hatfield of Oregon during their respective campaigns for the Senate, mishandling of a station contest, illegal corporate political contributions, and improper billing procedures. There was sharp reaction to the FCC decision. Charges that it violated the First Amendment to the Constitution, that it was a case of excess punishment, and that it used Burden as an "example" were common. Burden was permitted to continue to operate the stations pending an appeal, which he eventually lost. Estimates of the potential financial loss to Burden because of the action climbed into the millions of dollars. If decisions on denial of license renewal are upheld by the FCC, the only capital recovery an owner can make is for the equipment and real estate, since the license itself is nonexistent.

As with any governmental agency, the FCC must be flexible in the face of pressures from both the industry it regulates and the public it serves. The future is going to bring many more difficult decisions on the part of the Commission. As new technology continues to affect our lives, and as Congress continues to define its regulation of electronic mass communication, the work of this regulatory body will become significantly more important.

section 315

Of those sections found within the Communications Act of 1934, perhaps none has been more discussed than Section 315. It has had a profound effect on the operations of political broadcasting. Section 315 concerns the ability of political candidates to gain access to the air waves during political campaigns. It states:

> If any licensee shall permit any person who is a legally qualified candidate for any public office to use a broadcasting station, he shall afford equal opportunity to all other such candidates for that office in the use of such broadcasting station: *Provided*, that such licensee shall have no power of censorship over the material broadcast under the provisions of this section.

Pros and Cons of Access

Section 315 has received serious criticism from candidates and broadcasters alike. To better understand these feelings, imagine that you have just filed candidacy for your city council and plan to make arrangements to purchase advertising time on one of the radio stations in your community. You make an appointment with the sales manager to discuss the amount of money you have to spend and the type of political announcement you'll make. You look at the station's rate card and discover that by purchasing 100 commercials, you will obtain a discount. You aren't sure you can afford 100 commercials and are relieved to hear the sales manager say that you can purchase a lesser number of commercials and still receive the discount rate. He explains that under Section 315, you are entitled to the "lowest unit charge" and therefore will receive the station's "discount rate" for purchasing 100 commercials even though you will only purchase 50 commercials. The discount rate for 100 commercials is $5.00 per commercial. You can afford to purchase 50 commercials, for a total of $250. You agree to the contract and then explain that you want to use the station's facilities to produce your commercials. The sales manager quotes you a per-hour rate for the use of the facilities. Returning the next day to produce your commercials, you tie up the facilities for about two hours. Finally with the help of the program director, you produce an acceptable commercial. After you leave, the sales manager goes in to talk with the general manager.

Sales Manager: Well, that job is finished. We tied up the main studio for two hours and all for $250 in advertising. I could have used the same time to produce a commercial for the hardware store worth $500 in advertising.

General Manager: Yes, I know. This Section 315 is getting to be a real headache. We haven't heard the end of it, either. You know that when the opponent hears that commercial, she'll be in here wanting to buy time, and we'll be faced with the same tied-up facilities and low sales that we were on this one. What do you think? Would it be a good idea simply to refuse to sell political advertising next year and instead offer free time to all the candidates?

Sales Manager: Do you have any idea how many people are running for city council? This place would be like a zoo. We would have every candidate in here who wanted to state a case. This way, the cost of purchasing commercials at least keeps the crowd down.

General Manager: Yes. It also keeps our profits down.

The conversation between the sales manager and the general manager illustrates just one of the issues surrounding Section 315— money. The station doesn't actually realize much profit from political commercials. In addition, because the station is required to permit all candidates for any one office to purchase time, every candidate is assured equal access and equal rates. On top of this, since a radio station is only allowed to program so many minutes per hour of commercials, and since Section 315 says stations must grant candidates access to these minutes, many other advertisers who would pay more for commercials and who may be long-term, good customers may have to be pushed off the air to accommodate political advertisements. But remember the positive side of Section 315. Without it candidates with smaller campaign budgets might not have been able to use the broadcast media to bring their campaign to the public.

Exempting News Programming

One area which is exempt from the provisions of the law is news programming. Section 315 states that the equal time provisions do not apply to

1. bona fide newscasts;
2. bona fide news interviews;
3. bona fide news documentaries (if the appearance of the candidate is incidental to the presentation of the subject or subjects covered by the news documentary); or
4. on-the-spot coverage of bona fide news events (including but not limited to political conventions and activities incidental thereto). ... A 1975 ruling by the FCC added press conferences broadcast live in their entirety to this exemption.

If you interviewed a candidate and aired his or her remarks in a newscast, it would be up to you whether or not to air the comments of the opposing candidate. Although you would want to exercise your responsibility to seek out both sides of an issue, the opponents could not demand equal time based on Section 315. An example of this exemption occurred with the *CBS Morning News*, which covered a story about an ex-convict running for sheriff in the state of Virginia. The story showed the candidate campaigning, interviewed him, and told of his background, which had included time served at a number of prisons for felony convictions. When the report was broadcast, there was even a campaign poster behind Hughes Rudd, the CBS news commentator, which said "vote for" and the name of the candidate. Although the man was an officially declared candidate, the news about his campaigning came under the exemption provisions of Section 315.

A station, of course, cannot totally refuse access to candidates and close itself off from its community. For instance, it cannot refuse free time and also refuse to sell political advertising. That would be denying "reasonable opportunity for the discussion of conflicting views on issues of public importance." The main purpose of Section 315 is to assure minority candidates and candidates with limited funds at least a minimal access to the broadcast media. Although there is continued criticism of the law, so far it's the best measure the FCC has to assure candidates an opportunity to be heard.

the fairness doctrine

The Fairness Doctrine goes beyond political broadcasting to the overall treatment of controversial issues. The issues are not limited to politics as codified in Section 315, but can range beyond them to include other issues that are deemed of major importance to the community served by the broadcasting station. The Fairness Doctrine evolved in 1949 out of a reversal of a previous decision concerning the right of broadcasters to editorialize. The first decision, called the Mayflower Decision, said on January 16, 1941[2]

> that with the limitations in frequencies inherent in the nature of radio, the public interest can never be served by a dedication of any broadcast facility to the support of his own partisan ends. Radio can serve as an instrument of democracy only when devoted to the communication of information and the exchange of ideas fairly and objectively presented. A truly free radio cannot be used to support the candidacies of his friends. It cannot be devoted to the support of principles he happens to regard most favorably. In brief, the broadcaster cannot be an advocate.

The Fairness Doctrine Is Issued

In the spring of 1948, the FCC began a series of hearings on the subject of editorializing by the broadcast media. Out of these hearings arose the Fairness Doctrine which dealt with the responsibility of every broadcaster to provide station facilities for the expression of controversial issues and all sides of those issues.[3] In a statement on the matter, the Commission noted on June 1, 1949, that editorializing was "consistent with the licensee's duty to operate in the public interest." The Commission went on to emphasize the responsibility of the licensee to seek out opposing views on controversial issues, commonly referred to as the "seek out" rule. The 1949 report also charged the licensee with the responsibility to "play a conscious and positive role in bringing about a balanced presentation of opposing viewpoints."

Since 1949, the FCC has periodically issued a series of statements on the interpretations of the Fairness Doctrine. Among these is the "personal attack" statement concerning the rule of procedure for verbal attack on the air. To understand this issue, assume you are the student head of a committee supporting a bond issue to obtain a new parking lot near the campus. On television one night, a spokesman for an opposing viewpoint is heard on a community discussion program. He lashes out against the bond issue and your organization, claiming the parking lot is of no value whatsoever to the community, that a group of uninformed students are supporting the parking lot, and that no sensible individual should vote for it. The next morning, you receive a certified letter in the mail. It is from the television station notifying you of the comments against your organization and the bond issue that were made the night before on the discussion program. The station offers you the opportunity to respond to the comments. You accept and appear on the discussion program to present your side of the story.

By notifying you of the derogatory comments, the station was meeting its responsibility to "immediately" notify you. In answering the comments, you could either have appeared personally or have appointed a spokesman to represent you on the program. We'll assume this issue to be of substantial importance in the community. If, on the other hand, the issue had been a minor one, the station might not have notified you. The question is, how does one distinguish a major from a minor issue or a controversial issue of some import from a rather trivial one? These are difficult questions and ones that the FCC doesn't usually referee. The responsibility for selecting issues to be discussed remains mostly with the individual stations.

The 1974 Report

Reopened hearings on the Doctrine in 1974 led to the FCC's issuing the "Fairness Doctrine Report: 1974." That report specifically exempted product advertisements from the Doctrine's jurisdiction. The 1974 report also attempted to create an atmosphere of flexibility in interpretation of the Doctrine. What the FCC, the broadcasters, and the public had been grueling over was that there were no guidelines for any of the groups to follow in defining such important concepts as "a controversial issue" or "reasonable opportunity for contrasting viewpoints."[4] The Commission summed up its feelings on these matters as follows:

> The Fairness Doctrine will not ensure perfect balance and debate, and each station is not required to provide an "equal" opportunity for opposing views. Furthermore, since the Fairness Doctrine does not require balance in individual programs or a series of programs, but only in a station's overall programming, there is no assurance that a listener who hears an initial presentation will also hear a rebuttal. However, if all stations presenting programming relating to a controversial issue of public importance make an effort to round out their coverage with contrasting viewpoints, these various points of view will receive a much wider public dissemination.

Time will tell if the 1974 Report is going to lessen or increase the debate over the Fairness Doctrine. When cable television systems fully utilize their multi-channel capacity, and when citizen groups take advantage of their opportunities to help determine programming on these channels, then the restricted broadcasting "spectrum" will expand as will its potential for disseminating information. Perhaps there will come a time, then, when both the implied and stated controls that comprise the Fairness Doctrine can be virtually eliminated.[5]

prime-time access

Research has long shown that the highest viewing times for television in the United States are in the evening hours between 7:00 p.m. and 11:00 p.m.—the prime-time hours. Since these hours are so valuable, in terms of programming, advertising, and public access, the networks have usually "kept" these hours for their own use. In an attempt to restructure this dominance, the FCC created the prime-time access rule in 1970. In theory, the rule was designed to trim the amount of time devoted to prime-time network programming and substitute locally originated programming in its place. The idea was to foster the creativity of local television personnel. One FCC Commissioner at the time, Nicholas Johnson, was highly supportive of the bill. But the FCC forgot an important fact—the high-caliber creative people capable of producing local programs on a par with those of major production houses simply could not be found at every local television station. Moreover, syndicated programs permitted stations to meet their access obligations to the FCC. By the end of two seasons, the verdicts were in. The critics called the rule a flop. The supporters, like Commissioner Johnson, claimed it hadn't been given a chance. In a surprise development, television program directors across the country issued support for the measure through their professional associations. Finally, after modifications, challenges, and court cases, the revised rule allows local television stations to air three hours of network programming six days a week and four hours on Sunday. This compromise also gives production houses an outlet for some of their "not-so-successful" programs, and local stations that have developed quality programming have been encouraged to continue it.

the family-viewing concept

Closely aligned to the prime-time access rule is an arrangement volunteered by the networks with the FCC's blessing known as "family-viewing time." Instituted in the fall of 1975, it was the result of a series of FCC hearings on the amount of violence and sex contained in prime-time viewing hours during which children were watching. Under the networks' plan, only those shows suitable for family-viewing were to be aired during the first hour of prime time. Under the prime-time access rule, that was the time period before 9:00 p.m. Critics quickly pointed out that the theory assumed two things: (1) that west of the Eastern time zone, children went to bed at 8:00 p.m.; and (2) that while networks agreed to decrease the amount of violent programming during the family-viewing hours, "anything could go" after those hours.

Another problem with the family-viewing concept lay in the assumption that network executives were qualified to judge what type of programming was suitable for children to watch. This concept had overtones of First Amendment censorship. Critics abounded. The Writer's Guild, Directors Guild, Screen Actors Guild, and independent companies sued the FCC, the NAB, and the three commercial networks, charging the rule stifled creativity in the television industry. Editorial cartoonists had a field day with the idea (Figure 18–2). The magazine *TV Guide* commissioned the Opinion Research Corporation to find out what the public thought of family-viewing time. Results showed 82 percent favored family-viewing time, 7 percent opposed it, and 11 percent had no opinion.[6] That report was also soundly criticized. But even with debate and court

Figure 18–2. Cartoons such as this one by Jerry Barnett of the *Indianapolis News* were typical of the criticism leveled at the family-viewing-hour concept. (Barnett, *The Indianapolis News.*)

proceedings, the family-viewing concept gained a strong toehold on television programming.

regulating cable

The barrage of rules and regulations that has evolved since cable television became a major carrier of media content would boggle your mind. Federal legislation is almost equal in amount to the combined regulation governing commercial radio and television broadcasting, and when we add to this body of law the maze of local and state regulations concerning the operation of cable systems we may truly stand back in amazement. At least with standard broadcasting stations, the federal government has the responsibility for making and enforcing the laws. Such is not the case with cable. Regulations enacted by local municipalities abound, establishing standards for the local cable operator on everything from fees to program content. They have legislated to which poles cables can be attached, where they must be underground, why cable operators can't work on actual television sets, and numerous other regulations. Officials at all levels of the regulatory ladder have discovered the potential of cable systems, and state and FCC lawmakers also want a say in controlling them. There are no clearly defined rules or court precedents giving the FCC *exclusive* jurisdiction. Thus, in many areas there are significant conflicts, if not confusion, over exactly who has jurisdiction over the case.

Regulatory Conflicts

At the local level, control stems from the communities' realization that the cable system has much more potential than merely bringing distant entertainment radio and television to the community. It can reach local school children with information about their schools. It can broadcast meetings of the city council and bring the workings of municipal government into living rooms with a realism that the local newscast or newspaper would find hard to match. With so many channels available to community groups almost anyone can gain access to a local cable channel and proceed to disseminate a message to area cable subscribers. Moreover, there is the problem of categorizing cable in relation to other media. Legal precedent has suggested that the printed press and broadcast press are equal under the First Amendment rights of free speech and free press. However, is cablecasting the same as broadcasting? What would happen, for instance, if a cable company's news programs became justifiably critical of the city council, in a community where the city council had control over the cable company's franchise? These and other questions have posed many regulatory quandaries. Simple answers are just not available.

When a municipality becomes involved in cablecasting, problems of jurisdiction among the three governmental levels are usually bound to occur. Wherever state and local laws conflict, the state law will almost always have the advantage in an appeal. Similarly, in a conflict between state and federal laws, the federal law will usually take precedent. Thus, to avoid problems with possible appeals, many states and localities have borrowed regulations that closely resemble federal legislation.

State laws governing cable fall into three categories—*full preempt statutes, appellate function statutes,* and *advisory statutes.*[7] Of the three, the most encompassing is the full preempt statute. Here, the state assumes full control of licensing decisions and, in effect, "preempts" the municipalities' rights to determine licensing and programming. In other words, the state becomes the primary governing authority, and the loyalty of the cable operator is toward the state. In the appellate function statutes, the state has the authority to review local decisions concerning cable operating and franchising. "State approval does *not* preempt federal review (before the FCC). However, state disapproval *may* effectively preempt ultimate municipal authority. . . ."[8] Advisory statutes are the least encompassing. Massachusetts has a "pure" advisory statute. In other words, the state cannot normally regulate cable "in any way except when 10 percent of system subscribers petition the State CATV Commission for review."[9]

Channel Access

One area of legislation in which the federal government has clearly established jurisdiction is in access to the cable system. Unlike broadcasting where the spectrum is limited, hardware developments in cable have made it possible for more than two dozen channels to exist in many markets. The FCC has been decisive in mandating the importance of local access to cable systems and has facilitated the use by local community groups of cable systems for little more than the cost of the facilities. To further their point, the FCC has warned cable operators that these costs must be reasonable, so as not to infringe on the concept of "low-cost" access.

As a responsible consumer of mass communication, you will have many opportunities to take part in local hearings dealing with the operation and franchise renewal of cable systems. Whenever these develop in your own community, take the time to research the federal, state, and local regulations which may affect your local cable franchise.

control of satellite communication

The control of satellite communication, and specifically the use of satellites to beam television signals to earth stations, is a topic which is embroiled in international discussions spanning not only the broad field of communication but also politics, science, technology, theology, and morality. The Federation of Rocky Mountain States Technology Demonstration has used satellites to send television signals, commonly called "direct" broadcast satellite communication, from Denver, Colorado, to high schools in remote areas of the Rocky Mountain Region (Figure 18–3). In exactly the same way, satellites beam signals to schools in India—they could in fact be used to beam signals to any school anywhere on earth. This is, however, just one application of direct satellite communication. Satellites also make it possible to beam programming of the major American television networks to Europe and to encompass the entire United States in a network that would eliminate land-line systems. At first, prospects such as these may seem relatively uncontrover-

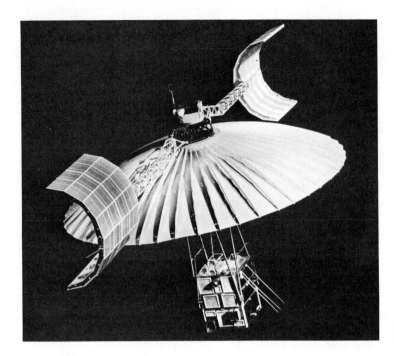

Figure 18–3. The ATS satellite. (Photo courtesy NASA.)

sial. After all, the First Amendment guarantees free speech and free press and has been used as a basis for guaranteeing the overall free flow of information in general. Yet the First Amendment is just the tip of an iceberg under which hulks many a controversy surrounding not only the control of direct broadcast satellites but also every issue in which the freedom of the individual is pitted against the welfare of the community.

Legalities and Cultural Integrity

Americans are also conditioned to the idea that the First Amendment to the Constitution is a universally held principle of law and morality—it isn't. Its jurisdiction applies only within United States boundaries. When other countries become involved, as they immediately do with direct broadcast satellite communication, new issues of international law and understanding crystallize. These issues have been summarized by Paul L. Laskin and Abram Chayes in an essay prepared under the auspices of the American Society of International Law and published by the Aspen Institute for Humanistic Studies.[10] In their summary was the contention that there is no way to assure that television programs sent from direct broadcast satellites will remain inside national boundaries. For example, a nation surrounded by a ridge of high mountains may effectively keep within its boundaries television signals sent from land-based transmitters. However, signals from satellites do not respect such natural terrain and can spill over into bordering nations. Even new developments in satellite technology which permit signals to be directed within areas of approximately 100 miles in diameter still cannot provide directional coverage to match the irregular political boundaries. Most satellite coverage areas must be circular. When spillover does occur, it can easily threaten a nation's culture, integrity, or even its security.

There is also the fear that the superpowers may be in a position to dominate world development of satellite communication. Because the United States, for example, has the technology as well as the economic base to develop a worldwide system of satellite communication, other countries, especially the underdeveloped ones, are resistant to the potential wholesale of American programming, especially programming from the major commercial networks. These nations also fear bad American programs drive out or keep out the good.[11]

Commercialism is another contested issue. Countries in which commercials are not a major part of the television fare fear that the influence of United States programming will ignite a commercial bombardment. There is also the fear that commercials of one country may tend to create a desire for goods of that country and, as a result, provide unfair competition to local industries. In addition, certain societies fear that commercial programming will create a thirst for consumer goods and project consumer-oriented societies too positively. Such examples will have the effect of disrupting national plans for orderly social and economic development.

International Law

Added to these considerations is the difficulty of formulating any aspect of international law. Laskin and Chayes note: "Where the Anglo-American countries, for example, proceed pragmatically, formulating the rules of legal behavior as they acquire experience, the civil law tradition tends to rely on the codification of rules in advance of action."[12] Such concepts become important when trying to establish systems whereby agreements will *precede* the beginning of direct satellite communication into a country, or if the regulatory function is to begin *after* the broadcasts commence, determining when there may be a need to control them.

Clearly, the solutions to these issues are not easy. In the United States, the only two documents which really reflect any attempt to govern satellite communication are the Communications Satellite Act of 1962 and the Communications Act of 1934 as amended. The 1962 legislation was primarily concerned with setting up COMSAT, creating a common channel of communication and control with other nations, and ultimately fixing the position of the United States with INTELSAT. The 1962 law followed precedents established by the 1934 legislation in that the FCC's responsibility for regulating television programming within the boundaries of the United States would logically carry over to programming beamed outside United States boundaries. Beyond this stance, however, control is vague if not nonexistent. This regulatory gap in American policy toward direct broadcast satellite communication is not necessarily negative. Premature control could place satellite communication in the same ballpark with cable television, which both industry and government officials have contended is being stifled by overregulation. The incentive to develop new hardware and software systems stagnates when constant rewriting of government regulations leaves companies uncertain of definitive guidelines. To prevent this from happening to satellite communication, many of the issues and incentives for developing an international system of direct broadcast satellites have purposely been retained in the discussion stage.

control of motion pictures

At the turn of the century when it became clear that motion pictures were here to stay and that the public was willing to pay the price to keep the industry profitable, serious competition began to develop. Theater production companies, distributors, and theater operators swamped the Hollywood scene. Unlike now, motion pictures were not then considered a legitimate form of mass communication any more than they had been when they were presented through the peephole of the penny arcade.

Early Legislation

In 1915, the Supreme Court in the case of *Mutual Film Corp.* vs. *Ohio* ruled that motion pictures were primarily a business, and were therefore not a link in the public's chain of information and therefore not safeguarded by the First Amendment. With that fact firmly established, the Federal Trade Commission set about to try and break up the sizeable monopolies that it contended were beginning to develop. Major motion picture companies wanted pieces of all the action, from the production of the film, through distribution, and on into the retail outlets. These dominant firms thus began to purchase control of all facets of the industry, and the era of the late teens and the early 1920s was characterized by corporate expansion and overzealous competition that placed the entire industry on shaky financial ground. However, that was temporary. Realizing the threat of federal control, the industry tried to avert it by forming the Motion Picture Producers and Distributors Association (MPPDA) headed by Wil H. Hays, a political crony of President Warren G. Harding. With Hays in the driver's seat of the MPPDA, the industry moved forward without much control and managed to survive without its First Amendment protection. But for all practical purposes, it also had no competition. That soon changed. Television surfaced, and the need to venture downtown to the lavishly furnished movie house was superceded by a comfortable evening in the living room in front of the television set. To hold their audience, films had to become more controversial.

In 1952, the Supreme Court ruled that films did in fact have some protection under the First Amendment. In the case of *Burstyn* vs. *Wilson*, the Court overturned a New York decision which had prompted the Board of Regents to censor the film *The Miracle* as being sacrilegious. The issue actually before the Court, however, was freedom of religion rather than First Amendment protection for film, for the Court's decision stated that to permit *The Miracle* to be censored would open up other opportunities for censorship of religious themes.[13] The court clearly sidestepped the issue of whether New York had the power as a state to censor film in the first place. Yet the ruling did open the door for other challenges.

Local Pressures

Throughout the history of motion pictures, the Supreme Court and many lower courts have tried to avoid the issue of direct control over what is shown in local theaters or in the public classrooms of any state, especially when the issue involves an immature audience. Sometimes, the mere threat of censure is enough to keep certain films out of town. If you were operating a local motion picture theater and had the option of running a film filled with sex and violence, you would probably face a rather clearcut dilemma. You can show the film and net a sizeable profit. But then you might incur the ire of some local citizens who picket in front of your theater and even demand action from the city council. That type of publicity would be bad for business in the long run. Thus, you decide to play it safe and continue showing films which are less objectionable to the community. Of course, the way your community reacts may be exactly the opposite of a neighboring community's reaction. In 1973 the Supreme Court returned to the lower courts a number of obscenity cases, stating in effect that the responsibility for determining these issues should be on the shoulders of local communities. In the future, matters concerning what is acceptable for public consumption will be determined more by local and state government. Normally, the more numerous the motion picture theaters in a community, the broader the spectrum of motion picture fare and the more permissive the regulations. The responsibility of viewing, in these cases, rests on the shoulders of the public. This responsibility has been aided by the well-known rating code of the Motion Picture Association of America (MPAA). First instituted in 1968, the code lists four types of films, each with a letter classification. They are G—general audience, all ages admitted; PG—parental guidance suggested; R—restricted to those accompanied by a parent or guardian; and X—no one under seventeen (older in some areas) admitted. These codes have at least given the motion picture industry something to consider when producing a motion picture.

advertising and the FTC

We need only look at a collection of antique advertising memorabilia to see why current advertising controls exist. A perusal of old medicine ads, for example, would bring to view labels for everything from horse liniment to castor oil, all capable of curing everything that could possibly ail man, woman, or beast. Their claims to cure were only outdone by those to prevent, claims that, figuratively speaking, promised the fountain of youth overnight—or in three doses! When the medicine wagon rolled through the frontier West, there wasn't much concern over the outlandish claims that the barker spieled into the sunset. However, when the twentieth century saw mass circulation magazines roll off the presses, when it heard radio commercials jingling their way across the countryside, and when television began to stimulate "miracle" results, advertising was due for some regulation. If you had watched television in the 1950s, you might have seen commercials for cereal or for tennis shoes whose claim to fame one would imagine was the role these products could play in a science fiction melodrama.

Criticism and Compliance

When the Federal Trade Commission was formed in 1914, its first duties did not center around advertising regulations. It was primarily concerned with guarding against corporate monopolies. In later years, however, the FTC became deeply involved in controlling deceptive advertising. We have already learned of one such

Dioxogen

An Advertisement to Mothers

BEWARE of Whooping Cough, Diphtheria, Measles, Scarlet Fever!

There is no more reason for your children to have these and all the rest of the childhood germ diseases, with their fearful after effects,—

Than there is for them to break their arms and legs.

Dioxogen is bottled common sense.

Its free use prevents all these and most other childhood ills.

For Dioxogen *kills* germs.

Doesn't just wash them farther along.

See that the little folks use it freely as a gargle and mouth wash.

Teach them to run to the Dioxogen bottle when they hurt themselves.

Dioxogen is a *germicide*—not merely an antiseptic. It is absolutely harmless too.

Three Sizes

Small	(5⅓ oz.)	—25c.
Medium	(10⅔ oz.)	—50c.
Large	(20 oz.)	—75c.

Dioxogen

98 Front Street   New York City

Remarkable claims such as these for Dioxogen are just one of the reasons for the development of controls for advertising.

385

involvement, the case against ITT Continental Baking Company and the claims about its Profile Bread. The agency has had its share of ups and downs over the years, and in 1969 and 1970, both consumer advocate Ralph Nader and the American Bar Association criticized the agency's performance. The FTC consequently undertook a major reorganization, establishing a separate division to handle food and drug advertising within the FTC's Bureau of Consumer Protection. The agency's enforcement powers range from simple letters reprimanding those who the FTC feels have violated its rules to the stronger "cease and desist" orders. Through regular press releases to nationwide news media, the FTC notifies the public of its actions; the dates, times, and places of agency hearings; the companies involved; and any final action taken by the FTC or by the judges hearing appeals on FTC decisions. It was not until consumer awareness developed that FTC press releases received such extensive news coverage. Now, however, with an increase in the number of "special reporters" and consumer watchdogs, virtually no development in this area goes unnoticed.

Celebrity Endorsements

One of the most publicized FTC orders occurred in 1975 when the agency clamped down on product endorsements by celebrities. Prior to that time, it had been common practice for any celebrity to lend his or her name to a product, whether or not the celebrity used that product. The classic case portrayed New York Jets football star Joe Namath reclining on his side while the camera panned slowly from his toes to his hips as he was clad in a pair of ladies pantyhose. This commercial and many others came to an abrupt end when the FTC set forth "guidelines" for advertisers casting a negative light on such practices and warning about the possibilities of lawsuits should they imply celebrity endorsements for any product the celebrity didn't actually use. The "guidelines" further stated that the celebrity need not even verbally comment on the product; the fact that he or she was seen in the same advertisement with the product was reason enough, according to the FTC, for the public to assume the celebrity was endorsing it. In the same year, the FTC also moved in on General Foods Corporation, arranging a consent order (agreement between parties) to stop the use of ads with former naturalist Euell Gibbons claiming Post Grape-Nuts reminded him of wild hickory nuts. The fear of the FTC was that children seeing the ad might eat wild foods which were harmful.

The future of FTC regulation will closely align with the amount of

Football star O. J. Simpson advertising Hertz rent-a-cars. FTC guidelines specify such celebrities must also use the products they advertise. (© Hertz System, Inc., 1975. Reprinted by permission.)

self-regulation that the media uses in screening advertisements before they reach the public. For the consumer, the FTC is one of the few federal organizations which clamps down on unfair practices by companies dealing directly with the public. Some consumers have criticized the FTC for being all talk and no bite. Others have suggested it oversteps its bounds when it regulates advertising content, saying its actions smack of censorship. Regardless of the legitimacy of the criticism, there have been sufficient court tests of the agency's regulatory powers *and* enough voluntary compliance to justify the FTC's current posture as the enforcer of truth in advertising.

postal regulations

The United States Postal Service plays an important role in the control of direct mail. Postal regulations actually fill legal volumes, but they apply essentially to three different classes of mail—first-, second-, and third-class postage—as well as distinguish between what can and cannot be mailed. If you were conducting a direct-mail campaign, you would need to be concerned with these regulations. Suppose, for example, that you decide to publish a newspaper that deals with campus issues on your state's colleges and universities. Since you need to secure some subscribers, you decide to send a letter to all the students attending college in your state. You discover that you can send your mail first class and either send it through a postage meter or stamp each letter individually. Yet you can also secure a first-class bulk permit, printed on the outside of each envelope you send, but then you would need to sort your mail in geographical areas before depositing it at the post office. You still would be paying the same first-class rate for this bulk permit. You decide to use a postage meter and forego the first-class bulk permit. If you wanted to save on postage rates, you could have chosen to use a third-class bulk permit. This permit would have permitted a major savings on postage, but you would have been responsible for sorting and bundling the mail into specific zip code areas before you took it to the post office. You would also have needed at least 200 pieces of mail in each mailing, and these would have all had to be the same size and weight. The priority service you receive with first-class mail would not have been available with third-class bulk mail. Although the Postal Service would try to sort your mailing as quickly as possible, your third-class bulk mailing would be handled only after other classes of mail were sorted. This might mean delays for your mail, especially near holiday periods.

Now let's assume that your business venture has progressed to the point where you have published your newspaper and are ready to mail it. You won't want to use either first- or third-class mail to do so. The first-class postage would be too expensive, and the third-class service might deliver your newspaper to subscribers after your news was old. Thus, you mail your newspaper by second-class postage—a special class of mail primarily for newspapers. With this class of postage, you are able to receive the advantages of priority service because you are mailing a newspaper. You would, however, need to sort your newspapers into zip-coded geographical areas before depositing them at the post office, and you would also have to publish your newspaper at least once per week to qualify for this class.

Other postal regulations affect direct-mail, mail order, and other mail-distribution practices in still other ways. For instance, it is illegal to send something C.O.D. (Cash on Delivery) if the person receiving the merchandise didn't order it. In other words, you couldn't send your newspapers C.O.D. and just haul in the money on those that decided to accept and pay for delivery. In most cases, it is illegal to distribute unsolicited advertisements for contraceptives by direct mail. However, this does not apply to mailing magazines which might contain advertisements for contraceptives. Intoxicating liquors cannot be sent through the mail and neither can such concealed weapons as handguns or switchblade knives. As new technology increases the speed and ability to disseminate messages, postal regulations will continue to play an important part in the function of the mail as a means of mass communication.

summary

The foundation of regulatory control of American mass media is the First Amendment to the Constitution, which guarantees freedom of the press and speech. The electronic media that have evolved in the course of the twentieth century are, however, a far cry from the colonial presses that the founding fathers had in mind when they wrote the First Amendment. In the public interest, therefore, Congress sought more definitive controls to regulate the new media and accordingly formulated such legislation as the Wireless Ship Act of 1910, the Radio Act of 1912, the Radio Act of 1927, and the Communications Act of 1934. Of this legislation, the 1934 law created the Federal Communications Commission, the governmental body primarily responsible for the control of electronic communication.

The Commission is under the direction of seven FCC Commissioners, each serving a seven-year term.

Two of the most familiar regulations which concern standard radio and television programming are Section 315 of the Communications Act of 1934 and the Fairness Doctrine, a special 1949 ruling of the FCC. Section 315 covers political broadcasting, and the Fairness Doctrine sets up guidelines for unbiased treatment of controversial issues. The prime-time access and family-viewing concepts have both been designed to control the quality of television programming.

Regulation of cable is accomplished by local, state, and federal statutes. Although appeals usually give priority to federal regulations as decreed by the FCC, many local and state governmental bodies have jurisdiction over such things as subscription fees and the granting of cable franchises. Regulatory control of satellite communication remains largely uncharted. Since satellite signals cannot always be made to conform to national boundaries, much of the discussion of satellite control is embodied in the principles of international law. Guidelines for the motion picture industry in the United States, originally established by the Federal Trade Commission and dealing with questions of monopolistic practices, have now become a matter of interpreting the Constitution, especially regarding censorship. Advertising, for the most part, comes under the jurisdiction of the Federal Trade Commission. The Postal Service is the regulatory body responsible for the control of direct mail.

opportunities for further learning

GALLOWAY, JONATHAN E., *The Politics and Technology of Satellite Communications.* Lexington, Mass.: D. C. Heath and Company, 1972.

KAHN, FRANK J., Ed., *Documents of American Broadcasting.* Englewood Cliffs, N.J.: Prentice-Hall, Inc., 1968.

KRASNOW, ERWIN G., and LAWRENCE D. LONGLEY, *The Politics of Broadcast Regulation.* New York: St. Martin's Press, 1973.

LEDUC, DON R., *Cable Television and the FCC.* Philadelphia, Pa.: Temple University Press, 1973.

TOOHEY, DANIEL W., RICHARD D. MARKS, and ARNOLD P. LUTZKER, *Legal Problems in Broadcasting.* Lincoln, Nebraska: Great Plains National Instructional Television Library, 1974.

legal issues
and the
working press

CHAPTER NINETEEN

As we learned in Chapter 1, the mass communication process does not occur in a vacuum. Many different forces of control affect the final message the public receives—government regulations, codes of ethics, and court orders, among others. This chapter and the two that follow examine some of the legal, judicial, social, and ethical controls upon the media.

theories of control

Before dealing with specific laws, rules, and ethical codes, we'll attempt to place these various controls in perspective as they apply to media, messages, and receivers of mass communication. To do so, we'll touch upon four theories for the operation of mass media. We'll also examine a model to help us understand the varying degrees of control that can be placed on both media messages and their audiences.

391

Four Theories of the Press

In their book, *Four Theories of the Press*, Siebert, Peterson, and Schramm outline the four theories for the operation of the mass media.[1] The first of these systems, termed *authoritarian*, is characterized by media which are either "private or public" and "are chiefly instruments for effecting government policy, though not necessarily government owned." The media of the Fascist or totalitarian states of Mussolini and Hitler would be indicative of this theory. The second, the *libertarian* rationale, espouses a press privately owned and an "instrument for checking on government and meeting other needs of society." The libertarian theory is common to Great Britain and was applicable to the United States during the period from the eighteenth to the twentieth century. Attitudinal changes within American mass media during the twentieth century, however, spawned the theory of *social responsibility*. The social responsibility theory is indicative of privately owned media "unless the government has to take over to insure public service." Siebert, Peterson, and Schramm state that the "media must assume the obligation of social responsibility; and if they do not, someone must see that they do." We have already encountered some of the elements of the social responsibility theory when we discussed journalistic societies and codes of ethics that attempt to foster self-regulation. Similarly, technological advances and the limited broadcasting spectrum have prompted some government controls in the public "interest, convenience, and necessity." The fourth rationale for the operation of media is functioning in the Soviet Union and is called the *Soviet Communist Theory*. In the U.S.S.R., the media are owned by the state and function as instruments of political propaganda.

We will be concerned primarily with the various types of control operating within the United States. Keep in mind that although we can theoretically posit four distinct systems of regulation, none operates to the complete exclusion of the other three. A nation's media system may represent a combination of several theories, and a single medium may be subject to controls from more than one theory. Our print media, for example, fall mainly into the social responsibility category. Yet our broadcasting media are influenced by both libertarian principles and those of the social responsibility theory because, although privately owned, the government through the FCC makes sure broadcasters assume responsibility for the operation of their stations. The purpose of presenting the four theories is not to pigeonhole each medium into its own neat and tidy classification, but rather to nurture an awareness of the various types of controls that act upon the media and how these controls operate across both media and national boundaries.

Model of Open and Closed Mass Media Systems

Another way to view the control of mass communication is through the model developed by Osmo Wiio, Professor and Director of the Helsinki Research Institute for Business Economics.[2] In Wiio's model, mass communication is viewed on a two-dimensional, open-closed continuum of the receiver system (the audience) and the message system (the media) as shown in Figure 19–1. The left vertical line of the model represents the audience, and the bottom horizontal line represents the message system. A numerical range of 0.0 to 1.0 is used to characterize the degree of control, with 1.0 representing the most open system and 0.0 representing the most closed system. Thus, the most *closed* system, for example, a Type 3 private telephone system, is actually private communication, not mass communication at all. Type 2, uncontrolled mass communication, which directs its messages to anyone who can hear them, represents the other end of the spectrum, a completely *open* mass communication system. Take a few moments to recall some of the media and audiences we have already discussed. Each medium operates under varying amounts of control and directs itself to an audience at some position on the open–closed continuum. For example, a company magazine is more closed both in terms of message and audience than is a major metropolitan newspaper. Cer-

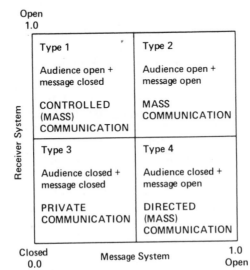

Figure 19–1. Wiio's model of mass communication.

tain messages within the same medium may also be more tightly closed than others. Consider the local television cable system that provides a fairly wide range of programs for its viewers. Some channels, however, may be accessible only to those viewers who pay an additional fee to the cable system. In this case, the system itself represents a more open position on the model, and a given cable channel represents a more closed position. In addition to the four theories outlined by Siebert, Peterson, and Schramm, also keep in mind the Wiio model when you attempt to weigh the relative differences among controls affecting mass communication. Again, it is important to realize that the four theories and the model are not meant to be neat classification systems of media. They are presented to help you conceptualize the various dimensions of control that affect the mass media process. As you read about the specific laws, codes, and regulations which follow, consider how they would interrelate with the theories and model we've just discussed. In addition, keep in mind that many of these "controls" are not controls in the traditional sense, but are actually safeguards which assure our system's "openness."

reporters' shield laws

When we left Harry in Chapter 11, he had just been served a subpoena by the deputy sheriff. The subpoena ordered him to appear and tell the judge where he received his information about the narcotics transfer. For Harry, it meant one of three things. He could ignore the subpoena and not appear in court. That would eventually result in a return visit from the deputy sheriff, only this time with handcuffs instead of a subpoena. Or, Harry could appear in court and testify where he received the information about the drug transfer, but that would mean going back on his promise to his friend Sam. This action would also probably result in Sam's arrest and signal the end of Sam's cooperative role as news source for Harry. If Harry refuses to testify, his third possible course of action, he risks the possibility of a stiff fine or a jail sentence. None of the alternatives is promising. Even if Harry appeals his fine and jail sentence, it will be a costly, time-consuming process.

Harry is fortunate, however. The newspaper Harry worked for would pay his legal fees. The next day, Harry consulted with an attorney. During that consultation, Harry told his attorney he would refuse to divulge his source of information, using his state's shield law as a basis for his decision. The shield law had been passed by the last session of the legislature and gave protection to journalists who did not want to divulge sources of confidential information. Although opponents of the bill claimed the First Amendment to the Constitution offered sufficient protection under its "free speech" and "free press" guarantees, supporters of the bill weren't quite as sure. They had watched reporters in other states go to jail for refusing to divulge their sources. As a result, the new law had passed, but there had been no test of its effectiveness. It looked as though Harry's case might be the first.

Finally, the day came for Harry to appear. He faced an aggressive prosecutor, and seated in the courtroom was an anxious police chief who had cracked the case. As Harry approached the witness stand, he was nervous. The prosecutor approached the stand and, looking Harry in the eye, reminded him of the story he had published about the drug transfer. He then asked Harry where he had received that information. Before Harry could answer, the attorney for the defendant in the case rose to his feet and objected. The judge asked on what grounds. The defendant's attorney then cited the exact wording of the new shield law: "No person connected with or employed by any media transmitting any information to the

"WHERE'D YOU GET YOUR INFORMATION, HARRY?!!!"

public shall be required by a legislative or judicial officer to compel testimony disclosing the source of any published or unpublished information obtained by any person in the course of gathering, receiving, or processing information for any medium of communication to the public."

Working on a hunch, the prosecutor replied, "But, Your Honor, the defendant has already disclosed the source of this information to other people he works with at his own newspaper, and it is therefore no longer confidential."

The prosecutor was right. Harry had talked with others at the office about the information he received from Sam. The defendant's attorney quickly replied, "Your Honor, the law specifically states that the fact that he has disclosed the source of this information to others does not mean that it ceases to be confidential. The Act also specifically states in Section 2 that it applies regardless of whether a person has disclosed elsewhere any of the information or source."

The prosecutor's arguments weren't over, however. He stepped forward and began a new line of reasoning.

"Your Honor, the defendant's attorney is arguing for a law which, if interpreted in the manner he suggests, would be a direct violation of the Fifth Amendment to the Constitution, which guarantees that no one will be deprived of 'life, liberty, or property, without due process of law.' Also, the defense attorney's interpretation of the law is in direct conflict with the Sixth Amendment which guarantees the accused the right to a speedy and public trial. Interfering with the due process of the law cannot be tolerated, or every reporter in this city will be inclined to make a mockery of this court."

The defendant's attorney quickly rose to his feet. "Your Honor, the rest of the reporters in this city are not on trial in this case, and there is little reason to assume a ruling in favor of the witness would result in a mockery of this court."

The judge looked pained. He had heard both sides of the issue and decided the decision was best delayed until after lunch. The court recessed until 2:00 p.m.

Harry started to think of the possible outcome. Going to jail wasn't something he relished. Perhaps it would be best to divulge the source of his information. After all, Sam wasn't involved in the robbery. He was only good as a source of information about criminal activities; Harry had other sources he could rely upon to do his job. If the judge overruled the objection, and Harry still refused to divulge his source of information, he would undoubtedly be cited for criminal contempt, an action against the dignity and in the presence of the court. But as he thought about it, he also realized there was no way he could face his peers again if he divulged his source.

Reporters didn't like going to jail any more than other people, but it would take a long time for Harry to resolve in his own mind why he "sold out" his professional ethics.

Time passed quickly, and the judge returned. The court was called into session, and the judge summoned the two attorneys to the bench. Although he indicated decisions such as this were difficult because they lacked judicial precedent within the state, he was sustaining the objection and would not require Harry to divulge his source of information about the drug transfer. It was this very thing that the state's shield law had sought to prevent in view of the difficulty in interpreting the Constitution in these matters. What had been difficult and trying hours were now swept away in a wave of relief. Harry thought about Sam, his profession, the people back at the office, and how elsewhere in other circumstances he might not have been so lucky.

The Scope of Reporters' Shield Laws

Had Harry been in another state or in front of another judge, the outcome of the decision might not have been so favorable. Reporters' shield laws are relatively recent, their emphasis occurring in the early 1970s when the courts with interesting frequency began jailing journalists for not divulging their sources of information. One of the most publicized cases involved *Los Angeles Times* reporter William Farr, who refused to divulge the source of information he had received from an attorney during a murder trial. Farr served some time in jail. As a result of several other similar cases, a number of states began realizing that the Constitution didn't ensure journalists sufficient protection, and there was a real need to either legislate new reporters' shield laws or beef up old ones. By 1976, more than twenty states had shield laws. Two states whose legislatures instituted typical changes were Indiana and Oregon. Indiana had had a shield law on the books since 1941, but it became outdated. This, accompanied by the reasons mentioned above, prompted the legislature to change the law in 1971 and 1973. The new law read as follows:[3]

> SECTION 1. IC 1971, 34-3-5-1 is amended to read as follows: Sec. 1 Any person connected with, or any person who has been so connected with or employed by, a weekly, semiweekly, triweekly, or daily newspaper that conforms to postal regulations, which shall have been published for five (5) consecutive years in the same city or town and which has a paid circulation of two per cent (2%) of the population of the county in which it is published, newspaper or other periodical issued at regular intervals and

having a general circulation or a recognized press association; a wire service as a bona fide owner, editorial or reportorial employee, who receives or has received his or her principal income from legitimate gathering, writing, editing and interpretation of news, and any person connected with a ~~commercially~~ licensed radio or television station as owner, official, or as an editorial or reportorial employee who received or has received ~~his or her principal~~ income from ~~legitimate gathering, writing, editing, interpreting,~~ announcing or broadcasting of news, shall not be compelled to disclose in any legal proceedings or elsewhere the source of any information procured or obtained in the course of his employment or representation of such newspaper, periodical, press association, radio station, or television station, or wire service, whether published or not published in the newspaper or periodical, or by the press association or wire service or broadcast or not broadcast by the radio station or television station by which he is employed.

The key to the interpretation of the Indiana law and the resulting effect on both the news media and the public can be seen by examining the words in the revised 1973 bill which have been crossed out. In crossing out those key words, the legislature sought to broaden the scope and strengthen the law. For instance, in the 1941 statute, a newspaper which was just starting would have had little protection under the law. It would have had to be in circulation for at least five years. Moreover, it would have had to be at least successful enough to have a paid circulation of two percent of the population. In other words, the newspaper had to show that it was a successful commercial enterprise, both in terms of profit and longevity. Moreover, under the law, if you had been a reporter for an educational radio station, you would not have been protected. Your radio station would have had to be a "commercially" licensed operation for the shield law to apply. Also, your "principal income" would have had to be from the medium that employed you. If you had been a part-time employee at a local radio station whose principal income derived from another source, you would not have been protected. If you had been a volunteer intern at a commercial radio or television station and had uncovered a major investigative story which necessitated keeping your sources confidential, you would not have had the protection. Interestingly enough, it was a college student journalist working as a page in the Indiana Legislature in 1973 who called to the attention of the legislative committee revising the bill the necessity for deleting the words "commercially" and "his or her principal." The law now permits educational radio and television stations as well as student interns who are paid only nominal sums to come under the jurisdiction of the bill.

Although Indiana's 1941 shield law may seem rather shortsighted by today's standards, it was felt conclusive enough for that era. Today, however, there are many other considerations. Technology and judical precedent have created a need for more inclusive shield laws.

An example of this inclusiveness is the Oregon shield law.[4] For instance, in the Oregon law, the scope of the media covered under the statute is much broader than in the Indiana law. Although a court might interpret the Indiana law as being equally as broad, the Oregon law specifically states that: "Medium of communication has its ordinary meaning and includes, but is not limited to, any newspaper, magazine or other periodical, book, pamphlet, news service, wire service, news or feature syndicate, broadcast station or network, or cable television system. . . ." Here we see that if Harry had been a reporter for a local cable television system, he would have been protected under the Oregon statute. Even the author of a book is explicitly protected under the Oregon law.

Working with Shield Laws

Laws as encompassing as Oregon's are rare. Not all states are explicit in their definition of media, and reporters who are working for magazines or writing books are not always protected to the full extent of newspaper journalists. Although judicial precedent has firmly established radio and television as being "press" in the traditional sense, there are still many legal frontiers to be conquered before shield laws can be said to have universal application.

Reporters are also faced with the fact that orderly judicial procedures must be followed when a court order demands that a reporter reveal confidential sources of information. Courts have also ruled that reporters are not exempt from appearing and testifying before grand juries. Even the strongest shield laws may not prevent a judge from issuing a contempt order, and although a reporter may win a case on appeal, he or she may in the meantime spend considerable time in jail and be faced with mountainous legal fees.

The Daniel Schorr Case

Not only can the courts become embroiled in the shield-law issue, but legislative bodies can also get into the action. One of the more publicized cases involved CBS correspondent Daniel Schorr, who was accused in 1976 of leaking a secret government report to the New York paper, the *Village Voice*. Schorr was subsequently relieved of his reporting duties at CBS, but the network kept him on the payroll and reportedly picked up the tab for his legal fees. The whole incident evolved when a government report was made available to Schorr and then, shortly thereafter, Congress voted to make the report secret. Schorr decided that the public should be aware of the contents of the report and was accused of arranging through an attorney with the Washington, D.C., based Reporter's Committee for Freedom of the Press to have the report published in the *Voice*. Congress didn't wait long before calling for funds to head up a full-scale investigation to find the source that supplied Schorr with the report. The investigation flopped, Schorr remained silent, and the issue was dropped. The entire incident brought up the question of the ability of reporters to protect the confidentiality of news sources and, when this condition exists, how far sources can go in supplying reporters with information without worrying about repercussions. Questions immediately came forth such as: Which is more important, the public's right to know or the protection of government secrets? Can or should a legislative body or the courts have the power to force reporters to divulge sources of information? When should they and when shouldn't they? Additional questions include: What is to stop an unscrupulous source from simply using a reporter and supplying him or her with false information—information that is damaging to someone's character—with the victim having no recourse? Arguments such as these are in the forefront of charges by those who claim we shouldn't have shield laws, which give reporters a god-like halo, an immunity from society's basic laws. Others argue that if reporters are afraid to do investigative reporting because they do not have the protection of a shield law, then there is ample opportunity at all levels of our society for corruption to abound.

As a consumer of mass communication, you should take the opportunity to become aware of any legislation in your state designed to protect the confidentiality of news sources. This type of regulation, and freedom-of-information laws dealt with next in this chapter, perhaps as much as any regulation or safeguard affecting the press, has a direct effect on the type of news the public receives.

freedom of information laws

Closely related to reporters' shield laws are freedom of information laws. Both are designed to help guarantee the ability of the news media to disseminate truthful, accurate, and complete information. Freedom of information laws attempt to assure the press access to (1) meetings of governmental bodies and (2) documents which are "classified" or part of public officials' files and reflect on possible corrupt activities in government. These laws exist not only on a national level, as was so vividly brought to the public's attention during the Vietnam War and Watergate era, but also at the state level. As with shield laws, the scope of freedom of information laws varies greatly from state to state. In 1974, Congress amended the 1966 Freedom of Information Act permitting the public and the press to gain access to records which had previously been kept secret. At the state level, Rhode Island, Vermont, and West Virginia currently lack open records laws, while Mississippi, New York, and West Virginia are the only states presently without specific legislation to guarantee access to meetings.

For the news media, the most common contact with freedom of information laws is in the area of open meetings. Investigative journalism is, of course, concerned with open records legislation, but the average reporter preparing information for daily public consumption is also concerned with whether or not he or she will be admitted to the local meeting of the city council or whether the executive meeting of the zoning board is going to shut the door to the news media. A report authored by Dr. John Adams of the University of North Carolina and funded by the American Newspaper Publishers Association classified open meetings laws.[5]

The ANPA report listed eleven different classifications:

1. Include a statement of public policy in support of openness,
2. Provide for an open legislature,
3. Provide for open legislative committees,
4. Provide for open meetings of state agencies or bodies,
5. Provide for open meetings of agencies and bodies of the political subdivisions of the state,
6. Provide for open County Boards,
7. Provide for open City Councils (or their equivalent),
8. Forbid closed executive sessions,
9. Provide legal recourse to halt secrecy,
10. Declare actions taken in meetings which violate the law to be null and void,
11. Provide for penalties for those who violate the law.

Of all the classifications, the four most common types of open meetings legislation presently in operation involve open state agencies, open county-local agencies, open county boards, and open city councils. For the average reporter, these are the most common types of governmental bodies to which he or she would need access.

Two other key areas where the press would like to see open information laws enforced are executive sessions and actions taken in meetings which violate the law. When important decisions must be made before they can be voted upon in public, many governmental bodies may call executive sessions. The problem with these closed sessions is that they can easily become a habit with these bodies. When such issues as budgets, firing employees, planning raises, and similar items arise, public reaction and concern can be significant. Voting and deciding behind closed doors and then merely "rubber stamping" the decisions at the public meetings of these agencies deprives the public of the information they need to play their rightful part as constituents of elected officials. The real teeth in open meetings laws is found in points 10 and 11. Any law is only as good as its ability to be enforced. Laws are strong where they void any action taken in closed session and go a step further when they provide penalties for those who violate the law. When the news media have this type of legislation protecting their ability to report, the free flow of information to the public is much more open. In an effort to encourage open meetings laws, two organizations — Common Cause and The Society of Professional Journalists, Sigma Delta Chi — authored "model" laws that the states could use as a basis for either passing or strengthening their open meetings laws. This action was important because many of the problems surrounding this issue have hinged on the differing interpretations of the laws. Although the amended Freedom of Information Act will tend to overshadow state regulations, there still needs to be some uniformity of open meetings legislation between the states before any legal "foundation" for freedom of the press can exist. You have the opportunity, through your own individual efforts and through professional associations, to help determine what your own state can do to assure the "free flow of information" from governmental bodies to the public.

cannon 35: media in the courtroom

Broadcasting has come a long way since the microphones of WGN dressed the table in the Tennessee courtroom in July of 1925 as schoolteacher John Thomas Scopes was tried and found guilty of teaching evolution. Since the electronic media became commonplace, many trials have served as the proving grounds for laws dealing with the coverage of those proceedings. When Bruno Richard Hauptmann came to trial in 1935 for the kidnapping of the young son of famed flyer Charles Lindbergh, the courtroom turned into a carnival. It was a scene reminiscent of a theatrical premiere and a county fair all rolled into one. The judge finally barred cameras in the courtroom, but one reporter managed to sneak one in anyway and took a picture of the proceedings which appeared in newspapers across the nation. Thirty years later in a less dramatic atmosphere, an appeals judge ruled that television in the courtroom during the trial of Texas financier Billie Sol Estes did not prejudice the outcome. Yet when the decision was appealed, the Supreme Court overturned the verdict and strengthened the foundation of judicial precedent that forbade cameras in the courtroom. Although individual agreements have been made between the news media and judges in some areas of the country, the trend is by no means universal. For the public, coverage of judicial proceedings amounts to a "commentator's version" and an "artist's conception" of the scene inside the court.

The basis for this judicial precedent is that cameras and/or electronic equipment will distract from the dignity of the court. This argument is succinctly stated in the famous Cannon 35 of the American Bar Association which was passed in 1937 after the bizarre coverage at the Hauptmann trial. The Cannon was amended in 1963 to encompass television. Cannon 35 states:

> Proceedings in court should be conducted with fitting dignity and decorum. The taking of photographs in the courtroom, during sessions of the court or recesses between sessions, and the broadcasting or televising of court proceedings detract from the essential dignity of the proceedings, distract the participants and witnesses in giving testimony, and create misconceptions with respect thereto in the mind of the public, and should not be permitted. Provided that this restriction shall not apply to the broadcasting or televising, under the supervision of the court, of such portions of naturalization proceedings (other than the interrogation of applicants) as are designed and carried out exclusively as a ceremony for the purpose of publicly demonstrating in an impressive manner the essential dignity and the serious nature of the naturalization.

The theme of Cannon 35 has become law in every state except Colorado, Oklahoma, and Texas.[6]

In the 1965 Supreme Court Appeals Case of Billie Sol Estes, the justices expanded upon the reasons for barring the use of cameras in the courtroom, and with particular implications for television, put forth various arguments favoring a continuation of the ban. Justice Clark described the scene in the Texas courtroom.[7]

> Indeed, at least 12 cameramen were engaged in the courtroom throughout the hearing taking motion and still pictures and televising the proceedings. Cables and wires were snaked across the courtroom floor,

three microphones were on the judge's bench and others were beamed at the jury box and the counsel table. It is conceded that the activities of the television crews and news photographers led to considerable disruption of the hearings.

Justice Clark went on to deal with four areas of argument supporting the decision of the Court: (1) The impact of television on the jurors. Feasibly they could be swayed by televised portions and new trials could be affected by the coverage of earlier proceedings. (2) The quality of testimony would be impaired. Witnesses could, for instance, be "demoralized and frightened." (3) Television would place additional responsibilities on the trial judge. Along with supervising the trial he would also have to supervise the televising. (4) Television could become "a mental—if not physical—harassment, resembling a police line-up or the third degree." Other High Court Justices were equally adamant in their appraisal of the presence of cameras in general and television in particular in the courtroom. Chief Justice Warren, with Justices Douglas and Goldberg concurring, stated that, "The televising of trials would cause the public to equate the trial process with the forms of entertainment regularly seen on television and with the commercial objectives of the television industry." The Justices opined, "The next logical step in this partnership might be to schedule the trial for a time that would permit the maximum number of viewers to watch, and to schedule recess to coincide with the need for station breaks."

Dissenting opinions in the case were filed by Justices White, Stewart, Black, and Brennan. The thrust of Justice White's reasoning was that evidence of previous effects of televised trials was too sparse to make judgments on constitutional principle. Justice Brennan felt the decision was "*not* a blanket constitutional prohibition against the televising of state criminal trials." In the same case, Justice Harlan, concurring with the majority, said, "the day may come when television will have become so commonplace an affair in the daily life of the average person as to dissipate all reasonable likelihood that its use in courtrooms may disparage the judicial process."

Since the Billie Sol Estes case, various members of the news media and judges have reached agreements about television cameras in the courtroom. New developments in miniature circuits have greatly reduced the size of former cumbersome equipment. Cameras that are capable of functioning without auxiliary lighting have also reduced judicial resistance to electronic equipment. In addition, small, inconspicuous microphones can now cover judicial proceedings without disrupting the court. As we said, however, these softenings of judicial resistance are the exception rather than the rule. In an effort to aid the broadcast press in gaining access to judicial chambers, the National Association of Broadcasters' Freedom of Information Committee has actively gone on record supporting the admittance of the broadcast press in covering public proceedings.

NAB standards for public proceedings

The NAB also enacted the *Standards of Conduct for Broadcasting Public Proceedings*. The *Standards* provide the judiciary with evidence of a written set of guidelines to convince them that what Cannon 35 tries to protect, the broadcast press will not endanger. The *Standards* courtroom guidelines to the broadcast news media state:

> The sanctity of public trial and the rights of the defendant and all parties require that special care be exercised to assure that broadcast coverage will in no way interfere with the dignity and decorum and the proper and fair conduct of such proceedings. In recognition of the paramount objective of justice inherent in all trials, broadcast newsmen will observe the following standards:
>
>> They will abide by all rules of the court.
>>
>> The presiding judge is, of course, recognized as the appropriate authority, and broadcast newsmen will address their application for admission to him and will conform to his rulings. The right to appeal to higher jurisdiction is reserved.
>>
>> Broadcast equipment will be installed in a manner acceptable to the court and will be unobtrusively located and operated so as not to be disturbing or distracting to the court or participants.
>>
>> Broadcast newsmen will not move about while court is in session in such a way as to interfere with the orderly proceedings. Their equipment will remain stationary.
>>
>> Commentaries on the trial will not be broadcast from the courtroom while the trial is in session.
>>
>> Broadcasting of trials will be presented to the community as a public service, and there will be no commercial sponsorship of such trials.
>>
>> Broadcast personnel will dress in accordance with courtroom custom.

The future of both still cameras and television cameras in the courtroom will depend upon two things — a development of judicial precedent for such equipment and the continued local examples of cooperation which can set the pace for national trial coverage. In some cities, judges have already given the broadcast press and their equipment access to the courtroom. Perhaps as these new developments continue, and as broadcast journalists and photographers prove they truly are "professionals" by using common sense restraint in reporting even the most sensational trials, then there will be serious cooperation between the judiciary and the fourth estate.

gag rules

In their attempt to assure a fair trial and secure the "dignity" of the court, some judges have placed restraints on the press by keeping them from reporting those aspects of the trial which the judges feel might interfere with the judicial process. Such actions are commonly called "gag rules" and create a direct conflict between the news media and the judiciary in the issue of free press versus fair trial. Gag rules have ranged from attempts to keep all news media from reporting any and all aspects of a trial, to orders stifling just one particular reporter. In many cases, reporters have been held in contempt of court for publishing or broadcasting information the judge has deemed unacceptable for public consumption via the news media.

The contemporary issue of gag rules has its foundation in the case of the Cleveland, Ohio, physician, Dr. Sam Shepard, who was charged in 1954 with murdering his wife. It was the first major national trial to take place since the new medium of television had evolved. Shepard was the subject of considerable pre-trial publicity including numerous editorials. He was found guilty. Twelve years later, the Supreme Court reviewed the case and reversed the decision on the basis that Shepard could not have received a fair trial because of the pre-trial publicity that surrounded the case.

In a similar case, the Supreme Court in 1961 said a fair trial had been denied to a man based on the pre-trial publicity which took place in Indiana in 1955.[8] In the Indiana case, the police were as much to blame as the press because when they arrested this particular suspect, who had been charged in a series of murders, they took the liberty of issuing their own press release. Thus, even outside the county where the killing allegedly occurred, the *Indianapolis Star* referred to the suspect in custody as a "maniac killer" and likened the crime to a "technique employed by Chinese military executioners."[9]

The Scope of Gag Rules

In recent years, gag rules have become increasingly common. Although there seems to be little Constitutional foundation to such rules, and they are almost always voided when appealed, this has not hampered their frequent issuance. For instance, in California,

Superior Court Judge J. A. Leetham barred journalists from reporting the identity of witnesses in a murder case. The same "gags"
were placed on defendants, documents, and exhibits. The gag rule
was eventually struck down by an Appeals Court.[10] An Ontario, California, judge issued a "gag" rule against publication of the names of
certain witnesses, also in a murder trial. A well-publicized gag rule
also resulted when a Baton Rouge, Louisiana, judge, Gordon E.
West, prohibited reporting news of a pre-trial hearing involving a
civil rights worker. Two reporters, Gibbs Adams of the *Morning Advocate* and Larry Dickinson of the *State Times*, defied the gag rule
and were consequently fined and held in contempt of court. The
rule was overturned by an Appeals Court, but the contempt citation
was upheld, leaving the clear directive that, although a gag order
may later be struck down in an appeal, it should be obeyed until
that appeal has been completed.[11] In Texarkana, Arkansas, an editor
was found in contempt of court for reporting the verdict in a rape
case. That decision was also overturned by a higher court.[12]

Reporters and news-gathering organizations banded together in
1975 in Nebraska when a judge barred reporting of testimony taken
in the murder trial of Erwin Charles Simants. Judge Hugh Stuart, of
the district court of Lincoln County, ordered the ban, noting it was
necessary for the defendant to get a fair trial. The Nebraska state
supreme court upheld Judge Stuart's order after it was appealed by
various Nebraska media groups. From there it went to the United
States Supreme Court where it was finally overturned. Among news-
gathering organizations joining in support against the gag order of
Judge Stuart were the three major commercial broadcasting networks, the Nebraska Broadcasters' Association, AP, and UPI. Over
twenty print organizations also joined in the effort.

The Judicial Dilemma

Although these judicial decisions may seem arbitrary to you, place
yourself behind the bench for a few moments and consider what
might go through your own mind. You are considering a controversial murder case which has received considerable publicity.
You, as a judge, have the responsibility to guide the attorneys in the
search for truth. It is your responsibility to secure the defendant a
fair trial and to see that everyone is equally represented in the case.
You know from previous decisions that if you do not adhere to the
rules of the court, the final decision in the case will be appealed,
and your own actions will be held accountable in the appeal. If
there is considerable pre-trial publicity and an appeals court rules
that the defendant is entitled to a new trial, then this reflects on the

operation of your own courtroom, especially if during the trial the defendant's attorney requested a change of venue (location) for the trial based on that very pre-trial publicity. Perhaps you are an elected judge and are caught between giving the press complete freedom to do and say what they please and thus risk the dignity of your court, or attempt to gag them and thus incur their ire which could have an effect on your chances in the next election. Even if the press is responsible in your community, you may still wrestle with the question of what should be done and how it will affect your political career. On the other hand, you may be asking yourself, "If I issue a gag rule and in my opinion protect the dignity of the court, then when the gag rule is subsequently struck down, what does that action create?" In trying to protect the dignity of the court and the due process of law under one constitutional amendment, you successfully bridge the thrust of another one. Thus, from behind the bench, it's a real dilemma, one which is not easily solved.

Now place yourself in the shoes of the reporter assigned to cover the case. From the morning the case first appeared on the police log, you have worked to provide complete and impartial information about it. You have based your activities not only on the fact that you have a job to do but also that the public has a right to know. As a journalist, you have the responsibility to report the activities of the government and the courts and to point out any deficiencies which might exist. Now comes the day of the trial. The judge issues you an order to not publish any information about the case. You are faced with some rather unpleasant alternatives. You can defy the judge and publish the story. You can also land in jail and be fined in the process. On the other hand, you can abide by the judge's ruling and tell your peers back at the office why you sold out. Suppose you decide at least to take the issue to a higher court to try and have the gag rule reversed. Chances are you will be successful, but in the meantime, you will have missed the story. At the very least, you will have spent valuable time and money and may face the situation again when the judge decides to issue another gag rule. There is no easy solution to your dilemma any more than there is an easy solution to the judge's dilemma.

In some circumstances, the news media can be caught *between* judges and attorneys. Let me explain. While working as a reporter and covering a court trial, I encountered a local judge who was hearing a case against a group of people charged with trespassing as the result of their participation in a "sit-in" at a state-owned building. Before the trial, the judge issued a public statement warning others who might be inclined to become involved in similar activities to be aware of the consequences. He reasoned "in the back of his mind" that it was "probably a subversive group which was training this small minority" and that the group could incur serious penalties for such activities. The judge's statement was publicized by media throughout the state and by at least one wire service. The attorney for the defendants then issued a public statement denouncing the judge's remarks as "a most outrageous violation of judicial ethics as is imaginable." The next day in court, the defense attorney was placed in contempt of court, because the statement he made about the judge was publicized by local media.

All parties to the incident were engaged in what they felt was appropriate activity. The judge's comments were published as being newsworthy remarks of a key figure in the case. They reported the defense attorney's comments as a natural followup to the judge's remarks. The defense attorney felt an obligation to comment since his clients had not yet come to trial, let alone been found guilty. The judge felt the dignity of the court had suffered. By issuing the contempt citation, he succeeded in creating an atmosphere whereby attorneys would think twice before releasing to the news media anything critical of the court. The judge labeled the contempt citation a case of "indirect" contempt. It was also a very effective "indirect" gag rule—There was no way the press could report comments about the case if no one made any comments.

Voluntary Cooperation

Occasionally the press has agreed to voluntary silence arrangements with the judge. For example, in Cartersville, Georgia, Judge Jefferson L. Davis simply calls a conference with the reporters whenever he wants information withheld from publication. He explains why, and the arrangement seems to work.[13] Yet Cartersville is not Los Angeles or New York, and what may work in a small Georgia community may not prove feasible in a major city. Moreover, many journalists would claim it shouldn't work! That's not the role of a journalist.

In an article in *Time* magazine the following incident was reported. When two persons accused of murder were brought to trial in Pennsylvania, the judge informed the press that the cases for the two defendants had been separated, and each was to receive a separate trial. The press agreed to withhold reporting the first trial so as not to prejudice the second trial. The news media, including radio and television stations as well as newspapers, went along with the judge and not only failed to cover the proceedings but even omitted any public mention of the trial. When it was all over, the press was divided on whether or not they had made the right decision.[14]

The problem of assuring a free press but at the same time according a defendant a fair trial is a dilemma far from nearing a solution. Gag rules will probably continue to be issued, and journalists will probably continue to defy them, as will judges persist in citing members of the news media for contempt. This is one of those gray areas in regulatory posture that places law, journalism, and the Constitution right in the middle.

summary

This chapter has dealt with theoretical bases for media controls and has given specific examples of control on the working press. The theories of control discussed were the authoritarian, libertarian, social responsibility, and Soviet Communist theories. We have also utilized the Wiio model of mass communication which analyzes media systems along two dimensions of an open-closed continuum—the messages and the audiences. In discussing specific regulations which affect the working press, Chapter 19 has examined reporters' shield laws, those laws protecting the confidentiality of reporters' news sources. Because of the lack of specificity of the Constitution with regard to safeguarding the confidentiality of news sources under First Amendment provisions, individual states have enacted shield laws to strengthen their own commitment to freedom of the press. Closely related to shield laws are freedom of information laws which guard against secrecy in such things as government record keeping and meetings. The measures that control the press in their coverage of judicial proceedings include Cannon 35 of the American Bar Association and gag rules. Cannon 35 is designed to prevent cameras in the courtroom, and gag rules are issued by judges to thwart journalists for reporting news of court proceedings.

opportunities for further learning

GILLMOR, DONALD M., and JEROME A. BARRON, *Mass Communication Law: Cases and Comment,* 2nd Ed. St. Paul, Minn.: West Publishing Co., 1975.

MARNELL, WILLIAM H., *The Right to Know: Media and the Common Good.* New York: The Seabury Press, 1973.

NELSON, HAROLD L., and DWIGHT L. TEETER, *Law of Mass Communica-*

tions: Freedom and Control of Print and Broadcast Media, 2nd Ed. Mineola, New York: The Foundation Press, Inc., 1973.

SIEBERT, FRED S., THEODORE PETERSON, and WILBUR SCHRAMM, *Four Theories of the Press.* Urbana, Ill.: University of Illinois Press, 1956.

STEVENS, GEORGE E., and JOHN B. WEBSTER, *Law and the Student Press.* Ames, Iowa: The Iowa State University Press, 1973.

toward

self-regulation

CHAPTER TWENTY

For any system of mass communication to be reasonably free from government control, it must establish its own internal system of control. Usually these alternative forms of control, termed "codes," are enforced via various sanctions and penalties. These range anywhere from living with one's own conscience to formal public censure, loss of membership in professional associations, and in some cases fines levied by the member's media organization. Chapter 20 attempts to familiarize the reader with a sampling of these codes and self-regulatory measures. The treatment here is by no means complete. However, with an awareness of these codes, their functioning and effectiveness, you as a responsible consumer of mass media will now be ready to participate in their formation and/or operation. Our discussion begins with one of the more familiar codes, that of the National Association of Broadcasters (NAB).

the NAB radio and television codes

In addition to the legislation formulated by Congress and the FCC, the broadcasting industry, through the National Association of

Broadcasters (NAB), adheres to self-regulation. The industry began the process of self-regulation back in 1928 when a code for radio was promulgated. Its first major revision occurred in 1937, and through the years, the NAB's Radio Code and Television Code have spelled out specific guidelines for its voluntary subscribers to follow.

The overall administration of the Radio and Television Codes is vested in the Code Authority whose director is appointed by the president of the NAB and approved by its board of directors. The executive staff of the Code Authority is responsible for enforcing the codes and periodically monitoring member stations. Basically, the codes are concerned with broadcast *advertising* and *programming*. The opportunity to subscribe to the code is open to "Any individual, firm or corporation which is engaged in the operation of ..." a broadcasting station or network "... or which holds a construction permit ..." for a radio or television station. Membership in the codes entails an agreement by the station to abide by NAB advertising standards and also permits the station to use the code seals (Figure 20–1) for on-air promotions and station literature such as promotional brochures and letterheads.

Radio Programming

Each of the codes tends to reflect the unique aspects of either radio or television in its provisions. For example, when the Radio Code specifies guidelines for news programming, it is well aware of radio's instantaneous ability to air news from almost anywhere and the difficulties that can result when radio is in competition with another medium.

The Radio Code deals with six aspects of news coverage: (1) news sources; (2) news reporting; (3) commentaries and analyses; (4) editorializing; (5) coverage of news and public events; and (6)

Figure 20–1. The seals of the Radio and Television Code of the National Association of Broadcasters.

the placement of advertising in the news. The section on news sources is especially concerned with assuring the "reliability" of news sources. Along with the overall presentation of news, the code warns that using "Morbid, sensational, or alarming details not essential to factual reporting should be avoided." Moreover, the code states, "Programs of news analysis and commentary should be clearly identified as such, distinguishing them from straight news reporting." Similar safeguards apply to editorials. In the coverage of public events, the code calls for broadcasters' judgments to be ". . . consonant with the accepted standards of ethical journalism and should provide accurate, informed and adequate coverage."

Controversial public issues, community responsibilities, and political broadcasts are three other areas covered by the Radio Code. Basically, the code encourages the airing of controversial issues, with ". . . fair presentation to opposing sides of issues."

Further clarification is expressed in the Radio Code's wording that such requests ". . . be considered on the basis of their individual merits, and in the light of the contributions which the use requested would make to the public interest." The Radio Code also states that such discussions, when they are aired, should be clearly defined as public issues. Political broadcasts are also within the code's realm, and both candidates and parties are called upon ". . . to observe the canons of good taste and political ethics, keeping in mind the intimacy of broadcasting in the American Home." Here, again, the code gives the broadcasters some protection when approached for air time by radical dissident groups. Although denying access to any group based on political views is treading on dangerous legal ground, the Radio Code at least permits the broadcaster to request responsible behavior.

The Radio Code sets up guidelines for encouraging the use of radio to promote cultural and educational growth in the community. It protects against broadcast attacks on religious faiths and establishes guidelines for dramatic radio programs. This particular section of the Radio Code has come into focus again in recent years with the renewal of radio drama series. Radio Code subscribers are alert to the possible effects of programs ". . . containing elements of crime, mystery, or horror. . . ." Remember, it was radio that conveyed the famous 1938 broadcast of Orson Welles' *War of the Worlds* which sent many listeners into panic. To guard against incidents of this sort, the code discourages presenting any programs that depict excessive violence.

The Radio Code also deals with children's programming. Broadcasts directed at children are to be based ". . . upon sound social concepts and should reflect positive sets of values which allow children to become responsible adults, capable of coping with the challenges of maturity." They should also ". . . contribute to the healthy development of personality and character." Along with discouraging subjects such as excessive violence and sex, the Radio Code specifies that, "The treatment of criminal activities should always convey their social and human effects."

Along with outlining the *do's* and *don't's* of children's programming, the Radio Code also provides guidelines for general programming. Broadcasters and networks are charged with being ". . . vigilant in protecting the audience from deceptive broadcast practices." Special areas for broadcasters' attention include subjects dealing with gambling, the handicapped, minorities, the courts, legal and medical advice, narcotic addiction, cigarette smoking, marriage, and the use of profanity on the air. The standards for profanity are flexible, however, and broadcasters need to be alert to changing word meanings. What may be acceptable at one point in time can, in a few years and by virtue of frequent use among certain age groups, take on a profane meaning. Similarly, the code states, "Special sensitivity is necessary in the use of material relating to sex, race, color, creed, religious functionaries or rites, or national or ethnic derivation." There are also strict guidelines concerning mysticism. The Radio Code lists as unacceptable those programs which pertain to ". . . fortune telling, occultism, astrology, phrenology, palm reading, numerology, mind reading, character reading, or subjects of a like nature . . ." especially when such programming ". . . encourages people to regard such fields as providing commonly accepted appraisals of life."

Radio Advertising

Although the general guidelines also apply to radio advertising, the code sets forth specific procedures for radio commercials. For instance, in dealing with the placement of advertising in news programming, the Radio Code states, "A broadcaster should exercise particular discrimination in the acceptance, placement and presentation of advertising in news programs so that such advertising should be clearly distinguishable from the news content." That phrase has discouraged stations from using the voices of news personnel in commercials and from using tones and similar "news" sounds in introducing commercials, and has prompted stations to ensure a significant "sound break" between the end of a newscaster's remarks and the beginning of a commercial. For example, assume a radio newscaster follows a news story with a commercial which begins with the words "News-Flash!" and then continues to describe a new model just off the Detroit assembly lines. This station's listeners could easily mistake the commercial testimonial for a news story. Such programming would therefore be unacceptable under the guidelines of the Radio Code.

The general NAB policy toward advertising is stated in that section of the Radio Code labeled "Advertising Standards." Here are set forth such things as the responsibility of the broadcaster to refuse the facilities of the station when there is "... good reason to doubt the integrity of the advertiser, the truth of the advertising representations, or the compliance of the advertiser with the spirit and purpose of all applicable legal requirements."

This section also enumerates products unacceptable for radio advertising, such as hard liquor. In the past, a common practice in children's radio programming had been for advertisers to make a pitch to children to purchase certain products as a means of keeping favorite programs on the air. Although these programs have long since lapsed into radio history, the Radio Code still charges broadcasters to guard against these practices.

Television Advertising to Children

One of the most controversial issues examined by the NAB Codes is the subject of children's advertising. The issue gained public exposure in 1973 during hearings of the Senate Select Committee on Nutrition and Human Needs. Appearing before the committee was NAB Code Authority Director Stockton Helffrich, who explained the history of the involvement of broadcasters with the issue of children's advertising. Although it wasn't the expressed purpose of the committee to investigate children's advertising per se, the issue was in the forefront of the proceedings, and both broadcasters and the food industry became alert to the types of appeals being used to attract children to the grocery shelves. At the same time, the NAB acted and adopted the "Children's Advertising Statement of Principles" in June of 1973. Among other things, the Principles suggested that products advertised should serve a "positive function" and "... avoid being exploitative of or inappropriate to a child's still developing cognitive abilities and sense of values." The Principles also called upon manufacturers to be able to provide documented evidence of the "... truthfulness and accuracy of advertising claims." The peer group pressures faced by children were also specifically recognized, and advertisements which purported to give a child an advantage over his or her peers merely by possessing a product or to disadvantage a child who didn't have the article, were strictly forbidden. Fear appeals directed toward children were also off limits, as was material which contained ". . . a portrayal of or appeal to violent, dangerous, or otherwise antisocial behavior."

Meanwhile, concern over the content of children's advertising increased in academic circles as well. Educators presented research studies on such topics as the violence content of commercials, the image of children in advertising, and advertising appeals. Accompanying this was the concern of the FCC over children's programming in general. After two years of discussion, which included NAB-funded research on children's perception of television, the NAB Television Board of Directors voted changes in the Television Code. These amendments added to already explicit guidelines, rules dealing with the issues and ideas that had been the theme of the Children's Advertising Statement of Principles. With these inclusions, the Television Code's revised provision X-3, which became effective in September of 1975, read:

> The broadcaster and the advertiser should exercise special caution with the content and presentation of television commercials placed in or near programs designed for children. Exploitation of children should be avoided. Commercials directed to children should in no way mislead as to the product's performance and usefulness.

> Commercials, whether live, film, or tape within programs initially designed primarily for children under 12 years of age shall be clearly separated from program material by an appropriate device.

> Trade name identification or other merchandising practices involving the gratuitous naming of products is discouraged in programs designed for children.

> Appeals involving matters of health which should be determined by physicians should not be directed primarily to children.

In its provision X-4 the code goes on to guard against sales promotions by characters (both real and cartoon) found in children's programs. The provision also applies to ". . . lead-ins to commercials when such lead-ins contain sell copy or imply endorsement of the product by program personalities or cartoon characters."

Indicative of the ability of the code to remain flexible in view of changing issues both in society and within the industry was the 1975 revision of the rules governing lottery advertising. Prior to that time, the code had ruled against such advertising. Since the Federal Lottery Act now permits advertising of state-supported lotteries in the home state and in adjacent states, first the NAB Television Board of Directors and then its radio equivalent voted to amend the language of their codes. The new provisions permit advertising of state-supported lotteries as long as such advertising does not unduly exhort the public to bet. Where lotteries are prohibited, the broadcast of lottery information remains unacceptable.

Television Programming

Essentially, the overall theme of the NAB Television Code is the same as that of the Radio Code—service to the community and a sensitivity to the community's needs. The Television Code must also be flexible in the face of rapidly changing program content. It must mediate between being *too* restrictive and, on the other hand, not according the industry enough of a say in its own efforts toward self-regulation. In this regard, the Television Code states, ". . . none of the provisions of this Code should be construed as preventing or impeding broadcast of the broad range of material necessary to help broadcasters fulfill their obligations to operate in the public interest." On the other hand, it cautions broadcasters to exercise care in the selection of program "subjects" and "themes" and to make certain that their programming is not ". . . for the purpose of sensationalism or to shock or exploit the audience or appeal to prurient interests or morbid curiosity."

Like the Radio Code, the Television Code sets definitive guidelines for children's programming. The Television Information Office, an independent association partially funded by the NAB, has brought the Code's provisions to the attention of the public and broadcasters alike (Figure 20–2). Ads in major newspapers as well as flyers from the Television Information Office alert parents to programs that are endorsed by the NAB as suitable for children to watch.

In addition, the Television Code calls upon broadcasters to take into account the ". . . range of interests and needs of children." It acknowledges that television has a role in preparing the child for his role in adult society. Trying to strike a compromise, the code stresses positive values in programming yet still backs off from specifics by noting that children ". . . should also be exposed at the appropriate times . . ." to programming which represents ". . . a reasonable range of realities which exist in the world sufficient to help them make the transition to adulthood." Such language is open to varying interpretations based on what is appropriate for a given local area.

In treating violence on television, the code states that ". . . violence, physical or psychological, may only be projected in responsibly handled contexts, not used exploitatively." The code further states that programming ". . . involving violence should present the

Some things your kids can see on TV in the next two months. And some things they can't.

Children watch lots of television.

Most watch it for fun. But they can also find many hours of enrichment and information, too.

Like most television programs, the ones for youngsters are generally supported by advertising. But commercials in programs designed primarily for children must meet special standards—the guidelines of the broadcasters' Television Code.

Here are some don'ts from the Code: Children can't be shown risking harm. And they can't be told to ask their parents to buy things for them. Ads mustn't mislead. And they mustn't confuse young viewers or cause dissatisfaction by comparing one toy with another. Program hosts can't sell to young-

sters during their programs, and famous people whom kids admire can't endorse items. Products must not be overglamorized, but shown as they are. Words like "just" or "only" can't be used to make prices seem attractive. And if a doll's clothes or batteries for a toy must be bought separately, the ad can't hide that fact. Medical remedies can't be sold in or near children's programs.

The Code is one way broadcasters meet their responsibilities to youngsters.

Another way is with programs that are entertaining and enriching for children and for the family.

The selective viewer will find an ample range of choices in the list below.

The Baboons of Gombe. Jane Goodall and the World of Animal Behavior. Friday, Feb. 1 (8-9 pm).

It's A Mystery, Charlie Brown; There's No Time for Love, Charlie Brown. Friday, Feb. 1 (8:30-9 pm); Sunday, March 17 (7:30-8 pm).

What's the Supreme Court All About?

Today is Ours. CBS Festival of the Lively Arts for Young People—Poems of the Black Experience. Saturday, Feb. 23 (1-2 pm).

The Wizard of Oz. Judy Garland, Ray Bolger, Bert Lahr, Jack Haley. Sunday, Feb. 24 (6:30-8:30 pm).

he Bottom of

The White Collar Worker. Changing status of office workers. Sunday, March 17 (10-11 pm).

American Film Institute Salute to James Cagney. Tribute to one of filmdom's legends. Monday, March 18 (9:30-11 pm).

The Energy Crisis: American Solution

Figure 20–2. Ads and other informative literature of the television information office call attention to television programming. (Television Information Office.)

consequences of it to its victims and perpetrators." Similarly, crime must not be displayed so as to "invite imitation" and such things as "... narcotic addiction shall not be presented except as a destructive habit."

The Television Code is specific in treating broadcast journalism. It calls for the news schedule to be "... adequate and well-balanced." Along with encouraging "fair" and "factual" reporting "without bias," it discourages sensationalism, especially concerning crime or sex. Reporters themselves are cautioned about news conferences where a person other than the journalist determines the questions to be asked. It also calls on the reporter to announce on the news program where there has been any "... advance agreement materially restricting an important or newsworthy area of questioning."

Code Enforcement

Adherence to both Radio and Television Codes is enforced by a systematic monitoring (either listening or watching) system. Subscriber radio stations are monitored near their license renewal periods and TV stations, twice each year. The NAB then notifies the station if it is operating within the guidelines established by the Code Authority. In certain situations, special attention will be paid to specific types of programming. If, for instance, the Code Authority feels there has been an increase in certain types of questionable commercials at a station, then the Authority may ask for the transcripts of those commercials. Along with determining a station's own self-regulatory posture, such detailed analysis keeps the Authority cognizant of changes that may be taking place within the industry. Still, when a broadcasting station decides not to join the code, there is little the rest of the industry can do to pull it into line. When an economic crunch hits, a station may be less willing to turn down an advertisement dollar for a commercial unacceptable to the code. Similarly, if the difference between the profit and loss column of a station begins to shrink, management may cancel its subscription to the code altogether, thus saving the subscription fee.

When subscription support is present throughout the system, the real advantage of codes for the broadcasting industry lies in two areas. First, they tend to deter dubious advertising and programming. Second, they can be an effective alternative to government regulation. The NAB keeps in close touch with the actions and pulse of the FCC. Where possible, it will actively try to assure the FCC and other government agencies that there is self-regulation in the broadcasting industry and that government regulation is therefore not necessary.

self-regulation and the working press

The press, because of its foundation in the First Amendment, has been the least controlled of any American institution of mass communication. Although there have been certain regulations placed upon broadcast journalism through the Communications Act of 1934, the news media have generally operated with only conscience as a guide. Unfortunately, some journalists are less scrupulous than others, and in many cases this laissez-faire atmosphere has resulted in journalism of less than good taste. Yet, there is an attempt on the part of some professional organizations to encourage responsible journalism practices, more through social and professional sanctions rather than concerted attempts at enforcement. Three codes among many which reflect these thoughts are The Code of Ethics of The Society of Professional Journalists, Sigma Delta Chi; the Code of Broadcast News Ethics of the Radio/Television News Directors Association (RTNDA); and the Code of Ethics of the American Society of Newspaper Editors.

The Society of Professional Journalists, Sigma Delta Chi

The Society's code charges journalists to exercise boldness in reporting the news but cautions them to do so responsibly. This particular code was cited frequently during the Nixon era when journalists were facing jail sentences for refusing to divulge their sources of information. It's divided into six major areas: (1) responsibility, (2) freedom of the press, (3) ethics, (4) accuracy and objectivity, (5) fair play, and (6) pledge.

Under *responsibility*, the code reminds the journalist of two forces. These are in the "mission of the mass media," which centers around the public's right to know, and the high trust that the public places in the news media. *Freedom of the press* is expressed as the "... right of people in a free society." The code endorses journalists "... responsibility to discuss, question, and challenge actions and utterances ..." of government and institutions, both public and private. The *ethics* section is concerned with such things as journalists' refusing freebies, moonlighting, and personal life styles which might reflect negatively on the profession. News judgment, overcoming obstacles in gathering news, and protecting the confidentiality of sources are also covered. The *accuracy and objectivity* section stresses "truth" as the ultimate goal and charges journalists to distinguish between news and opinions, to recognize editorializing, to keep informed, and to label clearly their "... own conclusions and interpretations." *Fair play* treats the right to reply, invasion of privacy, handling details of vice and crime, correcting errors, and accountability to the public. Compliance with the code is entirely voluntary, being signified by a *pledge* charging journalists to "... censure and prevent violations of these standards."

Radio/Television News Directors Association (RTNDA)

The RTNDA is comprised primarily of men and women whose responsibility it is to direct the news operation of a broadcasting station. Membership dues are based upon the size of the station's news staff, and associate memberships are available to educators and other practicing broadcast news professionals. The Code of Broadcast News Ethics of RTNDA centers around ten articles, within which are found the major issues affecting most working broadcast journalists. Many of these articles parallel those of the Code of the Society of Professional Journalists. For instance, similarities are found in the areas of rights of privacy, overcoming obstacles, keeping informed, confidentiality of sources, and censuring other professionals who violate the code. The RTNDA's unique qualities surface in such areas as broadcasting court proceedings.

This section calls for journalists to "conduct themselves with dignity" when covering such proceedings, as did the NAB's Standards for Broadcasting Public Proceedings that we presented in Chapter 18. Other articles within the RTNDA Code deal with the individual's right to a fair trial, the use and abuse of news bulletins, and guarding against sensationalism.

American Society of Newspaper Editors

Similar to both the codes of Sigma Delta Chi and RTNDA is the Code of Ethics of the American Society of Newspaper Editors. It stresses, "A journalist who uses his power for any selfish or otherwise unworthy purpose is faithless to a high trust." Two other sections deal with freedom of the press and the independence of the press. The latter states, "Promotion of any private interest contrary to the general welfare, for whatever reason, is not compatible with honest journalism." Editorialism is a topic the code also covers when it warns that ". . . editorial comment which knowingly departs from the truth does violence to the best spirit of American journalism; in the news columns it is subversive of a fundamental principle of the profession." Other concepts the code deals with include the use of headlines and fair play—the opportunity for the accused to be heard.

Code Enforcement

The Achilles' heel of every journalism code is, of course, the actual ability to enforce sanctions on violaters. With protection of the free press well established in law, there are few ways to force reporters to make public the "secrets," "confidential sources," and other "protected" information that may be necessary to investigate some aspect of a journalist's ethical conduct. The journalism profession is full of stories, some rumor and unfortunately some fact, of serious breaches of professional ethics in spite of the professional organizations' noble guidelines. Fear of retaliation, lack of concern, and desire to avoid publicity for the competition, all combine to make direct attack or censure by one medium on another rare. It is not, however, nonexistent. An example of such an attack took place in 1975 when a newspaper employee was caught rummaging through the garbage cans of the Secretary of State, Henry Kissinger. The Los Angeles Times Syndicate ran a cartoon drawn by Oliphant (Figure 20–3) which labeled a hobo with his hand in the garbage, the "Trash Press." Other journalists also condemned the action.

'I IS DEFENDIN' DA PEOPLE'S RIGHT TO KNOW — DAT'S WHAT!'

Figure 20-3. (Copyright, Los Angeles Times. Reprinted with permission.)

In addition to those we have discussed, various journalism reviews and professional publications, for example, the *Columbia Journalism Review* actively challenge the professional conduct and ethics of the press.

It should be pointed out that, although codes are an alternative to regulation, some journalism circles have considered doing away with codes altogether if they are seen by the courts as actual standards by which journalists should practice their profession. That in itself isn't necessarily bad, but when courts use the codes to determine the degree of "recklessness" in such issues as libel or invasion of privacy cases, then some reporters feel codes may defeat their purpose. Ask yourself: Would the lack of codes of ethics under these circumstances be beneficial or harmful to the press? To society?

self-regulation and advertising

Self-regulation in advertising emerges in the guidelines expressed in the Standards of Practice of the American Association of Advertising Agencies, Inc. (A.A.A.A.). Yet even before the Standards comes the scrutiny placed upon ad agencies seeking membership in the A.A.A.A. The Association investigates an agency's operating practices as well as its contractual commitments with clients before ever granting it membership. Once this investigation is complete and membership is granted, then the agency is expected to follow the Standards of Good Practice. Within the Standards is the "Creative Code," which guards against impropriety in developing advertising messages for clients. Member agencies are charged with the responsibility to avoid producing advertising which to their knowledge contains:

> False or misleading statements or exaggerations, visual or verbal. Testimonials which do not reflect the real choice of competent witness. Price claims which are misleading. Comparisons which unfairly disparage a competitive product or service. Claims insufficiently supported, or which distort the true meaning or practicable application of statements made by professionals or scientific authority. Statements, suggestions, or pictures offensive to public decency.

The enforcement of the Code rests with the Board of Directors of the A.A.A.A. As with any Code, the A.A.A.A. Code does not apply to non-member ad agencies and has little effect on advertising from companies that deal directly with media outlets instead of working through an agency.

the public and pressure groups

In a small midwestern community, a group of citizens gather on a quiet evening at the local high school auditorium. For the past three weeks, the meeting has been publicized through posters on community bulletin boards, articles in the local paper, and the "community calendar" of the local radio station. On stage in the auditorium is a color television set on loan from the neighborhood appliance store. Finally, after more than one hundred people have been seated, a member of the community approaches the podium and starts to talk about television. He then turns on the set to give the audience a sampling of what area residents are watching at that moment. His speech is followed by remarks from a professor at the local college, and the meeting concludes with a comment from a local banker. For the next hour, the audience will split into discussion groups to talk about the effects of television in their lives. They'll meet three more times over the next two months, and when the meetings end, they'll be ready actively to communicate with anyone in the industry—from the local television station manager to one of the FCC commissioners.

This gathering is just one of many similar groups responsible for a grassroots movement taking a critical down-home look at big-time television. They range from small community groups to the national Action for Children's Television (ACT), which lists its membership in the thousands. The national groups such as ACT attack the media at the jugular vein—the FCC, Congress, sponsors, and the writers and producers of television programming. Others, such as the Human Family Institute, offer substantial prize incentives to writers of scripts demonstrating the enrichment of traditional human values. Many of the local and national organizations derive financial support from the larger foundations. These groups not only write letters, but are also just as apt to board a bus and arrive on the steps of a government agency or a network executive's office. Their efforts have not gone unnoticed. The NAB Television Code had ACT in mind when it set up guidelines prohibiting cartoon characters and stars of children's programs from also appearing in commercials.

At the community level, inside the office of the local television or radio station manager is the ideal point at which to institute self-regulation. It is here that some of the smaller community groups are becoming just as effective as their national counterparts. Some national organizations even have local affiliate chapters whose chief role it is to communicate with local broadcast management. Such pressure at the local level can be very effective, since each local television station sends feedback in the form of decisions to carry or reject network programming. Numerous rejections by local stations of network material can hurt the ratings of a network production and feasibly cause its cancellation.

What is the result of such public attention? Is it having positive or negative effects? For the citizens' groups, there is now an impressive record of victories at high levels. The FCC has become very concerned with such things as children's television, both programming and commercial content, and this feedback has prompted voluntary changes within the industry. As happens in a country where a free press exists, the activities of citizen groups have been accorded considerable media attention even by those who are on the blunt end of the criticism. Some industry representatives complain that these groups are the ruination of the industry. They argue that the programs being aired are broadcast *because people want to see them*. They cite the impressive figures of the rating services to back their postulations and criticize the pressure groups for not understanding the first thing about the workings of the media in a free society. The pressure groups counter with the argument that pressure from the public is much more satisfactory than pressure from government. Gradually a citizen-industry working relationship is being built up.

If pressure groups are to be successful, both they and the industry will have to keep in mind that over-reaction only leads to polarization. The lesson is also pertinent for industry. When a community group becomes militant and refuses all compromise, then there is little reason to believe they won't isolate themselves from both the industry and other members of the community to the point of losing all previous gains. When industry representatives on the other hand, charge citizen groups with irresponsible activity and do not engage in self-regulation, then they also will experience the consequences of that same isolation. The lesson is pertinent for both industry and reformers. Public pressure groups are a phenomenon that goes beyond the traditional role of the "unseen, unheard" consumer. If the dialogue that has been developed by these groups remains rational and responsible on both sides, then new channels of communication may open up to give the citizen more say in what reaches the family living room.

summary

Codes are statements of suggested practice which serve as an alternative to government regulation where media operate in a free society. Two of the most widely known and influential codes are the Radio and Television Codes of the National Association of Broadcasters. The NAB Codes deal primarily with two types of media content—broadcast programming and advertising. Both codes have a well-developed monitoring and enforcement system. Working journalists of the print and broadcast media have the opportunity to belong to numerous professional associations. Three discussed in this chapter are The Society of Professional Journalists, Sigma Delta Chi; the Radio/Television News Directors Association; and The American Society of Newspaper Editors. These organizations have codes of ethics dealing with such issues as the confidentiality of news sources, the search for truth, fair treatment of issues in the press, and overcoming obstacles to serve the public. Ad agencies, through the American Association of Advertising Agencies, Inc., subscribe to a Standards of Practice. An important part of these Standards is the "Creative Code" which tries to guard against such things as false and misleading advertising statements. The public can also become involved in prodding the media into self-regulation by their membership in numerous public pressure groups which meet and take action to influence media content.

opportunities for further learning

KAYE, EVELYN, *The Family Guide to Children's Television: What to Watch, What to Miss, What to Change and How to Do it.* New York: Pantheon Books, 1974.

Television Code, 19th Ed. Washington, D. C.: National Association of Broadcasters, 1975 (under constant revision).

Radio Code, 18th Ed. Washington, D. C.: National Association of Broadcasters, 1975 (under constant revision).

media ethics

and

social issues

CHAPTER TWENTY-ONE

Any technological or social force that reaches down to affect the majority of society's members is bound to produce a number of controversial topics. Although there are many issues that directly confront the role of media in contemporary society, seven have been singled out for treatment in this chapter. Each discussion is not an answer or solution to these issues. Rather, it is hoped that the reader will reflect on the problems, perhaps discuss them with fellow students, possibly even fill in pieces of the puzzles he or she may be familiar with from past experiences or readings. We will begin with media ethics and conclude with a more philosophical approach to the future of mass communication espoused in the writings of Marshall McLuhan.

media ethics

A student reporter sits at his desk finishing a story for the next day's edition of the campus newspaper. By-lining the story which has

428

taken a week to compile, he decides at the last minute to use a quote from a professor's lecture, feeling it will add to the story. He neither tells the professor the quote will be published in the campus newspaper nor makes any attempt to interview him about other points of view he may have. He also quotes other people from information he has received secondhand. Even a damaging opinion about a campus administrator is attributed to an "unnamed," high-ranking military official who happens to be stationed at the school's ROTC detachment. The next day, the professor, in another class lecture, gives the other side of the issue about which the student was reporting. But there is no reason to print excerpts from that lecture because the material doesn't fit the slant of the student reporter's story. Besides, the newspaper already went to press. No follow-up story is ever printed.

A few weeks later, a Colonel who headed the ROTC detachment is relieved of his command, the resignation of the professor is called for in an editorial in the local paper, and the president of the school receives angry calls from members of the state legislature. A year later, when a multi-million dollar libel suit is filed against the campus newspaper by the professor and the Colonel, the real facts of the story come out. The "unnamed," high-ranking military official turns out to be the student reporter's roommate who is a Cadet Captain in the ROTC. The court also hears how the professor's lectures were quoted out of context. The student testifying under oath speaks in his defense and says he didn't realize that what he was doing was wrong. Along with awarding damages to the plaintiffs, the judge also sentences the student reporter to take some courses in ethics. The example of the student reporter is fictitious.

Specific Cases

Another example is not fictitious. Consider the case of the *Indianapolis Star*, which during the 1968 presidential primary in Indiana, published an editorial from *The New York Times*, deleting, however, a section unfavorable to Indiana's favorite son candidate, then Governor Roger Branigan (Figure 21–1). The thrust of the resulting editorial was a critical stance toward former Senator Robert Kennedy, a candidate and later victor in the Indiana primary, but a rather uncritical review of Branigan. Jules Whitcover, a reporter for the Newhouse News Service, brought the matter to the attention of the profession with an article in the *Columbia Journalism Review* that examined the reporting quality of Indianapolis newspapers during the campaign.[1] Whitcover's analysis was none too favorable and cited other questionable reporting practices by the same newspaper. The version his supporters were weakly led and on the defensive, Senator Eugene J. McCarthy, the winner, had no difficulty running up bills totaling more than $500,000. When a campaign is hard fought, the only limit to the spending is the wild blue yonder.

In the three-cornered struggle now nearing a climax in Indiana, the power of money works in favor of Senator Robert F. Kennedy, who can draw upon the resources of a huge family fortune. Gov. Roger D. Branigin, the "favorite son" candidate, is the leader of a state party organization which controls thousands of patronage jobs and which still engages in the ancient and disreputable practice of levying a 2 per cent party tax on the salaries of state employes. Senator McCarthy, without a personal fortune and without a party machine, has thus far done surprisingly well in attracting funds for his campaign.

The state Democratic chairman supporting Governor Branigin asserts that Senators Kennedy and McCarthy will spend $2 million each. Wildly implausible as that is in Mr. McCarthy's case, the Kennedy forces admit that they will spend $500,000, and no one would be surprised at an expenditure by them twice or three times as great. The truth is no one will ever know

weakly led and on the defensive, Senator Eugene J. McCarthy, the winner, had no difficulty running up bills totaling more than $500,000. When a campaign is hard fought, the only limit to the spending is the wild blue younder.

In the three-cornered struggle now nearing a climax in Indiana, the power of money works in favor of Senator Robert F. Kennedy, who can draw upon the resources of a huge family fortune. Governor Roger D. Branigin, the "favorite son" candidate, is the leader of a state party organization. Senator McCarthy, without a personal fortune and without a party machine, has thus far done surprisingly well in attracting funds for his campaign.

The state Democratic chairman supporting Governor Branigin asserts that Senators Kennedy and McCarthy will spend $2 million each. Wildly implausible as that is in Mr. McCarthy's case, the Kennedy forces admit that they will spend $500,000, and no one would be surprised at an expenditure by them twice or three times as great.

Figure 21-1 *New York Times* (left); *Indianapolis Star* (right).

of the editorial which had been published in the *Times* referred to candidate Branigan as "the leader of the state party organization which controls thousands of patronage jobs and which still engages in the ancient and disreputable practice of levying a 2 percent party tax on the salaries of state employees." When the *Indianapolis Star* reprinted the editorial from the *Times*, that passage was omitted. The editorial reprinted on the front page of the *Star* carried the headline, "Is Indiana For Sale? Asks the New York Times." Whitcover quoted the *Times'* editorial page editor, John B. Oakes, as characterizing the *Star's* action as "reprehensible, unethical and the kind of newspaper practice that blackens the reputation of American journalism." Kennedy won the primary; Branigan went back to practicing law, retired from active politics, and died in 1975.

It is important to point out, however, that not everything that happens in one area of a newspaper necessarily reflects on the rest of the staff. Almost seven years later, a team of tough investigative reporters for the *Indianapolis Star* went to work on a major police corruption story inside the Indianapolis police department. Having battled several lawsuits, they emerged with a series of stories which not only brought them a major share of journalism awards in the state but national awards as well, including the coveted Pulitzer Prize.

The broadcast media has not been immune from such ethical quandaries either. The well-known and criticized Chicago "pot party" staged by WBBM TV drew fire from a number of critics. The station's purpose was to show that there were young people, who, with some regularity, were smoking pot in Chicago. The station filmed people smoking marijuana and telling why they smoked it. The problem was that the pot party had been prearranged for the television cameras. The question becomes, if this was the only way that the medium could show what was taking place and provide an accurate reflection of what these people were experiencing, was it a breach of ethics to stage the party?

Not every questionable ethical practice occurs in the reporting functions of media. A case in point occurred with *The National Observer*. The *Observer*, which had done a front-page article on the subject of journalism ethics three months earlier in July of 1975, found itself in a very embarrassing situation caused by a readership survey questionnaire that had been sent to 3,000 of its subscribers. The eight-page questionnaire asked everything from what you liked in the *Observer* to what your income was and what jewelry you owned. The questionnaire and its results would have become a quiet part of the *Observer's* research files until a University of Wisconsin professor happened to put the questionnaire under ultraviolet light and found an identifying code number in the upper left-hand corner of the questionnaire. It meant that the questionnaire could be traced back to its sender. When the editor of the *Observer*, Henry Gemmill, received a letter from the professor who had uncovered the hidden code number, Gemmill was appalled and brought the whole issue to the attention of the public in a full-page explanation entitled, "The Invisible-Ink Caper." It covered the back page of the November 1, 1975, issue. Gemmill assured those who had filled out the questionnaire that he believed they would suffer no harm from the incident, and in the process was candid about his personal feelings of distaste for the entire matter.

Public Response
Generally, however, the public does not strike back against what it feels are unethical practices. Public inaction can be attributed to two factors: on the one hand, people may be unaware of the unethical conduct; on the other, they may feel powerless against the press or the red tape of media business in general. Although national news councils exist to which people and organizations can complain about unethical activities, proportionately few have taken their complaints to these bodies. Others have used a different retaliatory approach. One such instance was an advertisement purchased in a number of major newspapers by the Mobil Oil Corporation. Capitalizing on the *Jaws* motion picture phenomenon that swept the coun-

try, Mobil placed an ad under its trademarked "Observation" series which claimed the profits of Mobil Oil had been inaccurately reported by columnist Jack Anderson. In bold-faced type at the top of the first paragraph was the word "Shark-bait." The article went on to describe how Mobil could sympathize with "owners of beach cottages, hotels and water-ski shops who suffered from the 'Jaws' exaggerations" (Figure 21–2). The second paragraph detailed a specific charge of alleged inaccurate reporting by Anderson and was bold-faced with the words, "We were 'jawed' by Jack Anderson." Four other paragraphs highlighted Mobil's case. Regardless of the accuracy of either Anderson's or Mobil's claims, Mobil felt it had received the brunt of unfair reporting and attempted to show the other side, even if it meant buying advertising to do it.

⊚bservations™

Shark-bait. The terrifying motion picture "Jaws" probably caused millions of Americans to scan the oceans apprehensively before venturing into the water last summer. But the truth is that even death by bee sting is more likely than being eaten by a shark. An estimated 120 Americans were killed last year by lightning, yet worldwide there were no more than 50 recorded attacks by sharks, and less than a third of these attacks were fatal.

As oil people, we sympathize with the owners of beach cottages, hotels and water-ski shops who suffered from the "Jaws" exaggerations. We know from experience how quickly movies, TV and the press can establish fiction as fact — and how hard it is to correct the damage to one's reputation from untruths. A sample of the problem:

We were "Jawed" by Jack Anderson. Oil company profits, said this columnist recently, are "more fabulous than the pirate treasures of the Blackbeard era." He said that Mobil made "$3.6 billion net profit" last year. He was not only wrong; he overstated our actual net income by more than $2.5 billion.

Figure 21–2 (© Mobil Oil Corporation, 1975.)

Cases of questionable conduct are common in many media circles. Stories of a broadcast news reporter identifying police detectives to a group of civil protesters, reporters on the payroll of a government agency threatening the agency with bad publicity if their raises didn't come through, reporters working for politicians while also being active members of the press—these sagas are all too common. They have provoked a serious crisis in media ethics which has created a major credibility gap with the public. Why do they take place?

ethics and decision making

There has been considerable speculation about the credibility gap among academicians and working media professionals alike. Yet most of the discussion centers around excuses for the failure of moral leadership rather than solutions to the problem. Some suggest that unethical journalism is a combination of circumstances and forces. The college student reporter, for example, without proper training and proper advisement, reads professional newspapers which liberally use such phrases as "unnamed sources" or "reliable sources" whose "truth is self-evident." Without any background in the ethical responsibilities attached to professional reporting, certain campus reporters try to impress their peers by adopting those same reporting methods for local stories, using every Tom, Dick, and Harry who has an opinion on any subject as an "unnamed" source. This is not to suggest that all campus news media are suggestible and irresponsible or, conversely, that those reporters who work at leading newspapers or broadcast complexes throughout the nation are immune to breaches of ethical conduct. It simply points out how the public becomes the loser in these cases.

There are many forces that taken singly or together can precipitate unethical conduct. For example, if a small media outlet doesn't, or can't afford to, pay its staff a decent wage, employees are usually forced to seek out additional employment. Such employment can open up the potential for conflict of interest. There is many a journalist who could not be objective about reporting a boss's arrest for fraud, especially when the reporter needs the money to keep his or her family in food. Although many journalism veterans would not hesitate to ban such reporters from the profession, these same veterans probably have not faced a similar situation and would be the first to tell a new journalism graduate to take a job at any small newspaper or broadcast outlet just to gain experience, regardless of the pay.

There are also some very tough journalistic decisions which involve ethical considerations. For instance, the necessity to publish information about a terminally ill cancer patient as her relatives fight for permission to remove her from life-support machines may not be pleasant for anyone concerned. It may also be a very private family matter, which makes it even more difficult to have the responsibility of calling it to the attention of the public. The decision Harry's editor made not to use the story about the suicide was another example. If the person had been a public figure, the editor's feelings on the matter might have been different. Those feelings might also have been different if the person had taken his or her life in a public place, such as jumping off a well-traveled highway bridge. The problems which face the press in covering human activities become even more complex if the people are prominent in government, education, or industry. Here, still other forces act upon the media, creating conflicting goals and decision-making perplexities.

Such ethical dilemmas were put into perspective by a professor of sociology at the University of Texas, Gideon Sjoberg. Professor Sjoberg contends that ". . . the major ethical orientation of most people in the modern world is that of system loyalty or system maintenance. Indeed, commitment to the nation-state has been the basic ethical orientation during the past century and a half of most politicians, citizens, and scholars of the West. In contradistinction to this system ethic, we need one that transcends any given social system."[2] Professor Sjoberg warns of the dangers in a system-specific ethic ". . . wherein loyalty to the system is the dominant concern, . . ." these dangers ". . . loom ever more serious with the proliferation of large-scale organizations."

He cautions that all " . . . large-scale bureaucracies seem to generate a secret side, and part of that secret tends to become a dark side where a great deal of manipulation takes place." Much of this manipulation, Sjoberg contends, maintains the bureaucracies for those who hold power. It is in this area that many investigative journalists circulate and function. The crux of the problem, however, is that by working within this secret side and developing overt or covert relationships with inside sources, journalists can lose their ethical perspective. For instance, a journalist can find himself or herself becoming so sucked into the system, that he or she fails to be objective and thereby perpetuates its secret purposes.

Communication researcher and anthropologist Alfred G. Smith notes, "An ethic that stresses compatibility among the parts of a system, conservation of the system, limited change, and control, may lead it to control the system to its own advantage."[3] Such journalists become purveyors and communicators of only positive information about the system. Consider the journalist who travels the police beat, reporting the daily activities of the department. To obtain this information, the reporter must usually develop a close association with the police. They become friends, associates, "buddies," and even godfathers or godmothers to each other's children. When one of these "close friends" becomes involved in a police corruption scandal, what happens? Can the reporter dislodge himself or herself from the system-specific ethic to report the corruption? Will he or she be heralded by the police department for reporting this or be chastised, as Professor Sjoberg contends, for "disrupting the social order." Stop and consider your own ethics. What if it were necessary for you to work in this situation? Would you be able to report corruption in the police department if you had become close friends with the officers? Would you be able to report police bribery if you were working on an investigative story in which you needed the police as sources? What if you were dating a police officer? Would you be able to report corruption in the department if you were married to the police chief?

The answers to these questions grow increasingly complex. The role of any gatekeeper is not one of easy solutions to simple problems. He or she sits between a multitude of events with the awesome responsibility of determining which event will reach the public with consequences of untold impact.

media's portrayal of women

The women's rights movement has been responsible for much more than merely identifying women as a target audience. It has produced a groundswell of attention toward the way media portrays women. We already learned how the NAB revised its Codes to prohibit sex discrimination in radio and television programming. Similar action has taken place in other media as well.

The major controversy over the portrayal of women in mass media has tended to center around television, most obviously because of the dominance of the medium, but also because other media, such as specialty magazines, do treat women as the competent, contemporary people they are. Research has tended to substantiate the fact that the criticism television receives for portraying the female in a stereotyped, subservient role is justified.

Although any study can be criticized on methodological grounds, research has shown some definite trends in television's projection of women. Professors Alice E. Courtney and Thomas W. Whipple of

York University in Toronto, Canada, summarized four research projects investigating the image of women in television commercials.[4] One of the four studies was done in Canada, the others in the United States. Results were fairly consistent. The first of these applied to the *appearance* of males and females in television commercials. Results showed ". . . men were overwhelmingly present as voice-overs, the announcing or authority figures employed . . ." in television commercials. A positive point was found in the proportion of males and females as product representatives in television commercials; three studies investigated this concept and found a fairly equal balance between males and females. Three research studies investigated occupational data. Courtney and Whipple's survey showed that females were ". . . over-represented in family/home occupations while males dominate the media/celebrity and business/sales/management occupations. Furthermore, women are still seen in a more limited variety of occupational roles than they actually perform." Courtney and Whipple point out, though, that this imbalance seems to be changing. However, this was not the case when examining the portrayal of women in the family structure. Here Courtney and Whipple contended that there was ". . . little evidence in the world of TV commercials to show that the family structure may be changing or that women are capable of performing responsible tasks other than those associated with the family and home."

Another ongoing research project was conducted by Nancy Tedesco of the University of Pennsylvania.[5] Studying major television characters over a four-year period—"those who play leading roles representing the principal types essential to a story appearing on prime-time, non-cartoon, network dramatic programs"—she found males were portrayed as ". . . more mature, more serious, and more likely to be employed than females." Moreover, she found that males ". . . have advantages and get into violent situations. They are powerful and smart, and their independence requires that they be relatively unattached (not married) and thus able to take risks." Females tended to be almost the exact opposite. She found they lacked independence, ". . . they are not usually found in adventure situations; they are younger, more likely to be married; and less likely to be employed."

The image female children project in television commercials is similar to that of adult females. Research by Cornell Chulay and Sara Francis investigated the image of the female child on Saturday morning television commercials.[6] Results of their research concluded that 79 percent of 294 commercials analyzed used a male announcer. The appearance of the female child was "stereotyped."

Her dress never had a wrinkle in it, and there was never a hair out of place. In other words, she was ". . . sugar and spice and everything nice." Boys, on the other hand, were frequently seen in "casual" and "disordered" clothes. Boys were also pictured in an outdoor setting while girls were frequently seen playing in a room. Chulay and Francis summarized their research by saying that television was ". . . trying to orient the female child to the traditional role she should play in society. This role sees her as a mother with her child, or as a woman preoccupied with her appearance. She is portrayed as the conventional little girl programmed to grow up to be the typical housewife and mother."

It should be pointed out, again, that some of these televised media portrayals are changing. Female characters are creeping into more professional roles. Overall, however, the televised image is still not that of the contemporary, professional woman. Some of the underlying reasons for retaining the homemaker stereotype rest in the economic foundations of broadcasting rather that in its programming. For instance, the working professional woman is not normally the person viewing daytime television. The viewer is generally the housewife, and commercials are therefore often designed to exemplify this role.

Despite the publicity television has received in this area, other media have also come under criticism for their portrayal of females. At the University of Illinois, Cheris Kramer directed research which investigated the stereotypes of women's speech found in cartoons published in *The New Yorker, Playboy, Cosmopolitan,* and the *Ladies Home Journal*.[7] Students who analyzed the speech of women in the cartoon captions found it to be "ineffective and restricted." It could not ". . . deal forthrightly with a number of topics, such as finance and politics. . . ." Kramer went on to report that students ". . . in writing about how they determined the sex of the speaker of the captions characterized the stereotyped women's speech as being stupid, naive, gossipy, emotional, passive, confused, concerned, wordy, and insipid."

As noted earlier in this text, the outdoor industry's ad portraying a woman in a bare-backed, black velvet gown with the caption likening a hard liquor to the feel of black velvet has not been a favorite of various women's groups. Moreover, many textbooks have come under fire for continually using examples showing women in subordinate roles to men. How media will portray women in the future will be determined by how many changes media planners make on their own, how much pressure is placed upon them by women and men, and what economic indicators suggest about the profit or loss of changing portrayals. Although economic indicators may seem like a poor excuse for discouraging changes, it is indeed a powerful motivation and one to be reckoned with, especially when dealing with media decision makers.

violence in the media

While recently summer vacationing near a lake, I watched a group of young boys appear wearing swimming suits. One of the boys had a high-handlebarred bicycle, the kind with which you can do "wheelies"—riding with the front wheel off the ground. As they approached the dock which protruded into the lake about thirty yards, I noticed they were carrying a large heavy board about ten feet long. They also had two cement blocks. I watched as they placed the cement blocks on the end of the dock and positioned one end of the board on top of the blocks, forming an inclined ramp elevated about two feet. Then as the others cheered, one boy rode the bicycle the entire length of the dock, up the ramp and into the air. At the height of his ascent, the boys on the dock shouted, "yea Evel!" But the show wasn't over. As the bike and rider splashed into the lake, two other boys quickly donned their face masks. The bike rider had barely surfaced before the two boys in face masks yelled, "Emergency Squad" and plunged in to retrieve the bicycle. Fortunately, no one was hurt displaying the well-publicized antics of motorcycle daredevil Evel Knievel. However, mimicking what has become common media fare on television can have serious consequences.

Violence in media can be traced back to ancient pictographics which displayed such sacrificial acts as carving a heart out of a person's chest, ceremonial torture methods used to bestow adulthood on children reaching puberty, and other activities that by today's standards, if explicitly shown, would never make late night television. Awareness of the effects of violent programming in general and on television in particular began in 1952 during television's formative years when Senator Estes Kefauver's subcommittee investigated juvenile delinquency. Testimony by authorities charged television with being responsible not only for showing violence but also prompting juveniles to imitate it. The issue might have vanished from public attention except for that afternoon in 1963 when a sniper's bullets killed President John F. Kennedy. Ironically, it was television which brought three days of national mourning into American living rooms in what was hailed as the medium's finest hours. That same medium would later be blamed by its critics for causing the warped minds which were responsible for similar events.

The Surgeon General's Report

The bloodshed was not over. Black leader Martin Luther King was next to fall to an assassin's bullet. Then another assassin placed a 22-caliber bullet on target and brought death to Senator Robert Kennedy, as he was celebrating with hundreds of campaign workers his victory in the 1968 California presidential primary. The entire era had been spiced with dinnertime detail on the Vietnam War plus political protests at the 1968 Democratic Presidential Convention. What many saw as inevitable finally occurred as the American government examined the issue of violence on television and committed $1 million to a study with additional funds for administrative and publishing costs.[8] The project, entitled "The Surgeon General's Study of Television and Social Behavior" involved leading social scientists and produced a multi-volume work which, when completed, posed as many questions as it had answered. The summary report of the study stated:[9]

> There is a convergence of the fairly substantial experimental evidence for short-run causation of aggression among some children by viewing violence on the screen and the much less certain evidence from field studies that extensive violence viewing precedes some long-run manifestations of aggressive behavior. This convergence of the two types of evidence constitutes some preliminary evidence of a causal relationship.

From the above statement, it is easy to see how the press and critics jumped on the report with varying interpretations. The reactions ran from *The New York Times'* headline of "TV Violence Held Unharmful to Youth," to then FCC Commissioner Nicholas Johnson's likening the network executives responsible for programming to child molesters. Research cited in the report included the work by George Cerbner on determining the amount of violence which was actually present on television.[10] Gerbner's research, which has been ongoing since 1967, identifies and categorizes the amount of violence which appears in television. Despite the difficulty in determining the effects of violence, this research and the methods involved have proved especially woeful to media critics and professionals alike in actually rating violent content and using it as a launching point to determine everything from trends in programming to evidence for and against the controversial family-viewing concept.

Since the report was released and the public's attention drawn to the issue, the press has been filled with reference to televisions' causal relationship to violent behavior. One television movie which came under criticism was *Born Innocent* with its rape scene. When a similar rape incident occurred in San Francisco after the program had been aired on national television, NBC found itself with a law suit. A similar incident occurred in an Indianapolis suburb. In Los Angeles, police asked NBC to set up a special showing of one of their *Police Story* episodes after crimes were committed which were similar to an episode in the television series. U.S. Senator Bill Brock of Tennessee released the results of a survey that claimed the vast majority of Tennessee juvenile court judges felt there was a causal link between television violence and juvenile crime.

Violence on the Networks

Along with the behavioral science research studies looking at the effects of violence, Professors George Gerbner and Larry Gross, both of the Annenberg School of Communications at the University of Pennsylvania, have continued research into the amount of violence on television. A recent report of the two scholars provided comparative violence trends for a nine-year period ranging from 1967 through 1975 (Figure 21–3). Their research has showed a continued emphasis on violence during weekend daytime (children's)

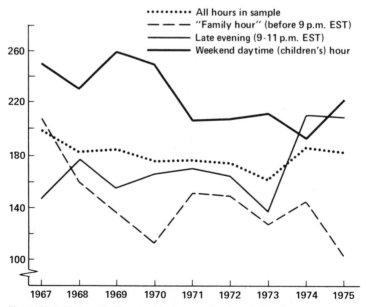

Figure 21–3 Violence indices for the three networks combined for different hours of dramatic programming over nine years. The violence index is a combination of such factors as number of programs with violence, amount of violence, and number of perpetrators and victims. (George Gerbner and Larry Gross, *Violence Profile #7*. Philadelphia: Annenberg School of Communications, 1976.)

hours. Included in the violence index employed by Gerbner and Gross are incidents of humorous violence such as would typically be found in cartoon fare. This factor has been a point of discussion and criticism by some, CBS in particular, which does not use humorous incidents of violence in some of the violence surveys it conducts. In publishing the 1975 results, some comments about the Gerbner and Gross report centered around the effect of the family-viewing concept on televised violence. Figure 21–3 shows some of the changes in violence that have occurred over different time periods. Although Figure 21–3 may seem to indicate a marked increase in violence in the late-evening time periods while a decrease occurred during the family viewing hours, keep in mind that the increase in the late evening time period is mostly between the 1973-1974 range, which was prior to the imposition of family-viewing hour requirements.

Violence and the Print Media

The broadcast media are not the only offenders in the media-violence interface. When Gerald Ford was on a Presidential swing through California, a young woman was arrested for allegedly pointing a gun at Ford. Lynette (Squeeky) Fromme splashed the covers of *Newsweek* and *Time*, which prompted Congressman John Rhodes to criticize the news weeklies for playing up the incident. Rhodes said, "I would like to suggest to my friends in the press that this situation demands greater discretion in the reporting of terrorist-inspired events. The press has a duty to report the facts and I am not suggesting censorship of any kind. I *am* suggesting that the press approach its job with a greater sense of responsibility . . . and not degenerate into a position where the selling of magazines and newspapers becomes *more* important than the national interest, and the future safety of our President and other prominent persons." In a subsequent edition of *Newsweek*, the magazine admitted receiving considerable mail accusing it of glorifying Fromme and giving her "cover girl" status.[11] Not long after Fromme was arrested, another woman, Sara Jane Moore, was taken into custody in connection with another attempt on Gerald Ford's life.

Some textbooks have even come under fire as links in a chain leading to violent acts. A citizen wrote a letter to the editor of a major metropolitan newspaper relating how her neighbor's pet had been hanged, then cited a descriptive passage in a textbook used in the local school system. The passage graphically told of the agony of a kitten being hanged.

The outcome of the media violence debate is far from over, and the evidence about its causal effects is far from conclusive. Attempts have been made to bring the graphic portrayal of violence under control and at least to limit its opportunities for exposure among children. The government of Mexico flatly banned twenty American television series from Mexican airwaves because they were considered to be too violent. Among those dropped were *Kung Fu, Mannix,* and *Dragnet.* To alleviate the problem, the United States tried the family-viewing hour concept. The results of that effort were discussed in Chapter 19. A number of FCC Commissioners have expressed displeasure over the content of television violence. Yet representatives from the television industry argue that some of the highest ratings are accorded programs in which the incidence of violence is frequent. The future will undoubtedly see more discussion and debate as systematic research begins to separate fact from conjecture.

censorship

The issue of censorship will always be in the forefront of any discussion of mass media. The forces which act toward greater control of media content and those which act against it are present in all societies. We tend to think of censorship as something negative, but we have yet to define this phenomenon that spans all media and all types of media content.

Earlier in this text, we learned how colonial governments virtually controlled the fledgling publishing industry in early America. Today we would have little difficulty in defining such control as a form of censorship. If an eighteenth-century newspaper wanted to publish articles critical of the government, the owner would usually find himself out of work; his government subsidy would be cut off, his presses might be confiscated, and there was always the possibility that he would be deported to England. In retrospect, we can see that it took the American Revolution to free the press from its shackles. And yet if there had been no government control over the press during its formative years, would the republic have survived and prospered as much as it did? Did our republic need a period of time simply to gain a foundation and population, even if it was the recipient of a daily diet of censored news? If the American Revolution had occurred earlier than it did, would the country have had the solidarity to conquer suppression? These rhetorical questions could be debated for hours. Yet when India's Prime Minister Indira Ghandi censored the press during nationwide upheavals in 1975, many gasped in amazement at how such a dictatorial attitude could be displayed. An ambassador from India appearing on a television news program was not nearly as taken back by the action, commenting that in the early stages of a democracy when certain political forces could actually harm it, censorship was necessary.

During the Civil War, we again saw the press shackled, this time by generals who were unhappy with the newspaper coverage they were receiving. In other wars in which Americans took part, notably World War II, the press voluntarily complied with government orders to withhold news from the public. In such cases, are the members of the press guilty of censorship just as much or more than the officials who order the news embargo? Are such embargoes ever justified? Would you comply with such an embargo if you were a reporter covering the battlefront?

We have already learned about shield laws which protect the confidentiality of news sources and freedom of information laws which guarantee the press and public access to public records. What about laws against censorship? What about the reporter who is subpoenaed before a grand jury to identify his or her source of information for a story? Can a zealous prosecutor use this same threat of subpoena to wrest this information from a reporter before the journalist is even called before the grand jury? Having been through this experience, will the reporter tend in the future to avoid the hassle represented by such a threat by shunning controversial stories? Is the prosecutor then, with this threat of subpoena, guilty of news censorship? Is the judge who issues a gag order preventing or trying to prevent pre-trial publicity guilty of censorship?

The molders of our Constitution could not have foreseen the advent of electronic media. When these media did make their impact felt, government found itself the umpire in assigning portions of the electromagnetic spectrum to specific radio and television stations. The FCC and its regulatory actions came about by necessity. When sex-talk shows scintillated the airwaves, the FCC let explicit on-air discussion of sexual activities go only so far. It then decreed that continuing such programming could provoke action against the licensee. Court cases and rulings such as the Fairness Doctrine have now established a legal precedent for determining the content of broadcast programming. Yet, there has been little solid legal ground on which to justify similar controls in the print media. Consider the broadcast manager who operates a station in a large city where there are ample opportunities for the public to obtain diversified programming. The FCC can admonish the manager that he or she has certain programming guidelines to follow. But, wait a moment— is this government control any different than the control placed upon the pre-revolutionary press? Are the actions of the FCC a form of censorship?

What about the small newspaper which receives a sizeable share of its advertising from a large business in the community? Can the threat of withdrawing that advertising make an editor think twice about giving the big business unfavorable publicity? Is this form of economic censorship any different from what the early colonial printer faced when he printed news unfavorable to the politicians subsidizing his enterprise?

What about the student press? At many colleges and universities, the campus newspaper as well as the campus radio and television station receive subsidies from the parent institution. What happens when these media grow critical of the college or university adminis tration? The loss of such subsidies, especially when the broadcast media are noncommercial and prohibited by law from selling com mercials to raise money, can become instantly crippling.

Other censorship issues focus on the internal operations of mass media. Take a labor dispute, for example. Perhaps the labor union strikes after newspaper management refuses to consider a union-proposed wage package. As negotiations progress, it is clear that non-union labor will be called in to run the presses. Thus, on the day before the strike, the presses are "accidentally" damaged be-yond immediate repair and cannot operate. Is this action a form of censorship? Is it a means of stopping the free flow of information to the public? Does censorship exist when the purpose of an action is not directly to inhibit the free flow of information but to protect workers' rights?

None of these answers is easy. Remember, censorship can be ob-vious. It can be the court order that keeps a newspaper story from being published. It can be the network executive's decision to scrap an evening television show the executive views as too sexually ex-plicit for a home viewing audience. Yet even these rather obvious forms of censorship can be seen as decisions in the public interest, actions that protect other constitutionally guaranteed freedoms. In this "in between" area lie many of the cases involving censorship. Continued discussion of individual situations as well as a reason-able definition of the issues are necessary to make sure that deci-sion makers do not stray too far in either restricting our freedoms or ruining our social order.

The National News Council

It was at the height of the Watergate era, when newsmen were being jailed and the administration of former President Richard

Nixon was protesting the press coverage it was receiving, that the National News Council became a reality. Supported by a grant from the non-profit Twentieth Century Fund, the Council was charged with the responsibility of considering the accuracy and fairness of news disseminated by national news-gathering organizations. Anyone can bring a complaint before the Council as long as they waive filed legal proceedings against the news-gathering agency in regard to the complaint.

From its very beginning the Council elicited both pro and con arguments. NBC claimed the liabilities of such a council outweighed its assets.[12] Elmer W. Lower, president of ABC News claimed it was unnecessary; J. Edward Murray, associate editor of the Detroit *Free Press* noted he personally was not opposed to the principle of the News Council; and Warren Phillips, president of Dow Jones, which publishes the *Wall Street Journal* and the *National Observer,* said, "We think that our record over many years demonstrates that we do not require help from a self-appointed, quasi-public committee to continue to do this job and to serve the public interest."[13]

After some well-publicized criticism, the Council finally became a reality in early 1973 and in July of that year formally announced its fifteen members representing people from a wide range of backgrounds. William B. Arthur, a former editor of *Look,* was named executive director. Roger J. Traynor, a former Chief Justice of the California Supreme Court, became chairman and the former city editor of WCBS-TV, Ned Schnurman, was named associate director. Three years later the Council increased its size to eighteen members, permitting two additional representatives from the media and one from the general public.

Ironically, Richard Nixon's criticism of the press coverage of his administration was not handled by the News Council, primarily because it couldn't gain the cooperation of the Nixon administration officials to substantiate the charges. Nixon's press secretary, Ronald Zeigler, "told the Council directors it would be inappropriate for him to participate in the inquiry."[14] Other cases have come before the Council.[15] A CBS television documentary about the life of former President Franklin Delano Roosevelt was criticized for misleading the viewers into assuming troops had killed marchers during a Washington, D.C., protest in 1932. The Council said the complaint brought against CBS was warranted. The *Washington Post* also received council scrutiny when the *Post* edited a UPI story and thus, the Council claimed, changed the reported thrust of a speech by a woman's rights advocate.[16]

In 1976, the scope of the Council expanded beyond the national press to include press which may not be national in initial circulation but which deals with issues of a national concern or concern for journalists. Certainly the future of such a body will be dependent upon the ability of the Council to get three things—money, public support, and media support. Without any one of these, it can't succeed. The thought by some that the Council might turn into a type of hatchet body was not justified. While criticizing some media, it found other complaints not warranted. Currently the Council operates much like a watchdog without teeth. It can investigate and comment, but it cannot take action against the media, short of attempting to publicize its findings.

invasion of privacy

Sitting in your room, you reach over to switch the channel on the television set from the instructional television program you have been watching as a class assignment. You feel you know the material being shown in the program and are ready to be tested on it in class. As you turn the dial to another channel, a warning light flashes on a master control console located in the basement of a building at the other end of the campus. There, a lab assistant

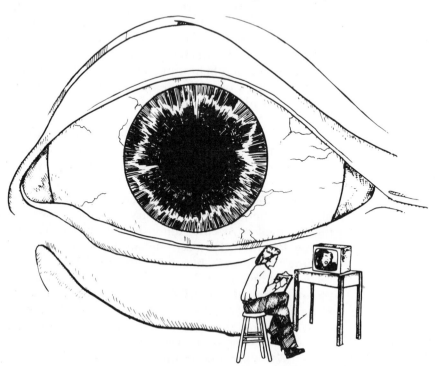

quickly traces the source of the alarm light to your room and, in a special notebook, records a check next to your name. It's not the first time you've changed channels in the middle of a televised course assignment. At the end of the semester, you receive a lower grade than the one you expected. In a consultation with the instructor, you are told you didn't watch the assigned programs and made fun of the course to friends who would stop by your room. That's why your grade was lowered. You discover that a two-way interactive cable system was hooked to your television set which made it possible for the master control to monitor what channels you watched and also listen in to conversations in your room. You are shocked and file a lawsuit claiming your privacy has been invaded.

Our example brings to light some of the concerns that recent technological capabilities have placed in the minds of the public. Many people feel we are no longer "secure" in our homes as guaranteed by the Fourth Amendment to the Constitution. We have become the watched instead of the watchers, the invaded instead of the invaders. The thought of an unseen, unknown, ever-present "big brother" looms over us as we become pawns to a technological society. And although the example in the preceding paragraph was fiction, it is well within the confines of technology at this very moment. Increasingly, we are faced with policy decisions which affect our rights to privacy and our ability to maintain confidential such items as our medical records, financial statements, and educational transcripts.

Among the media under fire in this issue, cable television perhaps more than any other has captured the limelight, primarily because of its two-way operability. Already hardware exists to monitor when television sets are on or off and to what channel a set is tuned. Hooked to central computers, these systems can be used for opinion polling and similar data gathering exercises. Obviously, one of the first concerns that the public expresses is how to control such a system. The federal government, the logical governing body, has in recent years discredited itself with news of snooping into citizens' private affairs and violating the same safeguards it has been charged with protecting. Reports from Washington reveal that the CIA, in the name of national security, has been actively involved in opening mail—approximately a quarter million letters—and the National Security Agency (NSA) has even monitored messages sent via overseas telephone and cable in attempts to locate people suspected of being involved in political dissent. Computers in the NSA were programmed to activate on such key words as "assassination" and identify the sender and receiver of such messages. Certain communication companies have been charged with routinely turning some messages sent through company facilities over to government officials. Such massive surveillance measures create a gloomy picture for those who feel that technology has already invaded our privacy and shows no signs of retreating. The immediate question becomes, how is invasion of privacy stopped once it is started?

mass media past, present, and future: McLuhan's perspectives

In the early 1960s, a Canadian professor of English literature with a background in science and technology began offering a perspective on the role of media in society. For ten years, between 1962 and 1972, Marshall McLuhan's writings and articles written about him filled everything from discussions of the street cultures in San Francisco to pages of *The New York Times.* He was the subject of serious broadcast interview programs and popular comedy routines. He was adored, idolized, and discarded. Critics called him everything from the greatest original thinker in centuries to a charlatan of intellectual thought. He reached the peak of his popularity in 1967. Shortly thereafter, the media movement gave way to the environmental movement, campus unrest, and the Vietnam War. After 1967 McLuhan dropped out of sight except for minor revivals of his ideas in esoteric publications. Although theories attributed to him stirred great scholarly debate at the beginning of the 1970s, the excitement soon died down. In its place a concerted effort toward professional education evolved and a concern over the individual's ability to survive economically, as opposed to the view that one could live on ideas and "happenings." Nevertheless, there are some important thrusts to McLuhan's thoughts. Whether his ideas have failed to achieve the limelight in recent years as a result of a passé attitude toward his philosophy, or whether we are in a transitional state waiting for his predictions to come true, we should still take a few moments to view the very broad subject of mass communication, the media, and civilization from his perspective. His role in initiating the testing of hypotheses and attempting to coordinate such hypotheses into a composite theory about man and technology can profit today's student of mass communication.

The Ages of Technological Determinism

Certainly anthropology, if not archeology, has long since known that human beings were not always the creatures they are today. The

Figure 21-4 Media philosopher Marshall McLuhan. Photo by Robert Lansdale.

newness in McLuhan's thinking lies in the way he relates human evolution to the senses.

McLuhan supports the contention that we have been the product of technological determinism—technology forcing us into our future. In the pre-literate era of our development, we used all of our senses equally to relate to our environment. We were just as apt to react to touch as we were to sight, sound, or smell. No order or priority existed among our senses, and they were, for the most part, in balance with one another. We could, therefore, absorb the total experience of our environment. We were part of a tribal culture in a global village.

The second era of McLuhanistic development occurred as we left the pre-literate stage and moved into the era of communication symbols, from the pictographics on the walls of caves to the development of the alphabet. This transition into the first stage of man's communicative technology caused a serious disruption in what had been a well-balanced relationship. For one thing, the very presence of the alphabet brought about an imbalance in the human perceptual system, a shift toward a predominantly visual orientation. We began to evolve along unidimensional lines—our thinking became linear, our advancement became linear, and we began to use the linear technology of the alphabet as a means of securing and searching out other discoveries. The tribal group culture of the pre-literate era was replaced with an individualized culture of the linear-visual period. We could participate in communicative acts without the presence of other people.

The next great invention was the printing press. Now, although humans were still oriented to the visual dimension, communication could begin on a mass scale. For a time, the new technology disrupted the status quo, as thoughts and ideas penetrated all levels of society on a scale and with an impact much greater than in the past. Print media became the "goggles" of society through which we viewed and learned about our world experience. Yet these "goggles" also perpetuated our one-dimensional perspective. We all know, for example, that although many profound words define love, nothing in print successfully captures the actual feeling of love. This discrepancy between the printed word and a life experience was a theme running through McLuhan's work and probably one of the chief reasons for his popularity. Members of the street cultures read and studied his philosophy and searched for a more sensual experience in life.

To McLuhan, print at its best was communicative but repressive. It hindered more than helped, and thrust us into a technological world and later a revolution. We could store ideas, compute ideas, and express ideas with print. As the new print technology spread, an almost competitive neurosis developed alongside an uncontrollable nationalism. Our visual culture spawned more visual culture; our technological determinism spawned more technological determinism. What had begun with pictographics and was immeasurably accelerated by the printing press, served merely to increase our linear world perspective and to spur the general process of industrial development. McLuhan contends that assembly line factories were the result.

The most disruptive age that we have encountered, according to McLuhan, is the electronic age. Here humankind was propelled into many new communication processes, both in terms of media and systems. These systems included the telegraph and ocean cables, especially the Atlantic Cable which linked the United States and Great Britain. The new media—radio, television, and the computer—connected countries and cultures in a massive, instantaneous manner. We have now come full circle, in a sense—we are once again a global village where everyone is connected and attuned to the same "tribal" drums.

Media Hot and Cool

Media in this electronic age, McLuhan contends, are basically of two types, hot and cool. Cool media demand the active, tactile participation of the individual. Although at first glance this might convey the idea that "touching" and turning the knobs on a radio is experiencing a cool medium, while sitting and watching television would be experiencing a hot one, just the opposite is the case. If we grant McLuhan's hypothesis that our culture is primarily visual, and since, as we learned earlier, it is necessary for our eyes and brain to assimilate the actual picture on a television from the lines and dots, then we are mentally "touching" television and it is thus a cool medium. Radio, on the other hand, is a hot medium. It does not demand as much of our senses or our involvement as television. The same is true with newspapers or magazines. They are all hot because they are unidimensional.

McLuhan also contends that serious conflicts can exist when the wrong medium is matched with the wrong message. A hot message on a cool medium will be less favorable than matching a cool medium with a cool message. As an example, McLuhan predicted the end of the Vietnam War because the public would be so sick of seeing a hot message (the War) on a cool medium (television), that they would finally react and demand an end to it. He also credited the 1960 loss of the American presidency to Richard Nixon because in the great television debates with John Kennedy, Nixon was clearly a hot personality on a cool medium. Later, observing Nixon on an evening variety show playing the piano in a casual, impromptu manner, McLuhan contended that his image could be favorably transmitted to the viewers and the voters.

Criticism of McLuhan

The majority of McLuhan's published thoughts about media occurred during the 1960s. They appeared in such profusion within such a short time period that his ideas almost seem to be expressed first and pondered later. Some of his writings are less satisfactory than others, more poorly formulated. Attention to them decreased in the early '70s, but they have recently received renewed interest.

Some basic conflicts in his theory development can readily be seen. For example, McLuhan criticized radio as a serious intrusion into minority cultures. However, research shows it has been a significant educational medium for such cultures. In addition, although McLuhan describes television as a cool medium because it forces us to use our brain and eyes to complete the picture before us, he criticizes movies for being a hot medium. Yet the procession of rapidly moving motion picture frames passing before our eyes necessitates a similar "visually tactile" experience. McLuhan has been criticized for being unclear in much of his published works. His defense in some cases has been to claim that he was limited by the single dimension of the print medium in expressing thoughts that were part of a much larger experience of the senses. McLuhan uses the term "rear view mirror" to express our involvement with our senses and society. Yet, we could apply this same criticism to his "rear view" thinking, grounding much of his thoughts on the historical foundation of the past.

McLuhan and the Future

Our encounter with McLuhan would have little relevance if we did not at least offer some perspective on the future validity of his contentions. McLuhan has said that as one medium arrives, it creates disruption; the medium overtaken then becomes an art form. History has generally tended to confirm this. Scrolls from biblical times have now become priceless art treasures, as have the books printed on the first printing presses. History has also recorded that when the new print media did arrive, there was in fact a disruption of society.

The age of electronics has created an equal concern and disruption at all levels of society. The telegraph, for example, accelerated our decision making. No longer were economic market quotations received days late. We suddenly had "instant" decisions and predictions available for immediate analysis. Life in our industrial society thus moved faster and became more competitive. The telegraph became what McLuhan called the central nervous system of our communication network. But voice transmission and the advent of radio soon eclipsed dots and dashes. This new medium created further disruption as it paved the way for the truly electronic media. Newspaper "extras" ceased to be sold on the street corner. They became the instant news bulletins of radio. Parents shuddered in horror as teenagers seemed to care about little except having a transistor radio glued to their ear. The masses tuned to the rhetoric of acid rock, or brought claims that the medium responsible for disseminating these unnatural sounds resulted in all sorts of ills among young adults. In retrospect, we see that an art form is already taking shape among the electronic media. Telegraph apparatus is an artifact of antique stores, and the radio drama of the 1930s has become part of the nostalgia of the 1970s. Reproductions of early radios fill department stores, and one can even purchase a working replica of the large, "church steeple" radio of the 1940s.

Television caused a similar disruption. A scant decade after its debut, government commissions conducted full-scale hearings on how television affected violent behavior, how it affected childhood development, how it corrupted our morals, and countless other "disruptions" in our society. Perhaps it's ironic that the debate on those issues goes on simultaneously as television is being considered a serious art form. Experimental video centers are using television as a medium of artistic expression for everything from multimedia "experiences" to video feedback, in which a television camera takes a picture of its own monitor (Figure 21–5). Video cassettes and video discs capturing the nostalgia of early television programs are available much like recordings of early radio. Some programs, such as the famed *Mickey Mouse Club*, even returned to television after having appeared as nationally popular programs twenty or so years ago. If television is becoming an art form, then what medium will supersede it? Computers?

Computers have brought with them the same disruption and acceleration in pace that accompanied the entry of other media into general usage. Already they are used as systems of communication, and the wired-city concept, where everyone will have access to a central computer, opens up even broader avenues of communication for this medium. Yet we have resisted the advent of computer technology. At the very least, we regard it as a common nuisance. At most, we fear being taken over by it.

It is important, however, to focus upon the future. What if McLuhan was correct? How will this technological determinism affect us in the last quarter of the twentieth century? Consider the ever increasing velocity of technological development that we have so far observed. The time between the introduction and demise of new media has continually shrunken, until we are now living in an

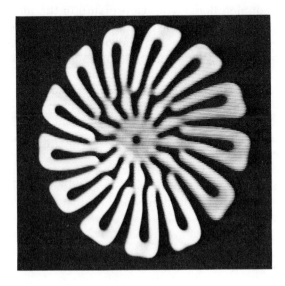

Figure 21–5 Video feedback. Television as an art form?

era of overlapping media. What effect is this having on our lives, and what new media are yet to appear? What will happen to the media that currently exist? How great will be the disruption? Will we be overtaken by media? Certainly questions such as these are much easier to ask than to answer. However, our lives are totally interrelated with mass media. Perhaps nothing has affected our past or will affect our future so much as this tremendous capability to communicate all sorts of information across cultures almost instantaneously. We must begin now to prepare ourselves to develop a satisfactory relationship with the media based on fulfilling human needs and goals.

summary

Chapter 21 has looked at the ethics and social issues confronting mass media. On the subject of media ethics, we saw how questionable actions took place within both the print and broadcast media. We also saw that within any single medium lies the potential for responsible, professional, ethical practices or blatant violation of those principles. Violence has been depicted in media since the beginning of civilization. Current attention adhered to the subject after "The United States Surgeon General's Report on Television and Social Behavior" inferred there was a causal link between violence depicted on television and overt behavior. The media have also been criticized for their portrayal of women. Although research indicates this may be changing, the overall image television, in particular, tends to project is that of the stereotyped housewife. Censorship of the media is an age-old philosophical issue. Pro-censorship arguments champion the need to protect social order, while anti-censorship arguments herald the necessity for the free flow of information in a democracy. To avoid the threat of possible government regulation or censorship and as an experimental effort to provide criticism for the press, the Twentieth Century Fund has provided initial funding for a National News Council. One of the most controversial issues facing media planners is the public's fear of invasion of its privacy. Although this fear is particularly keen with two-way cable television, other types of technology, such as computers, are also a perceived threat to many people. Policy making on such issues often comes to a stalemate when the need for government control is pitted over and against the necessity to prevent abuse of that control.

Canadian philosopher Marshall McLuhan speculated about the development of media in society and advanced the theory that we are caught in a process of technological determinism that has seen the pre-literate era give way in turn to the era of visual dominance, the era of the printing press, and the era of electronic media. McLuhan looks at media as either being hot or cool and stresses the importance of matching the proper message with the proper medium. Many of McLuhan's perspectives on mass media, regardless of the controversy surrounding them, seem to approach some validity as we view the future of mass media in society.

opportunities for further learning

BRENTON, MYRON, *The Privacy Invaders.* New York: Coward-McCann, Inc., 1964.

BROWN, LEE, *The Reluctant Reformation: On Criticizing the Press in America.* New York: David McKay Company, Inc., 1974.

CARTER, DOUGLAS, and STEPHEN STRICKLAND, *TV Violence and the Child: The Evolution and Fate of the Surgeon General's Report.* New York: Russell Sage Foundation, 1975.

CLINE, VICTOR B., Ed., *Where Do You Draw the Line?* Provo, Utah: Brigham Young University Press, 1974.

LESSER, GERALD S., *Children and Television: Lessons from Sesame Street.* New York: Random House, 1974.

McLUHAN, MARSHALL, *Understanding Media: The Extensions of Man.* New York: McGraw-Hill Book Company, 1964.

MILGRAM, STANLEY, and R. LANCE SHOTLAND, *Television and Antisocial Behavior: Field Experiments.* New York: Academic Press, 1973.

STEARN, GERALD EMANUEL, Ed., *McLuhan Hot and Cool.* New York: The Dial Press, Inc., 1967.

careers in mass media

CHAPTER TWENTY-TWO

Throughout this book, you have ventured into many of the careers in mass media. You have worked in broadcast management, traveled with Harry the reporter, walked the road to a hit record, been inside a wire service bureau, started a magazine, joined in a television production, and observed several other enterprises. The purpose of this chapter is to sharpen your awareness of some of the specific careers currently possible in the field. If it does nothing more than broaden your horizons, it will have been successful. As with any discipline, it is too easy to develop tunnel vision when considering career opportunities. Because parents, professors, counselors, and others may have a special interest in or experience with only one aspect of a professional field, students tend to see career opportunities only through their limited perspective. The author once overheard a colleague ask a student, with complete innocence, "Why do you want to study radio and television and graduate to be a camera operator?" The comment was not vindictive. The professor honestly believed that besides actors, actresses, and news commentators, the only other job in broadcasting was that of camera operator. Within broadcasting and its support industries alone, there are literally hundreds of other possibilities.

Similar comments have come from guidance counselors. One advised a journalism major to investigate other career possibilities because there weren't any job openings for newspaper reporters. That limited perspective was wrong on two counts. First, there are jobs as reporters if a student is willing to start somewhere other than the *Washington Post* or CBS. A few exceptional students have even started with major news media. A journalism publication recently ran an article about careers in journalism and how graduates were faring in the job hunt. In the next issue, the editor of a respected major weekly publication of national scope replied he had not yet to have a single journalism graduate apply for a job on his publication. It pointed out the problem. A large percentage of the students were trying to land a small percentage of the jobs.

The second error the guidance counselor made was assuming that the only job a journalism graduate could obtain was that of a newspaper reporter. Overlooked were all the other jobs in journalism—work on corporate publications, newsletters, magazines, freelancing, and the list goes on and on. Overlooked also were related careers in such fields as advertising, public relations, broadcasting, photography, and many others. Added to this is the fact that the study of mass media, regardless of the specialty, is excellent preparation for all types of careers. The use of closed-circuit television in a hospital operating room and videotape in a courtroom are experiences every doctor or lawyer will encounter sometime in his or her career. The home extension agent who never appears on television or never is faced with talking to a newspaper reporter is rare indeed. Study of the media, whether as a major, a minor, or as an elective, is valuable regardless of one's future career.

If the careers discussed here spark your curiosity, then take the time to investigate them further. Go beyond the pages of this book to talk with people in the media. Solicit knowledgeable career guidance and personally take an honest look at yourself. Understand your strengths and weaknesses. Remember that persistence, ambition, and skill can unlock many doors, and, most importantly, *there's always room for talent*. Even if you don't seek a career in the media, there is every chance that whatever vocation you choose, you will become acquainted with people involved in mass communication. You will find your associations with these people, whether on a personal or a professional basis, far more satisfying if you understand something about their work.

Deliberately omitted from these pages are discussions of average salaries, typical starting wage, lifelong income, and other money matters. Such information becomes obsolete with the monthly changes in the economy. It differs widely with qualifications and from business to business and job to job. In addition, a shortage or an abundance of personnel can occur in a given industry within less time than it takes a book such as this to go to press or be revised. The answers to these questions should come from people in the business. It's also important to keep in mind that skills, training, and career opportunities overlap. For instance, the beginning illustrator will have many of the same hurdles to cross as a beginning editorial cartoonist. The television producer in commercial broadcasting will need many of the same skills as the television producer for a large industrial firm. Keep all of these things in perspective as you learn about careers in mass media.

breaking into broadcasting

When people think of careers in broadcasting, all too often they envision the local television anchorperson on the 6:00 p.m. evening news sitting before the cameras, relating the events of the day and switching back and forth between a sports announcer and a weather girl, all the while spicing the news with correspondent reports from afar. These superficially glamorous impressions have seduced many students into a celebrity syndrome; if they don't make it to the evening news in a major market, they consider themselves a failure. If the experience makes them try another field of broadcasting, perhaps it is a blessing. Because there is more to broadcasting than being an announcer or a camera operator, and much more than the evening news.

The Sales Force

There are approximately 8,000 radio stations in the United States and about one-tenth as many television stations. Some stations don't employ any news personnel; some automated stations employ neither announcers nor disc jockeys. But virtually all commercial stations employ sales personnel. Commonly called "account executives," these people customarily receive the highest salaries outside of management, and rightly so, because on their shoulders rests the responsibility of keeping the station in business, i.e., on the air. Interestingly enough, few college graduates think of broadcasting in terms of a career in sales. Most are oriented toward on-air positions for which college courses that lean toward the creative side seem to prepare them. This is not to suggest that creative training is not important for sales. On the contrary, it would be difficult to communicate how a new product will be displayed in a commercial of special effects, dissolves, and sound transitions without knowing a little about television production and continuity.

What kind of career can the broadcast account executive anticipate? Like free-lance writers and illustrators, the sales executive must be self-disciplined. He or she must be able to work all day without constant supervision and must be familiar with every aspect of a station's function, from ratings to reverb. Perseverance is another key quality of such personnel. The prospective client who says "no," the business executive who doesn't have time to see you—you can allow none of these experiences to discourage you. Keeping a positive attitude, feeling an exciting challenge about meeting people, and being prepared to compete fiercely are qualities that spell success in sales. It is not surprising, either, that some of the most successful account executives are women. Some industry professionals predict that by 1985, women will be responsible for more than half of the broadcast sales compiled by local radio and television stations in the United States. Some of the reasons given for this forecasted accomplishment include the ability of women to listen attentively and their ability to talk with prospective clients, the majority of whom are men.

For a number of reasons, account executives frequently move into station management. They have constantly kept abreast of all facets of the station's operation; they've had to. Having spent time continually talking to the business community, they are also keenly aware of how changes in programming can affect attitudes toward the station. They are able to interpret broadcast ratings and understand promotion and public relations. Since they are continually dealing with all sorts of people, they usually display an ability to handle subordinate employees. All of these qualities add up to management capabilities.

Broadcast Management and Ownership

For those who do reach management, the rewards are substantial. Although it takes some experience and proven leadership qualities to reach management in major markets, starts by young, sharp people a few years out of college are not impossible. Small market stations are an excellent springboard to larger responsibilities. And although there are only a limited number of broadcasting stations, talent for management is in constant demand even at the network level. Few successful small or medium market station managers have not had offers for positions with more pay and greater responsibility. Some seize these opportunities. Others stay in smaller markets with profit-sharing plans or part ownership.

Lin Bolen, former NBC Vice President of Daytime Programming, now owns her own production firm of Lin Bolen Productions. Management level positions for women are becoming more frequent for those who are qualified.

For those who do venture into ownership, there is the satisfaction of being at the helm and of reaping the rewards of one's own efforts. The successful owner can watch the station appreciate in value as he or she increases its billings. Some people combine ownership with management; others hire managers to oversee their properties. Still others have developed major broadcasting chains. These chains are not always the metropolitan giants with the familiar call letters. Some are small stations in limited markets where the amount of annual billings may not be as great, but reduced labor costs add up to a sizeable profit margin. Management carries with it the satisfaction of making the decisions and guiding the station in a coordinated effort toward an established goal.

Television Journalism

Most of the glamour, and a lot of the money, is concentrated at this end of the broadcast spectrum. Thus, career opportunities are restricted to the talented few who can make news judgments, write well, speak distinctly, coordinate a pictorial with a written statement, and condense a tremendous amount of information into a relatively short time—minutes and even seconds. In major market television, it sometimes means having an attractive face. Although there are many pro and con arguments about why television journalism needs this "good looking" approach to the news, few stations have dropped this consideration. Some people who have achieved long-standing respect as professional reporters manage to confront the camera with bald heads and ruffled curls. They are the exception rather than the rule. For those who do have experience and reach network heights, the salaries are staggering. Former NBC *Today* host Barbara Walters moved to the ABC evening news for a reported five-year contract worth $5 million.

Behind the scenes, however, there are also writers, directors, producers, camera operators, and support news personnel whose basic training is in journalism. Many of the anchorpersons employed at small or medium market television stations have reporting responsibilities, and jobs in these areas are not only rewarding but provide an excellent learning situation. With the advent of electronic news gathering (ENG), the ability to work under pressure and constant deadlines is also an important prerequisite. The evening news deadline which brought the reporters and film crews back to the television station by mid-afternoon is slowly becoming a thing of the past. With the ability of television news to go on the air from anywhere at any time, rapid judgment and snap decisions are a common occurrence.

Radio Journalism

Radio news reporting demands many of the same qualities as television journalism. In radio, there is literally a deadline every minute. A news story can be aired in the amount of time it takes to dial a telephone or pick up the microphone of a two-way radio. The ability to write clearly, speak clearly, and make responsible and quick news judgments are requirements for success in this medium as well. And simple mathematics quickly shows that there are far more opportunities to break into radio news than into television news. The key is to understand the medium. Professional radio news does not consist merely in gathering, writing, and airing news copy. The tape recorder has become the radio reporter's typewriter. Skillful interweaving of audio actualities with narration of the news results in a truly professional newscast, which can mean the difference between simply landing a job and keeping it. This type of talent can also mean the difference between remaining stationary or jumping to a larger market with more responsibilities. Careers in radio journalism abound, and surprisingly enough, the market is still uncrowded for those who are talented and willing to start in smaller markets.

Broadcast journalism is another inroad to management. Many a successful news director has been given the opportunity to assume management responsibilities, coordinating his or her authority over other operations of the station. In some larger stations, the head of the news department is a top-level executive, compensated as well as any general manager. Some news directors or managers actually have more subordinates than other management personnel.

The Radio Disc Jockey

Most people have at sometime in their lives entertained the thought of becoming a radio disc jockey—the personality who plays the records, chats with the audience, says the one-liners that seem to fall effortlessly onto the airwaves, and has the ability to quit talking at just the right moment to give way to music, a peppy jingle, or a commercial. Those thoughts of stardom have become reality for some. In major markets, disc jockeys command huge audiences and are just as well known and have just as loyal a following as the biggest television or Hollywood stars. Names like Larry Lujack, Dick Biondi, Murry the K, Clark Weber, and Fred Winston are household words in the cities they serve.

For those major market stars, the salaries are big. For those in smaller towns, it can be minimum wage. In between are shattered dreams and a succession of jobs. If you have decided on a career in

Larry Lujack, nationally famous disc jockey. Careers as disc jockeys range from minimum wage positions in small markets to slots in major cities which pay big money for stars like Lujack.

this field, be prepared to start at the very bottom and expect tough competition if you want to advance beyond the Elmsvilles or Watertowns. It will take years, unless you have extraordinary talent, to develop the skill necessary to command an audience in metropolitan area markets. Think for a moment about competing with as many as thirty other disc jockeys for a share of the listening audience's attention!

It is easy to see why many disc jockeys accept other jobs in broadcasting or out of the business altogether. Those who are moderately successful and have the ability to understand the complete gamut of radio programming find rewarding careers as program directors where they supervise the overall programming of the station. More often than not, a day's work for this person will include an air shift as well as scheduling commercials and overseeing other on-air personnel.

Sports Announcing

If you're sports minded, have the ability to speak clearly, and understand a game inside and out, a career in sports announcing may be for you. Here again, the competition is stiff and it is necessary to start in smaller markets. Understandably, the station's popularity and, consequently, your success may be tied to the popularity of the home team. A city of sports fans eagerly following every game of a winning team will also listen to radio and watch television coverage of the team. A losing team, just as it hurts attendance at the stadium, will also affect ratings.

In recent years, women have been making big inroads as sports announcers. The more famous ones, such as Jane Chastaine or NBC's Claudia Pauley, have achieved network popularity. Women sports announcers have also become far more accepted on local radio and television stations. There have been a few obstacles as well as humorous moments in this transitional period for women sportscasters, but most athletes and audiences have now grown accustomed to women in this traditionally all-male field.

Engineering

For people with a bent toward electronics, careers as electronic broadcast technicians and engineers abound. Moreover, with the continued barrage of new technology affecting all types of media, this area of skilled technical work is constantly expanding. Every radio and television station must employ a qualified, FCC-licensed person who is responsible for both the maintenance and overall operation of the station's equipment. The broadcast technician fills the role. The same person in a supervisory role assumes the title, engineer or chief engineer. In addition, the engineer's regular duties include special frequency measurements and other required FCC equipment monitoring functions, as well as skills in computer technology where applicable. Besides the station's transmitting equipment, engineers are also charged with keeping such items as amplifiers, tape recorders, antenna systems, turntables, mobile radio equipment, and similar electronic hardware in operating condition. Operating condition means much more than just working order. For a highly trained engineer, it means keeping it tuned to perfection, much like a musician tunes a fine instrument. In television, the slightest audio distortion is a major problem, and the slightest interference in a radio station's sound must be remedied immediately. Subtle visual or aural disturbances can prompt thousands of listeners or viewers to change stations. Thus engineers are responsible to a much greater degree for quality broadcast programming than most people realize.

An engineer may also be an inventor of sorts. For example, every station has its own peculiar characteristics that may require a unique piece of equipment to handle a special broadcasting need. Here, the engineer must be able to understand the needs of the station and build, often from scratch, the special equipment to do the job. In other cases, he or she will have to understand, construct, and repair equipment from *schematic diagrams*—blue prints for electronic circuitry. Installation of equipment and understanding

The work of the broadcast engineer varies from monitoring equipment and making sure the station meets FCC regulations to the actual repair and construction of electronic equipment. (WAZY.)

the ways it will be used are also important particularly in constructing new stations or rewiring a broadcasting complex.

Qualifications for jobs as broadcast technicians and engineers almost always include obtaining a First Class Radiotelephone Operator's license, issued upon successful completion of their examination. People who have dabbled in amateur radio usually find such exams relatively easy. Other people obtain their "first," as it's called in the industry, by attending special technical schools which offer short courses lasting from six weeks to six months. But merely having the FCC First Class license does not mean that an engineer is qualified to repair and build equipment. These skills come from regular study in four-year or community colleges offering engineering courses. Both Associate and Bachelor's degrees are available. Others who have the ability and want advanced training may attend graduate schools. An ability to grasp mathematical principles and work formulas is essential. Enjoying working on electronic equipment is, obviously, a prerequisite.

Broadcasting is not the only industry which needs people skilled in electronics. Many of the nation's newspapers employ highly trained engineers to service their computer systems and other electronic hardware. Schools with educational television or radio facilities also have their own trained personnel, especially for maintenance purposes. Students inflict an unusual strain upon equipment because of the heavy use factor, and fast, reliable repairs are continually necessary to serve any educational broadcasting complex. People who enjoy meeting management and have a knowledge of electronics can find positions in sales. Every major electronic company hires new people in these fields to monitor electronic merchandise, sell new equipment, and fill the liaison function between industry's new products and the consumers' (here, broadcast stations') special needs. Cable and satellite communication are two other examples of career choices for engineers.

For those with skills in both music and electronics, there are jobs as recording engineers. When a new song is recorded, the recording engineer has the critical task of controlling as many as two dozen different audio channels, all designed to mix into a cohesive sculpture of audio artistry which eventually may yield a hit record. These highly paid positions require a talent found among only a very small percentage of the population, and job openings in these areas are much more limited than in broadcasting. Only recently have schools begun to develop flexible curricula to produce this type of trained and creative specialist.

Broadcasting in its entirety has many more careers than the few mentioned here. There are jobs in scheduling, or traffic, departments; larger stations employ promotion directors and have independent public information divisions; research departments are also becoming more common. If you are interested in a career in broadcasting, take the time to visit a major station and learn more about the total range of career opportunities.

so you want to be a newspaper reporter

The mock help-wanted ad is indicative of what many feel it takes to be a successful newspaper reporter.[1] Yet these criteria are not universal. Most feel there is no substitute for experience. Others feel that without a degree stressing journalism basics—reporting, writing, layout, and graphics design—there is no proper foundation upon which to build up experience. Still others feel those basics are not nearly so important as acquiring a liberal education in the arts, humanities, and social sciences. The basics, they feel, except for knowing how to write, can come later. In perspective, you would have little difficulty finding journalism legends from any of these backgrounds.

Training

Those things which *are* agreed upon are some of the qualities listed in our help-wanted ad, those requiring ". . . interest, versatility, and skill to reduce complex issues to lucid, simple English for demanding readers. . . ." The journalist must also work under deadlines and pressure and face both with equanimity. Your career as a newspaper journalist might start modestly as a general assignment reporter

> WANTED—Individual with innate curiosity, intelligence, college education (not merely degree), writing ability, typing proficiency. Must have capacity to dig for news and to write it accurately, fully and intelligibly even under deadline pressure. Must possess interest, versatility and skill to reduce complex issues to lucid simple English for demanding readers seeking not merely facts but comprehension in era of unparalleled complexity, perplexity, ferment, change.

who, after gaining some respect from the city desk, manages to land assignments which challenge your abilities, even if it's writing the obituary columns. The news of any newspaper is the lifeblood of the publication. Gathering and reporting the news demands teamwork from a trained, highly professional group of people who understand the complexities of society and can translate them into accurate, comprehensible information.

The different jobs a reporter can hold are as varied as the components of a typical newsroom. For instance, the general assignment reporter is just that—available for general assignments usually delegated by the city desk editor who oversees the reportorial functions of the newspaper. Special beat reporters are also assigned to cover the police beat, education, the courts, sports, and similar functions. Naturally, the larger a newspaper becomes, the more diversified its departments. The small town daily may find a single reporter handling every one of those beats and general assignments as well. Copy editors are responsible for checking the final copy before it is set in type and also for writing the headlines. The newspaper's managing editor shoulders final responsibility for coordinating all these functions, and, in some cases, acts as liaison between the reporting staff and the editor. The editor, along with other trained reporters and sometimes advisory boards, is responsible for the editorial content of the paper. The editor also makes the top management decisions. So wherever you want to hang a hat, a newspaper career is available with many opportunities for moving into new responsibilities.

Despite the differing opinions about how many "basic skills" a prospective newspaper reporter should acquire in college, some things are rather certain. A liberal arts background in a wide variety of areas is exceptionally helpful. It stands to reason that if you are going to review the performance of a symphony, then it's helpful to know something about music. Similarly, when you are reporting on the city council, knowing something about local government is essential. When you need to interpret complex data, a minimal knowledge of statistics will help you. In fact, sitting in front of a visual display terminal either typing a story, filing it, or recalling it for editing is much easier with a basic understanding of computer science. Understanding the qualities of effective interpersonal communication is a must for conducting interviews. Research methodology is also important and gaining considerable attention in journalism programs. The methods employed by social science researchers are now being applied with increasing frequency to the everyday practice of gathering and reporting the news.

Experience

Gaining experience while going to school can put you a jump ahead in the job competition. Just as working at a campus radio or television station can teach you about broadcast journalism, working at the campus newspaper can train you for newspaper journalism. Although there is no substitute for actual on-the-job experience, a responsible faculty adviser can contribute immeasurably to a student's career preparation. By this I mean a faculty adviser who is *deeply* involved in *every* issue—teaching, discussing stories, helping to edit, and advising students on matters of news judgment. Where this type of learning experience is provided, the benefit for students can be tremendous. One word of caution, however—lack of advisement can be just as big a liability as good advisement is an asset. Lack of advisement can also get the newspaper into libel suits. Thus, when necessary, you as student journalists should take the initiative to seek help with your stories and advice from trained professionals.

Although journalism schools are well attended and competition is tough, there continue to be numerous openings for newspaper reporters. More journalism graduates enter the field of newspaper reporting than most other media fields. There are two good reasons for this. First, more people are employed in newspaper reporting than in broadcast journalism. Second, the newspaper industry as a whole has done an excellent job of developing a good liaison with colleges and universities, more so than broadcasting, which in part is due to the relative "newness of the medium." If you are serious about a career as a reporter, begin now to plan your life accordingly. Learn all you can about the industry. Take courses which will teach you how to write and broaden your perspective for your future assignments. Work on your campus newspaper or volunteer your time doing odd jobs at your local newspaper. A final tip—take advantage of internships with newspapers whenever they're available.

newspapers: more than reporters

Although the reporter is the heart of a newspaper, there are other career opportunities that await those who have different interests. Sales is one. As in broadcasting, newspaper account executives are also some of the highest paid people on the newspaper staff. Again, these people must be self-starters, able to set up and follow their own schedules. Equally important, they must be familiar with all the functions of the newspaper and develop a special "sense" for the visual layouts used in advertising.

Advertisements are the bread and butter of any newspaper. For, although the consumer pays a price to purchase the newspaper, this revenue doesn't even begin to cover the costs of the average newspaper. Newspaper advertising expenditures far outweigh those for radio and television nationwide. In some major cities, it is not unusual for the gross annual profits of some newspapers to be greater than the total combined annual billing of *all* of the radio and television stations in the same market.

How does one break into newspaper advertising? Some people switch from the reporting side. Others enter the business via a sales background in some other field. One thing is certain: the advertising neophyte must immediately familiarize himself or herself with everything about the newspaper—how it functions, the community it serves, and the competing media. A knowledge of computer science and business is also becoming increasingly important, since many large newspapers are now converting their advertising departments to computer-based systems which actually design ads using a variety of type styles and layout possibilities. Knowledge of business is important because you'll be communicating with business people in either soliciting or designing their advertising messages. Knowing how these people perceive the advertising function of your medium is important, as is knowing where their advertising dollar fits into *their* profit and loss columns. It's knowledge like this that can spell success.

editorial cartooning

Nationally syndicated editorial cartoonists are some of the most recognizable people in journalism. Among the staff, they often command as much respect as a newspaper's editorial board. They can also say in one picture what pages of print would consume. Their skill is one of subtleties. They reflect on society in pictures. With little more than the shading around the character's eyes, they can rupture a political campaign, enrage a business leader, and cajole a readership into a bellyful of chuckles. Since the era of the Yellow Kid, they have steadily become more and more influential. Bill Mauldin, the Pulitzer Prize winning cartoonist for the Chicago *Sun-Times*, won national acclaim when he was 23 years old and started the comic strip "Willie and Joe." It was World War II humor at a time when it was desperately needed. Today, Mauldin has been joined by others whose distinctive styles are recognized by every reader of the editorial page.

Most major newspapers employ an editorial cartoonist. Getting started is tough; getting accepted is even tougher. It takes consistency and the ability to draw well. You need to be able to capture, although in the abstract, the distinct features of a person's face, and then mold that face like a sculptor molds clay into caricatures which communicate personality. You also need a keen awareness of the news and its interpretations. Illustrating these abstract issues is important, for a picture in itself is not enough. It must convey a dynamic presence to the reader.

The person who aspires to be a cartoonist must often combine that vocation with another to carry himself or herself through the lean years. You may find yourself working full time during the week and preparing your cartoons on the weekends. You may even find yourself in competition with the syndicated cartoonists to whom your newspaper subscribes. The key to success in this field is the ability to reflect upon the *local* scene, something the syndicated cartoonists can't do. The local election, the police firearms scandal, the school board's refusal to negotiate — these are issues that a proficient editorial cartoonist can capture and turn in to the city desk. As your material is used, your chances for acceptance grow. When this happens, you may find your cartoons becoming a regular feature on the editorial page.

photography: in the action

If you enjoy photography, there are openings for photojournalists at virtually every newspaper. Photographers are also needed for major magazines, and the opportunity to free-lance opens up still additional outlets for your work. Television stations, although many are converting to videotape, employ photographers to work with reporters in capturing both the sounds and the films of news stories. And although veteran film photographers would shudder to see videotape lumped with film, many skilled photographers have bridged the transition and can work with both.

Photographs usually highlight the major stories, and these are the ones a photographer is often assigned to cover. Yet there are other equally interesting assignments. Special feature stories may include complete photo layouts of everything from this year's fashions to scenes of the ski country and backwoods wilderness. But few photographers put their cameras away at the end of a working day, and those who don't, have captured some of the memorable scenes of international journalism.

THE XENIA DAILY GAZETTE

Commemorative Edition ★ *Thursday, April 3, 1975* ★ *48 Pages—Price 82*

Camera buff

snaps 'monster'

In addition to being public information director at Greene Memorial Hospital, Fred Stewart, Beavercreek, is a photography buff. That, he says, is what led him up to a second story stairwell to take a picture of the monster tornado that hit Xenia Wednesday afternoon.

"I was sitting in my basement office, which has a window," Stewart said. "I looked out and saw it getting dark and went up to the first story stairwell in the south wing.

"I had seen a couple of twisters in Oklahoma, but this didn't look like one," he said. "I saw a dark

cloud over Xenia but no funnel. But then I heard the noise, like a bunch of freight trains.

Stewart said he ran down to his office, got his camera, and went back up to the second story stairwell. Since his window faced east, he couldn't see downtown Xenia but what he saw was bad enough.

"It looked like it was going to come straight to the hospital," he said. "But then it veered off and hit Pinecrest Gardens. The air was filled with debris. I shot four frames before I headed back to the basement."

Stewart said he always thought tornadoes as having "pinpoint heads," but he said he thinks differently now. "It was just so big, I was astonished."

He said by the time he got downstairs and put his camera up, the disaster code had been sent through the hospital. He said they expected injuries, "but not like we got. I just thought maybe it hit Pinecrest. I didn't know about downtown.

The photo was made while the funnel was over the hard-hit Pinecrest Gardens housing development, southeast of the hospital.

One year ago today, Our Town became the focal point of attention from around the world...a devastating tornado, nearly a mile wide in scope and bulldozing its way for miles through our community, changed Xenia's destiny, perhaps, for all time...The terrible ordeal left 33 killed or dying, etched itself indelibly into the minds of all of

us who survived...The Daily Gazette, in commemorating that day now 12 months into the past, publishes this edition for posterity — giving opportunity to reappraise the experience by reading again that first week as reported by the staff of this newspaper...

It was an amateur photographer who snapped this front-page picture of the Xenia, Ohio, tornado.

If you are considering a career in photography, it's wise to begin practicing. Even amateur equipment can give you a feel for the composition of a good photograph. If you have the opportunity, enroll in courses in photography or photojournalism. Learn everything you can about equipment, film, developing, and technique. Talk to professional photographers; read magazines on photography as well as books.

Breaking into photography follows much the same pattern as entering other mass media professions. Plan to start at the smaller, obscure media outlets. Sometimes a small town can be the very source for an award-winning human interest picture. Speaking of awards, compete for them. Photography competition is part of the profession, and some contests are even open to amateurs. Entering them will give you a perspective on how your work stacks up with others, and a list of "first places" never hurt anyone's resumé. Take photographs for your campus newspaper. If you have the equipment, try shooting some film or videotape for your campus television station—there's always the chance that your picture will make a front-page story. When the tornado struck Xenia, Ohio, the front-page picture of the oncoming twister was shot by an amateur photographer. When NBC produced a documentary on the tornado, it was movie film shot by an amateur that aired over network television. Similarly, the major record of the assassination of President John Kennedy was film shot by an amateur photographer. Although major events such as these are not always the rule, a camera in the right place at the right time can give you many opportunities to have your work reach the public.

making it in magazines

When the mass circulation magazines *Look* and *Life* folded, some people thought it was clearly a bad omen for the magazine industry. Television had replaced the medium as a viable communicator to the masses, and there was little future for the unlucky soul who had placed his or her future in magazine publishing. After all, when an American publishing institution could fold, any publication could go under. Any publication *can* go under, but the assumption that the magazine industry is not in healthy straits is far from accurate. While *Look* and *Life* were folding, new specialty magazines were sprouting. Even the *Saturday Evening Post* reemerged to an audience of middle-aged Americans. With a beginning theme of nostalgia, Americana, and patriotism, the *Post* managed to find a readership and become, once again, a regular addition to the newsstands. And for the suburban resident with a half acre or so to tend, *Country Gentleman* appeared, but this time aiming for a new audience radically different from the grain-belt readers of years past. Before the first issue of the new *Country Gentleman* had run off the presses, subscriptions had passed the 100,000 mark.

Some facts and figures immediately paint the career picture in magazine publishing. For example, there are an estimated 28,000 specialized magazines in the United States, including internal and external corporate publications. The readership is estimated at about five billion. They supply information to everyone from atomic scientists to beauticians. There are jobs for writers, photographers, graphics design experts, illustrators, and marketing and advertising account executives, to name a few. Is the work interesting? Kathy Klassen, managing editor of *Holiday* enthusiastically says, "The job of magazine editing may be one of the neatest on earth. In terms of providing an outlet for creative expression, I can't imagine a more challenging position. There's always a need, a vital one, for new ideas, new material, exciting presentations. Vital because if you don't come up with innovative approaches, the competition will." She goes on to say that magazines are a multidimensional production. "The magazine itself is not just what you say, but how it's said, and how it is presented. It's a packaging job. Everything must hang together. Visual material, the type style, copy, position in the book, etc. It's a totally organized, synchronized design."

The Illustrator

The "visual material" Kathy Klassen is talking about is often the work of the magazine illustrator. Perhaps the most famous master of the craft was Norman Rockwell, who became famous through the *Saturday Evening Post*. Rockwell, however, was an exception to most of the rules. He had a style very much his own. Today, even without seeing his famous printed signature at the bottom of a painting, one glance identifies it as a Rockwell. Moreover, the *Post* was as much Rockwell as Rockwell was the *Post*. But for an illustrator to achieve and stay with an identifiable style is not necessarily the key to success or even the key to finding a paycheck. Rockwell's illustrations became serious art. Most illustrations do not, although there are many illustrators who are serious artists.

What does it take to be a successful illustrator? "An illustrator must remain flexible," says Lucian Lupinski, artist in residence at the new *Saturday Evening Post*. "You must please the temperament of the times. When you paint for a client, you must paint for him. I have worked for clients, and they have given me clippings and said,

Lucian Lupinski, artist in residence at the *Saturday Evening Post.*

'I'd like my stuff to look like this.' The client is always right. Some feel changing their style to suit a client is belittling. I don't." Lupinski, who also free-lances, has some advice for this realm of illustrating as well. He suggests, ". . . you must be versatile in several styles. And you should be able to adapt to a style you have not done." There are art directors who can come up with a clipping from some foreign publication and ask you to copy that style. Be prepared and be willing to try it. But above all, "An illustrator should study all styles, impressionistic, abstract, all of them. And also create some original styles. I've created drawings by adding sand or even sugar in my paint to get the right effect." Understanding the story you're illustrating is also important. Learn what visual images come from the script and then convey these onto canvas.

Although being an illustrator demands artistic talents, it also requires a knowledge of printing processes, since these will determine what the finished illustration looks like when it appears in print. "It is important to understand everything possible about the printing processes. Learn all you can," advises Lupinski. "Visit printing plants. Chat with printers about new processes. If you know the different processes then you can determine how to use your color and black and white art wisely. . . . Clients may see beautiful art, but they are mostly interested in the good quality in the final reproduction. Let's face it, that is what the public will see."

Many illustrators break into the business simply by arranging an interview at a magazine and showing samples of their work. Others become well-known illustrators on their own and enjoy the luxury of being asked to complete special jobs for clients. If you are thinking about a career as an illustrator, practice continually. Be persistent *and* be honest with yourself. Seek out the advice of teachers and professionals you feel are qualified to judge your talent. Then begin thinking about developing a *portfolio*—a file of your best work to show prospective employers. Don't be surprised if your first job is not as an illustrator. You may work at another job and continue to free-lance until you have the opportunity to join a magazine full-time or are successful enough to make a living as a free-lancer.

The Free-lance Writer

It takes self-discipline, but the freedom and rewards of being a free-lance writer are unique. The quality and versatility required of the free-lance illustrator are also a prerequisite for free-lance writing. There are different types of magazines, and each has a style somewhat its own. You'll write in one style for a hardware retail magazine and another for a magazine directed toward teenage girls, one for an economic review and still another for an outdoor hunting and fishing magazine. The key is to understand what the audience of each magazine wants to read, or what the editor thinks they want to read, and then write accordingly.

Overall, the most important thing is learning to write. Ability to change writing styles will prepare you to accept a variety of assignments. It is also important to do your homework. Kathy Klassen of *Holiday* advises, "Don't send 45-page articles when we can only use 2,000 words." With any magazine, you should "Review the back issues; this is especially important," says Klassen. If an article has already appeared in a recent issue, don't make the mistake of sending a similar piece to be considered for publication.

The opportunities for free-lancers in magazine publishing are growing, but talent is necessary. If you are good, you can usually find a publication and a niche that suits you. From there, you can move about within the field, garner new experiences to expand your horizons and, if the spark ignites you, move into management positions as well.

book publishing

There are doors that open onto the field of book publishing. The question usually raised is: How far into management realm do you want to travel? One of the first places to consider a book publishing career is in sales. Depending on the books your company sells and its means of distribution, most sales positions can lead to the corporate headquarters of a publishing company. From there, advancement is up to you. Book companies with different lines of books usually have different sales distribution systems. These run anywhere from door-to-door "peddling" to overseeing retail accounts.

The library or educational divisions of a publishing company also provide good field experiences. Here, you will call on teachers and professors who purchase textbooks for their classes. You may also visit public school libraries, where the librarian is responsible for purchasing most of the selections. You may also confer with textbook selection boards to discuss the adoption of certain texts by an entire city or school district. The professional exhibit division of the company will be another avenue for your sales endeavors. Attendance at professional conventions, major trade fairs, and similar gatherings is another must in order to keep in constant contact with potential customers.

From sales, you might decide to advance to the position of editor. Here, you would have the opportunity to actually develop a special line of books. Authors would become your clients instead of the public. By studying the qualifications and manuscripts of prospective authors, you would determine what to publish and then work with authors under contract to arrange reviews of their manuscripts and editorial assistance. You would also act as liaison between the authors and the sales force. There would be satisfactions, excitement, and a gamble in your work. On your shoulders would go the credit for developing a best seller, or the discredit of having made a boner of a decision.

Many other careers are available in the world of book publishing. Before a book appears on a bookstore shelf in its finished form, it has transcended many different phases. Copy editors check it for grammar and punctuation. Publicity people plan sales literature and promotional campaigns. These people work in conjunction with marketing and advertising people who continually monitor sales.

Within each of these divisions of any publishing company are career opportunities for any aspirant.

careers in advertising

Why choose a career in advertising? According to Walter Bagot, senior vice-president of agency operations of the Indianapolis-based ad agency of Garrison, Jasper, Rose & Company, it's "the challenge of different marketing problems practically every day of the week. We work across a great cross section of markets," he says. "One day we'll be dealing with problems facing a financial institution. The next day we'll be dealing with the home appliance field. The next day we might be talking about roller bearings. It is just that every day is a new opportunity, a new challenge. That's what excites me about it."

The Creative Environment

Being responsible for the creative and individual efforts of others is also part of a career in advertising. Beverly Green, president and owner of the Eugene, Oregon-based ad agency of Green/Associates Inc., says, "The basic responsibility is to provide a rich environment for people to work in so their talents can operate at the highest level. I like the excitement of the business when you see something very unique and very exciting produced, whether you've done it or not." The idea of the agency's work being a new experience is also a view held by Green. She feels, "A rule is to be broken the minute you find a better way of doing it. I try to encourage my people to believe that so they won't call upon a habit and keep reproducing the same hackneyed kind of copy and layout. An attitude of 'oh that worked last time, let's plug it in for the next client,' doesn't work. I want each client to get the essence of the creativity that we can give them to make their message unique, and that is half the battle."

The process of drawing out and bringing to fruit this uniqueness and creativity falls on the shoulders of many different persons. It involves people who are knowledgeable in different types of media and in creating different types of messages. There are, for instance, those who specialize in commercials for radio and television. Many agencies in larger markets have their own television recording equipment and produce the commercials right in the agency. Medium-sized or small agencies frequently use the facilities of local television stations or production houses. Regardless of

Ad agency owner and manager, Beverly Green.

the method, an agency must employ skilled people who can transform an idea into a composite product of sound, sight, and motion. The commercials airing on network television are almost always produced by advertising agencies, as are a great many of the local television commercials. Most creators of commercials have been associated with radio or television production in some way before joining the agency. Often they have attended college or university courses or have actually worked in radio, television, or an ad agency in a different capacity. If these innovators don't directly produce the commercials, then they are usually skilled at communicating their ideas to the broadcasting stations and production houses that do.

Print and graphic work is another agency function. Like a newspaper, an ad agency must employ persons skilled in preparing copy, writing creatively, and integrating individual ideas to convey a persuasive message via all the visual qualities of type and graphics design. What type style(s) to use, how to arrange the written material, how to use white space effectively—these are all important decisions which can determine the effectiveness of an ad and more importantly, what the client thinks of the ad, for this will determine whether the agency will retain the account.

Closely aligned to the work of copy and layout personnel is that of artists. The agency art director may be a skilled illustrator or have the knowledge to coordinate as well as locate free-lance artists to execute specific jobs for clients. Working closely with these free-lancers and often contributing his or her own work, the director coordinates this art work with house productions into the final ad. He may even have the final say in determining the ad's layout design. Keep in mind that most agencies permit flexibility in order to nurture creative talents among their personnel. Beverly Green notes, "You learn to give the areas of responsibility to those individuals who can best handle it, and it varies from year to year with an agency."

Marketing and Sales

Careers in the marketing and sales division of the agency involve everything from interviewing customers about brand preferences to checking sales figures on advertised products. These people provide the reliability of hard facts, the mathematical probabilities, the dollars and cents on what is effective and what isn't. They are usually skilled in different techniques of market research, such as statistics, research design, and data collection. Interpreting data from other sources is also part and parcel of the job. Broadcast rating services, newspaper readership surveys, and studies on magazine circulation are as much a part of their daily lives as morning coffee.

Media buyers are responsible for purchasing the time and space upon which or in which clients' advertising will appear. These people are astutely aware of the different trends in local markets, such as changes in radio and television ratings, rate schedules, and personnel. They also keep in touch with the latest information from *Standard Rate and Data,* a compilation of various media rate schedules and circulation costs. In this age of computers, they are able to understand computer programming concepts and can analyze various data spewn from these machines.

The task of the account service department of any agency is to refer a steady stream of clients to the agency. As with any sales force, this team must be acquainted with all aspects of the agency's business. They must be marketing people, artists, production wizards, and account executives all wrapped into one. They must be able to communicate to a client, often in competition with account executives from other ad agencies, the unique services their agency can offer.

What makes for a successful career in advertising? The answer can be best expressed by characterizing the kind of a person who probably would *not* fit into an advertising agency. Walter Bagot sums it up succinctly: "For someone who wants a very stable, ordered kind of an environment, I wouldn't think he would want to consider advertising agencies. Because the stability, all the fringe benefits, all the pension plans that permit you to retire at 62 and live happily ever after, aren't too awfully common in advertising. Someone who doesn't enjoy conflict and confrontation in the best sense of these words, the exciting sense of these words, might not want to be involved in the advertising business either."

public relations

In the past half century, there have been many changes in the relationships of individuals and institutions to society. Fifty years ago, a major corporation could do almost anything it pleased to operate its business and make a profit. Yet it often operated to the detriment of the community it served and the people it employed. Today, that attitude would plunge a company into hot water with the general public, the city council, the federal or state government, etc. To achieve this liaison with society institutions and individuals employ public relations people. The corporation that funds a city park, the fast-food chain that sponsors a charity fund-raising drive, the university that offers the services of its professors in a volunteer consulting program for its community, the political figure who must maintain good relations with his or her constituency, and the news media which must communicate *with* the public in order to communicate *to* it, all must employ people who understand and practice the public relations function.

The definition of public relations is somewhat nebulous since it involves so many varied functions, depending upon the particular public relations campaign or institution involved. Back in 1948, Denny Griswold, editor of *PR News*, defined it by saying:

> Public relations is the management function which evaluates public attitudes, identifies the policies and procedures of an individual or organization with the public interest, and plans and executes a program of action to earn public understanding and acceptance.

Today, that definition encompasses a diversity of job titles. For instance, instead of merely calling people "public relations personnel," the terms "director of public information," "public affairs officer," "coordinator of university relations," and similar titles deck office doors.

The scope of public relations has also widened. The social awareness of the consumer, the overt protests that activists can command, the major needs of media doing in-depth features on important issues are all concerns of any public relations firm. Its functions are definitely not limited to seminars for community leaders and executive workshops.

The realm of careers in these fields are many, and the number of employees considerable. For instance, public information officers operate in virtually every branch and at all levels of government. At the federal level, such bureaus as agriculture, public health, the military, law enforcement, and Congress all employ directors of public information with sizeable staffs. Virtually every educational institution and every major corporation employ people in similar functions. Many corporations consider public relations so important that they create a separate division under the direction of a vice-president. Charitable and religious organizations must also involve themselves in public relations, as must hospitals. In some cases, these organizations have complete media divisions. These divisions are responsible for producing syndicated radio and television programs, producing documentaries, and even publishing books.

This leads us to the fact that a career in public relations requires many different media skills. Skills in news writing and editing, for example, are necessary in preparing press releases. To produce radio and television programs one needs a knowledge of the creative processes in these media. Most importantly the public relations team should conduct careful surveys of public opinion to understand the attitudes of its public. A fundamental knowledge of all mass communication systems, usually obtained by majoring in this subject area at the university, will be a tremendous asset when planning a public relations campaign. If you have an eye on corporate public relations, a working knowledge of business and economics is equally important, as is a thorough background in science and technology if your goal is to work in such specialized areas as agriculture or the health fields. Wherever you choose to apply your public relations skills you will need to understand your client's objectives and how best to complete the task facing you.

the other road to a hit record: careers in the recording industry

Let's assume that when you ventured down the road to Nashville in Chapter 9, you were one of the casualties instead of one of the successes. Yet the lure and excitement of the industry still cajoled you into searching out a career in the recording industry.

What is the recording industry like and who are the people who control it? The recording industry has been one of the least publicized areas of the vast communications industry. There are a number of reasons for this. One is that the industry has been founded on the savvy of entrepreneurs. These people didn't necessarily go to college to prepare themselves for a specific career; rather, they ended up in the business because they happened to like music, may have puttered around with a small rock group, or hung out at the local nightspots singing country-western music. Gradually, they met people in the industry and finally managed to corral a job. Other roads to the top include branching out from the performance sector into management, or working up through the ranks of the professionals, learning and fulfilling the tasks of each step along the way. As the business has become increasingly complex, however, more and more positions are being filled by trained specialists rather than the self-made entrepreneurs of the past.

The industry itself has started a concerted liaison program with colleges and universities, mostly through the efforts of the National Academy of Recording Arts and Sciences (NARAS) in Nashville. Through NARAS encouragement, curricula of study in the com-

Careers in the recording industry can involve creative hours spent in facilities like this. (Photo: Yael Brandeis, courtesy Le Studio.)

mercial music business have been developed at many colleges in the United States. Even at those colleges having no contact with NARAS, there is an abundance of career-specific courses. In addition to general music, courses in broadcasting, mass communication law, business and economics, and several other areas of study can prove helpful on your rough road to the top. As mentioned earlier, the industry needs recording engineers as well as people to serve in its distribution, promotion, and sales capacities.

What does it take to get in the door, and where are the opportunities? Henry Romersa, formerly the executive director of NARAS, cautions that a college degree is not a guarantee for success. According to Romersa, the person who wants to get started must "hang around where the action is; in other words, the recording studios and the publishing houses. He then gets his foot in the door, and from that point on, advances. That is what the industry understands. He would make a mistake waving his bachelor's degree around in people's faces. He would make a mistake going in telling everyone how great he is. But if he is smart, he would take his knowledge and go on that personal basis and get to know the people in the business."

As to where the opportunities lie, Romersa predicts, "that in the Southeast where American music basically started, with jazz, dixieland, and rock, there is going to be more opportunity for young people than in some of the other recording studios in the United States. And I would suggest that if anyone were interested in a career in the commercial music business, stay in the Southeast and try to get as close to the industry as possible. I think they would have a better chance there than they would practically anywhere else."

Although the recording industry is the crossroads of NARAS-type programs, the student should be aware of openings in allied fields. It takes astute business minds who understand music to direct the day-to-day operations of symphony orchestras, of university performing-arts centers, and of city arts complexes. Careers in the general realm of arts management are open to people who can combine their artistic awareness with an understanding of management principles. The advice for venturing on to all these "other" roads to a hit record is familiar by now—talent and perseverance.

the rewards of teaching

Public schools, at levels from kindergarten through college, are becoming more and more aware of the mass media as a major social force in our society. Even elementary school students are experimenting with videotape recorders, and the subject of network news is just as apt to come up in these classrooms as in a college seminar. In many elementary and secondary schools, courses about mass media have been added to the curricula. In high school print journalism classes the school newspaper frequently serves as a vehicle for both curricular and extracurricular activities, and where facilities are at hand, courses in radio and television production have also made their mark. Courses in mass media at the college level are, of course, growing at a record pace. All of these require trained instructional personnel.

If you have a desire to teach, you will be faced with a number of decisions. At what level do you want to teach—elementary, secondary, college, or even junior college or technical? Where do you want to teach? Is the inner-city or the rural area your choice? And most importantly, what do you want to teach? Do you want to instruct in the area of radio and television, or do you want to teach classes in news writing and supervise the student newspaper? Carefully examine all of these alternatives. A good starting point is to visit some of the larger schools in your area and find out what courses in mass media-related areas are being offered and which ones appeal to you. Talk with the education department in your school about requirements. Usually, courses in mass media can be integrated with courses in education to apply toward both graduation *and* certification.

Many states now require commercial media experience before granting certification to teach at the secondary school level. This means that if you want to teach radio and television in these states, you will have to work full-time in commercial broadcasting prior to certification. The length of this commercial media experience varies, but one year is normally the minimum.

There are many rewards to the teaching profession. The unique excitement of watching students learn and grasp new material, become aware of important concepts, and develop self-confidence and creative skills is unmatched in any other profession. There is also the fun of working around and with young people. One is constantly immersed in a renewed spirit of fresh ideas and challenges. The mental stimulation, the different personalities, and the satisfaction are all part of what makes teaching especially gratifying. Teaching about mass media is somewhat different from teaching other subjects. Mass media is contemporary. It's *now,* and the subject matter is always current and as futuristic as the instructor wants it to be. Teachers do put in considerable class preparation time, and added to such tasks as correcting papers and tests are such supplemental duties as preparing grants, serving on committees, advising student groups, organizing conferences, participating in admissions activities, and other functions placed upon them by their respective schools. But the key, as with any profession, is that if you enjoy what you're doing, you'll relish these challenges.

instructional television in education and business

Our discussion would not be complete without a brief mention of career opportunities in both education and business for people trained in instructional television. In education, for example, major instructional television (and sometimes radio) complexes are a standard part of all levels of the curriculum. Elementary schools have instructional media centers, and many metropolitan area high schools have complexes on a par with commercial broadcasting facilities. Teachers are more and more apt to supplement their lectures with television programs taped directly from the air or with specially produced television modules—short programs which teach a specific lesson. School districts across the country are employing people to work with these teachers, handle the equipment, and evaluate the effectiveness of instructional programs. Usually a master's degree is required, but the pay and responsibility are commensurate. There is also the opportunity of advancement to the position of media coordinator for an entire school district.

Business has also realized the value of instructional television. It is not unusual for a company to have a fully equipped television production facility capable of producing news features for the public relations division as well as training programs to inform workers in affiliates about new corporate developments or to teach them new skills. The application of television to business has proceeded alongside its use in governmental and educational institutions. There are many new opportunities for people qualified to produce training and public information programs. Business and education are two more examples of the many facets of our society which are reacting to that phenomenon called mass media.

summary

The skills for many of the careers discussed in this chapter and the techniques for breaking into these fields often interrelate. For instance, a budding illustrator will have many of the same hurdles to cross as the budding editorial cartoonist.

Careers in mass media are extremely diverse. As a case in point, broadcasting offers opportunities in sales, management and ownership, journalism, announcing, engineering, and others. Another field that draws many to its ranks is newspaper reporting. Two indispensable qualities for success in this endeavor are being able to write clearly and having an unquenchable curiosity. Along with the various beats open to journalists at a typical newspaper, there are also positions for copy editors, account executives, managing editors, editors, cartoonists, and photographers. Magazines are an outlet for creative writing of all sorts, much of which comes from freelancers. Many magazines also employ illustrators, many of whom, again, choose to free-lance. Book publishing offers careers in the areas of sales, editing promotion, marketing, and advertising, among others.

A career in advertising is synonymous with creative teamwork. Artists, writers, broadcast production personnel, and people skilled in marketing and sales functions all integrate their talents into a total effort for clients. Closely related to advertising is public relations, which operates to provide a public understanding and awareness of an institution or individual. Although careers in the recording industry are limited, new curricula are being developed to prepare students for more highly specialized jobs. If you have a desire to work with students and share in the enrichment of helping them to mature and learn, then a career in teaching is a possibility. With the increase in new technology, instructional television has become commonplace throughout the worlds of education and business, and career opportunities abound in these fields as well.

opportunities for further learning

GELFAND, LOUIS I., and HARRY E. HEATH, JR., *Modern Sportswriting.* Ames, Iowa: The Iowa State University Press, 1969.

KENDRICK, ALEXANDER, *Prime Time: The Life of Edward R. Murrow.* Boston, Mass.: Little, Brown and Company, 1969.

McKEE, JOHN DeWITT, *William Allen White: Maverick on Main Street.* Westport, Conn.: Greenwood Press, 1975.

SANDERS, MARION K., *Dorothy Thompson: A Legend in Her Time.* Boston, Mass.: Houghton Mifflin Company, 1973.

TYRRELL, ROBERT, *The Work of the Television Journalist.* New York: Hastings House Publishers, 1972.

UNWIN, PHILIP, *Book Publishing as a Career.* London: H. Hamilton, 1965.

notes

chapter two

[1] Eric W. Allen, "International Origins of the Newspapers: The Establishment of Periodicity in Print," *Journalism Quarterly*, 7 (December, 1930), 309–19.

[2] The serious student will want to consult Edwin Emery's text *The Press and America* (Englewood Cliffs, N.J.: Prentice-Hall, Inc., 1972).

[3] William M. Glenn, *The Sigma Delta Chi Story* (Coral Gables, Fla.: The Glade House, 1949).

[4] Jon G. Udell, *Economic Trends in the Daily Newspaper Business, 1946 to 1970* (Madison, Wisconsin: Bureau of Business Research and Service, 1970), p. 9.

[5] Frank Luther Mott, *A History of American Magazines 1865–1885*, Vol. 3 (Cambridge, Mass.: Harvard University Press, 1938), p. 5.

[6] Theodore Peterson, *Magazines in the Twentieth Century* (Urbana, Ill.: University of Illinois Press, 1964), p. 23.

[7] Ibid., p. 23.

chapter three

[1] Mark Hall, *Broadcast Journalism* (New York: Hastings House, 1971), p. 11.

[2] John Fink, *WGN: A Pictorial History* (Chicago, Ill.: WGN, Inc., 1961), p. 11.

[3] Ibid.

[4] Wilbur Schramm, "Reading and Listening Patterns of American University Students," *Journalism Quarterly,* 22 (March, 1945), 23-33.

[5] *Welcome South Brother* (Atlanta: WSB Radio, 1974), p. 17.

[6] *Cox Looks at the Future* (Atlanta, Ga.: Cox Broadcasting Corporation, 1975).

[7] "Annual Report of Research in Progress," Institute for Communication Research, Stanford University, 1972–73.

[8] Jan Leyda, *KINO: A History of the Russian and Soviet Film* (London: George Allen and Unwin Ltd., 1960), pp. 17–18.

[9] Lewis Jacobs, *The Rise of the American Film: A Critical History* (New York: Harcourt, Brace and Co., 1939), pp. 3–4.

[10] Donald Bogle, *Toms, Coons, Mulattoes, Mammies, and Bucks* (New York: The Viking Press, 1973), p. 10.

[11] Vernon Jarratt, *The Italian Cinema* (New York: The Macmillan Co., 1951), p. 17.

[12] See I. Nemeskaurty, *Word and Image,* trans. Zsuzsanna Horn (Budapest: Corvina Press, 1968).

[13] Joseph L. Anderson and Donald Richie, *The Japanese Film: Art and History* (Tokyo: Charles E. Tuttle Co., 1965), pp. 36–37.

[14] Gerald Mast, *A Short History of the Movies* (Indianapolis, Ind.: The Bobbs-Merrill Company, Inc., 1971), pp. 101–2.

chapter four

[1] See F. L. Shick, *The Paper Bound Book in America* (New York: R. R. Bowker Company, 1958).

[2] Richard Maisel, "The Decline of Mass Media," *Public Opinion Quarterly,* 37 (Summer, 1973), 159–70.

chapter six

[1] *CBS* v. *U. S.,* 316 U. S. 407 (1942); *NBC* v. *U. S.,* 316 U. S. 447 (1942).

[2] The lighter moments in the history of CBS are told in a special issue of the company newsletter *Columbine,* 2 (April/May, 1974).

[3] *Columbine,* 6.

[4] Excerpt from "Preface," p. vii, in *Public Television: A Program for Action,* The Report and Recommendations of the Carnegie Commission on Educational Television (New York: Harper & Row, 1967).

[5] Ibid.

[6] Ibid., i.

chapter nine

[1] Walter L. Thomas, *A Manual for the Differential-Value Profile* (Ann Arbor: Educational Service Company, 1966), p. 6.

[2] Thomas uses the term "power" instead of "prestige."

[3] 8 FCC 2d 381; 9 FCC 2d 921.

[4] *Banzhof* v. *FCC,* 405 F 2d 1082, D. C. Cir. 1968, cert. den. 396 U. S. 842.

[5] Loevinger, Lee, "The Politics of Advertising," an address before the Radio and Television Society, New York City, January 4, 1973. Unabridged Edition, published by the Television Information Office, New York City. February, 1973.

[6] James T. Lull, "Counter Advertising: Persuasability of the Anti-Bayer TV Spot," *Journal of Broadcasting,* 18 (Summer 1974), 353–60.

chapter eleven

[1] Early work on reaction to crisis was pioneered in 1954 by Enrico L. Quarantelli. More recent studies have included: A. H. Barton, "Social Organizations Under Stress," National Academy of Sciences–National Research Council Disaster Study 17. Washington D.C.: National Academy of Sciences, 1963; F. L. Barton et al., "The Social and Psychological Consequences of a Natural Disaster: A Longitudinal Study of Hurricane Audrey," National Academy of Sciences–National Research Council Disaster Study 18. Washington, D.C.: National Academy of Sciences, 1963; Dennis S. Milet and E. M. Beck, "Communication and Crisis: Explaining Evacuation Symbolically," *Communication Research*, 2 (January 1975), 24–49.

[2] *A Broadcaster's Guide to Planning for A National Disaster* (Washington, D.C.: National Association of Broadcasters, 1975), p. 2.

chapter twelve

[1] Herbert Zettl, *Television Production Handbook* (Belmont, California: Wadsworth Publishing Company Inc., 1968), p. 408.

[2] Cornell Chulay served as a student intern at the *Mary Tyler Moore Show* in 1974 as part of the internship program directed by the author. A student at UCLA, she contributed much of the information included in this section "Behind the Scenes of a Major Television Production."

[3] See also James K. Carroll and John R. Bittner, "A Developmental Model for Testing the Validity of Instructional Television Programming," *International Journal of Instructional Media*, 2 (1975), 211–25.

chapter thirteen

[1] See Elihu Katz and Paul Lazarsfeld, *Personal Influence: The Part Played by People in the Flow of Mass Communications* (Glencoe, Ill.: Free Press, 1955). See also Wilbur Schramm and Donald Roberts, Eds., *The Process and effects of Mass Communication*, Rev. Ed. Urbana, Ill.: University of Illinois Press, 1971.

[2] Paul Lazarsfeld, Bernard Berelson, and H. Gaudet, *The People's Choice* (New York: Columbia University Press, 1948).

[3] Ibid.

[4] Carolyn Sherif, Muzafer Sherif, and Roger E. Nebergall, *Attitude and Attitude Change: The Social Judgment–Involvement Approach*. Philadelphia, Pa.: W. B. Saunders Company, 1966.

[5] Robert Monaghan, Joseph Plummer, David Rarick, and D. Williams, "Predicting Viewer Preference for New TV Program Concepts," *Journal of Broadcasting*, 18 (Spring, 1974), 131–42. R. R. Monaghan, "Television Preference and Viewing Behavior," unpublished Ph.D. dissertation, Michigan State University, 1964.

[6] Elizabeth Yang and Joseph Plummer, "Mass Media Structure, Research and Creativity," program presented at the annual meeting of the Speech Communication Association, Chicago, 1974.

[7] Ibid.

[8] For a review of research on the concept of selective perception, see David O. Sears and Jonathan L. Freedman, "Selective Exposure to Information: A Critical Review," in *The Process and Effects of Mass Communication*, Wilbur Schramm and Donald F. Roberts, Eds. (Urbana, Ill.: University of Illinois Press, 1971), pp. 207–34.

[9] Everett M. Rogers and F. Floyd Shoemaker, *Communication of Innovations: A Cross Cultural Approach*, 2nd Ed. (New York: Free Press, 1971).

[10] Carl I. Hovland, "Reconciling Conflicting Results Derived from Experimental and Survey Studies of Attitude Change," *The Process and Effects of Mass Communication*, Wilbur Schramm and Donald F. Roberts, Eds. (Urbana, Ill.: University of Illinois Press, 1971), pp. 493–515.

[11] Elihu Katz, "Mass Communications Research and the Study of Popular Culture," *Studies in Public Communication*, Vol. 2 (1959). As discussed in David Chaney, *Processes of Mass Communication* (London: The Macmillan Press Ltd., 1972), pp. 11–36.

[12] Louis M. Savary and J. Paul Carrico, Eds. *Contemporary Film and the New Generation* (New York: Association Press, 1971), pp. 15–19.

[13] From David Chaney, in reference to H. Herzog, "What Do We Really Know About Daytime Serial Listeners?" *Radio Research 1942–1943*, Eds. Paul F. Lazarsfeld and Frank Stanton (New York: Duell, Sloan and Pearce, 1944), pp. 3–33.

[14] Bernard C. Cohen, *The Press and Foreign Policy* (Princeton, N.J.: Princeton University Press, 1963). Also Maxwell McCombs and Donald Shaw, "The Agenda-Setting Function of Mass Media," *Public Opinion Quarterly*, 36 (1972), 176–187.

chapter fourteen

[1] Philip H. Dougherty, "Advertising: Reaching Blacks," *The New York Times*, March 24, 1974.

[2] Kevin A. Wall, "New Market: Among Blacks, the Haves Are Not Overtaking the Have-Nots," *Advertising Age*, February 11, 1974.

[3] Ibid.

[4] Ibid.

[5] "Television Commercial Recall in Spanish Surname Households," Spanish International Network, 1969.

[6] John R. Bittner and Gary T. Hunt, "National News Dissemination to the College Student Audience," *College Student Journal*, 1 (Feb.–March, 1972), 97–99.

[7] Craig Aronoff, "Old Age in Prime Time," *Journal of Communication*, 24 (Autumn 1974), 86–87.

[8] For a source of articles and references on the subject, consult the *Journal of Communication*, 24 (Autumn 1974).

[9] James A. Peterson, "Guide to TV Viewing," *Modern Maturity* (April–May 1974), 44–46.

[10] Data for "International Comparisons" are from *Nielsen Newscast*, 20 (Summer, 1971), 1–7 and 21 (Spring, 1972), 4–7.

[11] *Nielsen Newscast*, 21 (Spring, 1972), 7.

[12] *Nielsen Newscast*, 20 (Summer, 1971), 5.

chapter fifteen

[1] D. Green, "Dear Mr. Editor . . .," *The Quill*, 58 (July, 1970), 16–19.

[2] Ibid.

[3] C. H. Davis and G. Rarick, "Functions of Editorials and Letters to the Editor," *Journalism Quarterly*, 41 (Winter, 1964), 108–9.

chapter sixteen

[1] Lawrence W. Lichty and George A. Bailer, "Violence in Television News: A Case Study of Audience Response," *Central States Speech Journal*, 23 (Winter, 1972), 225–29.

[2] Ibid.

[3] Terms used by rating services are not always standardized. The serious student is encouraged to consult the National Association of Broadcasters' publication *Standard Definitions of Broadcast Research Terms.*

[4] As in the case of A. C. Nielsen Company.

[5] Peter D. Fox, "Television Ratings and Cultural Programs," *Industrial Management Review,* 5 (Fall, 1963), 37–43.

[6] *Television Ratings Revisited* (New York: Television Information Office, 1971).

[7] From "How a Lot of Programs Grow Up to Become a National Schedule," and "The SPC" in *The People's Business,* 1 (July 1974), pp. 21 and insert.

chapter seventeen

[1] Edmund Landau and John Scott Davenport, "Price Anomalies of the Mass Media," *Journalism Quarterly,* 36 (1959), 291–94.

[2] Jon G. Udell, "Future Newsprint Demand 1970–1980" (Madison, Wisc.: Bureau of Business Research and Service, 1971).

[3] Jon G. Udell, "The U. S. Economy and Newspaper Growth: 1963–1973 and the Future Outlook," American Newspaper Publishers Association, *Newsprint and Traffic Bulletin,* No. 31, October 24, 1974.

[4] Udell, "Future Newsprint Demand 1970–1980."

[5] Gerald L. Grotta, "Prosperous Newspaper Industry May Be Heading For Decline," *Journalism Quarterly,* 51 (Autumn, 1974), 498–502.

[6] Andrew Kershaw, "The Next Ordeal or The Biggest Problem of the Next Ten Years," Speech delivered to the annual meeting of the Association of National Advertisers, Hot Springs, Virginia, October, 1974.

[7] Stephen Traiman, "CB Boom Drops Auto Radio Audience," *Billboard* (May 15, 1976), 1 and 47.

chapter eighteen

[1] Sydney Head, *Broadcasting in America* (New York: Houghton Mifflin Co., 1976), pp. 113–14.

[2] *In the matter of the Mayflower Broadcasting Corporation and the Yankee Network, Inc.* (WAAB), 8 FCC 333, 338, January 16, 1941.

[3] *In the matter of Editorializing by Broadcast Licensees,* 13 FCC 1246, June 1, 1949.

[4] See Frederick W. Ford and Lee G. Lovett, "Fairness Doctrine: 1974," *Broadcast Management/Engineering,* 10 (October, 1974), 16–19.

[5] A good reference for specific laws and regulations concerning broadcasting is Frank J. Kahn, *Documents of American Broadcasting,* 2nd Ed. (Englewood Cliffs, N.J.: Prentice-Hall, Inc., 1973).

[6] Neil Hickey, "Does America Want Family-Viewing Time?" *TV Guide* 23 (December 6–12, 1975), 4–8.

[7] Frederick W. Ford and Lee G. Lovett, "State Regulation of Cable Television, Part 1: Current Statutes," *Broadcast Management/Engineering,* 10 (June, 1974), 18, 21, 50.

[8] Ibid.

[9] Ibid.

[10] Paul L. Laskin and Abram Chayes, "A Brief History of the Issues," in *Control of the Direct Broadcast Satellite: Values in Conflict* (Palo Alto, Calif.: Aspen Institute Program on Communications and Society, 1974), pp. 3–14.

[11] Ibid.

[12] Ibid.

[13] *Joseph Burstyn, Inc.* vs. *Wilson,* 343 U. S. 495, 96 L. Ed. 1098, 72 S. Ct. 777 (1952).

chapter nineteen

[1] Fred S. Siebert, Theodore Peterson, Wilbur Schramm, *Four Theories of the Press* (Urbana, Ill.: University of Illinois Press, 1972), p. 7.

[2] Osmo A. Wiio, "System Models of Information, Communication, and Mass Communication: Revaluation of Some Basic Concepts of Communication," paper presented at the annual meeting of the International Communication Association, Montreal, 1973. See also, Osmo A. Wiio and Leif Aberg, "Open and Closed Mass Media Systems," paper presented at the annual meeting of the International Communication Association, Chicago, 1975, and Osmo A. Wiio, *Systems of Information, Communication, and Organization* (Helsinki: Helsinki Research Institute for Business Economics, 1975).

[3] Public Law No. 319, IC 1971, Sec. 1, 34-3-5-1, as amended and approved April 23, 1973.

[4] Senate Bill 206, Oregon Legislature Assembly, 1973. See also John R. Bittner, "Politics and Information Flow: The Oregon Shield Law," *Western Speech* 39 (Winter, 1975), 51–59.

[5] John B. Adams, *State Open Meetings Laws: An Overview* (Columbia, Missouri: Freedom of Information Foundation, 1974).

[6] Donald M. Gilmore and Jerome A. Barron, *Mass Communication Law: Cases and Comment* (St. Paul, Minn.: West Publishing Company, 1974), p. 453. A historical perspective on the cases and issues surrounding the issue of free press vs. fair trial is also found in Harold L. Nelson and Dwight L. Teeter, Jr., *Law of Mass Communication* (Mineola, New York: The Foundation Press, Inc., 1973), pp. 276–326.

[7] *Estes* vs. *State of Texas*, 381 U. S. 532, 14 L. Ed. 2d 543, 85 S. Ct. 1628 (1965).

[8] Gilmore and Barron, *Mass Communication Law*, p. 397. *Irvin* vs. *Dowd*, 366 U. S. 717, 6 L. Ed. 2d 751, 81 S. Ct. 1639 (1961).

[9] "Telltale 'Mark' Left Downstate," *The Indianapolis Star*, April 9, 1955, p. 2.

[10] Roger M. Grace, "The Courts v. the News Media: Is the Conflict Necessary," *Case and Comment*, 79 (March–April, 1974), 3–10.

[11] Stan Crock, "A Flurry of Gag Rules," *The Quill* 62 (March, 1974), 21. *United States* vs. *Dickinson*, 465 F. 2d 496 (5th Cir. 1972).

[12] Grace, "The Courts v. the News Media."

[13] Ibid.

[14] "York's Strange Silence," *Time*, November 18, 1974, 88–89.

chapter twenty one

[1] Jules Whitcover, "The Indiana Primary and the Indianapolis Newspapers—a Report in Detail," *Columbia Journalism Review* (Summer, 1968), 11–17.

[2] The quotation from Gideon Sjoberg was delivered at a conference on "Ethics and Communication" at the University of Texas at Austin, March 5, 1975, sponsored jointly by the University of Texas Center for Communication Research and the Shell Companies Foundation, Incorporated.

[3] Alfred G. Smith, "The Ethic of the Relay Men," in *Communication: Ethical and Moral Issues*, Ed. Lee Thayer (London: Gordon and Broach Science Publishers, London, 1973), pp. 313–24.

[4] Alice E. Courtney and Thomas W. Whipple, "Women in TV Commercials," *Journal of Communication*, 24 (Spring, 1974), 110–18.

[5] Nancy S. Tedesco, "Patterns in Prime Time," *Journal of Communication*, 24 (Spring 1974), 119–24.

[6] Cornell Chulay and Sara Francis, "The Image of the Female Child on Saturday Morning TV Commercials." Paper presented at the annual meeting of the International Communication Association, New Orleans, Louisiana, April, 1974.

[7] Cheris Kramer, "Stereotypes of Women's Speech: The Word from Cartoons." Paper presented at the annual meeting of the Speech Communication Association, Chicago, Illinois, December, 1974.

[8] For a general overview and insights into some of the background of the study, see Leo Bogart, "Warning: The Surgeon General Has Determined That TV Violence is Moderately Dangerous to Your Child's Mental Health," *Public Opinion Quarterly*, 36 (Winter, 1972–1973), 491–521.

[9] *Television and Growing Up: The Impact of Televised Violence.* Report to the Surgeon General, United States Public Health Service, from the Surgeon General's Scientific Advisory Committee on Television and Social Behavior (Washington: Government Printing Office, 1972).

[10] George Gerbner, "Violence in Television Drama; Trends in Symbolic Functions," in George A. Comstock and Eli A. Rubenstein, Eds., *Television and Social Behavior, Vol. 1, Media Content and Control* (Washington: Government Printing Office, 1972).

[11] "The 'Contagion' Issue," *Newsweek*, 86 (October 16, 1975), 77–78.

[12] "The Press Council Idea, A Worthy Cause or Waste of Time," *The Quill*, 61 (January, 1973), 20.

[13] Ibid.

[14] "News Council Backs Off," *The Quill*, 62 (March, 1974), 9, 11.

[15] "News Council Branching Out," *The Quill*, 64 (May, 1976), 10.

[16] Ibid.

chapter twenty two

[1] *Your Future in Daily Newspapers* (Washington, D.C.: American Newspaper Publishers Association Foundation, 1973), p. 11–12.

glossary of media terms

A.A.A.A. — American Association of Advertising Agencies.

Action line — a service of a newspaper or magazine which offers readers a forum to complain about some product, service, or company. The publication usually tries to help the complainant.

Advocacy advertising — stresses issues of public concern that usually arise as the result of by-products of illegal activities (i.e., crime as a result of drug abuse).

AEJ — Association for Education in Journalism.

Affiliate — a broadcasting station that is bound by a contract to associate with a particular broadcasting network or wire service.

AM — amplitude modulation.

Annual billings — money billed advertisers for commercials carried in a medium over a one-year period.

ANPA — American Newspaper Publishers Association.

Apogee — that point in a satellite's orbit farthest away from earth.

ASCAP — American Society of Composers, Authors, and Publishers.

Audio actuality — the recording of the "actual sounds" in the news for incorporation into radio newscasts.

Authoritarian — characterized by media which are either "private or public" and "are chiefly instruments for effecting government policy, though not necessarily government owned."

AWRT — American Women in Radio and Television.

Banks — or *buses*, groups of control switches on a master control console used to program various portions of an audio or video production.

BEA — Broadcast Education Association.

Billboard — (1) a wire service feed listing all the pre-recorded stories in the wire service's current audio file; (2) a major publication of the recording industry; (3) a slang term for outdoor advertising bulletin.

Blue box — slang term for interactive earth terminal used for direct broadcast satellite communication.

BMI — Broadcast Music Incorporated.

Booklet — a direct-mail piece which consists of a number of sheets of paper, is usually fastened with staples, and opens like a book.

Broadsides — a form of direct mail usually composed of single sheets of paper much larger than letters, folders, or leaflets. Broadsides are often folded in more than one direction and colorfully display their message.

Bulletin — (1) display boards used in outdoor advertising; (2) important news usually disseminated as an interruption in normal broadcast programming; (3) wire service (audio or video) feed to subscribers.

Buses — *see* banks.

Capital intensive — when maximum costs occur immediately after an investment.

CATV — community antenna television, or cable TV.

Clipping bureau — a business which peruses publications and cuts out all printed matter on a specific subject a client wants researched.

Coaxial cable — heavy cable consisting of an inner wire core surrounded by a layer of plastic, metal-webbed insulation, and a third layer of plastic.

Cold type — various typesetting processes not involving casting type from molten metal. The newest cold-type process is computer composition.

Compressed speech — via the use of special machines, the recorded voice is accelerated to compress a given number of words into a shorter time span than normal delivery would permit.

Contour — the geographic area covered by a broadcast station's signal.

Co-ops — also called *informal networks*, (1) broadcast news networks created by a group of radio or TV news personnel; (2) trade-out advertising agreements between advertisers and the individual advertising outlet.

Corrective advertising – advertising which rectifies, usually because of regulatory orders, false or misleading advertising.

Counter-advertising – advertising directed against a product or service.

CPB – Corporation for Public Broadcasting.

Cume – (or cumulative audience) the number of different persons or households which watch or listen to a given station or program during a certain time period.

Daytimers – radio stations required by the FCC to sign off at sunset.

Demographics – data concerning such things as age, sex, education level, income, and ethnic background.

Demo session – a preliminary recording session.

Diary – method of broadcast rating measurement in which viewers or listeners keep a record of the programs and stations they tune in at periodic intervals.

Directional antennas – a group of strategically placed broadcast antennas whose purpose is to transmit the signal in specific directions in order to achieve an irregular rather than a circular contour.

Directional stations – radio stations, primarily in the AM band, which utilize directional antennas to keep their signals from interfering with those of other stations.

Director – the person upon whose shoulders rests the creative responsibility for the entire production of a program.

Direct-wave propagation – radio wave pattern in which signals travel through direct line-of-sight transmission.

Dissolve – smoothly changing from an image produced by one television camera to an image produced by a second television camera, film, slide, or videotape.

Drop – that section of a cable which brings the signal from the trunk or subtrunk directly into a subscriber's home receiver.

Electromagnetic spectrum – an atmospheric yardstick with which to measure varying levels of electromagnetic energy, called frequency.

Electromagnetic waves – electrical impulses traveling through space at the speed of light. Used to transmit radio and television signals.

Electrostatic transmission – a system used to transmit wire service pictures. Subscribers receive glossy prints on dry paper ready for printing, thereby eliminating the need for the subscriber to develop the photo himself.

Embellishments – special cut-out designs which protrude beyond the basic rectangular shape of outdoor bulletins.

ERI — Electronic Response Indicator.

ETV — educational televison.

Feedback — reactions of a receiver to a message from a sender.

Floor manager — the person who communicates the commands of the director to the performers.

FM — frequency modulation.

Folders — a form of direct mail usually printed on rather heavy paper and with more extensive and expensive printing displays than leaflets.

Freebies — ranging from excursions to foreign countries to tickets to a church supper, these complimentary offerings are designed to entice journalists to cover a story.

Frequency — (1) broadcast rating term to indicate how often a viewer has tuned to a given station; (2) position on the electromagnetic spectrum.

Gatekeeper — any individual directly involved in the relay or transfer of information from one individual to another through the use of a mass medium.

Gatekeeper group — a group of gatekeepers among whom there is the opportunity for interaction to take place.

Gazetta — the Italian coin used as an admission price to hear a reader announce the day's news events.

Geostationary — or *synchronous,* an orbiting satellite that travels at the same speed in proportion to the earth's rotation, and thus appears to remain stationary over one point of the earth.

Head end — the human and hardware combination that is responsible for originating, controlling, and processing signals over the cable system.

Hertz — last name of Heinrich Rudolph Hertz commonly used as abbreviation for "cycles per second" in referring to electromagnetic frequencies.

Home terminal — receiving set for cable TV transmissions that can be either one-way or two-way.

Horizontal publication — a category of business publications aimed at a certain level of employee across several different industries.

Hot type — typesetting process using linotype machines to cast letters and sentences into type from molten metal.

Households using television (HUT) — a term used in broadcast ratings to describe every household using television.

House organ — a direct-mail piece in the form of a newsletter or company magazine that is sent to all members of a certain organization.

Hypoing — sometimes called *"hyping,"* heavily promoting something, usually to increase sales or ratings.

ICA — International Communication Association.

Image advertising — advertising designed to enhance a corporation's standing in the eyes of the consumer.

Impressions — the number of times a person is reached by an advertisement.

Industrial magazines — a type of business publication directed toward a specific industry, such as masonry.

Informal networks — broadcast news networks created by a professional group of radio or TV news personnel. These networks are also called co-ops.

In-house agencies — advertising agencies operating within a company solely to promote its products.

Institutional magazines — a type of business publication directed toward a specific institution.

In-the-can films — movies which have already been seen in movie theaters but whose income is assured through re-releases and release to television.

ITV — instructional television, programming specifically designed for use in a direct or supplemental teaching role.

Junkets — excursions for journalists, compliments of someone seeking news coverage of an event.

KHz — Kilohertz.

Kicker — closing story of a newscast, often a humorous anecdote.

Kinetoscope — forerunner of the motion picture developed by Thomas Edison, it was a crude device with a peephole through which a viewer could see pictures move.

Leaflet — a form of direct mail, usually a single sheet of light paper folded to fit into an envelope.

Libertarian — espouses a press privately owned and providing a check on government in addition to meeting other needs of society.

Louvers — outdoor bulletin panels which rotate automatically and produce as many as three different messages, each appearing for about ten seconds at a time.

Mailgram — Western Union trade-marked system to send a message via computer and regular postal service mail delivery.

Market research — research, usually conducted by advertising agencies, into the potential market for products.

Mass communication — process by which messages are communicated by a mass medium to a large number of people.

Master control console — heart of a television control room operation through which both the audio and video images are fed, joined together, and improved perhaps through special effects for the "on-air" image.

Master record — the master session is recorded on this record, from which additional records are pressed.

Master session—the final recording session in which a song is put onto tape. Costing many thousands of dollars, this involves full orchestration, major control console, and recording engineer.

Media brokers—persons in the business of selling media properties.

Media credibility—the effect that various media have on how mass communication messages are perceived.

Message intensity—the value or importance of an event or its potential impact in relation to other events or potential news stories.

Meter method—a broadcast ratings measurement in which a monitoring device installed on TV sets is connected to a central computer, which then records channel selection at different times of the day.

MHz—Megahertz.

Microwave—a very short wave frequency located above the area on the electromagnetic spectrum where standard broadcast transmission takes place.

Mix—to join and separate the pictures of various television cameras for a composite "on-air" image.

Mnemonic joining—a process of speech compression that overlaps portions of words.

MPA—Magazine Publishers' Association.

MPAA—Motion Picture Association of America.

NAEB—National Association of Educational Broadcasters.

News dissemination—the process by which news is diffused to the receiving public.

Noise—something that interferes with the communication process.

Offset—a printing process in which typeset copy is reproduced on a photographic, smooth-surfaced plate; the image is transferred to paper through a series of steps *not* involving a plate with raised typefaces.

Ombudsman—personnel who accept feedback from readers on any issue, from suggestions to complaints.

Opinion leaders—people who influence our thinking on a particular subject(s) because we respect their opinions.

Pass-around rate—the number of people who read a single copy of a publication.

Pay cable—a system whereby cable subscribers pay an additional amount beyond the standard monthly rental fee in order to receive special programming.

PBS—Public Broadcasting Service.

Perigee—the closest point to the earth of a satellite's orbit.

Personalized book—composed and printed by a computer, these gift items can be programmed to incorporate specific names and places that are directly relevant to the recipient.

Picture wire — wire services through which photo transmission takes place.

Pilots — sample broadcasting programs produced either by networks or production companies for possible programming adoption.

Pirated tapes — illegally recorded music sold in violation of copyright and contractual agreements with artists.

Plant — the term for an outdoor advertising company.

Playlists — form of feedback for the recording industry in which individual radio stations list the songs that are popular in their listening area for a given time period.

Portfolio — a file of an applicant's best work to present to prospective employers.

Producer — the organizer of a television show or film.

Production companies — commonly called production houses, these businesses produce broadcasting programs for adoption either by networks or individual stations via syndication.

Product research — research, usually instigated by advertising agencies, into a company and its product.

Professional magazines — a type of business publication directed at readers in a specific profession, such as law.

Program managers — persons responsible for selecting programs for airing, scheduling their air time, and overseeing the production and direction of locally produced programs.

Projection — an estimate of the characteristics of a total universe based on a sample of that universe.

Psychographics — study of the psychological characteristics of the mass audience.

Public broadcasting — the operation of the various noncommercial radio and television stations in the United States.

Public service advertising — PSAs are designed to support a nonprofit cause or organization. Most of the time or space for this advertising is provided free as a service to the public by the print or broadcast media.

Random sample — a selection whereby every item in a universe has an equal chance of being chosen.

Rating — (*or share*) a percentage of the total number of households or persons tuned to a station or program during a certain time period.

Reader profiles — research surveys designed to ascertain both the demographic and psychographic characteristics of specialized audiences.

Reader service card — a device that gives magazine readers an opportunity to request additional literature and information about an advertiser's products by circling a corresponding number on a reply card.

Readership survey — detailed analysis of a newspaper's audience.

Regional networks — a system that provides broadcast programming and information to specific geographic regions of the country.

Relay satellite — Echo I became the first of these man-made devices capable of bouncing messages back to earth.

Repeater satellite — the United States' Courier 1-B became the first of a series of satellites that could both receive and retransmit signals back to earth.

Reply cards — a direct-mail piece that caters to the recipient by enclosing a self-addressed card or envelope for convenient reply.

Research service — businesses that specialize in providing research on current topics for subscribers, primarily newspaper and broadcast executives.

RTNDA — Radio Television News Directors Association.

Sales networks — a group of broadcasting stations linked together by a financial agreement to benefit all member stations by offering advertisers a joint rate.

Sampling — the process of examining a small portion of something to estimate what the larger portion is like.

Saturation — the percentage of the total number of households that subscribe to a given medium.

SCA — Speech Communication Association.

Schematic diagrams — blueprints for electronic circuitry.

Scrapbook service — one service a clipping bureau provides, namely to mount all of the clippings in an attractive scrapbook.

Seditious libel — criminal libel against the government.

Semantic noise — interference with the communication process because of a misunderstanding caused by a cliché or slang.

Share — (or rating) is a percentage of the total number of households or people tuned to a station or program during a certain time period.

Sky wave propagation — radio-wave transmission pattern in which the signals travel up, bounce off the ionosphere, and rebound from the earth in a continuing process.

SNAP — Society of National Association Publications.

Social responsibility — theory espousing privately owned media "unless the government has to take over to insure public service."

Social responsibility advertising — publicity that warns consumers to be responsible about things which can hurt them.

Soviet communist — system of state-owned media functioning as a propaganda instrument of the government.

Special effects generators — devices that can create special visual effects for television programming.

Speculators — people who buy a media property and hold it for a short time while heavily promoting it to increase sales.

SPJ, SDX — Society of Professional Journalists, Sigma Delta Chi.

Split — a given news report compiled by a wire service.

Standard advertising — its motive is to sell and to create in the consumer a feeling of need and want for a product or service.

Station program cooperative (SPC) — concept in public broadcasting which utilizes direct feedback in the form of financial commitment from affiliate stations to determine which programs will compose about one-third of the programming distributed by PBS.

Subgroups — the "mass within a mass" upon which the concept of the mass audience is based.

Sub-trunk — secondary cables branching out from the main trunk in a cable TV system to carry the signal to outlying areas.

Supering — positioning a picture from one television camera on top of another picture from a second camera. This special effect is controlled by the master control console.

Switcher — or *technical director,* person responsible for the operation of the master control console.

Synchronous — or *geostationary,* a satellite that travels at the same speed in proportion to the earth's rotation, and thus appears to remain stationary over one point of the earth.

Syndicates — companies whose business it is to promote and sell comics, columns, and other special features to newspapers.

Target audience — any group of persons who have a common bond, that bond being shared demographic and/or psychographic characteristics.

Technical director — sometimes called *switcher,* person responsible for the operation of the master control console.

Television household — a broadcast rating term used to describe any home with a television set, as distinguished from a household using television.

Tip sheet — list of important events that will probably make news in the coming weeks. Usually provided by research services.

Trade magazines — a type of business publication directed toward specific businesses, such as hardware stores.

Trade-out — an exchange of merchandise for a service; e.g., in advertising, a merchant will trade the use of a product for an equivalent amount of advertising in print or broadcast media.

Translators — television transmitting antennas, usually located on high natural terrain.

Trunk — main line of a cable system.

Two-step flow — process by which information disseminated by mass media is (1) received by a direct audience and then (2) relayed to other persons secondhand.

Universe – the whole from which a sample is being chosen; in broadcast ratings, this can be the sample area, metro area, or rating area.

Value structures – a normative, conceptual standard of the desirable that predispositionally influences individuals in choosing among personally perceived alternatives of behavior.

VDT – visual display terminals. Data from electronic keyboards and computers appear on a device similar to a television screen.

Vertical publications – a category of business publications designed to reach people at all levels within a given profession.

Weekly carriage report – a local station's broadcast schedule.

White space – that portion of a printed advertisement devoid of printing or illustrations; i.e., blank space.

WICI – Women In Communication, Inc.

Wireless – term used to describe early radio.

index

Freebies, 198, 497
Freedman, Jonathan L., 489 n.
Frequency, 83, 497
Frequency modulation (FM),
    46, 47, 48, 85, 86, 88,
    125, 497
  stations, 117
  stereo, 47
Frequency rating, 310
Friendly, Fred W., 128
Friends of the Earth, 177
Fuchs, Wolfgang, 148

Gable, Clark, 62
Galloway, Jonathan E., 390
Gandhi, Indira, 442
Garnett, Bernard E., 287
Garrison, Jasper, Rose &
    Company, 477
Gatekeeper, 10, 135, 161, 162,
    497
  group, 497
Gaudet, Hazel, 247, 489 n.
Gazetta, 16, 497
Gelfand, Louis I., 486
General Foods Corporation,
    386
Georgia Gazette, 16
Geostationary orbit, 98, 497
Gerbner, George, 439, 440,
    441, 493 n.
Germany, 16, 17
Gibbons, Euell, 386
Gillmor, Donald M., 410,
    492 n.
Golden Era of Radio, 31
Gordon, George, 244
Grace, Roger M., 492 n.
Grain Information News (GIN),
    137
Gray Panthers, 283
Greeks, 67
Green, Beverly, 162, 477, 478
Green, Maury, 65
Green/Associates Advertising,
    Inc., 162, 477
Greenburg, Bradley S., 287
Gregory, John, 136
Grey, David, 226
Griffith, D. W., 57, 58
Grin And Bear It, 143
Griswold, Denny, 480
Gross, Larry, 440, 441
Groth, Otto, 17, 18
Grotta, Gerald L., 491 n.
Ground Skimmer, 36
Group-owned stations, 127
Guimary, Donald L., 332
Gumps, The, 144
Gunsmoke, 114, 122

Hale, William Storm, 364

Hall, Mark, 487 n.
Halographics, 62
Hamilton, Andrew, 19
Happy Hooligan, 144
Harding-Cox election, 366
Hardware Retailing, 33, 37
Harless, James, 221
Harris, Benjamin, 18
Harrison, Stanley, 39
Hartke, Vance, 370
Hatfield, Mark, 370
Hays, Will H., 383
Head, Sydney, 491 n.
Head end, 93, 497
Hearst, William Randolph, 143,
    144
Heath, Harry E. Jr., 486
Hello Dolly, 351
Herrold, Charles David, 43
Hertz, Heinrich Rudolph, 42,
    64, 497
Hertz rent-a-car, 387
Hickey, Neil, 491 n.
Hidden messages, 186
Hidetoshi, Kato, 287
Highbrow audience, 263
Highway Beautification Act,
    355
Hit charts, 153
Hitchcock, Alfred, 57
Hit Parade, The, 80
Hoffer, Jay, 364
Hohenberg, John, 209
Holiday, 473, 475
Holt, Rinehart, and Winston,
    Inc., 127
Home terminal, 94, 497
Homo sapiens, 2
Hones, Alexander, 130
Hoover, J. Edgar, 141
Horizontal publications, 38,
    497
Horn, Maurice, 147
Hottelet, Richard C., 114
Hot type, 23, 24, 497
House Beautiful, 162, 282
Households using television
    (HUT), 309, 497
House organ, 38, 497
Hovland, Carl I., 261, 490 n.
Howe, Quincy, 304
Hudson Home Publications,
    298
Hudspeth, Tod, 98
Hulteng, John L., 209
Humanitarian value appeals,
    165, 168, 188
Hunt, Gary T., 490 n.
Hurst, Walter E., 364
Hypoing, 343, 497

I Am Woman, 281

Iconoscope electron television
    tube, 50, 51, 111
Idaho, 9
Illinois Bell Telephone
    Company, 273
I Love Lucy, 114
Image advertising, 173, 181,
    182, 498
Impressions, 498
InCity, 337, 339
Independent agents, 155
Independent Television
    Corporation, 123
Indianapolis 500, 114
Indianapolis News, 377
Indianapolis Star, 406, 429,
    430
Indirect messages, 184, 185,
    186
Industrial magazines, 498
Informal network, 124
In-house agencies, 159, 341
Innis, Harold A., 14
Institute of Outdoor
    Advertising, 76
Instructional television (ITV),
    54, 275
Intellectual value appeals, 165,
    168, 188
INTELSAT, 99, 382
International Communication
    Association (ICA), 498
International film, 58
International News Service,
    132
Interpersonal communication,
    2
Intrapersonal communication, 7
Intra-studio communication
    system, 230
Ironside, 122
It Happened One Night, 63
ITT Continental Baking
    Company, 180, 386

Jacobs, Lewis, 488 n.
Jakes, John, 347
Japan, 285, 286
Jarratt, Vernon, 488 n.
Jaws, 62, 63, 431
Jennings, Ralph Merwin, 332
Jewish News, The, 38
Jimmy 'The Greek' Snyder,
    145
Joey Bishop Show, The, 162
Johnson, Joseph S., 65
Johnson, Lyndon, 77
Johnson, Nicholas, 332
Jones, Kenneth K., 65
Journalism awards, 161
Juliet Jones, 141
Junkets, 198